IDOL MEAT IN CORINTH

SOCIETY
OF BIBLICAL
LITERATURE

DISSERTATION SERIES

Charles Talbert, Editor

Number 68
IDOL MEAT IN CORINTH
The Pauline Argument
in 1 Corinthians 8 and 10
by
Wendell Lee Willis

Wendell Lee Willis

IDOL MEAT IN CORINTH
The Pauline Argument
in 1 Corinthians 8 and 10

Wipf & Stock
PUBLISHERS
Eugene, Oregon

Wipf and Stock Publishers
199 West 8th Avenue, Suite 3
Eugene, Oregon 97401

Idol Meat in Corinth
The Pauline Argument in 1 Corinthians 8 and 10
By Willis, Wendell L
Copyright©1985 by Willis, Wendell Lee
ISBN: 1-59244-726-0
Publication date 6/15/2004
Previously published by Society of Biblical Literature, 1985

Contents

CONCLUSIONS

.

Acknowledgments

I am very honored that this study, despite its forbidding length, has been selected for publication in this series. In respect to this, I wish to acknowledge the help of the staff of Scholars Press, in particular, Dr. Davis Perkins, who guided the initial editing work.

The dissertation was originally undertaken for the Graduate Program in Religious Studies at Southern Methodist University. It was a joy to be in that program because of the humane and caring attitude of both faculty and fellow students. I am most grateful for this wider forum to express my appreciation to those at SMU who offered insights and encouragements. I regret only that space limitations preclude explicit mention of others whose contributions were as real, if less frequent.

First, I wish to express my thanks to Dr. Victor Paul Furnish, who guided me in this initial venture into an exploration of Pauline ethics, a field in which his own work has been so significant. I am thankful for his support, guidance, and especially for his warm friendship, which made this work relationship so pleasant. My debt extends also to his skillful suggestions on form and expression, which have immeasurably improved the study. I, of course, take sole responsibility for the inaccuracies and infelicities which remain.

Appreciation is also extended to Dr. Harold Attridge whose considerable mastery of the Greek sources has enriched the study. I also express gratitude for his guidance for my maiden voyage into the world of Greek inscriptions.

I use this opportunity to recognize the John Hicks Fund from Perkins School of Theology which supported me for an important period of study at the American Schools of Classical Studies Library in Athens. While there I benefited also from members of the Corinth excavation team. I am especially grateful to Dr. Nancy Bookidis, who generously read drafts and answered questions.

Finally, I wish most of all to express my awareness of my debt to my family: To my wife, Sandra, who has endured my absences and anxieties, yet patiently supported me throughout the project (including this re-working). Also to my sons: Joshua, Nathan, and Adam, who have given of their rightful time that daddy might finish his book. Thankfully, their wish is now fulfilled.

Citation of Sources

In this study the Loeb Classical Library editions are used for both texts and translations of Greek and Latin authors unless otherwise indicated. These texts and authors are cited using the abbreviations employed in Gerhard Kittel, *A Theological Dictionary of the New Testament,* Volume 1, xvi-xxix.

Standard abbreviations for journals and selected standard reference works are listed according to the style used in the *Journal of Biblical Literature.* Where this style lacks a recommendation, the format of the *Theological Dictionary of the New Testament* is followed for abbreviations. Only in a few instances where no abbreviation is suggested by these standard works have I ventured to make my own, and then so noted. For journals not commonly used in the field I have chosen to give unabbreviated titles for the benefit of the reader.

Introduction

THE PROBLEM OF THIS STUDY

A. State of the Problem

During his missionary work in mainland Greece Paul established a Christian community in the city of Corinth (1 Cor 3:6, 10; 4:15, 16). Perhaps because of his role as founder, Paul maintained a continuing relationship with Christians there, including an active correspondence. Of the letters which Paul wrote to the Corinthinians, at least two (depending upon how one decides about partition theories) survive. In part of the letter now known as 1 Corinthians Paul replied to several questions raised by the Corinthians in a letter sent to him. This study is concerned with one of these questions: what is the proper stance for Christians toward εἰδωλοθύτον (1 Cor 8:1)?

In dealing with Paul's instructions to the Corinthian church regarding the eating of "idol meat," several questions arise. First, what is meant by the word εἰδωλοθύτον and why is it an issue? Second, what was the Corinthian question about this idol meat? What attitudes and practices lay behind their query? Third, what is Paul's response to their inquiry? What does he feel should or should not be done? This question includes two further ones: why does Paul advise as he does, and how does he seek to secure the Corinthians' acceptance of his instructions? All these issues, and some additional ones, combine in the problem of idol meat as it is addressed in 1 Corinthians.

B. The Importance of the Problem

This study is important primarily as a contribution to the understanding of one specific issue which arose in Paul's Corinthian congregation and of the internal dynamics of the relationship between the apostle and the church as they faced that issue. This investigation requires consideration both of the character of this particular early Christian community and of the theology of its founding apostle, Paul.

There are some secondary concerns for which this study may be important. First, there is the question of Christianity's relationship to its surrounding culture. The specific issue of idol meat in Corinth raises this question at an incipient stage in Christian history. Since the question of "Christianity and culture" is an abiding one, perhaps a study of this specific problem may shed light on the larger topic.

Second, as is clear from a simple reading of 1 Corinthians 8 and 10, there was obviously some disagreement within the Corinthian church over the question of idol meat. This disagreement within the church had led to animosity between Christians of differing understandings, including perhaps some "name-calling," and it led eventually to the Corinthian letter to Paul seeking his advice. Therefore this study is important as an investigation of conflict within a Christian community and of Paul's approaches to such conflict.

Third, this study is important for understanding Paul's characteristic approach to Christian ethical problems. In his response to the Corinthian crisis regarding the eating of idol meat Paul is dealing with a concrete problem in Christian ethics. Although this specific issue as Paul faced it belongs to the past, there are ethical concerns which Paul adduces in the course of his argument which may have enduring significance. The discussion of 1 Corinthians 8 and 10 is one example of the inner relation between Paul's theology and his ethical teachings.

PREVIOUS STUDIES OF THIS PROBLEM

Unlike some topics in Pauline studies, the problem of idol meat in 1 Corinthians has not been the object of extensive study. Beyond the treatments in various commentaries, there is only one monograph which deals in a thorough way with these chapters, the unpublished dissertation of W. T. Sawyer, "The Problem of Meat Sacrificed to Idols in the Corinthian Church."[1] Although Sawyer's study considers many of the same problems found in the present investigation, there are important differences which make the two projects distinct.

---

[1] W. T. Sawyer, "The Problem of Meat Sacrificed to Idols in the Corinthian Church" (Th.D. dissertation, Southern Baptist Theological Seminary, 1968).

First, Sawyer's dissertation regards the problem of idol meat in Corinth as only one part of a general struggle in the early church between the freedom allowed by the Pauline gospel and the legalism of some "Judaizing" Christians who opposed it. The present study examines the problem of idol meat in its specific setting at Corinth, rather than interpreting the problem by a larger reconstruction of early Christian history.

Second, because of his basic interest in the problem of "Judaizing" in the Corinthian church Sawyer's investigation is heavily weighted toward a consideration of the influence of Jewish food customs and regulations. He neglects the very significant Hellenistic background which is important for understanding how the issue would have developed in a Greek city like Corinth. This Hellenistic background is emphasized in the present study.

In addition to Sawyer's study, several articles have treated 1 Corinthians 8 and 10 and the problem of idol meat in some detail. Each of these will be considered in the process of the present study, but they are relatively few in number and relatively brief.

Beyond these specific studies there are a number of articles and monographs which relate either directly or indirectly to aspects of 1 Corinthians 8 and 10. There are studies of some important words in these chapters, such as συνείδησις, κοινωνία and σῶμα, as well as of such topics as the Lord's Supper, the image of the body of Christ, Paul's hermeneutical methods, and the theological orientation of Corinthian Christianity. Finally, these chapters are also considered in discussions of still broader topics, such as Paul's continuing relationship with the Corinthian church, the question of sacrificial meat elsewhere in the New Testament and later Christian writings, Paul's ecclesiology, and Pauline ethical thought. These studies, too, have been consulted insofar as they shed light on the special problems which are taken up in the present investigation.

OBJECTIVES OF THE STUDY

The present investigation has several particular objectives which correspond to the various aspects of the problem as those have been set forth above. The first objective is to understand what the problem of idol meat at Corinth involved. This means knowing both what was referred to by εἰδωλόθυτον (and ἱερόθυτον, 10:28), and also why this topic was of interest to the Corinthians.

Another objective of the study is to establish the attitude of the Corinthians to this issue. What course of conduct had they followed or proposed to follow and how did they seek to defend their position? It will be argued below that these questions can be at least tentatively answered, even though the only source of information is Paul's reply. This is so because in his letter Paul seems to allude and/or respond to points made by the Corinthians which reveal their arguments and attitudes.

A third objective of the study is to explain the reply of Paul to the Corinthian inquiry. The exegesis will examine the structure of Paul's argument and the types of appeals which characterize his guidance on this ethical question. In this way a particular example of the relationship between Paul's theology and his ethical teaching will be studied.

Finally, in the process of the exegesis and in the conclusions this study will seek to identify fundamental norms and themes which are operative here as a part of Paul's ethical thought. Several ethical themes found in 1 Corinthians 8 and 10 occur elsewhere in Paul's letters. This study will locate these ethical themes in 1 Corinthians 8 and 10 and point to their larger significance in Pauline thought. Of special interest for the present study is how Paul's ethical concerns are related to his understanding of the nature of Christian community (i.e., his ecclesiology).

THE SCOPE AND METHOD OF THE PRESENT STUDY

A. Scope

This study will focus on 1 Corinthians 8 and 10 and the analysis of the development of Paul's argument there. Other passages which also deal with the topic of sacrificial meat, such as Acts 15, 21 and Revelation 2, will not be studied directly. However, Romans 14 and 15 will be noted whenever that discussion illustrates or clarifies 1 Corinthians 8 and 10.

Neither will the present study examine directly Jewish food regulations. It will be argued in the course of the exegesis that, however one decides about the later discussion of Romans 14 and 15, 1 Corinthians 8 and 10 do not reflect a debate over Jewish food laws.

Not even all the issues raised in 1 Corinthians itself can be investigated here, although these will be taken into account insofar as they impinge on the study of chapters 8 and 10. For example, although the questions raised by F. C. Baur about the "parties" in Corinth will not be the object of direct study, it will be argued that on the issue of idol meat there seem to be only two viewpoints within the church. It is not helpful to term them "parties" or to seek to explain their views by identifying their founders.

Finally, it has been deemed advisable to forego any detailed study of the various cult shrines in and near Corinth which are known to have featured dining facilities.[2] This would take us too far afield from the central objectives of our study. Moreover, the results of the excavation of one of the most important of these, the shrine of Demeter and Kore on the northern slope of Acrocorinth, have not yet been fully evaluated.

B. Method

The two major points of this work reflect the method of the study. Part I, "Sacrifice, Cultic Meals and Associations in Hellenistic Life," investigates the setting for the question about idol meat as it arose in the Corinthian church. Although limitations preclude a complete examination of the massive evidence—archaeological, inscriptional and literary—related to cult meals, some investigation is necessary for understanding 1 Corinthians 8 and 10. In Part I a review of the most important evidence about the meaning of cultic meals is made, and prominent assessments of this evidence by classical scholars are noted.

The second and most extensive part of this study deals exegetically with 1 Corinthians 8 and 10. For this purpose the two chapters are divided into four units: chapter 8; 10:1-13; 10:14-22; 10:23--11:1. It will be shown in the exegesis that these units represent definable, although not isolated, steps in the overall development of Paul's argument.

---

[2]The main excavations are: the sanctuary of Demeter and Kore, the caves at Isthmia, the lower dining rooms at the Asklieipion, and the South Stoa terrace. Reports giving details of these excavations and interpreting the remains are found in volumes of *Hesperia* and the ongoing publications on the Corinth archaeological work published by the American School of Classical Studies in Athens.

Part I

Sacrifice, Cultic Meals, and Associations in Hellenistic Life

INTRODUCTION

In 1 Cor 8 and 10 Paul deals with the problem of Christian participation in meals associated with pagan sacrifice in Corinth. The present study proceeds to investigate exegetically the arguments between Paul and the Corinthian Christians on this issue. The structure and theology of Paul's argument are the foci in the present investigation. This necessarily limits pursuing many other approaches. For example, no attempt is made in the present study to identify the "parties" in the Corinthian church, their possible origins, founders or distinctive positions.[1]

However, even these necessary limits of space in this study must allow for some consideration into the role of sacrifice and cult meals in Hellenistic life. The discussion between Paul and his Corinthian inquirers involves common aspects of Hellenistic life, especially meals which normally followed a sacrifice. As will subsequently be shown a meal was a customary part of sacrifice in antiquity. Conversely, most dining occasions beyond family meals also involved sacrifice. Before one can appreciate the Corinthians' inquiry and understand Paul's reply, it is necessary

---

[1] As is found in C. K. Barrett, "Things Sacrificed to Idols," *NTS* 11 (1968), 138-153; Max Rauer, *Die "Schwachen" in Korinth und Rom nach dem Paulusbriefen* (Freiberg: Herder, 1923) and Sawyer, "Meat Sacrificed." For a thorough survey and critique of this type of approach, see John C. Hurd, Jr., *The Origin of 1 Corinthians* (New York: Seabury, 1965), 43-47. Like Hurd, the present study concludes that trying to interpret 1 Cor 8 and 10 by locating distinct groups and/or distinct leaders within the Corinthian church is unfruitful.

to have some understanding of the cultural situation which is reflected in
1 Cor 8 and 10 regarding sacrifice and dining.

A. Preliminary Remarks on Sacrifice

Although there was in the first century A.D. an active critique of
sacrifice as an appropriate means to honor the gods,[2] sacrifice enjoyed a
long-standing acceptance in Greco-Roman life. Space forbids more than
the briefest rehearsal of the origin and development of sacrifice in Greek
religion. For the same reason any direct examination such as was undertaken much earlier in this century must also be omitted.[3]

Generally one may distinguish between bloodless and blood (animal)
sacrifice.[4] Since the problems between Paul and the Corinthians involved
"sacrificial meat" (εἰδωλόθυτον, ἱερόθυτον) the bloodless sacrifice is not
important for the present study. The immense efforts of previous scholars seeking to understand the origins of animal sacrifice,[5] and to distinguish between sacrifices by the terminology used to describe them,[6] by
the deities (celestial or chthonic)[7] who received the sacrifice, or by the

---

[2]For a brief survey and bibliography, James Thompson, "Hebrews 9
and Hellenistic Concepts of Sacrifice," *JBL* 98 (1979) 567-578.

[3]For a valuable summary see the article, "Sacrifice," in James
Hastings, ed., *Encyclopaedia of Religion and Ethics* (New York: Charles
Scribner's Sons, 1908-21) Vol. 11. Especially E. O. James, "Introduction,"
1-7, and L. R. Farnell, "Sacrifice, Greek," 12-18. Hereafter this work
cited as *ERE*.

[4]For a general discussion of the broad range of things given in
sacrifice see Farnell, "Sacrifice (Greek)," *ERE* 11.12-18. Also K. Latte,
"Opfer und Gebet," *Römische Religionsgeschichte* (München: Beck, 1960)
375-81. Also E. O. James, *Sacrifice and Sacrament* (New York: Barnes
and Noble, 1962).

[5]See Farnell, "Sacrifice (Greek)," for a review of the controversy
regarding the totemistic theory of the origin of sacrifice as it affected
study of Greek religions. Also, J. A. MacCulloch, "Sacrament, Primitive
and Ethnic," *ERE* 10.897-902. The classical presentation of the totemistic
theory is W. R. Smith, *The Religion of the Semites* (Cambridge: A. C.
Black, 1889).

[6]Jane Harrison, *Prolegomena to the Study of Greek Religion*, 2d
(Cambridge: University Press, 1903). Also Royden K. Yerkes, *Sacrifice in
Greek and Roman Religions and Early Judaism* (New York: Charles
Scribner's Sons, 1952) 106ff.

[7]Harrison, *Prolegomena*, 58f.

motives of those who sacrificed[8] similarly are beyond the scope of our evaluation. Moreover, these issues are largely moot since such "primitive" theoretical distinctions are granted to have disappeared long before the rise of Christianity.[9]

However one understands their origin, communal meals following sacrifice were normal from before the time of Homer. For example, in *Odyssey* 24:212ff., the returning Odysseus tells his servants: "Do you now go within the well-built house, and straightway slay for dinner the best of the swine."[10] The verb translated "slay" is ἱερεύω and thus illustrates the close connection between sacrifice and supper.

While there are some variations noted, blood sacrifice had a fairly standard form from pre-Homeric times. Yerkes has outlined the procedures for a *thusia* which will serve to recall what actually took place in sacrifice:

1. The preparation (lustration, barley grain ceremony, prayers, casting the hair from the animal in the fire, slaying and flaying the victim, procession)
2. The *thusia* proper (burning of the god's portion, libation, eating of the *splagchna*)

---

[8]In addition to the works cited in notes 3-5, see also, L. R. Farnell, "Sacrificial Communion in Greek Religion," *Hibbert Journal* 2 (1904) 308-13. Farnell favors a modified version of W. R. Smith's interpretation. He admits Smith's "sacramental" understanding is not found in Homeric religion, but thinks it was known in the pre-Homeric period. Jane Harrison, *Themis* (New York: Meridian Books, 1962; 1st ed., 1912) 136ff., rejects Smith's view as still too tied to traditional assumptions about the gods. In *Themis* Harrison appears to change her own earlier observations in *Prolegomena*.

A critical assessment of the views of Smith, and the totemist school, as well as a valuable review of the evidence for distinguishing between forms and recipients of Greek sacrifice is A. D. Nock, "The Cult of Heroes," *Essays on Religion and the Ancient World* (ed. Zeph Stewart; Cambridge: Harvard University Press, 1972) 2.575-602. Nock sees Greek sacrifice as basically a gift, and the meal a feast for the worshippers which is occasioned by the meat which is available after sacrifice. Hereafter this work cited as *ERAW*.

[9]Harrison, *Prolegomena*, 55.

[10]Throughout the present study when classical sources are quoted the texts and translations are taken from the Loeb series unless otherwise indicated. Harrison, *Prolegomena*, 55, implies that *Od.* 24.215 suggests the meal was the goal of the sacrifice.

3.   The feast (roasting the victim, the banquet libations, music and dancing).[11]

From this description, supported by specifics from the original sources, it is clear the communal meal was a major aspect of Greek sacrifice.   Already in Homer the meal seems to have been at least as important as the offering upon the altar.[12]   The sacrifice was not just for the god's benefit (only the flesh burned upon the altar was exclusively for him or her), but also for the benefit of the worshippers, who received the flesh from the sacrifice.[13]

B. Sacramentalism and the Interpretation of 1 Corinthians

Before turning to a more detailed study of the occasions of dining involving sacrifice which occurred in Hellenistic life, it seems worthwhile to review briefly the importance this topic has had in the interpretation of 1 Cor 8 and 10. At the beginning of this century it was commonly held among many interpreters of early Christianity that Hellenistic sacramentalism had been decisive in the development of Christian theology and worship, especially of Pauline Christianity.[14]   This line of interpretation was very important in attempts to understand the discussion found in 1 Cor 8 and 10.

Although a subsequent critique of the "sacramental" interpretation of Pauline Christianity and its alleged dependence on Hellenistic mystery religions resulted in the demise of the *religionsgeschichtliche Schule*,[15] it seems the influence of this approach has not vanished. For example, in his

---

[11]Yerkes, 99f.

[12]*Il.* 1.447-74; 9.220f.; *Od.* 3.430-74. Cf. Hesiod, *Theog.* 535ff.

[13]D. H. Gill, "Trapezomata: A neglected aspect of Greek Sacrifice," *HTR* 67 (1974) 117-137, especially 123.

[14]For a summary of the importance of the mystery religions in New Testament interpretation at the beginning of this century, see W. G. Kümmel, *The New Testament: The History of the Investigation of Its Problems* (Nashville: Abingdon, 1970) 245-80. Also Stephen Neill, *The Interpretation of the New Testament: 1861-1961* (London: Oxford, 1964) 153-67.

[15]The rise and demise of the *religionsgeschichtliche Schule* is traced by Carsten Colpe, *Die religionsgeschichtliche Schule* (FRLANT 60; Göttingen: Vandenhoeck & Ruprecht, 1961). See also Hugo Rahner, *Greek Myths and Christian Mystery* (New York: Harper and Row, 1963).

important, modern critical commentary on 1 Corinthians, Hans Conzelmann writes concerning Paul's use of the phrase τραπέζα κυρίου in 1 Cor 10:21, that this accords with general pagan practices, in which "one sits at the 'table of the god' . . . entertains the god, partakes of him."[16] Since Conzelmann interprets the Christian meal as parallel to the pagan one, and interprets Paul's instructions in light of both, how he understands the pagan meal is crucial.

The "sacramental" interpretation of pagan cultic meals was regarded as proven beyond debate by earlier scholars. The only debate was regarding to what degree these pagan sacramental concepts influenced the Christian "sacraments" of baptism and the Lord's Supper. When and where the pagan understanding of such meals was equated with the Christian one, this led to an argument against the unity of 1 Cor 8 and 10.[17] For, it was argued, 1 Cor 10:1-22 evidenced a sacramental argument opposing Christian participation in the parallel sacraments of pagan cults. This "sacramentalism" believed to have been set forth in 1 Cor 10:1-22 was contrasted with the "ethical" arguments of 1 Cor 8 and 10:23-11:1. It will be argued in the present study that this alleged conflict misunderstands both the character of pagan cult meals and Paul's arguments in 1 Cor 8 and 10.

Paul has been regarded, especially half a century earlier, as the source for the sacramental interpretation of the Lord's Supper. To give one example of this view:

> Paul cannot have drawn his doctrines of the mystical ceremonies to baptism and the Lord's Supper from the traditions of the Christian community, because this tradition before his time knew nothing of these doctrines; . . . on the other hand, Paul himself appears in 1 Cor X to use the analogy of the pagan sacrificial meal.[18]

Paul was regarded as the Christian theologian who translated (or destroyed) the religion of Jesus (in the Synoptic gospels) into Hellenistic

---

[16]Hans Conzelmann, *1 Corinthians* (Hermeneia; Philadelphia: Fortress Press, 1975) 174.

[17]Johannes Weiss, *Der erste Korintherbrief* (KEK 5; Göttingen: Vandenhoeck & Ruprecht, 1910) xxxix-xliii.

[18]Otto Pfleiderer, *Primitive Christianity* (New York: G. P. Putnam's Sons, 1906) 1.63. See 1.337-339 and 417-426 for the details of his presentation stressing Paul's adoption of pagan mystery religion concepts.

categories.[19] It was he who made what had been "at first a repast of brethren similar to those which Jesus had formerly taken with his disciples" into "a veritable sacrament, the rite by which the union of believers in their immortal Savior was more particularly effected and deeply felt."[20] Loisy then concluded, "Thus the system is complete: in it worship as in its belief, Christianity is a religion of mystery."[21]

Perhaps the most influential presentation of the thesis that Paul derived his eucharistic practice and theology from a pagan sacramentalism was made by Wilhelm Heitmüller in his brief study, *Taufe und Abendmahl bei Paulus*.[22] He argued that Paul's doctrine of the Lord's Supper was that of a sacrament in which the worshippers devoured the deity, a belief which Heitmüller felt was essentially the same as that of syncretistic paganism.[23] Similar interpretations of Paul, stressing his dependence on Hellenistic mystery religions for a sacramental theology are well known.[24]

Many Christian scholars undertook a critique of this proposed development of sacramental theology in Paul and its alleged dependence on pagan mystery cults. Most of these critiques stressed either the limited influence of the pagan mysteries, or the decisive differences between them and Pauline (Christian) theology. However, as has already been noted with regard to Conzelmann's comments on 1 Cor 10:21, there remains a residual belief (suspicion) of some Christian indebtedness to the mystery religions precisely in the matter of sacramentalism. Moreover, as will be seen below, the sacramental interpretation of pagan religious

---

[19]Richard Reitzenstein, *Hellenistic Mystery Religions* (Pittsburgh Theological Monographs, 15; Pittsburgh: Pickwick Press, 1979, original ed. 1910) 77-79. Also Wilhelm Bousset, *Kyrios Christos* (Nashville: Abingdon Press, 1970; original ed. 1913).

[20]Alfred Loisy, "The Christian Mystery," *Hibbert Journal* 10 (1911) 56.

[21]Ibid. Johannes Weiss, *Earliest Christianity; A history of the period A. D. 30-150* (New York: Harper and Row, 1965; original ed. 1937) 2.648, generally agrees, but feels Paul stopped short of following sacramentalism to its logical consequence.

[22]Wilhelm Heitmüller, *Taufe und Abendmahl bei Paulus* (Göttingen: Vandenhoeck & Ruprecht, 1903).

[23]Ibid., 35-37, 51-53.

[24]Boussett, *Kyrios Christos,* 153-167, gives a classical presentation of Paul's crucial role in the Hellenization of Christianity. S. Angus, *The Mystery Religions and Christianity* (New York: Charles Scribner's Sons, 1925) esp. 129-133, gives a balanced presentation in support of this thesis.

meals tended to go unchallenged. As a result a problematic understanding of pagan cultic meals has misled many interpreters of 1 Cor 8 and 10.

C. Occasions for Cultic Meals

Meals among worshippers were a common feature of sacrifice in Hellenistic religions. While sacrifice was not a daily, or even weekly event in Hellenistic life, neither was it a thing of great rarity. There were a variety of sacrificial occasions, including: sacrifice to a particular deity (of which there were many);[25] state festivals;[26] also various private associations with a religious, or at least a quasi-religious, base.[27] Since they are less familiar, more must be said about private associations here.

---

[25]Both "public" deities such as Jupiter or Athena, or more "private" cults such as Asclepius or Dionysus.

[26]The most famous of which was perhaps the Panathenea, spoofed by Aristophanes, Nu. 11.385ff.; compare Thucydides, 2.38. The Roman equivalent would have been the civic lectisternium, a national festival which included ample meals. See Livy, 5.13.5f.

Other important public festivals were held in various Greek cities and regions, including the panergyreis. Martin Nilsson considers these to have been very important in Greek life. They were at one time, fairs, sporting events, and religious occasions. "They took place in some sacred precinct, they were dedicated to some god, and they were accompanied by sacrifice." Martin P. Nilsson, Greek Folk Religion (New York: Harper, 1961; originally pub. Greek Popular Religion, 1940) 97.

Other public festivals were more irregular, celebrating such things as military victories or kingly generosity. See Ammianus Marcellinus, Julian, 22.12.6, 7; 25.4.17; already in Homer, Od., 17.330ff.

[27]There were many types of associations, although in the Hellenistic period, if not before, the formal designations had lost precision. Such groups were known as: σύνοδοι, φυλετικά, δημοτικά, θίασοι, φρατρία and ὀργεῶνικα. Athenaeus 5.186f., shows the virtual interchangeability of these terms in his day (c. A.D. 200). On these associations see Peter Hermann, et al., "Genossenschaft," Reällexikon für Antike und Christentum (ed. Theodor Klauser; Stuttgart: Hiersemann, 1950--), 1976 Supp. 83-155.

Of course, it was possible to have private sacrifices to which citizens were invited, Xenophon, An. 5.52.8-10. See also Cato, Agri. 132. Because of the cost of such events, they would have been quite rare.

The public festivals would have provided the most bounteous feasts for the largest numbers, but the private sacrificing associations would have been more frequent. From pre-classical times social groups shared a sacrifice and a common meal. These groups included tribal or political subgroups, sacrificing associations, groups formed on the basis of fraternity (φρατρία) or contributions (ἔρανοι). Plato's συμπόσιον was the model for dining associations of various philosophical groups who shared meals as well as common ideas. All these were, broadly speaking, religious associations (θίασοι).[28]

These various societies which met for common sacrifice and meals were always religious, at least to the extent that their meetings were held under the aegis of a patron deity (although they might be formed on something else held in common, for example, ethnic origin or profession). "They acted as friendly societies holding common funds for charity, and in particular offering security for burial."[29]

In fact, festivals which included a shared meal are the most common feature of the various associations just named. Some were apparently devoted to the dead and held at their graves.[30] Others were for heroes.[31] Private banquets were also associated with well-known deities. Apuleius's *Metamorphoses* describes a meal in which the hero, Lucian, partook following his conversion to the goddess Isis "of many names."[32] Private banquets have also been mentioned which were associated with Asclepius,[33]

---

[28]Stirling Dow and David H. Gill, "The Greek Cult Table," *AJA* 69 (1965) 113. Also M. N. Tod, *Sidelights on Greek History* (London: Blackwell, 1932) esp. 71-93. Also, Martin P. Nilsson, *Cults, Myths, Oracles and Politics of Ancient Greece* (Lund: C. W. K. Gleerup, 1951) 153-65. Nilsson also discusses the distinctions between these various associations and the blurring of the distinctions in the Hellenistic period.

[29]E. A. Judge, *The Social Patterns of Christian Groups in the First Century* (London: Tyndale, 1960) 40.

[30]Gill, "Trapezomata," 122. He also cites Martin P. Nilsson, *Geschichte der griechischen Religion* (2d ed., *Handbuch des Altertumswissenschaft*; München: C. H. Beck, 1941) 1.135, 187.

[31]Gill, "Trapezomata," 122. Also Nock, "Cult of Heroes."

[32]Apuleius, *Met.*, 11.

[33]Aelius Aristides, *Or. Sacr.* 2.27, recounts such a meal. Aristophanes, *Pl.* 676ff., lampoons such meals and their presumed devotion. His lines would not have been funny, unless some were known to have taken the meals more seriously. Meals at the shrine of Asclepius in Corinth are known.

Dionysus,[34] Zeus Hypsistos,[35] and especially the mention of Sarapis in the papyri.[36]

It is not necessary to say more now about these associations which will be discussed at the close of this chapter. They, as well as the cults of various gods, illustrate the variety of opportunities in Hellenistic life for dining following a sacrifice. The frequency of such dining would have varied according to one's social situation and circle of friends. But there would have been ample opportunity for most people (citizens, freedmen, and even slaves) to have some occasion to participate in such meals. J. P. Kane, whose article first opened for me the interpretation followed in this study, summarizes well on Hellenistic cult meals:

> Some form of cult meal was one of the fundamental features of Greek religious festivities, and took the form of a meal devoted to, presided over, or shared with, the gods. Usually meat or other food was offered to the god and then—apart from reserved portions—consumed by the participants. This was so at the public festivals organized by the City State, and in smaller political and social groups, whether public or private (*orgeones, thiasoi,* and *eranoi*). It was so in the pre-Classical, the Classical, the Hellenistic, and the Roman periods. The practice is referred to in Greek authors and inscriptions, and dining halls and cult tables have been excavated within the sacred precincts of the Greek gods.[37]

D. The "Table of the God"

The "table of the god" (τραπέζα τοῦ θεοῦ) is alluded to in 1 Corinthians 10 by Paul's expressions τραπέζης κυρίου and τραπέζης δαιμονίων. He probably uses the latter expression to denote the table of the

---

[34]See the cult regulations for the Iobacchoi, SIG³ 1109. Wilhelm Dittenberger, *Sylloge Inscriptionum Graecarum*³ (Lipsae: S. Hirszel, 1915-24) 3.267-74, hereafter cited SIG³. For an interpretation of the inscription, M. N. Tod, "NVGAE EPIGRAPHICAE," *Classical Quarterly,* 23 (1929) 1-6.

[35]A. D. Nock, "Gild of Zeus Hypsistos," *ERAW* 1.433, n. 129.

[36]Several examples in the Oxyrhynchus Papyri are discussed later in this chapter.

[37]J. P. Kane, "The Mithraic Cult Meal in its Greek and Roman Environment," *Mithraic Studies* (ed. John R. Hinnels; Manchester: University Press, 1975) 2.321.

god found in pagan shrines. This table was a standard feature of Greek sacrifice, yet has not received much attention in studies of Paul's teaching in 1 Corinthians. However, it is important, not only because Paul expressly refers to it here, but also because it may have been the source of some of the meat considered in his exchange with the Corinthians.

In the Hellenistic blood sacrifice the meat was distributed in three, not two, ways. The god's portion (μηρία) was burned upon the altar, and certain parts were allotted to the worshippers for their consumption. But a third portion was also dedicated to the god and placed upon his special table.[38] This portion was termed the τραπέζομα. In theory it was for the deity to consume, but in practice it was consumed by the worshippers and/or the cult officials.[39] This portion of the sacrifice placed upon the "table of the god" was distinct from that put on the altar.

David Gill, in a study of the cult tables, notes their infrequent mention in ancient literature,[40] but their frequent appearance in inscriptions and archaeological remains.[41] Gill shows that it is possible to draw a much fuller picture of these tables and their function from sacred laws and cult inscriptions. These show that the food on the table of the god was treated in the same way as the portions which were assigned to the sacrificers. The tables were cared for by a variety of cultic personnel (the epimeletai, the priests, the archon, the mesogeioi).[42] In many cases the priests in charge received this portion assigned to the deity, in addition to their own allotment.[43]

---

[38]Gill, "Trapezomata," is the most thorough study of this portion "deposed" for the god. The Latin equivalent is the *mensa sacra*, although Tacitus 13.17 calls Nero's family table by that name.

[39]Gill, "Trapezomata," 124. This portion placed on the god's table is variously termed: τραπεζώματα, θεομοιρία, and ἱερὰ μοῖρα.

[40]Dow and Gill, 124f. But see Aristophanes, *Av.* 518f. and Plutarch, *Frag.* 95 (Sandbach ed.).

[41]Gill, "Trapezomata," 125. Also Dow and Gill, 109. This article examines the construction of the cult table and its equipment. See also Yerkes, 108, who quotes SIG[3] 1106, a c. 300 B.C. inscription from Cos. Other relevant inscriptions are found in SIG[3] 996.1-16; 1022; 1038; 1042.

[42]Dow and Gill, 126.

[43]Ibid., 127. This table could be the source of meat used both for cultic dining and perhaps also sold in the market (1 Cor 10:25). Several writers mention men sharing from provisions left on the god's table. E.g., Diodorus Siculus 4.74.2; Julian, *Or.* 5.176d. Athenaeus 372 refers to the custom at Delphi that the one who offers the largest onion at the yearly *theoxenia* for Leto receives a portion from her table.

The origin of the table of the god is not certain. Gill suggests that it came from an awareness that the god actually received a meager portion in the *thusia*, and so was granted an additional portion at the subsequent sacred meal.[44] A. D. Nock suspects that the Greeks simply could not see wasting so much good meat by immolating it.[45] The cult table would have been a possible source for meat sold in markets, and would have been especially significant for the various private associations (*orgeones, thiasotai, eranisti,* etc.) which gathered for regular (often monthly) banquets.[46]

In summary, the τραπέζα δαιμονίων mentioned in 1 Cor 10:21 refers to a common feature of Greek sacrifice. It was not the altar, but a table on which a portion of the meat was placed. This portion, although dedicated to the deity, was consumed by the worshippers, or given to the priests. It may have been the origin of the view that the gods ate the meal with the worshippers, and the sacramental interpretation of Hellenistic mystery religions.

MEANINGS SUGGESTED FOR CULTIC MEALS

What these meals following pagan sacrifices may have meant for those who participated is both very important, and yet very difficult, to determine. Much of what is known derives from archaeological remains, and although these do testify to the existence of such meals, they give little information on the meaning of the meals to the participants.

Similarly, while inscriptional remains give valuable information about the conduct and organization of such gatherings, including private associations, they too provide little direct insight on the meaning of the meals. The scattered references in literary remains also inform largely by implication. Because the meaning of the meal is not given explicitly, we are forced to find it by a process of inference. The result has been major disagreement on the proper interpretation of the evidence.

Aristophanes spoofs, *Pl.* 655.81, the priests taking from the table of the god (ἀπὸ τῆς τραπέζης τῆς ἱερᾶς) and the altar (βωμός) as well.

[44]Gill, "Trapezomata," 135f.

[45]Nock, "Cult of Heroes," 597.

[46]SIG[3] 1042, a sacred law from Attica regarding a private shrine for Men prescribes that those sacrificing receive half from the table of the god and assemble an ἔρανος for Men. Other examples are in Gill, "Trapezomata," 125-32.

In spite of the difficulty of determining the meaning of these meals, their importance is very real. This is especially true for students of the New Testament and early Christian worship. For example, it is often the case that how such pagan meals are understood influences how the Lord's Supper is understood in the New Testament.

The meaning of cultic meals in Hellenistic religion has been conceived basically in the following ways (with due allowance for differing emphases by individual scholars): (1) the *Sacramental*, (2) the *Communal*, and (3) the *Social* interpretations. Before investigating the best evidence for the sacramentalist interpretation, it is well to be clear about these alternatives.

(1) The *Sacramental* view is that in the cult meal the worshippers consumed their deity who was contained (really or symbolically) in the sacrificial meat. The worshippers thereby appropriated for themselves his peculiar traits and powers and established a most intimate union with him. The most famous example of the effect of this interpretation on the study of 1 Corinthians is the excursus, "Kultmahle" in the Lietzmann commentary on the Corinthian letters, first published in 1907.[47]

In fairness to Lietzmann, it is important to realize that he is only one example of a view widely held in his time. The particulars of the sacramentalist view of pagan meals were developed and endorsed by leading scholars in classical studies, as well as by important figures in New Testament studies. It is a tribute to Lietzmann's erudition and persuasive style that his excursus has played such a decisive role in New Testament studies ever since, although the excursus is only a page and a half in length.

Lietzmann discusses both the sacramentalist and the communal interpretations as present in Hellenistic piety. He thinks the sacramentalist view, while rare, influenced Paul's warning to the Corinthians. He says, concerning these sacramental meals, "Das macht die Warnung des Pls verständlich: beim Abendmahl nehmt ihr den Herrn Christus in euch auf, beim Götzenfest fährt der Dämon in euch."[48]

J. A. MacCulloch,[49] and others, present a variation of the sacramentalist view by suggesting that the general meaning of cultic meals was

---

[47]Hans Lietzmann, *An die Korinther I, II* (HNT 9; Tübingen: J. C. B. Mohr [Paul Siebeck], 1907) 49-51. Revised 4th ed.; W. G. Kümmel.
[48]Ibid., 50.
[49]MacCulloch, "Sacrament," 901f. Like Farnell, he cites W. R. Smith to support his conclusions.

communal (the worshippers sharing a meal with the deity), but in certain cults, e.g., Dionysiac, the first view is held, in which the deity himself was eaten in his incarnation. According to this *Sacramental-Communal* view the sacramentalism of certain mystery cults was what made them unique. MacCulloch refers especially to the Dionysiac cult.[50] Other influential scholars who subscribe to this modified view of a limited sacramentalism include E. R. Goodenough,[51] and Franz Cumont.[52]

Nonetheless, the sacramentalist view has largely fallen into disfavor today. Even when contemporary scholars do suggest this interpretation it is with caution and strict limitations. A. D. Nock noted in a review of E. R. Goodenough's *Jewish Symbols,* volume seven, "Many would reject the totemism and the communication of divine life [in the sacrificial communion as pictured by Goodenough and W. R. Smith], but would accept the idea of partaking together of the flesh of the victim."[53] Thus, we now turn our attention to the second view, the *Communal*, which is the prominent one today.

(2) The *Communal* interpretation: a meal shared with the deity. In this view the cult meal was a solemn occasion of worship in which the god and the worshippers together consumed the sacrifice. In what was earlier noted about Greek sacrificial practice, it is clear that the customary meal accompanying sacrifice included a share both for the deity and the worshippers. The most obvious example of this was that a portion was immolated (literally, "smoked") to the god.[54] But also there was the portion for the "table of the god." From the fact that both the gods and men benefited from the sacrifice, it is often concluded that a "sense of inner fellowship" between gods and men resulted.[55] MacCulloch states well this view, that the cultic meal was "a meal eaten in common with the god. He [the god], being satisfied with his share of the feast, as it were,

---

[50]Ibid., 899.

[51]Erwin R. Goodenough, *Jewish Symbols in the Greco-Roman World* (New York: Pantheon Books, 1958) 7.5f., 16ff.

[52]Franz Cumont, *The Mysteries of Mithra* (New York: Dover, 1956; 1st ed., 1903). *Idem., Oriental Religions in Roman Paganism* (Chicago: Open Court, 1911).

[53]A. D. Nock, "Review of E. R. Goodenough, *Jewish Symbols,*" *ERAW,* 2.916. Also, "Cult of Heroes," 597-600.

[54]Yerkes, 94.

[55]Farnell, "Sacrifice (Greek)," 15.

invites his worshippers to eat with him."[56] It is the presence and participation of the god at the meal which makes it sacred; therefore men are
his hosts or guests and thus in fellowship with him.[57]

Interestingly, this second view, which seems so modest in contrast
with the sacramental one, is more often assumed than argued. But A. D.
Nock has already raised important objection to the Communal meal view,

> ... participation in the flesh of a sacrificed victim did not
> involve conscious table fellowship with the supernatural
> recipient of the other parts of the animal, and, although a god
> was now guest, now host, man kept his distance.[58]

(3) The *Social* interpretation: a meal eaten before the deity. I turn
now to a third possible interpretation of the cultic meals in Hellenistic
religions. It has a subtle, yet very real, difference from the prominent
communal interpretation. This difference may be summarized thus: in
the communal view the meal is an occasion of conscious worship in which
the sacrificers consider the meal sacred because the deity ate with them;
in the social view, while due regard was given the deity and a portion
allotted to him, the focus is on the social relationship among the worshippers. The deity is more an observer than a participant. (One is tempted
to say the communal view is more "sacramental" than the social one, but
the use of the word "sacramental" in describing Greek cult meals may be
basically unwise. It is a word too often fraught with various aspects of
later Christian theology.)

After a consideration of the evidence for sacramentalism in Hellenistic meals, evidence for the social interpretation will be considered. At
present it need only be noted that it is certainly true that cult meals
involved a deity (the meat came from a sacrifice).[59] But this need not
imply either a sacramental or communal understanding of these meals. In
many instances "whether we should consider them as a common meal of

---

[56]MacCulloch, "Sacrament," 897, thinks this is the meaning of sacrifice and meal in most cults, excluding the mysteries such as Dionysus.

[57]H. J. Rose, "Meals, Sacred," *Oxford Classical Dictionary*
(Oxford: Clarendon Press, 1970, 2d ed.) 658. Ancient references cited to
illustrate this view are numerous, yet their meaning is often uncertain if
one asks what the meals meant to the participants.

[58]Nock, "Cult of Heroes," 582.

[59]Although see Robert F. Healey, "A Sacrifice without a deity in
the Athenian State Calendar," *HTR* 57 (1964) 153ff.

god(s) and men, or a meal among men which was preceded by a gift of food to the god, is not fully clear."[60] This is the case although a god might be named as host or guest, or invited to the sacrifice which preceded.[61] Greek *thusiai* were doubtless accompanied by religious sentiment and sanction, but that they involved a sense of personal relationship with the deity is doubtful.[62] Even when a shared table is mentioned, it should not be assumed that the meal was a conscious occasion of communion with the deity.

PROPOSED EVIDENCE FOR
PAGAN SACRAMENTALISM IN CULT MEALS

The evidence most often put forward to support a sacramental interpretation of meals in Hellenistic cults is that taken from the mystery religions. Several scholars have suggested that the idea of a sacramental meal was developed in these mystery cults. Even A. D. Nock, who is basically quite suspicious of the "sacramental" interpretation, especially the suggestion that this shapes early Christian theology, seems open to a sacramental concept in the mysteries.[63]

---

[60]Gill, "Trapezomata," 123; MacCulloch, "Sacrament," 898. Nock, "Cult of Heroes," 586, notes that the dead were often invited to the meals. Pausanias, 4.27.4, recounts a feast of the Dioscuri among the Lacedemonians. The worshippers had "turned to drinking and sports after the mid-day meal" and were destroyed by two enemies. The Lacedemonians bowed and prayed as their slayers approached, thinking the Dioscuri themselves had come to their feast. Did their drinking at the feast affect their judgment, and does it reveal the mood of the worship?

[61]For example, Julian, *Or.* 5, ". . . in the sacrifices which we honor most highly the gods in which alone the gods deign to join us and share our table."

[62]Nock, "Cult of Heroes," 587, says "in fact, a personal relationship, other than one of dependence and gratitude, to a *numen*, is barely thinkable."

[63]A. D. Nock, *Early Gentile Christianity and its Hellenistic Background* (New York: Harper, 1964) 74f., mentions particularly the mysteries of Eleusis and the cult of Attis. He refrains from accepting even these as sacramental, but is more open to the possibility in them than in other Greek cults. Nock stresses that we simply do not have evidence which allows us to know how the mysteries were understood by their members.

There were many mystery cults in the Imperial period, but this study will be able only to consider the four most often used to support a sacramental interpretation: the mysteries of Eleusis, Dionysus, Mithras, and Isis-Sarapis.

A. Eleusis

Eleusis is an appropriate cult to consider first, both because of its antiquity and its wide influence.[64] The fame and influence of Eleusis was increased by various satellite shrines in the Hellenistic world. Eleusis was virtually the pattern for the various "mysteries" of the age. However, exactly what *occurred* in the cult of Demeter and Kore at Eleusis is not known, and speculations vary widely.[65]

The annual festival held at Eleusis surely included a meal, as well as other acts often held to be sacramental in character. But George Mylonas, who has given us a recent, most thorough investigation of the cult, states repeatedly that for many questions about these events accurate answers are just not possible from the extant evidence.

There was a fast which ended with the drink called the *kykeon,* but what it meant to drink this cup is not certain. Mylonas rightly objects to such highly interpretive translations of Hesiod's *Homeric Hymn to Zeus* (δεξαμένη δ᾽ ὁσίης ἕνεκεν πολυπότνια Δηώ) as Evelyn-White's, "so the great queen Deo received it to observe the sacrament" or Allen and Sikes', "to observe the rite."[66]

In the worship of Eleusis there were sacrifices to Demeter, Kore and other deities. The sacrifices were not held in secret, but were public events in Athens on behalf of the city and its inhabitants.[67] The mysteries, basically a drama, themselves were held within the sacred theater at

---

[64]On the cult of Demeter and Kore in Eleusis see W. K. C. Guthrie, *The Greeks and Their Gods* (Boston: Beacon House, 1950) 282f. Especially see the complete study by George Mylonas, *Eleusis and the Eleusinian Mysteries* (Princeton: University Press, 1961).

[65]The secrets of the Eleusinian mysteries were protected by Athenian civil law, as well as by fear of the gods. Mylonas, 224f.

[66]Mylonas, 259f. H. G. Evelyn-White's translation is in the Loeb edition. See also T. W. Allen and E. E. Sikes, *The Homeric Hymns* (Oxford: Clarendon Press, 1904). Mylonas thinks that the drinking of the *kykeon* was an act of religious remembrance, but implied no sacramental or mystical meaning.

[67]Mylonas, 260ff., also 238-41.

Eleusis. Some have conjectured that these secret rites included a sacra-mental meal, but this is only conjectural.[68] From what is known, Eleusis's mysteries were essentially something *seen*. There is no emphasis on either sacrifice or meals, although surely both occurred.

Mylonas summarizes in an appendix the interpretations of Eleusin-ian worship found in early Christian writers, as well as modern historians. He concludes that the church fathers (Clement, Hippolytus, Tertullian, and Asterios) who comment on the Eleusis worship are not reliable, but have conflated Eleusis with other cults, or misunderstood much of what was in fact Eleusinian.[69] In summary, there is insufficient evidence to use Eleusis as evidence that sacramental meals were a part of Hellenistic cults.

B. Dionysus

Perhaps the best evidence for sacramental meals as a feature of a Hellenistic cult is the cult of Dionysus. In particular there is the picture of the cult given in Euripides's play, *The Bacchae*.[70] This evidence has been used to prove that there was a meal in which the god himself, incar-nate in a wild animal, was eaten. Yet even here, one must remain cau-tious and not assume what has been hypothesized is thereby proven.

The earliest references to Dionysis are oblique. In Hesiod's *Homeric Hymns* it is said, "When Demeter saw them [Hermes and Per-sephone] she rushed forth as does a maenad down some thick-wooded

---

[68]Mylonas, 271. See also Bruce M. Metzger, "Considerations of Method in the study of mystery religions," *HTR* 48 (1955) 13f., who rightly says that it is begging the question to assume the Eleusinian cult meal (which is nowhere described) must have had a sacramental significance for the worshippers because it was a mystery religion. Metzger notes funda-mental differences between the Eleusinian cult drink and the Pauline Lord's Supper.

[69]Mylonas, 297-316.

[70]The *Bacchae* was written at the end of the fifth century B.C., and first performed in Athens after the death of its author. Two recent editions of the play take opposite interpretations of the evidence in the *Bacchae* for Dionysiac religion. E. R. Dodds, *Euripides: Bacchae* (2d rev.; Oxford: Clarendon Press, 1960); G. S. Kirk, *The Bacchae of Euripides* (Englewood Cliffs, NJ: Prentice-Hall, 1970).

The cult of Dionysus was also known as the Bacchic cult in the Hellenistic and Roman periods.

mountain."[71]   Maenads were a prominent feature in the cult of Dionysus and his myth, but little is made clear about them or about sacramentalism from this offhand remark.   The reference in Homer is similar.[72]   All these early references establish is the antiquity of Dionysism.

The character and significance of early Dionysiac worship is hotly debated, especially the meaning of the *omophagia* (the meal of raw flesh). E. R. Dodds is a representative of the view that the orgiastic worship of Dionysis pictured in *The Bacchae* has a basis in real cultic practices.   He comments on Diodorus 4:3 (which describes Dionysiac dances at Delphi), "Probably he is right, as regards his own time; but ritual is usually older than the myth by which people explain it, and has deeper psychological roots."[73]   This assumption of Dodds is especially important for the *omophagia* widely used to prove a sacramentalism in Greek cult meals.

Facing the slim documentary evidence of Dionysiac worship before Euripides, some scholars have tried to reconstruct the earlier cult by comparing similarities with other cults, both ancient and modern. Dodds, for example, notes parallels to ecstatic worship in the middle ages and in contemporary primitive peoples.[74]   He stresses the psychological roots of the *omophagia* and considers foundational to a proper understanding the reconstruction of Erwin Rohde.   He says that Rohde was "the first modern writer who understood the Dionysiac psychology. . . . His *Psyche* . . . is still the fundamental book."[75]

---

[71]Hesiod, *The Homeric Hymns: Hymn to Demeter* 1.386.

[72]Homer, *Od.* 8.266ff.   Kirk, 6, comments: "It may be doubted whether any integrated conception of the god . . . was commonly held during the fifth century, when Dionysus was already firmly established at Delphi under the aegis of Apollo and at Eleusis under the aegis of Demeter."   He also notes that "evidence is scarce for the period before Euripides, and afterward it proliferates almost uncontrollably."

[73]E. R. Dodds, *The Greeks and the Irrational* (Boston: Beacon Press, 1957) 271.   He concludes there "must have been a time when the maenads or thyriads or βάκχαι really became for a few hours or days what their name implies—wild women whose human personality has been temporarily replaced by another."   Diodorus wrote in the middle of the 1st century B.C.

[74]Dodds, *Bacchae*, xv.

[75]Ibid., xi.   Dodds refers to Erwin Rohde, *Psyche* (New York: Harcourt Brace and World, 1925).   According to Rohde, the ecstasy was intentionally induced by the dancing, shrieks, etc., to lead the worshipper to lose herself (or himself).   This psychologizing view is critiqued by W. F.

In his discussion of "Maenadism" Dodds argues that the ecstatic orgia was a real, not merely poetic or mythical, practice.[76] This is especially seen in his treatment of the *omophagia*. Summarizing his interpretation, Dodds says:

> I have tried to show that Euripides' description of maenadism is not to be accounted for in terms of the imagination alone; that inscriptional evidence (incomplete as it is) reveals a closer relationship with the actual cult than Victorian scholars realized, and that the maenad, however mythical certain of her acts, is not in essence a mythological character but an observed and still observable human type.[77]

It is important to realize that Dodds is not alone in presenting this interpretation, but represents a widely defended view. In the concluding section of his very complete *The Cults of the Greek States*, Farnell says of the *omophagia*:

> The inward significance of this strange religious act is still a matter of controversy. The explanation here adopted, that in its primary meaning it is an ecstatic sacramental act of communion, seems incontrovertible, but may not be a complete account of it.[78]

Otto, *Dionysus: Myth and Cult* (Bloomington, Ind.: Indiana University Press, 1965) 124f.

[76]Dodds, *The Greeks and the Irrational*, 270-80. In addition to the parallels from other cultures, he cites numerous inscriptions; Pausanias, 8.23.1; Aelian, *Var. Hist.* 13.2; and Firmicus Maternus, *Err. Prof. Rel.* 6.5.

Plato, *Ion*, 534, compares the coming of the spirit upon the Corybants and Bacchants with the inspiration of poets and dramatists. Thus the Dionysiac ecstasy is a metaphor.

[77]Dodds, *The Greeks and the Irrational*, 278.

[78]L. R. Farnell, *The Cults of the Greek States* (Oxford: Clarendon Press, 1909) 5.177, especially see notes 80-85. Farnell considers this ritual to be the clearest example of sacramental communion evidenced. Dodds, *Bacchae*, xvii, supports such an interpretation, and adds to Farnell's evidence a cult regulation from Miletus (Milet 6.22) dated 276 B.C. which he thinks proves the throwing of a living animal to a crowd for dismemberment and devouring as an act of Bacchic worship.

Martin P. Nilsson, *The Dionysiac Mysteries of the Hellenistic and Roman Ages* (New York: Arno Press, 1975) 7f., interprets the evidence, including the Miletus inscription, in much more mundane terms. See also

The basic theory behind the sacramentalist interpretation of the *omophagia* is that in the eating the worshippers ingest their deity. W. K. C. Guthrie states well this thesis on the *omophagia:*

> This primitive communion (which rests "on the possibility of obliterating the line between the human and the divine, whether for a long period or for a brief moment of ecstasy, blending the two natures in one") was achieved by consuming the flesh and blood of the god in his animal form, a culmination which we have seen referred to by Euripides.[79]

Dodds himself states a similar rationale:

> . . .the practice seems to rest in fact on a very simple piece of savage logic. The homeopathic effects of a flesh diet are well known all over the world. . . . If you want to be like god you must eat god (or at any rate something which is θεῖον). And you must eat him quick and raw, before the blood has oozed from him. Only so can you add his life to yours, for "the blood is the life."[80]

Dodds even suggests that the *omophagia* and *sparagmos* had once involved a human victim.[81] In his summary of this point he says, "we cannot be sure, and some scholars deny it. There are, however, scattered indications which point that way."[82] He notes that later Greek writers explained the *omophagia* as merely commemorative of the day when the

---

Kane, "Mithraic Cult Meals," who notes that this is the only inscription of a Dionysiac society from the Hellenistic and Roman periods which mentions the *omophagion.* See pages 336f.

[79]Guthrie, 49. Elsewhere, 45, he cites a fragment of Euripides's *The Cretans,* now found in Porphyry, *Abst.* 4.19, in which the Cretans tore a live bull apart with their teeth. Euripides's quote is used for apologetic purposes by Firmicus Maternus, *Err. Prof. Rel.* 6.15.

[80]Dodds, *The Greeks and the Irrational,* 277. The quote is from Deut 12.23.

[81]Dodds, *Bacchae,* 224. This comments on lines 1183f. in the *Bacchae,* where Agaue, while still a maenad, suggests having a meal of her slain son's head. See also Kirk, 121.

[82]Dodds, *Bacchae,* xvif., cites in support, Oppian, *Cyn.* 4.304; Plutarch, *Quaest. Graec.* 38 and D. L. Page, *Select Papyri* (Loeb), 1.134. The pseudonymous *Cynegetica* is probably 3d cent. A.D.; Plutarch, the end of the 1st cent. A.D., and the papryrus, 5th cent. A.D. Thus they all could easily be dependent on Euripides.

infant Dionysus was himself torn to pieces and devoured.[83] But he considered this interpretation to be too reductionistic.

Dodds is a clear and careful representative of the sacramental interpretation of the Dionysiac *omophagia* that argues that the worshippers believed themselves to consume the deity. But others have interpreted the evidence from Euripides and the Dionysiac cult quite differently.

Commenting on Dodds' arguments, G. S. Kirk says, "I wonder whether he has not gone too far in implying that, because many of the details of Dionysus' worship seem to be based on observation, the general picture [in Euipirides] is accurate, not necessarily for the late fifth century but for the archaic past."[84]

In his own edition of the *Bacchae* Kirk suggests that the *sparagmos* and *omophagia* interpreted as being Dionysus embodied in an animal is a "late development."[85] The phrase often quoted from line 139, "rejoicing in raw flesh," Kirk believes simply refers to an animal, and "the purpose ... was probably to bring the worshipper as close as possible to the life, power, and liberation of wild Nature which Dionysus represented."[86] He suggests that sacrifice is not as important in Dionysiac worship.

Kirk strongly objects to Dodd's translation of line 75 in the *Bacchae:* "O blessed is he who, by happy favour knowing the sacraments of the gods, leads the life of holy service and is inwardly a member of God's company." Kirk comments:

> Taking part in the devouring of raw flesh ... among a band of ecstatic women on Mount Cathaeron was really very unlike a Christian communion or mass. ... The very word "sacrament" is surely incorrect, unless it can be clearly shown that in eating a piece of goat the bacchants thought they were eating the god himself, or a symbol of him, rather than assimilating a bit of raw Nature.[87]

---

[83]Dodds, *The Greeks and the Irrational*, 277, commenting on those favoring a "commemorative" interpretation of the *omophagia*, says this is "as some would explain the Christian communion." One suspects here that Dodds' understanding of the Christian communion influences his views on Dionysus.

[84]Kirk, 7.

[85]Ibid.

[86]Ibid., 41.

[87]Ibid., 34. Like Dodds, Kirk seems to assume the "sacramental" character of the Christian cult meal. They are, no doubt, reflecting common Eucharistic thought in contemporary Christendom. However, this need not be assumed present in 1 Corinthians 10.

It must be understood that there is agreement among Kirk and
Dodds, and others, that in some way Dionysiac religion as pictured in the
Bacchae involved the eating of the raw flesh of an animal. What is con-
troverted is the (alleged) sacramental significance of that eating. Just as
Dodds is not the only scholar who holds the act to have been sacramental,
so also Kirk is not the only scholar to deny it. W. F. Otto had written
much earlier, "Nowhere in all the sources does the idea appear that the
devout partook of the flesh of the god for their benefit."[88]

Thus far the investigation has dealt with the picture of Dionysiac
rites found in the *Bacchae*, because the best evidence of a sacramentalism
is found therein. The evidence is sparse, however, and its meaning uncertain. Arguments can be made both for and against a sacramental understanding of the *omophagia*, especially if one relies on interpretations
taken from apparent or alleged parallels in other cultures. However, even
if a sacramental eating of the raw flesh was a part of Dionysiac religion
before Euripides, it was: (1) exceptional and (2) reduced to only a memory
in the time of Paul.

To complete this brief survey of Dionysiac cultic eating, it is
necessary to consider evidence after the time of Euripides. Dodds summarizes regarding the later domestication of the cult very well:

> In the course of the centuries which separate the first ap-
> pearance of the Dionysiac cult in Greece from the age of
> Euripides, it was brought under state control and lost much of
> its original character, at any rate in Attica. The Athenians
> of Euripides' time had no biennial winter rite, no mountain
> dancing, no ὠμοφαγία; they were content to send a delegation
> of women to represent them at the Delphic τριετηρίς. So
> far as we know, their own Dionysiac festivals were very
> different; they were occasions for old-fashioned country
> magic, as at the rural Dionysia, or for pious and cheerful
> drunkenness, as at the feast of the cities; or for a display of
> the civic and cultural greatness of Athens, as at the city
> Dionysia.[89]

---

[88]Otto, *Dionysus*, 132. Otto also says, 131: "Whatever one may
think of it [the theory of sacramentalism] is cannot be applied to the rite
of Dionysus unless one uses the most artificial hypothesis and the most
daring jump of logic." He also argues that the rending of Pentheus cannot
be interpreted as the human embodiment of Dionysus, for he is his enemy.

[89]Dodds, *Bacchae*, xxif. This loss of the orgiastic aspect of
Dionysiac worship he believes occurred at different times in differing

The later evidence from the Hellenistic and Roman periods shows the Dionysiac cult to have operated similarly to other *thiasoi*. The master of Greek religion, Martin P. Nilsson, gives a chronological study of the cult, and concludes that the Dionysiac (or Bacchic) mysteries resembled numerous other associations of Hellenistic and later periods, which assembled to enjoy themselves and feast under the pretext of honoring some god after whom the association was named.[90]

Evidence for Nilsson's interpretations of Dionysiac religion in Hellenistic Greece is found in Athenaeus. He reports that the victorious Mark Anthony erected a scaffold (in imitation of a cave) on the side of the Athenian acropolis. He outfitted this stage with various Dionysiac paraphernalia and greenery, then drank there from morning until night with his friends, proclaiming himself "Dionysus."[91] A later emperor, Gaius Caligula, similarly arrayed himself in Dionysiac costume and had himself proclaimed "the new Dionysus."[92]

Nilsson carefully reviews the Dionysiac, or Bacchic, societies of Imperial Italy and his conclusions support the non-sacramental understanding of Dionysism urged here. He notes that knowledge of the Bacchic mysteries in Italy is solely dependent on monumental art.[93] There is not space, or need, to rehearse again here his evidence, but his conclusions on Italian Bacchic cults are important for this study.

First, Nilsson notes that in Italy the cult sites of Dionysus were private homes, rather than temples as in the Greek cults.[94] Second, he says the careful art of Villa Item, Villa Farnesnia, the "Homeric" house, the Campana relief, and various sarcophagi, "all suggest a cult of upper class, financially secure people." Nilsson suggests that in Italy Dionysiac cults were a religion of a conservative class who sought to add a "little thrill of religion as a spice to the daily routine."[95]

---

locales. In Athens it was already gone by Euripides's time. Dodds says that the Dionysiac cult was perhaps the oldest of Greek dramatic subjects, and the play of Euripides was "a rehandling of a theme already familiar to generations of Athenian play-goers." Ibid., xxvii.

[90]Nilsson, *Dionysiac Mysteries*, 64. Nilsson also examines the extant evidence for the cult in its later stages, including inscriptional and archaeological remains.

[91]Athenaeus, 4.148.

[92]Ibid.

[93]Nilsson, *Dionysiac Mysteries*, 66. He examines the monuments individually and has reproductions of most, 66-106.

[94]Ibid., 144.

[95]Ibid., 147.

One difficulty with interpreting most Greek cults, and especially in the cult of Dionysus, is that the evidence comes from a wide variety of places and times, and allowance must be made for these differences. Some examples will illustrate the variety of ways in which Dionysus cults operated.[96]

Diodorus Siculus 4.3 suggests that possibly there were two gods known as Dionysus. One had a cult which celebrated semi-annually by roving bands of women waving the *thyrsus* and shouting "Euai!," as they acted the role of maenads. Another Dionysus, called Sabazius, had his birth and sacrifices and honors celebrated secretly by night in drunkenness and sexual debauchery.

Other examples of variety in Dionysiac worship include Plutarch's description of an Egyptian cult in which he equates Osiris and Dionysus, because their processions are similar, featuring wearing skins, carrying wands and employing ecstatic shouts.[97] Pausanias says that at Pellene Dionysus was surnamed "Torch" and worshipped in a festival called the feast (ἑορτή) of torches, celebrated with a torch-light parade and bowls of wine set throughout the city.[98] In another place Pausanias says at Alea the bi-annual festival of Dionysus included the flogging of the city's women.[99] Finally, Aelian says the people of Tenedos had a yearly festival to Dionysus the Man-Slayer which was conducted in a way very similar to the Athenian *bouphania*.[100]

Even in this variety of expressions of Dionysiac religion, it is granted that it had an unconventional mythology, at least. The reports of drunkenness and sexual immorality, regardless of their foundation, appear to have led to an official regulation and suppression of Bacchism in Italy.[101]

---

[96]Nilsson, *Dionysiac Mysteries*, 7, suggests that these differences represent regional variations in Dionysism. He also reminds us, 144, that we are dealing with a cult which covered over 500 years (in the Hellenistic and Imperial periods alone) and is spread geographically from Africa and Egypt through Asia Minor, Greece and Italy.

[97]Plutarch, *Is. et Os.* 364E.

[98]Pausanias, 7.27.3.

[99]Ibid., 8.23.1.

[100]Aelian, *Nat. An.* 12.34.

[101]Nilsson, *Dionysiac Mysteries*, 15-21, reviews the attempts to suppress the cult in Italy. See also A. D. Nock, "The Historical Importance of Cult-Association," *Classical Review* 38 (1924) 105-109. Livy 8.39f. is a major source on the attempt to suppress Dionysism in Rome.

In addition to the arguments against a sacramentalist meal behind the Dionysiac *omophagia*, it is important to note several indications of the domestication of Dionysism which expose its social character, at least in the Hellenistic and Imperial periods.

Nilsson notes that the titles and functionaries of the Dionysiac associations reflect the common practices of other Greek associations.[102] This can be illustrated from a second-century A.D. inscription of an Athenian Dionysiac *thiasos*, which describes offices in the cult, the honors and responsibilities which are involved, and tries to set limits on boisterous conduct in the meetings.[103]

Athenaeus gives a description of a Dionysus guild whose meeting involves basically eating barley cakes and a broth. On special occasions, when cattle were sacrificed, boys shared a meal with their fathers and the family slaves.[104] This meeting seems very tame, much like other tribal associations whose meetings are known from the classical period.

Another description of Athenaeus quotes Eratosthenes's *Arsinoe* which describes a Dionysiac cult in Alexandria. Arsinoe stopped a man carrying a flagon and olive branches and asked what the holiday celebrated. She was told it was called "Flagon-Bearing" which included a common meal at which each man brought his own flagon from home. Arsinoe then concluded, "That must indeed be a dirty get-together. For the assembly can only be that of a miscellaneous mob who have themselves served with a stale and utterly unseemly feast."[105] Her suspicions are also reflected in Aristophanes's *Wasps*. There two household slaves change the watch in an Athenian home. One notes the other is very drowsy and says, "Surely you're a maniac or a Corybant." The other replies, "Nay, 'tis a sleep from great Sabazius holds me" and produces a wine flask. The first then produces his own flask and replies "Aha! and I'm your fellow-votary there."[106]

---

[102]Nilsson, *Dionysiac Mysteries,* 55f., notes an inscription from Thrace which gives as cult officials: ἑστιαρχός (maitre de) and κρατηρι-άρχος (wine captain). Nilsson also notes the proliferation of titles and offices in the cult, comparable to trends in other Hellenistic cults. *Ibid.,* 51-64.

[103]SIG³ 1109. See Nock, "Historical Importance," 107, who notes here Dionysus is associated with Demeter and Kore. He thinks that by the Christian period Orphic, Eleusinian, and Dionysiac terms had become indistinguishable.

[104]Athenaeus, 4.149c.

[105]Ibid., 7.276b.

[106]Aristophanes, *Vesp.* 7-10.

From the evidence set out here, and the detailed study by Nilsson, it seems a judicious conclusion that from several centuries before the time of Paul, Dionysiac religion did not include sacramental meals (if it ever had) and the *omophagia* was only a myth to members. This does not deny that the possession of the myth made for a different character to the cult but argues that the idea of sacramental communion was not operative nor had been for centuries.[107] In conclusion, once again I quote from Kane:

> Scholars who have not based their judgment of this *sparagmos* (dismemberment), and *omophagia* (eating of raw flesh) on the context and vocabulary of the Greek sources, but rather on modern anthropological "parallels," similar experiences in other cultures, or the writing of mystics, have attempted to establish that it was a kind of sacramental act whereby the powers of the animal (and ivy?) devoured were acquired or in which an animal embodying Dionysus was eaten so that the participants could gain his powers or be united with him. But the classical sources are unanimous in placing far more emphasis on other facets of the Dionysiac frenzy than the *omophagia*, which is only rarely mentioned until it begins to exercise the fascination of the unknown upon the minds of scholiasts, lexicographers, and Church Fathers. *There is no reason why this act should be isolated and assigned a special, unique meaning of its own.*[108]

---

[107] As has been seen, Euripides's *Bacchae* has been the main source of the "sacramental" understanding of the cult of Dionysus. It ought to be remembered that Dionysus was the patron of comedies as well as tragedies, and he is pictured much differently in Aristophanes, *Frogs*. Yet it may be that Aristophanes has caricatured him no more than has Euripides. See Victor Ehrenberg, *The People of Aristophanes* (Oxford: Basil Blackwell, 1951) 253.

[108] Kane, "Mithraic Cult Meals," 335. Ivy was also a feature of Dionysiac religion. Plutarch, *Quaest. Rom.* 112, says the manaeds tore ivy from a tree and masticated it. Significantly, this is already a primitive curiosity in Plutarch, who is searching for an explanation of the popular custom of not touching ivy. Pausanias, 1.21.6, says in Archarne Dionysus Ivy was invoked in worship.

C. Mithraism

In the present brief review of proposed evidence of sacramentalism in Hellenistic religions, Mithraism is perhaps the latest example. Although the evidence for Mithraism is more extensive than either Dionysiac or Eleusinian mysteries, it too is highly debated among scholars in the area. Franz Cumont[109] and M. J. Vermaseren,[110] pioneering Mithraic specialists who have edited and published the standard collections of sources, argue that Mithraism featured in its worship a sacramental meal from pre-Christian times. Their arguments will be reviewed briefly below. Fortunately, the recent reassessment of their positions by J. P. Kane[111] pursues the same basic questions which concern this present study. Thus it is sufficient to refer substantially to Kane's review.

The sources available for reconstruction of Mithraism essentially are three: the Avestan texts from pre-Hellenic Iranian religion, the archaeological and artistic remains in excavated Mithraic sites, and very limited references in Christian authors. The first two sources are complicated by their dating. The Avestan texts are controversial also in the nature of their relationship to Mithraism (they actually come from ancient Persian religion). Kane insists that they are of very questionable reliability for interpreting Mithraism in the Hellenistic era.[112] Conversely, the archaeological evidence is all from the Imperial period or later, at least from the late first century A.D.[113]

The quotations from the church fathers, specifically Justin Martyr, *Apologia prima* 66,[114] and Tertullian, *De praescriptione haereticorum*

---

[109]Of his many studies on Mithraism, two most important are in English: Franz Cumont, *Mysteries of Mithra*, and *Oriental Religions*. Also see the assessment of his work cited below in note 111.

[110]M. J. Vermaseren, *Mithras, the Secret God* (New York: Barnes & Noble, 1963), summarizes his investigations and the conclusions he has accepted.

[111]Kane, "Mithraic Cult Meals," 314-17, on Cumont and 318-20 on Vermaseren, with reference to their positions throughout the article.

[112]Ibid., 314f., and 317.

[113]Ibid., 342-348, reviews the monuments.

[114]The text in Justin is related to a discussion of the Christian meal shared with new initiates. It runs: ὅπερ καὶ ἐν τοῖς τοῦ Μίθρα μυστηρίοις παρέδωκαν γίνεσθαι μιμησάμενοι οἱ πονηροὶ δαίμονες ὅτι γὰρ ἄρτος καὶ ποτήριον ὕδατος τίθεται ἐν ταῖς τοῦ μυουμένου τελεταῖς μετ' ἐπιλόγων τινῶν ἢ ἐπίστασθε ἢ μαθεῖν δύνασθε. Kane, "Mithraic Cult Meals," 315f., evaluates this source.

40,[115] are equally controversial although they are also the best evidence for a Mithraic sacramentalism. They too come from a much later period (100 to 150 years) than the problems Paul faced with the Corinthians regarding participation in pagan meals. Moreover, their very brief statements about Mithraism are probably based on a second-hand knowledge.[116] Finally, both Tertullian and Justin must be considered suspect because of their apologetic and polemical stance in these writings.[117]

Cumont, the father of Mithraic studies, is of the opinion that the Mithraic cult involved a sacramental banquet in which the powers of the god were obtained by his worshippers by eating his embodiment in a sacral meal. Cumont points to a relief (Konjica, 4th cent. A.D.) which he says shows a reenacting of Mithras slaying the bull. From this reenactment by the worshippers meat was obtained and used in "the common meal and the holy communion of the *mystae*."[118] However, Cumont's evidence for his interpretation of the relief is two-fold: (1) reports by the Christian writers who polemicize against Mithraism, and (2) the Avestan texts.[119]

Vermaseren, another leading authority, shares Cumont's sacramentalist interpretation of a meal following a ritual slaying of a bull. He says of the Mithraic *mystae:*

> They firmly believed that by eating the bull's flesh and drinking its blood they would be born again just as life itself had once been created anew from the bull's blood. This food and drink were supposed . . . to bring salvation to the soul which would in time achieve rebirth and eternal light.[120]

---

[115]Kane, "Mithraic Cult Meals," 316f., discusses the passage in Tertullian, in which serious textual problems and grammatical questions exist. If one read the text most supportive of a sacramental view it would be: *Mithra signat illic in frontibus milites suos, celebrat et panis oblationem.*

[116]Although Justin implies this is information easily accessible (ἢ ἐπίστασθε ἢ μαθεῖν δύνασθε) one cannot know if his sources were reliable.

[117]Kane, "Mithraic Cult Meals," 315-317.

[118]Cumont, *Mysteries of Mithra,* 155-60. He concludes, "From this mystical banquet, and especially from the imbibing of the sacred wine, supernatural effects were expected." (160)

[119]Kane, "Mithraic Cult Meals," 317f., notes the problems.

[120]Vermaseren, *Mithras,* 103, goes on to say that some writers, such as Loisy, think the bull was understood as Mithras who offered himself as a sacrifice, and that the worshippers then consumed the divine

Vermaseren acknowledges that the meal can be regarded as an event which occurs solely on a divine level between the gods, Sol and Mithras. "But the believers, according to certain texts, imitated the examples of their deity during the ritual."[121]

In addition to the sacramental meal allegedly shared by Mithraism and Christianity, Cumont and Hinnels argue that an acquaintance and dependence of earliest Christianity on Mithraism is proven by other similarities.[122] They mention in particular: regarding December 25 as the birthday of the god, a savior god who returns in fire, a resurrection and judgment, baptismal purifications, and power given to combat the evil spirits. Except for the observance of December 25 all these have precedent in Judaism, especially intertestamental Judaism.

It is important to be clear here. It is absolutely certain that meals were an important feature of the cult of Mithras.[123] What is debated is the significance of these meals. Laeuchli[124] and Kane[125] argue that there was no actual taurobolium in Mithraic worship during the Christian era. Kane says three kinds of meals occurred in Mithraism. One is an

---

body and drank his blood as in the Dionysiac mysteries, "but neither the temples nor the inscriptions give any definite evidence to support this view and only future finds can confirm it."

[121]Vermaseren, *Mithras*, 99. John R. Hinnels, "Christianity and the Mystery Cults," *Theology* 71 (1968) 20-25, is a recent defender of the sacramentalist interpretation of Mithraic meals, and of their influence on the origin of Christian theology.

[122]Cumont, *Mysteries of Mithra*, 190f.; Hinnels, "Christianity and the Mystery Cults," 20.

[123]Samuel Laeuchli, "Urban Mithraism," *BA* 33 (1968) 76. Dennis Groh, "The Ostian Mithraeum," *Mithraism in Ostia* (ed. Samuel Laeuchli; Chicago: Northwestern, 1967) 9-21, gives a very useful description of the general form of a Mithraeum. The earliest of the Ostian Mithraea is dated c. A.D. 160. Groh noted, 12f., the built-in *podia* (equivalent to Greek κλίναι) on the two long sides of the rectangular building take up much of the floor space. He concludes that this shows the importance of the banquet for Mithraic cults. However, this does not prove, nor does Groh imply, that the frequent banquets were sacramental.

[124]Samuel Laeuchli, "Mithraic Dualism," *Mithraism in Ostia*, 54f. He says that the sanctuaries in Ostia were too small for a real taurobolium, and suggests that the bull-slaying was remembered by a symbolic means.

[125]Kane, "Mithraic Cult Meals," 321.

initiation meal.[126]   A second is a cultic reenactment of the myth (as a drama) but without a sacramental eating of the god.[127]   Finally, the followers of Mithras had meals in their association similar to those common in Hellenistic religions and civic life.[128]   Kane thinks that the artistic representation of a sacrificial procession of animals in the Aventine Mithreaum represents the latter form of meal.[129]   This form of community meal, with the menu furnished by the members, also would account for the recovery of a large cache of varied animal bones in some Mithraea.[130]   It is similarly indicated by graffiti listing the expenses of a Dura site, which is headed up by purchases of meat and wine.[131]

In addition to the problem of interpreting archaeological and artistic remains of Mithraism, which is certainly necessary since they cannot interpret themselves, there is the problem of the internal development in the Mithraic religion. Laeuchli distinguishes three consecutive forms of Mithraism.[132]   The first is the pre-Hellenic Mazdean religion before it expanded westward. The second stage was Mithraism as it developed in Asia Minor and was there influenced by the cult of Cybele. The final stage was Mithraism in the Roman Empire. He then observes how this influences interpretation:

> Most of the extant Mithraic materials date from the third period. Many conclusions about earlier forms of Mithraism are conjectural, although we have important vestiges such as the famous Commagene inscription and the evidence in old Persian and Indian texts to guide us.[133]

---

[126]Ibid., 344. He thinks that this is what was noted by Justin Martyr and is illustrated by the Capua Vetere monument.

[127]Ibid., 345-47. He notes that in the reliefs picturing this, the human figures who act the roles wear masks which would have prohibited their eating.

[128]Ibid., 347-51. These meals, of course, begin with a sacrifice. Still, this does not imply the meal following the sacrifice was conceived sacramentally.

[129]Ibid., 320. Vermaseren, *Mithras*, 100, on the other hand, thinks that these paintings prove the sacramental character of the meals held there. The cult officials are standing in for the gods.

[130]Kane, "Mithraic Cult Meals," 347, 350.

[131]Vermaseren, *Mithras*, 102f. Laeuchli, "Urban Mithraism," 76, refers to a similar list from Ostia.

[132]Laeuchli, "Urban Mithraism," 74.

[133]Ibid., 73f. Kane, "Mithraic Cult Meals," is very suspicious of

While it is true of all the mystery cults, Mithraism appears to have had something which most resembled the Christian eucharist. That establishes sacramentalism in neither Mithraism nor Christianity.[134] The frequency and bounty of Mithraic meals attests to their importance in the cult. But that importance was probably the community experience felt by members who shared these meals, not a feeling of sacramental union with the god.[135]

In summary, even if it were proven that Mithraic meals were sacramental in character (which is scarcely to be granted), the attendant problems of dating and interpretation make it impossible to have any confidence about using this mystery to prove a sacramentalism in first-century Corinth, either among the Christians or their pagan neighbors. At the present, Mithraic cult meals offer insufficient proof of a pre-Christian sacramentalism in Hellenistic life.

D. Sarapis and Isis

Sarapis and Isis were originally local deities in Egypt whose myths and cults were closely related. However, in the Hellenistic age they had expanded beyond regional status to become widespread, with shrines around the Mediterranean, including Rome, in the first Christian century.[136] Impressive archaeological remains establish the cults' influence

---

using the Persian texts. On the other hand, Hinnels, "Christianity and the Mystery Cults," 21, argues for an active pre-Christian Mithraism in Syria and even Palestine. Thus the debate over dating goes on.

[134]Metzger, "Considerations of Methodology," 14f., notes that it was this similarity which led Justin and Tertullian to attack Mithraism. One could argue that if there was influence between the two cults, it ran from Christianity to Mithraism. That is, of course, what Justin alleges.

[135]Laeuchli, "Mithraic Dualism," 64; Kane, "Mithraic Cult Meals," 349-51; and even Cumont, Oriental Religions, 69, all note the great importance of the banquet for the sense of esprit de corps. Cumont says, "The religious bond of the thiasus or sodalicium took the place of the natural relationship of the family, the gens, or the clan." Of course, Cumont also stresses the sacramental understanding of some meals in the cult.

[136]F. E. Peters, The Harvest of Hellenism (New York: Simon & Schuster, 1970) 471-75, describes the development of these Egyptian cults in the Hellenistic period. He says it was a contrived effort by the Egyptian Ptolemy I Soter to enlarge Egyptian hegemony. This occurred about 312 B.C. Peters says the transformation of Isis and Sarapis into

in Corinth.[137]   In this period these deities had been transformed into mysteries. Because of this, and because it is certain their cults were in Corinth, they deserve to be considered in this overview of evidence for sacramentalism in Hellenistic religion.

In some ways the cults of Sarapis and Isis are uniquely represented among the Hellenistic mysteries. In the case of Isis, the story of Lucius in Apuleius's *Metamorphoses* gives the most revealing account of liturgy from a mystery cult.[138] This account reports two meals, which have often been regarded as sacramental. For Sarapis the evidence includes several papyri dinner invitations which at least illustrate the practice of inviting guests to a religious meal.[139] Also involving Sarapis is the hymn written by Aelius Aristides, which seems to describe a special significance to his cult meals.[140] As with the other mysteries considered above, the evidence permits varying interpretations of these cults and their meals.

The account of Lucius wandering as an ass and his subsequent return to human form includes a description of his conversion to Isis "of many names."   The conversion is located at the Corinthian port of Cenchreae.[141] As was common in the mystery religions, the date of his initiation was described as a "birthday." A torch-light procession, chanting robed priests, special robes and a garland worn by Lucius, and his epiphany atop a platform in the temple of Isis all comprise his initiation. From the description of Apuleius this initiation was concluded with a joyful and delightful banquet, which marked the attaining of the first degree in the cult. Then following a solemn two-day fast a second cult

---

mystery cults was accomplished with the assistance of an imported priest from Eleusis, a certain Timotheus.   That may explain the similarity between what is understood about the initiations at Eleusis and the description of Lucius's initiation. On the Hellenization of Isis, see also Herbert C. Youtie, "The *Kline* of Sarapis," *HTR* 41 (1948) 9-15.

[137]Dennis Smith, "The Egyptian Cults at Corinth," *HTR* 70 (1977) 201-231, reviews the evidence.

[138]Apuleius, *Metamorphoses*, 11.

[139]Whether these Sarapis invitations describe something similar to those mentioned in 1 Cor 10:27 or perhaps events referred to in 1 Cor 8 and 10:19-22 remains uncertain.

[140]Aelius Aristides, *Hymn to Sarapis*, 27. W. Dindorf, ed., *Aristides* (Hildesheim: Georg Olms, 1964, reprint of 1829 ed.). The relevant passage is on pages 93f.

[141]Apuleius, *Met.* 10.35.

meal marked advancement in the cult.[142] However, little is made of the meals, and there is no indication they were understood as a sacramental eating of the goddess, or even a sacrament shared with the goddess.[143]

There is no comparable account of meals in the cult of Sarapis, but there is in Aelius Aristides a report of his being commanded by Asclepius (closely associated with Sarapis in Hellenistic syncretism) to offer sacrifice to him. In his recounting of one such sacrifice Aristides says after a "full sacrifice" he was to set up sacred bowls and to share the sacred portions of the sacrifice with his fellow worshippers.[144]

In addition to the biographical report by Aristides and the information from Apuleius, there have been recovered from Egypt actual invitations to meals involving Sarapis.[145] These are very similar in form and content to many other papyri invitations to private, non-religious dinners.[146]

In form these brief invitations begin ἐρωτᾷ or καλεῖ[147] followed by the name of the host, the occasion and location of the meal, and its time

---

[142]Ibid., 11. J. Gwyn Griffiths, *The Isis Book: A Commentary on Apuleius' Metamorphoses Book 11*(Leiden: Brill, 1976) 318-19, commenting on Apuleius, compares its description of Lucius's meal with the papyri invitations and Aristides, *Hymn to Sarapis*.

[143]R. E. Witt, *Isis in the Graeco-Roman World* (Ithaca: Cornell University Press, 1971) 164, says "the convivial aspect of the ceremony of initiation must be always remembered." Similarly, Kane, "Mithraic Cult Meals," 334, says: "Nowhere is there any hint that these meals are sacraments conveying grace or power, uniting him to the goddess or bestowing immortality upon him." He suggests that Lucius's closest relationship to the goddess was by meditation and prayer.

[144]C. A. Behr, *Aelius Aristides and the Sacred Tales* (Amsterdam: Adolf M. Hakkert, 1968) 228. This account is from book two of the *Sacred Tales*. Here the sacrifice is to Aristides's patron god, Asclepius, rather than Sarapis. However, it may be Aristides was not distinguishing these gods sharply, rather regarding each as a manifestation of the One. See Peters, *Harvest of Hellenism*, 546.

[145]Those which mention Sarapis explicitly are: P. Oxy. 110, 523, 1484, 1755, 2791, P. Oslo. 157, P. Yale 587 and P. Fouad 76.

[146]For example: weddings (P. Oxy. 111, 524, 927, 1486, 1487); celebrations of civic life (P. Oxy. 926, 2147) or just a party (P. Oxy. 747).

[147]B. P. Grenfell and A. S. Hunt, eds., *The Oxyrhynchus Papyri* (London: Oxford Press, 1916) 12:244, say that καλεῖ replaces ἐρωτᾷ during the third century.

(usually "tomorrow, the 9th hour").[148]   The specific cases involving
Sarapis are worthy of examination, especially because they are occasionally cited in interpreting 1 Cor 8 and 10. I reproduce here the texts with
translations:[149]

P. Oxy. 110   'Ερωτᾷ σε Χαιρήμων δειπνῆσαι εἰς κλείνην τοῦ
                  κυρίου Σαράπιδος ἐν τῷ Σαραπείῳ αὔριον, ἥτις
                  ἐστὶν ιε, ἀπὸ ὥρας θ

                  Chaeremon requests your company at dinner at the
                  table of the lord Sarapis in the Sarapaeum to-
                  morrow, the 15th, at 9 o'clock.

P. Oxy. 523   'Ερωτᾷ σε 'Αντώνιο(ς) Πτολεμ(αίου) διπνῆσ(αι)
                  παρ' αὐτῶι εἰς κλείνην τοῦ κυρίου Σαράπιδος
                  ἐν τοῖς Κλαυδ(ίου) Σαραπίω(νος) τῇ ις ἀπὸ
                  ὅρας θ

                  Antonius, son of Ptolemaeus, invites you to dine
                  with him at the table of the lord Sarapis in the
                  house of Claudius Sarapion on the 16th at 9 o'clock.

---

[148]Because these invitations are for the next day (even one for
"today") it is likely they are a social formality, the actual inviting no
doubt done orally earlier.   Jack Lindsay, *Daily Life in Roman Egypt*
(London: Frederick Muller, 1963) 47.
[149]Both the texts and translations of the Oxyrhynchus Papyri come
from Grenfell and Hunt. The text and translation of P. Oslo. 157 from S.
Eitrem and L. Amundsen, *Papyri Osloenses* (Oslo: Det Norske Videnskaps-
Akademi, 1936) Fasc. 3, 246f.   The text of P. Fouad comes from Mariangela Vandoni, *Feste Pubbliche e Private nei Documenti Greci* (Milano:
Istituto Editoriale Cisalpino, 1964) 130.   The text of P. Colon 2555 is from
L. Koenen, "Eine Einladung zur Kline des Sarapis," *Zeitschrift für Papyro-
logie und Epigrapik* 1 (1967) 122.   In the last two cases I have made my
own translation.
        The text and translation of P. Yale 85 is from: J. F. Oates, A. E.
Samuel and C. B. Welles, *Yale Papyri in the Beinecke Rare Book and
Manuscript Library (Am. Stud. Pap., 2*; New Haven: Yale University,
1967) 1.264.

P. Oxy. 1484   Ἐρωτᾷ σε Ἀπολλώνιος δειπνῆσαι εἰς [κ]λείνην
                  τοῦ κυρίου Σαράπιδος ὑπὲρ μελοκουρίων τῶν
                  [ἀδελφῶν?] ἐν τῷ Θ[ο]ηρίῳ

                  Apollonius requests you to dine at the table of the
                  lord Sarapis on the occasion of the coming of age of
                  his brothers in the temple of Thoeris.

P. Oxy. 1755   Ἐρωτᾷ σε Ἀπίων δει-πνῆσαι ἐν τῷ οἴκῳ τοῦ
                  Σαραπείου εἰς κλεί-νην τοῦ κυρίου Σαράπιδος
                  τῇ ιγ ἀπὸ ὥρας θ.

                  Apion invites you to dine in the house of Sarapis at
                  the table of the lord Sarapis on the 13th at 9
                  o'clock.

P. Oxy. 2791   Ἐρωτᾷ σε Διογενής δειπνῆσαι εἰς πρωτογενεί-
                  σιου τῆς θυγατρός αὐτοῦ ἐν τῷ Σαραπείῳ αὔριον
                  ἥτις ἐστὶν παχῶν ἀπὸ ὥρας η.

                  Diogenes invites you to dinner for the first birthday
                  of his daughter in the Sarapeum tomorrow which is
                  Pachon 26 (? or 16) from the eighth hour onward.

P. Oslo. 157   Ἐρωτᾷ σε Σαραπίων γεγυμνασιαρχ(ηκὼς) δειπνῆ-
                  σίαι εἰς κλείνην τοῦ κυρίου Σ[α]ράπιδος ἐν τῇ
                  ἰδίᾳ οἰκίᾳ αὔ[ρ]ιον ἥτις ἐστὶν ιε ἀπὸ ὥρ(ας)
                  η.

                  Sarapion, ex-gymnasiarch, requests you to dine at
                  his house on the occasion of the lectisternium of the
                  Lord Sarapis to-morrow,which is the 15th, at the 8th
                  hour.

P. Yale 85   Ἐρωτᾷ σε Διονύσιος δειπνῆσαι τῇ κα εἰς
                  κλείνην Ἡλίου μεγάλου Σαράπιδος ἀπὸ ὥρας θ
                  ἐν τῇι πατρικῇι ἑαυτοῦ οἰκίᾳ.

                  Dionysios asks you to dine on the 21st at the kline of
                  Helios, great Sarapis, at the 9th hour, in the house
                  of his father.

P. Fouad 76   Ἐρωτᾷ σε Σαραποῦς δειπνῆσαι εἰς ἱέρωμα τῆς
               κυρίας Ἴσιδος, ἐν τῇ οἰκίᾳ, αὔριον, ἥτις
               ἐστὶν κθ, ἀπὸ ὥρας θ.

               Sarapis invites you to dine at the sacred rites of the
               lady Isis in the house, tomorrow which is from the
               9th hour.

With these should be compared:

P. Colon 2555 καλεῖ σε ὁ θεὸς εἰς κλείνην γεινο(μένην) ἐν
               τῷ θοηρείῳ αὔριον ἀπὸ ὥρ(ας) θ΄

               The god invites you to dine at the table which will
               take place tomorrow in the temple of Thoeris from
               the 9th hour.

In each case of the Oxyrhynchus Papyri, and also the case of P.
Oslo. 157 the invitation is εἰς κλείνην τοῦ κυρίου Σαράπιδος. P. Yale
85 reads slightly differently: εἰς κλείνην Ἡλίου μεγάλου Σαράπιδος.
Obviously in these invitations κλείνην τοῦ κυρίου Σαράπιδος is not a
place, but an event, for the locations vary.[150] In some cases the location
is the temple of Sarapis (P. Oxy. 110, 1755, 2791).[151] But in others it is
the house of the host (P. Oslo. 157 and P. Oxy. 523),[152] or the father of
the host (P. Yale 85), or even the temple of another deity (Thoeris, P.
Oxy. 1484; P. Colon 2555).

Similarly varied are the occasions stated for the meals. Most (P.
Oxy. 110, 523, 1755, P. Oslo. 157) do not specify the occasion of the
dinner. In two cases where the occasion is given they are a coming-of-age
celebration (P. Oxy. 1484) and a birthday party (P. Oxy. 2791). If one
restricts oneself solely to the explicit reasons, these dinners seem to have
been familial celebrations. It is certainly begging the question to assume
they refer to a sacramental cult meal.

---

[150]Milne, "Kline of Sarapis," 9, makes this observation. Also,
A. D. Nock, "The Gild of Zeus Hypsistos," ERAW 1.435.

[151]For P. Fouad 76 the translation of ἐν τῇ οἰκίᾳ is uncertain,
but it may refer to a house of τῆς κυρίας Ἴσιδος. Regarding P. Oxy.
1755, the editors, Grenfell and Hunt, 14.181, say it is unclear whether ἐν
τῷ οἴκῳ refers to the house of the host, or to a part of the Sarapis shrine.

[152]Thus Eitrem and Amundsen, Papyri Osloenses, 247, interpret ἐν
τῇ ἰδίᾳ οἰκίᾳ in P. Oslo. 157.

The important question for this study of sacramentalism in connection with these Hellenized Egyptian cults is what meaning did these meals have for those who gave them, and to those who attended. Some scholars have regarded these invitations as examples of a cult's worship, and not infrequently a sacramental meal.[153] Several points make this interpretation questionable.

First, the variety of locations for the meals associated with Sarapis suggests a very loose connection, if at all, with the cult's liturgy. Not only were these meals held in the temple of another deity,[154] but even in private homes. It has even been suggested the temple might have operated an adjunct restaurant.[155]

Second, the informal character of these invitations implies, although does not prove, they are not special occasions, except for the host and his guests.[156]

Third, only in one case, P. Colon. 2555, is the invitation from the god.[157] Since the papyrus comes from Oxyrhynchus it is a reasonable conjecture that Sarapis is the god involved, but it is not certain. The extending of the conjecture beyond the name of the god, to assume an occasion similar to what occurred to Lucius, or a sacramentalism (assumed) in Aristides's *Hymn to Sarapis* is to erect a large conclusion on an uncertain connection between unclear sources.[158]

---

[153]Helmut Engelmann, *The Delian Aretology of Sarapis* (Vol. 44 of *Études Préliminaires aux Religions Orientales dans L'Empire Romain*; Leiden: E. J. Brill, 1975) 43. He says: "All ancient mystic religions have provisions for such feasts, cf. the Dionysiac στιβάδες, the communion of the Mithraic devotees, the agape (love feasts) of the early Christians."

[154]P. Oxy. 1484. This is unlikely to have been because Sarapis had no convenient temple, for in Egypt these were plentiful. Peters, *Harvest of Hellenism*, 473.

[155]Milne, "*Kline* of Sarapis," 9. He cites B. P. Grenfell, Arthur S. Hunt and David G. Hogarth, *Fayûm Towns and Their Papyri* (London: Oxford Press, 1900) 33, who conclude from an inscription at Kom Ushim (Karnasis) that the temple of Pnepheros and Petesuchos operated a civic banquet hall. Milne regards οἴκῳ in P. Oxy. 1755 to describe such a facility.

[156]The attempt by Koenen, "Einladung," 124-26, to prove that all the Oxyrhynchus Papyri come from a festival season for Isis and Sarapis is unconvincing. The dates are seldom given, other than "tomorrow." The evidence is insufficient to decide for or against his proposal.

[157]Καλεῖ σε ὁ θεός.

[158]Such as does Koenen, "Einladung."

Fourth, the comments by outsiders on the meals of Sarapists, while clearly prejudicial, describe them as preeminently social affairs. Juvenal describes Egyptian religious festivals as characterized by continual feasting for a week.[159]   Similarly, Philo says the sacrificing associations (θίασοι) of Egypt, although called σύνοδοι and κλίναι, were in reality based only on strong drink, carousing, and wantonness.[160] Tertullian also contrasts the modest decorum of Christian meals with the excesses of the Sarapists. In the case of the latter, he says, the clouds of smoke from their festivals bring forth the fire department.[161]

In summary, regarding the Egyptian cults the evidence compels no indisputable conclusions. Setting aside the evidence from Aristides and Apuleius, it is most likely the meals mentioned in the papyri were predominantly social occasions of co-religionists.[162]

----

[159]Juvenal, *Satires* 15.40. In the same satire, he accuses the Egyptians of practicing cannibalism. Thus one might conclude his bias makes him a questionable source. However, conversely, one might say that if Juvenal had known of a sacramental eating of Sarapis or Isis as a doctrine of the cult, he might well have turned this to propaganda advantage.

[160]Philo, *Flacc.* 17 (136). The translator of the Loeb edition, F. H. Colson, comments, "The present passage [17] suggests that the religious side was often left very much in the background."

Earlier in the same book, 1 (4), Philo had said the Egyptian clubs "were constantly holding feasts under the pretext of sacrifice in which drunkenness vented itself in political intrigue." Because of this, he says, the predecessor of Flaccus, Iberus, had repressed the cults.

[161]Tertullian, *Praescr. Haer.* 40. In addition to the obvious pro-Christian bias of Tertullian, he may even be influenced by his own rather austere values. However, he was able to attack pagan "sacramentalism" where he suspected it in Mithraism. See above, n. 115.

[162]Milne, "*Kline* of Sarapis," 8. He is perhaps going too far when he terms these meals "secular." However, he may only mean by that term "not sacramental." One may reasonably assume these meals, like similar ones in Greek religious and fraternal associations, took some notice of the god. Milne suggests that we regard the "κλίνη of Sarapis" as a dining club. He summarizes: "There is nothing strange in a dining-club meeting alternatively in public institutions or in private houses; it would be natural for a member to use it for the purpose of celebrating family events; and ... guests might be invited to it by members."

Kane, "Mithraic Cult Meals," 333, has a similar view, although he thinks there were other occasions of dining related to Isis and Sarapis which were "moments of solemnity." He has in mind specifically the

The evidence from Aristides certainly suggests he held great import for meals involving Sarapis. The interpretation of Aristides largely centers on how one understands the phrase τοίνυν καὶ θυσιῶν μόνῳ τούτῳ θεῷ διαφερόντως κοινωνοῦσιν ἄνθρωποι τὴν ἀκριβῆ κοινωνίαν. Elsewhere in the present study it is argued that κοινωνία and κοινωνεῖν do not imply a sacramental "communion" with the god, as is often alleged of Aristides's words.[163] Even if one grants that Aristides refers to an unusually meaningful relationship with Sarapis, no sacramental conclusions follow for the meals of the cult.[164] Aristides also mentions in the same hymn festival dances, a common feature of all Greek banquets, and not suggestive of sacramentalism.[165]

It is equally difficult to be certain about the meaning of the initiatory meals of Lucius at the temple of Isis. However, in the description of Apuleius the meals do not seem to have played a prominent role. Witt seems correct in regarding them as the conclusion of the ceremony, rather than its apex. He suggests that the meals in the cult, following the pattern of other Hellenistic religions, were marked by "pleasant intercourse and conviviality."[166]

E. Conclusions on Sacramentalism in the Mysteries

This brief review has covered the most prominent and widespread of the Hellenistic mystery religions in the time of Paul. Other less influential mystery cults are known,[167] but they seem not to change the

---

experience of Lucius.

Opposing this non-sacramental view of the papyri invitations are: Eitrem-Amundson, *Papyri Osloensis*, 242; Ulrich Wilken, in Ludwig Mitteis und U. Wilkin, *Grundzüge und Chrestomathie die Papyruskunde* (Hildesheim: Georg Olms, 1963) Vol. 1, pt. 2, 130f.

[163]See in this study, 168-174.

[164]Kane, "Mithraic Cult Meals," 333. Similarly, Jack Lindsay, *Leisure and Pleasure in Roman Egypt* (New York: Barnes & Noble, 1965) 47, although he suggests an awareness of the god's participation. "The dinner merges with communion." As is always the case, what then is decisive is what is meant by "communion."

Also Nock, "Cult of Heroes," 597f.

Milne, "*Kline* of Sarapis," 8, suggests that Aristides regarded Sarapis as the patron of the society named after him.

[165]Youtie, 15.

[166]Witt, *Isis*, 164.

[167]For a convenient summary of other possible mysteries such as that of Zeus of Panamara (A.D. 2nd century) and that of the Great

conclusion that the sacramental interpretation of meals in the mysteries is based on slim and highly questionable evidence.

A. D. Nock has categorized ancient religious meals into three types, recalling the three categories of meals described above (18-21). First, there was the fellowship meal which involved nominal outward notice of the patron deity, hero, or founder. This conforms to the present study's category of the social meal. Second, there was the meal eaten together by members when a god or goddess was felt to be presiding. Nock cites Aelius Aristides, *To Sarapis* and P. Oxy. 110, 523 as illustrative. Finally, there was the ritual rending of animals followed by the meal of raw flesh (Dionysiac). Concerning the latter (the sacramental form in this study's definitions), Nock says: "Clear traces of this conception of sacramental communion in Greek ritual are not obtrusively frequent."[168]

However cautious as Nock's statement about sacramental meals is, it may still be too generous. As we have seen, there is only very limited proof for the third type of meal Nock lists. Indeed, Dionysiac religion is the evidence and that evidence is tenuous. The best evidence for sacramentalism in Dionysiac religion is Euripides's *The Bacchae*. However, in Euripides's time (late 5th cent. B.C.) the Dionysiac *omophagia* was regarded as abnormal and strange (his play is concerned with the suppression of a cult for its dangerous ideas and practices). It would be gratuitous to think that the cult meals of other Hellenistic religions and of Christians in Corinth had conformed to what was regarded as an anomaly over four centuries earlier.

It is, of course, true that it is very difficult to determine the meaning religious meals had for their participants. That no doubt varied from person to person. But from the evidence now available regarding the mysteries it would seem that they had religious meals, that these were commonly held in temple precincts, and that there is some implication of a special importance to some such meals. However, the sacramentalism commonly accepted earlier this century, and still often assumed today, is

---

Mother, see Kane, "Mithraic Cult Meals," 330-33. Also Nock, *Early Gentile Christianity*, 74f.

[168]Nock, *Early Gentile Christianity*, 72f. Since Nock elsewhere expresses great reluctance to find a sacramentalism in Dionysiac worship, there may be in this sentence a touch of irony.

not convincing and certainly cannot be assumed to be typical of the mysteries.[169]

In summary, the probability is that, even in the mysteries, religious meals were not regarded as sacramental occasions. In some of the mysteries, at some stages of their development, the communal understanding may have been prominent, and this may have set these cults off from their rivals. This seems to be most probably in the case of Dionysus in his pre-Christian stage, and for Mithras at a post-Pauline period. As Kane says: "The main point is that one requires evidence *even in a mystery cult* that a festal sacrifice is more than an occasion of table fellowship over which the god presides or to which he is summoned as guest."[170]

In addition, as will be shown in the following section of this chapter, there is a good deal of evidence from the late Hellenistic and Imperial periods for the social interpretation of cult meals in the Greco-Roman world. This evidence indicates that the general importance of table fellowship in civic, fraternal, occupational and religious associations was the social conviviality and good cheer. Some of this evidence comes from associations devoted to the mystery gods. These meals would have set the pattern for common meals and it is doubtful if the mystery religions—or the Christians—could have avoided this pattern, or would have wanted to do so.[171]

EVIDENCE FOR A SOCIAL INTERPRETATION OF CULT MEALS

It was suggested earlier in this chapter that basically three interpretations are proposed for Hellenistic cult meals: the *sacramental*, the

---

[169]Angus, *Mystery Religions,* 130f., warns against reliance on theories of totemism and mana, or "some mystic formulae preserved by Clement of Alexandria, Minucius Felix and Arnobius." The latter two Christian apologists are 3rd century.

Angus does think, 131f., that the member of the mystery cults, pagan and Christian, "believed that in some realistic, hyperphysical sense the sacrament was an occasion on which or means by which he was privileged to enter into fellowship with the divine life, by which he was reborn or endowed with immortality." Angus feels that there was little conscious reflection on this experience.

[170]Kane, "Mithraic Cult Meals," 332 (italics mine).

[171]Ibid., 3.

communal, and the *social.* Of these three, the sacramental is the most extreme and is more distinct from the communal and social than they are from each other. However, the sacramental interpretation has been more influential in modern scholarly discussions of 1 Corinthians 8 and 10.

One of the major arguments against the integrity of 1 Corinthians is that Paul appears to have a sacramental understanding of pagan meals in 1 Cor 10:14-21, and a more "enlightened," non-sacramental view in 1 Cor 8 and 10:22-31. This is one reason why it is important to examine the alleged pagan sacramentalism before the exegetical study of 1 Corinthians 8 and 10.

It is also important for the present study to find what significance pagan cult meals had in order to understand why some Corinthian Christians wanted to participate. If pagan meals were commonly regarded as sacramental, or even communal, occasions, it is difficult to understand why Christians would want to participate. (The proposal that the Corinthians were seeking to exhibit their immunity derived from the Christian sacrament is examined below, 139-141, and reasons given for its rejection.) However, if these meals were predominantly social occasions, the Corinthians' willingness to participate is very understandable, especially for those who knew the pagan deities were "nothings" (1 Cor 8:4).

It has just been shown that there are very few indications of a sacramental understanding of pagan religious meals, even in the mysteries. When the evidence is examined, it is seen to be insufficient to support the hypothesis of pagan sacramentalism, or at least the evidence can be reasonably doubted to compel such an interpretation. This leaves the communal and the social interpretations of such meals.

In virtually all meals of Hellenistic groups the gods are invoked in prayers and libations are poured. The gods are also the recipients of the sacrifice which precedes the meal. Some civic festivals featured the visit of the deity as the occasion for a feast.[172] Therefore even in the social understanding of these meals, it is granted that due regard was given, and a portion allotted, to the deity. Their presence at such meals was assumed. The difference, then, between the social and the communal interpretations of these meals is where the *focus* is believed to lie. The communal view stresses the relationship of the worshippers to the

---

[172]These were called θεοξένια, the Roman equivalent being the *lectisternia.* See "Theoxenia," A. Pauly and G. Wissowa, eds. *Realencyclopädie der klassischen Altertumswissenschaften* (Stuttgart: A. Drukenmuller, 1960--) 5.11.2, 2256-59.

deity;[173] the social, the relationship between the worshippers.

The evidence for the communal interpretation is substantially the same as that for the sacramental view. Indeed in the secondary literature the communal interpretation is seldom argued, but simply assumed whenever a sacramental significance is denied or considered missing. It is often suggested that this communal understanding originated in the cults of the dead, and/or the cult of heroes.[174] However, A. D. Nock has shown it is impossible to distinguish between the function of the cults of the heroes and other deities.[175]

Rather than retrace the evidence previously examined for a sacramental interpretation to see if it would support a communal interpretation, I turn to consider some evidence that the social understanding of religious meals was the common one in Hellenistic life. It may be granted at the outset that in some cults, on some occasions, some diners had a greater sense of the presence of the patron deity (for example, as indicated in Aristides's praise of Sarapis). However, the indications are that cult meals, including the mystery cult meals, were generally regarded fundamentally as occasions for social association and conviviality.

A. The Character of Fraternal Meals

The sacrifice was the principal ceremony of all Hellenistic worship, whether domestic, civic, or cultic. And the feature most characteristic of sacrifice was the meal which accompanied it. Because of this common association of sacrifice and meal, it is misleading to distinguish between secular and religious gatherings on the basis of their meals.[176] This can be clearly seen in the various guilds and sacrificing associations.[177]

---

[173]The communal interpretation is found in some sources. However, the intimacy of a shared meal with the gods is regarded primarily as an event of the glorious past. See Hesiod, *Frag.* 59 (Loeb edition, 186f.); Pausanias 7.11.4.

[174]Farnell, "Sacrificial Communion," 310. Also see Gill, "Trapezomata," 122, who notes that these meals were not restricted to the cults of the dead. For an example of a hero cult in Corinth, see O. Broneer, "Hero Cults in Corinth," *Hesperia* 11 (1942) 130-161.

[175]Nock, "Cult of Heroes."

[176]Angus, *Mystery Religions,* 196, says, "An ancient chamber of commerce could equally be a religious society."

[177]Guthrie, 268f. He is speaking of the classical period, but it need not be so limited. He says of public sacrifice, "Hundreds of animals

In the Hellenistic age there were many social groups formed as associations.[178] Some of these were very ancient, based on tribal divisions within the city-state, such as the γένος and φράτρης.[179] Others represented subdivisions within these larger groups, such as the ἐφηβές and νεοί.[180]

The ὀργεῶνες seem to have originated among colonists from other countries (hence not eligible for participation in the Greek demes). But some were apparently long-standing familial associations. These civic associations featured a common meal for their members, which was, of course, preceded by sacrifice.[181] Although according to strict definition the orgeones' sacrifices were paid for by the members of the associations and held in private shrines,[182] W. S. Ferguson has shown that at least one

---

would be slaughtered, and the gods were by no means the only or even the chief participators in the resulting feast of roast meat. It was distributed among the people." As Nilsson, *Greek Folk Religion*, 87, observes, "The people feasted at the expense of the gods, and they soon learned the advantages of this kind of piety."

[178]See the recent thorough treatment by Hermann, "Genossenschaft." Inscriptions pertinent to these various associations are collected in: Franz Poland, *Geschichte der grieschischen Vereinwesens* (Leipzig: Teubner, 1909); Erich Ziebarth, *Das griechische Vereinwesens* (Leipzig: Teubner, 1896); and Paul Foucart, *Des associations religieuses chez les Grecs* (Paris: Klinecksieck, 1873).

[179]In addition to Hermann cited in note 178, see Nilsson, *Cults, Myths*, 153-57, who discusses the φρατρία in regard to their origins and organizations.

[180]C. A. Forbes, *Neoi. A Contribution to the Study of Greek Associations* (Philological Monographs 2; Middletown, CT: American Philological Association, 1933), is a very thorough study of what is known about the organization, purpose and functions of such groups. They formed a corporate group, which could take corporate acts. They are often called σύνοδοι, a designation for a loose social group. Forbes says, 52, "It is certain . . . that the association of neoi were formed partly for just such pleasure" (citing Strabo, 14.1.20).

[181]W. S. Ferguson, "The Attic Orgeones," *HTR* 37 (1944) 61-140, is the basic study of the ὀργεῶνες. He concludes that in origin they were an imitation of the Athenian demes, but in pre-Hellenistic times they had become almost indistinguishable institutions. The old Attic γεντές were imitating the later ὀργεῶνες in both organization and practices. See also Nilsson, *Cults, Myths*, 156f., on the relationship between the φρατρία and ὀργεῶνες.

[182]Ferguson, "Attic Orgeones," 64.

(the association of the Thracian goddess, Bendis) was open to the public.[183]

In addition to these civic groups of which one was a member by birth, there were also numerous voluntary associations. These were a prominent part of Hellenistic life after the decline of the city-states.[184] Among them were guilds based on common occupations. These were not primarily economic organizations (such as a modern trade union) but social in the broadest sense.[185]

One cannot accurately distinguish these private associations, trade guilds, or cult-brotherhoods as secular or religious.[186] Both their self-descriptions and their functions overlap these categories. Some clubs were named for their founder, others for a national group, but most were named for one of the gods.[187] Their titles commonly include such adjectives as ἱερός, ἱερώτατος, or σεβάστος, whether they were trade associations, athletic guilds or "religious" cults.[188] Their meetings would include consideration of a patron god or goddess by sacrifice. A passage from Aristotle reveals how a secular vs. religious division is artificial:

> . . . some associations (κοινωνιῶν) appear to be formed for the sake of pleasure, for example religious guilds and dining-clubs (θιασωτῶν καὶ ἐρανιστῶν) which are unions for sacrifice and social intercourse (θυσίας καὶ συνουσίας).[189]

---

[183]Ibid., 102.

[184]Nilsson, *Cults, Myths,* 169. It is important to remember these political units were religiously based, and their gatherings considered religious festivals.

[185]Ramsay MacMullen, *Roman Social Relations: 50 B.C. to A.D. 284* (New Haven: Yale University, 1974) 18-20. On these guilds in Egypt see A. E. R. Boak, "The Organization of Gilds in Greco-Roman Egypt," *Transactions of the American Philological Association* 68 (1937) 212-220. Boak concludes these Egyptian guilds are modeled on Greek organizations. See also Milne, "*Kline* of Sarapis," 7.

[186]One must keep in mind that in the Hellenistic and Imperial periods the varying designations given such associations are virtually interchangeable. Athenaeus, 5.186f., equates such terms as σύνοδοι, φυλετικά, δημοτικά, θίασοι, φρατρικά and ὀργεωνικά.

[187]Tod, *Sidelights,* 75f.

[188]Ibid., 76f. See also Angus, *Mystery Religions,* 204.

[189]Aristotle, *Eth. Nic.* 8.9.5, 1160a 19-20.

The predominant mood at the gatherings of such associations was one of good cheer. "Presents were exchanged, altars and friends wreathed in roses, the diners beautifully drunk and dizzy with the noise and dancing."[190] Ferguson concludes that when the Athenian orgeones assembled, although there were sacrifices and prayers offered to a deity or deities, "the picnic, the barbeque, was probably the main attraction."[191] Tod's suggestion that these various associations may rightly be compared with such modern ones as Freemasons, Druids, Oddfellows and Buffaloes reveals much of their character.[192]

It is essential to remember that there was not a clear distinction between the religious and civic voluntary associations.[193] Therefore the conduct and the meaning of common meals in these associations expresses the general attitude toward such meals in other Hellenistic groups, including religious cults. They had a preeminently social importance in Hellenistic life. They set the tone for other meals, including those of cultic religions. Before examining the more direct evidence for the social interpretation of cult meals, it is important to be aware of this general milieu, which religious associations could scarcely have resisted, nor would have desired to do so.[194]

B. Positive Statements of the Social Character of Cult Meals

There is evidence already in Homer that the meal which followed sacrifice was characterized primarily by merriment and joyous association. A sacrifice of the hecatomb by Odysseus when his warriors began the Trojan war is a good example. Apollo receives a prayer; his share of the meat (thighs and fat) and a libation are immolated. But the focus in Homer's account is upon the fraternal meal which follows and stresses the

---

[190]MacMullen, 19.   Regarding the purpose of these guilds, he summarizes, 77, "Pure comradeship."

[191]Ferguson, "Attic Orgeones," 123.   He also summarizes, 129, "The annual reunion of orgeones was thus in a sense a family party."

[192]Tod, Sidelights, 78.   Cf. MacMullen, 77, "Moralists grumbled that they ate too much, to the point of inflating prices in the food markets; worse, that they drank too much, so that the associations common under the title 'Fellow Drinkers of . . .' were in reality."

[193]W. L. Westermann, "Entertainment in the villages of Graeco-Roman Egypt," Journal of Egyptian Archaeology 18 (1932) 27, describes these cult associations as the secularization of the religious association.

[194]Kane, "Mithraic Cult Meals," 349.

abundant supply of meat and drink followed by joyful singing.[195] Similarly, when Odysseus returns, a swineherd kills a pig for a feast to celebrate
and to share dinner with friends.[196] Homer's accounts illustrate Aristotle's statement that sacrifices and festivals were celebrated for "both
paying honor to the gods and providing pleasant holidays" for the participants.[197]

Other writers also clearly share the social understanding of religious meals. Thucydides recalls Aristotle when he says: "Moreover, we
have provided for the spirit many relaxations from toil: we have games
and sacrifices regularly throughout the year."[198] Livy's description of the
first Roman *lectisternium* stresses its social significance for the city,
especially its ample provisions and conviviality:

> They also observed the rite in their homes. All through the
> City, they say, doors stood wide open, all kinds of viands were
> set out for general consumption, all comers were welcomed,
> whether known or not, and men even exchanged kind and
> courteous words with personal enemies.[199]

A most revealing comment is given by Dio Chrysostom in a discussion of the importance of friendship:

---

[195]*Il.* 1.457-475. The same outlook toward sacrifice is found in
Virgil's retelling of this adventure in his *Aeneid*. In *Aen.* 8.283 a
description of a sacrifice and accompanying meal at a yearly festival is
illustrative: "These chosen youths, and the priest of the altar, in emulous
haste bring roast flesh of bulls, pile on baskets the gifts of Ceres,
fashioned well, and serve the wine of Bacchus. Aeneas and, with him, the
warriors of Troy feast on the long chine of an ox and the sacrificial
meat. When hunger was banished and the desire for food stayed, King
Evander spoke: 'These solemn rites, this wonted feast, this altar of a
mighty Presence—'tis no idle superstition, knowing not the gods of old,
that has laid them upon us.'" Cf. *Aen.* 8.265-85.

[196]*Od.* 14.418-436. Similar is *Od.* 24.213f., where the verb
ἱερεύειν is translated "slay for supper."

[197]Aristotle, *Eth. Nic.* 8.9.6. Similarly, Plato, *Leg.* 653D, says
that in pity the gods ordained feasts of thanksgiving as a time of respite
from human troubles.

[198]Thucydides, 2.38.

[199]Livy 5.13.5f.

What festivity could please unless the most important thing
of all [friendship] were at hand, what symposium could delight
you if you lacked the goodwill of the guests? What sacrifice
is acceptable to the gods without the participants in the
feast?[200]

Each of these authors speaks in very positive terms of the social
importance of religious meals and sacrifice. Yet none appears to be
arguing a case for this sociality. They illustrate the accepted value of
conviviality in the meals associated with sacrifice, beginning already with
Homer. The same outlook can be illustrated from regulations of cult
associations.

C. Evidence from Cult Regulations

Some inscriptions which give regulations for various cult associations are also informative, implicitly, about the social character of their
meals. For example, one finds a great concern about the equitable distribution of the sacrificial goods. At fraternal gatherings, such as the
Attic orgeones, the normal practice was for each member to receive a
full share and their children and slaves a half-share.[201] However, some
members were given special honor by being allotted a double share.[202]
The regulations about fair shares in the food supplies suggest the meal
was a major concern to the worshippers, and this is confirmed by other
sources.

An inscription from Athens gives some revealing rules of conduct
at the cult's meals. This is from an association called the Iobacchoi and
describes a feast of Dionysus (the same deity often used to substantiate
sacramentalism!).

----

[200]Dio Chrysostom, 3.97. The last line reads: ποία δὲ θυσία
κεχαρισμένη θεοῖς ἄνευ τῶν συνευωχουμένων; sociability is the most
important aspect of sacrifice—even to the gods.

[201]Benjamin Merritt, "Greek Inscriptions," *Hesperia* 11 (1942)
286f., citing Poland, 258.

[202]Youtie, "*Kline* of Sarapis," 22. Normally, the priest or priestess
receives an additional share. See SIG³ 271, 921 and 1097 for examples of
regulations regarding the distribution of meat at Athenian celebrations.
One might also receive additional portions in return for special services to
the cult. Youtie, "*Kline* of Sarapis," 21f. Ferguson, "Attic Orgeones,"
77f., notes that absent orgeones did not receive a share.

No one may either sing or create a disturbance or applaud at the gathering, but each shall say and act his allotted part with all good order and quietness under the direction of the priest or the archbacchos.

If anyone start a fight or be found acting disorderly or occupying the seat of any other member or using insulting or abusive language to anyone [there follows a list of fines].[203]

This general impression of conduct at a cult gathering, including cult meals, is confirmed by Ramsey MacMullen in his survey of Roman associations. He notes several inscriptions which encourage "tranquility and propriety" and which ask members to "take your ease without ill temper" avoiding "hubris and abuse."[204] To illustrate his assessment of the boisterous conduct at such meals, he quotes from a second-century regulation of an Italian association of worshippers of Diana and Antonius:

If anyone wishes to bring up any matter of complaint he shall do so in a business meeting, so that our dinner on the usual day may pass off serenely and joyfully. Whoever leaves his place to cause a disturbance shall be fined 4 sesterces; if he insults another or is disorderly, he shall be fined 12 sesterces.[205]

Finally, a similar ordinance from Roman Egypt gives a list of fines for those who fail to attend the monthly meetings, or who take another member's seat at the banquet, or in any other way act disorderly.[206]

In summary, inscriptional evidence of cult regulations from Greece, Rome and Egypt suggests that a widespread problem in cultic meals was the misconduct of the members. These fines prescribed imply

---

[203]SIG^3 1109. This translation comes from Tod, *Sidelights*, 88f. Tod comments that this is a good example of Greek guilds, "a curious medley this—religion, drama, good fellowship, banqueting!"

[204]MacMullen, 78, citing Varro, *De Re Rustica,* 3.2.16. He also refers to *Corpus Inscriptionum Latinarum* 14.3323 and 12.4393, in addition to SIG^3 1369 and 1109 (the latter quoted in the text above).

[205]MacMullen, 78, citing a condensation of *Corpus Inscriptionum Latinarum* 14.2112.

[206]P. Michigan 5.243. Cf. 244 and 246. H. C. Youtie and O. M. Pearl, *Tax Rolls from Karanis: Michigan Papyri (Humanistic Studies,* 42-45; Ann Arbor: University Press, 1935).

that this was not uncommon; their minimal amounts imply such misconduct was not too serious or unexpected.

D. Evidence from Literary Sources Regarding Misconduct

The most direct and abundant evidence for a social understanding
of the cult meals comes from criticisms of the conduct of those attending
the meals. These criticisms are not that the worshippers lack the solemnity appropriate to a religious gathering, but that their expected merriment goes beyond reasonable limits. There is often expressed a concern
that the sacrificial gathering not degenerate into an uproar.

The criticisms of Philo (*Flacc.* 17) and Tertullian (*Praescr. Haer.*
40) directed at the Egyptian cults have been noted above (44). Perhaps
the accuracy of their criticisms may be suspect because they are antagon-
ists of pagan cults and are polemicizing against them. However, other
writers who stand within those religious traditions are equally critical.
Aristophanes has the most criticisms to make of conduct at sacrifices and
meals, but others give similar views.

Perhaps the earliest literary source which reveals the attitude of
worshippers by its criticism is Hesiod's *Works and Days* 724-56. Robertson
examines this text, especially the phrase in line 756, μωμεύειν ἀΐδηλα,
and concludes this is a rebuke of worshippers who complain about the
"waste" of the portion burned to the god.[207] Robertson paraphrases: "If
you are present when offerings are ablaze on the altar, do not çarp at
what is consumed; this too the god rather resents."[208]

The other side of this outlook is expressed by Menander when the
god complains that the worshippers take the best and the most from the
sacrifice, leaving only meager scraps for the gods.[209]

Plutarch, in chastizing Epicurus's atheism for taking joy out of life,
inadvertently reveals how sacrifices and sacrificial meals were regarded
by some. The lengthy passage is worthy of quoting in full:

---

[207]Hesiod, *Op.* 755f., μηδ' ἱεροῖσιν ἐπ' αἰθομένοισι κυρήσας
μωμεύειν ἀΐδηλα θεός νύ τι καὶ τὰ νεμεσσᾷ.

[208]Noel Robertson, "How to Behave at a Sacrifice: Hesiod *Erga*
755-6," *Classical Philology* 64 (1969) 168.

[209]Menander, *Dyskolos*, 447-53, "Look at their mode of offering
sacrifices, the burglars that they are. They bring couches and wine-jars,
not for the god's sake but their own." Cf. the famous passage on the
origin of sacrifice in Hesiod, *Theog.* 535-70.

For it is not the abundance of wine or the roast meats that
cheer the heart at festivals, but good hope and the belief in
the benign presence of the god and his gracious acceptance of
what is done. For while we leave the flutes and the crowns
out of certain festivals, if the god is not present at the sacrifice as master of rites (so to speak) what is left bears no
mark of sanctity or holy day and leaves the spirit untouched
by the divine influence; rather let us say for such a man [as
Epicurus] the occasion is distasteful and even distressing.
. . . When he sacrifices, the priest at his side who immolates
the victim is to him a butcher.[210]

Although Plutarch is arguing against a lack of due regard for the
deity at sacrificial meals, his complaint implies that others were not as
motivated by piety as by pleasure. They did find most significant "the
abundance of wine" and "the roast meats."

The most evidence for a social understanding of sacrifice and cult
meals is found in the comedies of Aristophanes, the late 5th-century
playwright. In many passages his characters show a clear unconcern about
the gods, although a real fondness for cult meals.

Theoris cynically says Theognis's infatuation with becoming an
Athenian was based on his longing to "taste his Aparturian sausage."[211]
Two citizens argue in *The Knights,* and one complains of the gluttony of
the other at the meal in the Prytaneum.[212]   Ehrenberg notes that in
Aristophanes a man could be called "fond of sacrifice" (φιλοθύτης) as an
allusion either to his piety or greed.[213]

---

[210]Plutarch, *Suav. Viv. Epic.* 21.1102AB.   Priests are termed
μάγειροι elsewhere without any implication of rebuke.   Plutarch
complains that Epicurus says one ought to act religious for the benefit of
others who are.   "For out of fear of public opinion he goes through a
mummery of prayer and obeisances that he has no use for and pronounces
words that run counter to his philosophy."

[211]*Ach.* 146. The Aparturia was a clan festival open to members
only.

[212]*Eq.* 280f. It was a great honor to be invited to take part in the
state-supplied meal in the Prytaneum. Ehrenberg, 342f., says that in the
time of Aristophanes this once great and rare honor had come to be
regarded as something one could buy or sell.

[213]Ehrenberg, 259. He refers to *Vesp.* 82, where two slaves are
discussing the "vices" of honest men, such as being "dice lovers," "drink
lovers," or "lovers of law courts."

Elsewhere Aristophanes describes the behavior at cult festivals as characterized predominantly by drunkenness. This is seen in an invitation to supper by the priest of Bacchus, as one might expect.[214] In *The Eccleziazusae* strong drink is regarded as the only explanation for the misconduct, lengthy prayers and fights at civic meetings (which were, of course, held under religious aegis).[215] It is no surprise that Dionysus is termed "fellow drinker."[216]

Several times in Aristophanes sacrifice is described, and in those instances too the focus is upon the pleasure of the gathering. In the *Acharians* a messenger summons Dicaeopolis:

> Come at once to supper, and bring your pitcher, and your supper-chest. The priest of Bacchus sends to fetch you thither. And do be quick; you keep the supper waiting. For all things else are ready and prepared: The couches, tables, sofa-cushions, rugs, wreaths, sweetmeats, myrrh, the harlotry are there.[217]

A more extensive description is in *The Peace*, where a sacrifice is quickly accomplished, but the subsequent meal is fully described. While the worshippers roast the sheep, a passerby, Hierocles, arrives and an argument ensues over the cooking and meal:

Se.   What brings him [Hierocles] here?
Tr.   'Tis evident he comes to raise some opposition to our truces.
Se.   No, 'tis the savour of the roast attracts him ...
Hi.   What is this sacrifice, and made to whom?
Se.   Roast on: don't speak; hands off the haunch remember.
Hi.   Will ye not say to whom ye sacrifice? This tail looks right.[218]

---

[214] *Ach.* 1089, also see n. 106 above.

[215] *Eccl.* 135-55.

[216] *Ra.* 297. Ehrenberg, 259, concludes: "'to offer sacrifice' and 'to drink,' seem to be about the same thing."

[217] *Ach.* 1085-90. To this passage a scholiast comments: "Those invited to a feast furnished garlands, perfume, sweetmeats, etc., and the guest brought provisions." Cf. *Ach.* 243-279, a rather bawdy account of a rural Dionysiac festival. Cf. Athenaeus 574f.

[218] *Pax* 1020-50. Cf. *Ach.* 1000-1015 in which the smell of cooking eases the complaints of the chorus.

It is clear that the main concern of those sacrificing (and their inter-
rupter) is how the sheep is cooked. Their main fear is losing a portion to
Hierocles. The latter, at the same time, pays closest attention to the
preparation of the roast and wishes a dining invitation.

Another indication of the attitude toward the god's role at sacrifice in Aristophanes's plays is when the gods complain that men steal their
portions. Hecate complains that the monthly offerings left for her at
crossroads are stolen:

> Each month do the wealthy a supper provide,
>   to be used in my service divine,
> But the poor lie in wait for a snatch at the plate,
>   or e'er it is placed on my shrine.[219]

The most complete passage involving the theft of sacrifices is in
the *Plutus*, and has been noted above.[220] Charion recounts his night spent
in a temple when he imitated the example of the priest by swiping food
from the table of the god. His wife replies to his misconduct:

> Wife: Unhappy man! Did you not fear the god?
> Ch.   Indeed I did, lest he should cut in first,
>   Garlands and all, and capture my [soup] tureen.[221]

Of course, it is true that Aristophanes is writing comedy and not
reporting historical events or real speeches. Allowance must be made for
exaggeration for comic effect. Yet the lines would not have been funny if
their caricatures did not reflect familiar attitudes and conduct. Moreover, most plays, comedies and tragedies, were written for and performed
in association with religious festivals. Aristophanes did not fear, apparently, that his humor would be judged an impious falsification of the real
meaning of sacrifice and cult meals.

---

[219] *Pl.* 596f.

[220] See 17, n. 43.

[221] *Pl.* 683f. There are other references to men stealing sacrifices
for the gods. Aelian, *Nat. An.* 7.13 tells that a dog was highly honored in
Athens because he was responsible for the capture of a thief who had
robbed the temple of Asclepius.

Diogenes Laertius, 6.73, says that Diogenes the Cynic "saw no
impropriety either in stealing anything from a temple or in eating the
flesh of any animal." Is the "anything" which Diogenes took from the
temple the same as "the flesh of any animal"?

Another writer who makes frequent reference to sacrificial meals and other dining occasions is Athenaeus. His *Deipnosophists* is an eclectic, often disarranged, collection taken from earlier writings. He says the gods initiated their festivals for the enjoyment of men, so that "after first sacrificing to the gods, they let themselves go in relaxation."[222]

Athenaeus laments that in his own day one might be assigned a couch to share with a glutton and have one's dinner stolen. Or one could not enjoy the meal because of the boisterous conduct of others.[223]

Several times Athenaeus speaks of cooks or recounts words of cooks (μάγειροι).[224] They are described as a common feature at sacrifice.[225] Athenaeus recounts that a certain Alexander was urged to purchase his mother's cook who was well-versed in sacrificial rites.[226] In a quotation from Athenion's *Samothracians,* a cook claims his profession had contributed more to piety (εὐσέβειν) among mankind than any other, for they turned men from cannibalism when they showed the superior taste of roast sheep—following sacrifice.[227] In each of the passages the close connection between the work of offering sacrifice and fixing dinner

---

[222]Athenaeus, 363d. In one of his frequent word studies, Athenaeus concludes that strong drink is called μέθυ because at feasts in honor of the gods men "gave themselves up" (μεθιέντες) to jollity and relaxation.

[223]Athenaeus 186c. Here he is writing about a symposium, not a cult sacrifice. However, the symposium also had a quasi-religious character; it began with a libation. Also Athenaeus freely interchanges many terms for dining occasions, even equating them explicitly, which suggests no strict differences among them. 186a.

[224]The word μάγειρος can mean among other things "cook" or "butcher." It can also refer to a cult official who slays the animal in sacrifice and divides the flesh. An insightful discussion of the various roles and duties of people called μάγειροι and their cultic significance is in E. M. Rankin, *The Role of the ΜΑΓΕΙΡΟΙ in the Life of the Ancient Greeks* (Chicago: University Press, 1907).

[225]For example, Athenaeus 149a, 172f. (the "cooks" from Delos were famous for familiarity with sacred rites), and 579e. In 360f. Athenaeus discusses how words used to denote sacrificer or cook evolved in Greek. SIG³ 1021 lists among officials at a feast "water provider" (στεγανόμος) and "butcher" (μάγειρος).

[226]Athenaeus, 659f.

[227]Athenaeus 660e, f. The cook says, "It is we cooks who perform the rites of consecration; we offer sacrifice, pour libations, because the gods hearken more to us than to all others for having discovered those things which pertain most to the good life" (661c).

shows how similar these undertakings were regarded in popular sentiments.

Another character found at Hellenistic meals, both at private
parties and cult gatherings, was the parasite who lived from the dinners of
others. Athenaeus quotes from one parasite, Didorus, this claim: "The
parasite's life was an invention of Zeus the god of friendship, admittedly
the mightiest of the gods." He says that Zeus enters any home that he
wishes, rich or poor, and there eats and drinks to his fill, and then "he
goes back home without paying the scot."[228]

A final citation from Athenaeus will best illustrate the conduct
characteristic of Hellenistic fraternal meals. Lamenting the sad state of
conduct at meals in his day, Athenaeus says:

> People who gather for dinner-parties today, especially if they
> come from fair Alexandria, shout, bawl, and objurgate the
> wine-pourer, the waiter, and the chef; the slaves are in tears,
> being buffeted by knuckles right and left. To say nothing of
> the guests, who thus dine in complete embarrassment; if the
> occasion happen to be a religious festival (θυσία), even the
> god will cover his face and depart, abandoning not only the
> house but also the entire city.[229]

In summary, from this wide range of literary sources, spread over
centuries, it is clear that the dominant mood at common meals (private,
public festivals, even cults) was one of joyous feasting. These authors see
nothing inappropriate with this joyous attitude and complain only when
the merriment gets out of hand. The presence of the god(s) is assumed;
however, the focus is upon the worshippers and their association and
pleasure.

---

[228]Athenaeus, 239c. It seems unlikely both from the immediate
context and from other remarks in Athenaeus that he really is describing
the communal interpretation of the god's presence at the feast. His
remarks are not to encourage piety but to lampoon a troublesome aspect
of dining.
   [229]Athenaeus, 420e. Cf. also 363f-364b, where he laments that
the "serious deportment" of earlier times is no longer to be found. For
"the men of to-day, who pretend to sacrifice to the gods and call together
their friends and intimates, curse their children, quarrel with their wives,
drive their slaves to tears [and] threaten the crowd."

CONCLUSIONS

The preceding investigation permits the following conclusions regarding cult meals in Hellenistic life and their importance for the correct understanding of 1 Corinthians 8 and 10.

First, in spite of the widespread modern acceptance of the sacramental interpretation of pagan cult meals, there is insufficient evidence to support this theory. The eating of a sacrificial animal was not the means of acquiring the deity, nor a special power or trait of his—at least not in the Hellenic, Hellenistic and Imperial periods.[230]

After his survey of the evidence for a sacramental interpretation of cultic meals, Kane rightly concludes:

> There is no evidence at all that in these cults, including even the old Greek *orgia* of Dionysis, the ancient mysteries of Eleusis, or the later banquet of the Zeus of Panamara, such meals or other occasions of eating and drinking had a sacramental significance in the sense of conveying *ex opere operato* special powers, status or communion.[231]

Second, there is impressive evidence for a social interpretation: from writers approving the social pleasures of cult meals, from regulations in Hellenistic associations, and from critics of misconduct at such meals. Quoting again from Kane:

> So far as the limited evidence shows, cult meals were usually pleasurable social occasions rather than means of obtaining mystical union with a deity or special powers of any kind.[232]

---

[230]In the present study's investigation of sacramentalism, especially in the Dionysiac mysteries, it has been noted how influential the *totemistic* hypothesis has been. This approach is largely based upon the study of primitive tribes and an assumption that their understandings were shared by Hellenistic Greeks. M. P. Nilsson, "Second Letter to Professor Nock on the Positive Gains in the Science of Greek Religion," *HTR* 44 (1951) 143, has rightly recalled that one must remember the Hellenic and Hellenistic Greeks were not primitives.

[231]Kane, "Mithraic Cult Meals," 348f.

[232]Ibid., 343.

The norm of these banquets was an atmosphere of relaxed good cheer which accords with Greek religion.[233]

Third, it has been seen that sacrifices and common meals were normative features of Hellenistic cults and associations. Since these meals were characteristic expressions of Greek public life, it is altogether understandable that the Corinthian Christians would desire to be involved in them, at least to the degree they considered permissible.[234] Since they probably did not see such meals as religiously significant, their enlightened Christian monotheism would have been sufficient to overcome any qualms about eating—except among some members "weak in conscience." The social character of cult meals would also have emboldened the Corinthians to ask defensively of their founder-apostle reasons why they must abstain from such normal functions of life.

The assessment of the cult meals as occasions of good company, good food, and good fun makes it obvious why the Corinthian Christians would not have wanted to miss out. It probably was not regarded as pagan worship to participate in the various "socials" held in temple precincts.[235]

Fourth, because the pagan cult meals were not sacramental (a means of acquiring the deity and/or its special powers and traits) nor communal (an occasion of intimate relationship between the worshipper and the god), it is unlikely that Paul in 1 Cor 10:14-21 is trying to warn the Corinthians against dangers in pagan sacraments. It is not that he fears that they are ingesting a pagan deity. In brief, Paul is not opposing a pagan sacrament for the sake of the Christian one, for the pagan meal was not regarded as a sacrament.[236] Other explanations must be sought

---

[233]Ibid., 349.

[234]Ex-pagan Christians in Corinth would have had many social obligations from family or business (marriages, funerals, puberty rites) which would have involved sacrificial meals, normally in or near the temple grounds. Participation would be an expected part of family and social duty.

[235]Of course, Christians with a strong sense of their Christian "knowledge" (γνῶσις) and "privileges" (ἐξουσία) based upon having the Spirit may have had an additional incentive.

[236]Nock makes essentially this point in *Early Gentile Christianity*, 83, yet he allows for some aberrations in Greek cult meals which had the idea that "the strength of the deity dwells in the sacrificial flesh and passes into him who eats it." (He is citing Lietzmann's *Mass and Lord's Supper*, 73.) Nock certainly thinks that such a sacramental view is very limited and may be only implied: "What we infer from these indications

for Paul's opposition to Christian involvement in pagan cult meals (see below, 218-220).

Fifth, from the survey of pagan cult meals there are two tangential discoveries which are suggestive for the interpretation of 1 Cor 8 and 10, beyond what has been learned about the social importance of cultic meals.

From certain regulations it is seen that on some occasions, not all, members of cults were permitted to take their portions of sacrificial meat home.[237] One inscription from Pergamum allots meat from a public sacrifice to be used for the prize in accompanying athletic games.[238] This offers one source of meat from sacrifice (cf. 1 Cor 10:27) which a Christian might encounter at dinner in a pagan home.

Also an examination of the work of cult officials called μάγειροι shows that they are called in other contexts cooks and/or butchers. From their allotted portion for slaying the sacrificial animal, they sold meat in the market.[239] This is a possible source of the sacrificial meat mentioned in 1 Cor 10:25. By the nature of the case, in view of the slim evidence presented in 1 Cor 10:25-27, neither of these possibilities can be proven.

[of mana in sacrifice] is our inference, not ancient expressed belief or theory. It is something much less near the surface than the notion that the worshippers and the god eat together in fellowship; part is reserved for the god, the rest man takes."

[237]Franciszek Sokolowski, *Lois Sacrées des cités Grecques Supplement* (Paris: E. de Boccard, 1962) 140f., on a *lex sacra* from Didymes. Also W. A. Ferguson, "The Salaminoi of Heptaphylai and Sounion," *Hesperia* 7 (1938) 6. E. L. Hicks, "A Sacrificial Calendar from Cos," *JHS* 9 (1899) 329-330. E. J. and L. Edelstein, *Asclepius: A Collection and Interpretation of the Testimonies* (2 vols.; Baltimore: Johns Hopkins Press, 1945) 1.277 quote a passage from Herondas, *Mimiambi* 4.1-95, where a sacrifice to Asclepius could be taken home. See also, *ibid.*, 2.189 for a review of other regulations which prohibit removing meat from the temenos of Asclepius. An example of such prohibition is SIG[3] 736, on which see the comment of Yerkes, 108. Also cf. Pausanius 2.27.1 on similar regulations in cults of Asclepius in Epidaurus and Titane.

[238]C. A. Forbes, "Ancient Athletic Guilds," *Classical Philology*, 50 (1955) 238.

[239]Sokolowski, 149f. "And let the cooks/butchers (μάγειροι) sell the heads of the sheep when they have cleaned them." Cf. Artemidorus, *Oneirocr.* 56, where a butcher is said to cut up meat for sale in the agora. Cf. Rankin, *Role of* ΜΑΓΕΙΡΟΙ, 64, who cites Athenaeus 243f and 579e.

Part II

Exegesis of 1 Corinthians 8 and 10

1 CORINTHIANS 8: QUESTIONS FROM CORINTH

INTRODUCTION

A. Problems in Corinth

The topic of Christians eating sacrificial meat arises first in 1 Corinthians in chapter 8. The issue was apparently raised by the Corinthians in a letter sent to Paul, as is discussed below.

There are several important problems involved in the study of 1 Corinthians 8. First, what actually occurred in Corinth regarding the eating of sacrificial meat? How did what occurred affect the church members? Second, what did the Corinthians say about this in their letter to Paul? Third, what was Paul's reply and what guidance does he give? Fourth, how does what is said in 1 Corinthians 8 relate to the subsequent discussion in chapters 9 and 10?

Answers to these questions must be reconstructed from implications in 1 Corinthians. In some cases, the reconstruction involves what the Corinthians wrote in their now lost letter. Despite the impossibility of achieving certainty, this reconstruction is both a necessary and possible task in order to understand the discussion of eating sacrificial meat as it appears in 1 Corinthians 8 and 10.

B. Structure of the Passage

There are several considerations which support the present consensus that in 1 Corinthians 8 Paul actually quotes from a letter which he received from the Corinthians.[1]

---

[1] A valuable and comprehensive summary of the question of quotations in 1 Corinthians is by Hurd in *The Origin of 1 Corinthians*. The

First, such a letter is expressly referred to by Paul (7:1, περὶ δὲ ὧν ἐγράψατε). Second, the formula περὶ δέ, which occurs five times in 1 Corinthians (7:1; 8:1; 12:1; 16:1, 12) and otherwise only in 1 Thessalonians (4:9; 5:1), in every case in Paul's letters seems to reflect questions asked of Paul.[2] Third, the abrupt change in topics in 1 Corinthians 7, 8, 12 and 16 suggests Paul is following a predetermined agenda. Finally, as will be shown, the structure and content of 1 Corinthians 8 can best be explained by the hypothesis that Paul is answering a set of questions sent to him.

It must be acknowledged that the presentation of the Corinthians' viewpoint in all these cases could be Paul's own attempt to capsulize (perhaps unfairly) their views. Whether this is the case or whether Paul actually quotes their words is not decisive for understanding the chapter and in any case must be determined by the exegesis of 1 Corinthians 8.

It will be argued in the exegesis that 1 Corinthians 8 is organized around phrases taken from the Corinthians' arguments setting forth their reasons for their participation in pagan cult meals.[3] These quotations from their letter account for the structure of the chapter, because in each case Paul takes a statement from the Corinthians as his starting place and then responds to it.

Using the quotations as a guide, the present study, in agreement with several prior studies, divides 1 Corinthians 8 into three parts: 8:1-3, 4-7, and 8-13.

---

history of investigation of this question is found on pages 62-94, and a table summary on page 68.

[2]Regarding the formula, "περὶ δὲ . . ." Hurd, 63f., concludes, "The fact that this formula occurs six times in the last ten chapters of 1 Corinthians but elsewhere in the Pauline corpus only at 1 Thess 4:9 and 5:1 . . . emphasizes its importance to the structure of 1 Corinthians." B. W. Bacon, *The Story of St. Paul* (Boston: Houghton, Mifflin & Co., 1904) 270f. says: "Paul gives his answers *seriatim.* . . ."

C. E. Faw, "On the Writing of First Thessalonians," *JBL* 73 (1952) 221-22, explores this περὶ δέ form for quotations elsewhere in the New Testament, especially in 1 Thessalonians. For others who have noted the importance of the formula see Hurd, 64, note 2 and 90, note 2.

[3]Joachim Jeremias, "Zur Gedankenführung in den paulinischen Briefen: (3) Die Briefzitate in 1 Kor 8.1-13," *Abba* (Göttingen: Vandenhoeck and Ruprecht, 1966) 273-76 argues for this organizational principle.

1 CORINTHIANS 8:1-3: KNOWING AND LOVING

A. A Quotation from Corinth:
οἴδαμεν ὅτι πάντες γνῶσιν ἔχομεν

As Paul turns to take up the third topic of the inquiry from the Corinthians he begins by quoting from their letter.[4] The extent of that quotation is uncertain. 1 Cor 8:1b, ἡ γνῶσις φυσιοῖ, is clearly a Pauline qualification or rejection of the Corinthians' slogan and thereby marks the terminal limit of the quotation. However, where the quotation begins is not obvious. It could begin with περὶ δὲ τῶν εἰδωλοθύτον, if the Corinthian inquiry was in a list form.[5]

But if περὶ δὲ εἰδωλοθύτον is not part of the direct quotation, where does the quotation begin? Most scholars take ὅτι to introduce the quotation,[6] (a common Greek way to set off quotations, since the language lacks quotation marks).[7] In this view the actual words of the

---

[4] In addition to those scholars cited by Hurd in his table on page 68 one should add: C. K. Barrett, *The First Epistle to the Corinthians* (New York: Harper & Row, 1968) and Conzelmann, *1 Corinthians*.

[5] No one seems to have ventured this suggestion. It would fit nicely with the previous quotation in 7:25 and with subsequent ones in 12:1, 16:1 and 12. However, in 7:1 περὶ δὲ ὧν ἐγράψατε is clearly not a quote, although it does introduce a quote, "καλὸν ἀνθρώπῳ γυναικὸς μὴ ἅπτεσθαι." If this initial quotation sets the pattern, then the περὶ δὲ, although occasioned by the Corinthians' quotes, is Paul's formulation.

The formula περὶ δὲ should not be taken in a rigid way for it does not necessarily establish the limits of quotes from the Corinthians' letter. It does not occur, for example, in 11:2-16 which surely deals with a question asked by the Corinthians. The same is true of chapter 15 and the question of the resurrection of the dead. See Hurd, 90-94.

[6] For example, Hurd, 69; Barrett, *1 Corinthians*, 187 and Conzelmann, *1 Corinthians*, 140, among others.

[7] Walter Bauer, W. F. Arndt, F. W. Gingrich and Frederick Danker, *A Greek-English Lexicon of the New Testament and other Early Christian Literature* (2nd revision, Chicago: University Press, 1979) 558, 1(e): "the formula οἴδαμεν ὅτι is frequently used to introduce a well-known fact that is generally accepted." Also see F. Blass and A. Debrunner, *A Greek Grammar of the New Testament and other Early Christian Literature* (rev. Robert W. Funk; Chicago: University Press, 1961) § 470(1), "ὅτι is usually followed not only by the indicative instead of the optative (a tendency also in classical), but also by an exact representation of direct discourse, so that ὅτι serves the function of our quotation marks."

Corinthians begin with πάντες. However, there are some good reasons for thinking the quotation begins with οἴδαμεν.[8]

First, the words οἴδαμεν ὅτι are unique in syntax within the Pauline letters, which suggests that the style is not Paul's but that of someone else. Elsewhere Paul writes οἴδαμεν + ὅτι six times. In each of these cases the syntax is οἴδαμεν + δὲ/γὰρ + ὅτι[9] Only in 1 Cor 8:1 and 4 is the δὲ/γὰρ lacking. The sampling is not large enough to be conclusive but suggests that in 8:1, 4 the words οἴδαμεν ὅτι come from the Corinthians' letter.

Second, as has been noted frequently, Paul seems to be in self-contradiction in verses 1 and 7. In the former he says *all* have γνῶσις while in the latter verse he says *all* do not. This apparent contradiction can be explained adequately simply on the basis of rhetorical style, irony, or other reasons.[10] However, the contradiction really disappears if the quotation of 8:1 begins with οἴδαμεν . Then it is Paul's questioners who assert *all* have knowledge.

---

[8]Walter Lock, "I Corinthians viii.1-9, A Suggestion," *The Expositor,* fifth series VI (1897) 65-74.

[9]Rom 2:2; 3:19; 7:14; 8:22, 28; 2 Cor 5:1. Paul also uses οἶδα + ὅτι three times: Rom 7:18; 15:29; Phil 1:19. The observations about his syntax hold for these single person usages also.

[10]W. L. Knox, *St. Paul and the Church of the Gentiles* (Cambridge: University Press, 1939) 136, n. 7, says that Paul uses γνῶσις ironically in 8:1 and 8:4. Adolf Schlatter, *Die Korintherbriefe* (Stuttgart: Calwer, 1962) 98, says that Paul doesn't want to insult the Corinthians by questioning their γνῶσις. Jean Héring, *The First Epistle of Saint Paul to the Corinthians* (London: Epworth Press, 1962) 67, says that Paul is being defensive. "The apostle takes up their catch-phrase in order to let them understand first of all that they are not the only ones to 'have knowledge.' 'We also have it.'"

Others insist that Paul is aligning himself with the Corinthians by including himself in the word οἴδαμεν. For one example, Otto Merk, *Handeln aus Glauben* (Marburger Theologische Studien 5; Marburg: N. G. Elwert, 1968) 122, "Ihre richtige Erkenntnis, die Pls teilt (er schliesst sich in 8.3, vgl. auch 8.4 in die 1. Pers. plural mit ein). . . ."

Joachim Jeremias, "Briefzitate," 273-76, suggests reading οἶδα μὲν rather than οἴδαμεν in 8:1 and 4. This somewhat lessens the apparent agreement between Paul and the strong. However, the μεν is syntactically unrelated and somewhat awkward. Hurd, 120, uses this apparent agreement of Paul with the Corinthians' slogans, especially his apparent unwillingness to reject them outright, as a major piece in his reconstruction of the discussion between Paul and the Corinthians.

Third, if πάντες is regarded as beginning the quotation from the Corinthians, then Paul appears to agree with the "strong," yet he then moves immediately to correct their arguments. This tension is not crucial, since Paul could no doubt agree with their theoretical position without accepting their practice.[11] Yet it does leave Paul with a conflict between his theology and his practice.

Fourth, in his study of possible quotations in 1 Corinthians, Walter Lock argues that the Corinthians' words begin with οἴδαμεν, on the basis of the verb number. He says that the first person plural verbs come from the Corinthians while the second person plural verbs come from Paul.[12] In my view this argument, which should be noted, is less convincing.

These particular arguments are also confirmed by two general observations. First, as is well known, the Corinthians were much taken with their "knowledge" (leaving aside how the word γνῶσις is understood). A slogan beginning "we know" would certainly agree with their self-estimate. Second, Paul repeatedly rebukes the Corinthians with οὐκ οἴδατε. Although this phrase is familiar from the diatribe, it is still

---

[11] This is the common resolution of the conflict. See Conzelmann, *1 Corinthians*, 137, among others. On the apparent theoretical agreement of Paul and the Corinthians see in this study pages 15-17.

It cannot be overlooked that the approach of having Paul accept a position in theory but refrain from acting on it has a hermeneutical advantage for many modern Christians who find it preferable to follow a traditional style of Christian behavior, although holding quite different theoretical views. To what degree, if any, this influences interpretation is probably not discernible.

[12] Lock, 65ff., is not defensive here and apparently does not consider that the quote might begin with πάντες. He foreshadows Hurd's thesis when he says, "The history of most of these phrases would be this, that St. Paul had used them in his preaching to the Corinthians. . . . They are his phrases; he does not repudiate them, but he shows how they need adapting to particular needs."

Lock therefore still assumes Paul's agreement with the position stated by the strong. In addition to Lock and Hurd many others have seen Paul as the source of the Corinthians' arguments.

Hurd, 120, says, "In 8:1 the double 'we' is awkward, 'We know that we all have knowledge.' The subject of the two verbs does not appear identical. The first verb is best referred to the author(s) of 1 Corinthians."

It ought to be noted that the double "we" is much less awkward in Greek, since each "we" is a part of a verb, a normal style.

noteworthy that Paul employs it eleven times in 1 Corinthians and only once elsewhere.[13]

The extent of the quotation is not a decisive issue. But, it seems better to say it begins with οἴδαμεν both on grammatical and theological considerations. In this way 8:7 is less problematic, and one can avoid having to split Paul's thought into conflicting theoretical and practical halves.[14] It is more likely that Paul in 1 Cor 8-10 is seeking to hold together theory and practice, but his theology has a different center than that of the Corinthians, which is γνῶσις.[15]

In summary, Paul begins the discussion of eating εἰδωλοθύτον by quoting from the Corinthian letter where they argued, οἴδαμεν ὅτι πάντες γνῶσιν ἔχομεν.[16] Even if their words began with πάντες, the content of their γνῶσις is the same. Immediately in the opening verse Paul turns to correct their defense of their conduct.

---

[13]1 Cor 3:16; 6:2, 3, 9, 15, 16, 19; 8:1; 9:13, 24 and Rom 6:16. This is noted by Hurd, 85, who observes, "This is explicable enough in the face of the conceit of the Corinthian church, but the satire of it is even more marked if twice in their recent letter they had used the boastful οἴδαμεν." F. W. Grosheide, *A Commentary on the First Epistle to the Corinthians* (NICNT 7; Grand Rapids: Wm. B. Eerdmans Co., 1955) 188, aptly notes, "*We know* is an expression which fits the proud Corinthians." See also, Lock, 70.

Bauer, ed. Gingrich and Danker, *Greek-English Lexicon*, 558b, note that the phrase οὐκ οἴδατε could reflect a rhetorical convention in Paul's letters. Otherwise Paul uses οἴδατε to recall factual information known by the recipients of his letters: 1 Cor 12:2; 16:15; Gal 4:13; Phil 4:15; 1 Thess 1:5; 2:1, 2, 4, 11; 3:3, 4 and 4:2. In 1 Thessalonians too it is used paraenetically.

[14]This is repeatedly done, so that Paul, knowing that eating sacrificial meat is an adiaphoron, still is willing to forego it in specific cases. There is nothing inherently wrong with such an approach; 1 Cor 9:19-22 seems to suggest it. Nevertheless, one ought to be suspicious of such bifurcation of Paul's theology. In dealing with the present passage such a policy leads to such a statement as "Die in 8,1 erwähnte γνῶσις ist, an sich ganz richtig . . ." Merk, 122. This strongly reminds one of Kant.

On the integrity of Paul's theology and practice, see Victor P. Furnish, *Theology and Ethics in Paul* (Nashville: Abingdon, 1968) esp. 98-111 and 224-227.

[15]Conzelmann, *1 Corinthians*, 140, rightly observes, "The slogan, 'we know' has a specific content: εἷς θεός . . . along with the conclusion: accordingly the gods are non-existent. This provides the theoretical foundation for the practice of freedom."

[16]Lock, 67.

B. A Pauline Reply:
ἡ γνῶσις φυσιοῖ, ἡ δὲ ἀγάπη οἰκοδομεῖ

Paul begins his answer to the Corinthians' argument with a slogan of his own: ἡ γνῶσις φυσιοῖ, ἡ δὲ ἀγάπη οἰκοδομεῖ.[17] These two slogans in 8:1 capture succinctly the basic conflict between Paul and the Corinthians, not only about idol meat but other issues as well. They and he have a fundamental difference in how they understand the gospel. For the Corinthians it is γνῶσις, for Paul it is ἀγάπη. The result of these two contrasting standpoints is also a contrast: γνῶσις φυσιοῖ, ἀγάπη οἰκο- δομεῖ. Each of these terms gives insight into the way Paul understood the debate.

1. *Knowledge puffs up.* Much has been written about the back- ground and significance of the term γνῶσις in Paul's writings,[18] and this is especially true of 1 Corinthians.[19] Paul does use γνῶσις far more often

---

[17]Héring, *First Epistle*, 67, suggests that 8:1b, ἡ γνῶσις φυσιοῖ, ἡ δὲ ἀγάπη οἰκοδομεῖ, is a non-Pauline interpolation "added either by Sosthenes or by a reader who remembered the phrase about 'puffed up' gnostics in 5:2." Héring seeks to distinguish two types of γνῶσις, one true and one false. But Paul is not writing systematics, rather he is engaging in a debate. So he need not worry about attacking all γνῶσις, or protecting the "true" γνῶσις.

The exact character of the Corinthians' γνῶσις is, of course, hotly debated. Walter Schmithals, *Gnosticism in Corinth* (Nashville: Abingdon, 1971) is the most thorough attempt to relate Corinthian γνῶσις to the later Gnostic movement identified in polemic with church fathers.

Of course, Hellenistic writers were occupied with γνῶσις under- stood in varying ways. Barrett, *1 Corinthians*, 189, says, "The term was probably (at this time) a wide one, and the next few verses show that it included Christian speculative theology in general. . . . It seems, how- ever, to have been founded upon the doctrine of God; evidently the gnos- tics claimed to know God (cf. 1 John ii.4)."

[18]On the general usage of the terms, see Rudolf Bultmann, "Γινώσκω" *TDNT* 1, 689-719, who summarizes and gives most of the important evidence. Also Jacques Dupont, *Gnosis: La Connaissance religieuse dans les epitres de S. Paul* (Universitas Catholica Lovaniensis, Dissertationes in Facultate Theologica 2:40; Louvain: Nauwelarts, 1960) and Hans Jonas, *Gnosis und spätantiker Geist* (Göttingen: Vandenhoeck & Ruprecht, 2nd ed., 1964) 66.

[19]Especially Schmithals, *Gnosticism in Corinth*. But also Robert Jewett, *Paul's Anthropological Terms* (AGJU 10; Leiden: E. J. Brill, 1971) 40, who says that Paul's opponents at Corinth can be termed Gnostics "because of their belief in salvation through σοφία/γνῶσις and because of

than any other New Testament author (21 times to 8) and of the Pauline uses 16 are in the Corinthian letters, five in 1 Cor 8. As Barrett concludes:

> If figures prove anything, these figures show that it was primarily in the Corinthian situation that the idea of γνῶσις developed, and that the γνῶσις was much, though not exclusively, concerned with the problem of εἰδωλοθύτον.[20]

Since the relationship between γνῶσις and εἰδωλοθύτον is not an obvious one, and since it arose in response to an inquiry from Corinth, it is probable that the Corinthians made this connection in their argument. They are engaged in defending a course of action, real or proposed, in which Christians eat sacrificial meat, and they defend it on the basis of knowledge.[21]

Certainly a critical review and evaluation of the term γνῶσις is beyond the scope of the present study. Both Barrett and Conzelmann[22] point out that the γνῶσις at Corinth was probably neither simple rationalism, nor the more speculative theology of the later Gnostics. The content of the Corinthians' γνῶσις was "εἷς θεός" and the accompanying conclusion that therefore other Gods are non-existent, hence the eating of sacrificial meat is freely permitted.[23] This is clear, yet Conzelmann is right in observing:

> The specific understanding of the nature of the liberating gnosis is so far still an open question: it can be understood as enlightenment on the nature of the gods in the sense of popular philosophy, or as illumination of the pneumatic, or as a specifically gnostic insight into the depth of the world and

---

their consistently dualistic world view."

Bultmann, "Γινώσκω," 709, says that vocabulary and even approach come from Gnostics, but Paul fills the words with Old Testament election theology. Others, e.g., Barrett, 1 Corinthians, 18, 189, prefer to speak of an incipient form of Gnosticism.

[20]Barrett, "Things Sacrificed," 150f.

[21]The defensive tone of the Corinthians has been noted. See Conzelmann, 1 Corinthians, 140; Hurd, 65; Barrett, 1 Corinthians, 195.

[22]Barrett, 1 Corinthians, 195; Conzelmann, 1 Corinthians, 140.

[23]Conzelmann, 1 Corinthians, 140.

of being. . . . We must take account of the fact that these possibilities cannot always be strictly separated.[24]

Actually Paul does not undertake to investigate the basis and content of the Corinthian γνῶσις but its consequent result. What is wrong with their knowledge is that it "puffs up." Paul defines this γνῶσις by contrasting it with ἀγάπη, which "builds up."

Both φυσιόω, "puffed up," and οἰκοδομέω are important terms in the epistle. Φυσιόω occurs five other times in Paul—all in 1 Corinthians (φυσίωσις is found once, in 2 Cor 12:20), and οἰκοδομέω/οἰκοδομή occurs 18 times, half of which are in 1 Corinthians.[25]

The Corinthians had probably raised the issue of γνῶσις, but Paul himself originates the description of its effect as φυσιοῖ. As Hurd comments, "Clearly, therefore, this word expresses Paul's strong disapproval of the attitude of the too-wise Corinthians."[26] Paul sees the Corinthians as "inflated" in their self-estimate (5:2). Some are "puffed up" against their founder-apostle (4:18, 19) so that he is reluctant to come and discover this in person (2 Cor 12:19; note that in this verse Paul contrasts their attitude with his own. He does everything ὑπὲρ τῆς ὑμῶν οἰκοδομῆς).

The stance of φυσιοῖ is "against one another" (1 Cor 4:6, κατὰ τοῦ ἑτέρου) which is exactly the opposite of the work of love. This is said

---

[24]*Ibid.* Conzelmann distinguishes the Corinthian gnostics from later Gnostics in that the former employ their knowledge in a practical way, they do not have a concern for the "knower's reflection on himself nor seem to have developed any Gnostic theory on the relationship between the knower and the thing known in the process of knowing itself."

[25]1 Cor 8:10; 10:23, (a verbal parallel to 8:1); 14:3, 4, 5, 12, 17, 26, (all concerned with glossolalia) and 3:9. Elsewhere οἰκοδομέω refers to the goal or process of Paul's own work (2 Cor 10:8; 12:19; 13:10; Rom 15:20 and 1 Cor 3:9). In 2 Cor 5:1, οἰκοδομὴν ἐκ θεοῦ ἔχομεν is unique in its usage. Even this statistic may be misleading because two references in Romans (14:19 and 15:2) stand in some dependent relationship to the discussion in 1 Corinthians.

[26]Hurd, 76f. Dieter Georgi, "I Corinthians," *IDBSup*, 182, says that words like "pretend" (δοκέω), "boast" (καυχῆσθαι), and "puffed up" (φυσιόω) are "more than ethical metaphors. They . . . literally (but critically) circumscribe the sense of transworldly elevation the Corinthians tended to gain from their enthusiasm." Similarly Gerhard Friedrich, "Freiheit und Liebe im ersten Korintherbrief," *TZ* 26 (1970) 86, notes the connection between the Corinthians' arrogance and their pneumatology.

positively in 1 Cor 13:4:   ἀγάπη οὐ φυσιοῦται.. As in 1 Cor 8:1 ἀγάπη and γνῶσις are contrasted.

2. *Love builds up.* 'Αγάπη is a frequent concept in Paul, evenly dispersed in his letters. In addition to 1 Cor 8:1 it is used in 1 Corinthians in chapter 13 (vv. 1, 2, 3, 4, 8, 13) and 4:21; 16:14, 24; and 14:1 (which really belongs to chapter thirteen's argument). But the concept has a prominence in Paul's thought beyond these statistics.[27]

Althought in 1 Cor 8:3 Paul speaks of the Christian's love for God (also 1 Cor 2:9, an Old Testament reference), most often he speaks of God's love for man or of the love-relationship among believers. This is what he is describing in 8:1-3, especially the conduct that love demands from one believer for another. Other Pauline passages help illumine what is said very epigrammatically here.

Paul describes the higher goal of Christian faith as "pursuing love" (1 Cor 14:1), and urges Christians always to "walk in love" (Rom 14:15, where, as in 1 Cor 8:1, this is spelled out as being considerate of the brother). This "walk" means the total conduct of one's life. In those passages which speak of love for one's brother, Paul usually speaks of placing a priority on the neighbor's good (Phil 2:1-3) and of service to them (Gal 5:13, where ἀγάπη is specifically related to ἐλευθερίᾳ, also a concern at Corinth). It is precisely because ἀγάπη places a priority on the brother's good that it is the fulfilling of the Law (Rom 13:10) and embodies the life of Christ himself.[28]

The most familiar Pauline discussion of ἀγάπη is in 1 Cor 13. Conzelmann notes on 8:1, "The commentary on ἀγάπη is supplied by chap. 13. . . ."[29] In 1 Cor 13 ἀγάπη is specifically contrasted with charismata (including γνῶσις) and love's qualitative (13:13) superiority is seen in its effect on others.

Just as Paul characterizes γνῶσις as φυσιοῖ, so also the counter-term, ἀγάπη, is characterized by οἰκοδομέω. Vielhauer rightly says, what οἰκοδομέω means is first of all to be concluded from its antithesis to φυσιοῖ.[30]

---

[27]See Victor Furnish, *Theology and Ethics*, 199-203, and his *The Love Command in the New Testament* (Nashville: Abingdon, 1972) 91-117.

[28]Phil 2:1-3 says that love is esteeming others better than oneself, which is then grounded in the Christ-hymn of 2:5-11.

[29]Conzelmann, *1 Corinthians*, 140.

[30]Philipp Vielhauer, *OIKODOME. Das Bild vom Bau im der christlichen Literatur vom Neuen Testament bis Clemens Alexandrinus* (Karlsruhe-Durlach: Tron, 1939) 93, gives a succinct and apposite comment: "Die Erkenntnis bläht, d.h. ihre grosse Wirkung ist nur scheinbar, ihrer

It is possible that the Corinthians had argued in their letter that the weak must be "built up" to eat sacrificial meat as a growth to spirituality.[31] Like γνῶσις, οἰκοδομέω may have been a Corinthian term, but its occurrence elsewhere in Paul's letters (e.g., Gal 2:18; 1 Thess 5:11)[32] and the Pauline metaphor of the church as a temple/building shows it need not have its origin elsewhere. Of course, the Corinthians may have acquired the theological use of the word from Paul and applied it to their action of eating sacrificial meat on their own.[33] They may have urged both by slogan and conduct the "edification" of other Christians whose conscience did not permit them to eat sacrificial meat.

Paul's other uses of οἰκοδομέω are generally of two classes. The first are references to his own work as an apostle. This is presented as a metaphor in 1 Cor 3:10-15,[34] but also alluded to in 2 Cor 10:8; 12:19; 13:10 and Rom 15:20. Paul's work is the "building up" of the eschatological temple/house of God (1 Cor 3:16; 6:19).[35] In this way he is an example of what he urges of other Christians, such as here in 1 Cor 8.

The second group of Paul's uses of οἰκοδομέω are hortatory passages. In these he urges others to act for the furtherance of the kingdom as he does even when he does not specifically refer to himself as an example.[36]

Grösse und Stärke entspricht keine Realität, ihr Schein ist Täuschung; demgegenüber bezeichnet οἰκοδομεῖν wirkliche Förderung, Kräftigung, Stärkung. . . ."

[31]Conzelmann, 1 Corinthians, 151, n. 14, refers to Johannes Weiss (presumably, in Der erste Korintherbrief) and Lietzmann, Korinther, 39, says the Corinthians may have argued, one "erbaue sich an dieser Betätigung christlicher Freiheit." He is commenting on 8:10, which is discussed below, pages 103-105.

[32]Neither of these two references seems related to the problems at Corinth; nor does Rom 15:20, which refers to Paul's ministry.

[33]So Otto Michel, "Οἶκος," TDNT, 5, 140f. Vielhauer, OIKODOME, 97f., says they "misunderstood" Paul's earlier preaching on building up, just as they did on γνῶσις, σοφία, and ἐλευθερία.

[34]Michel, 140, cites as parallels: Epictetus, Diss. 2.18.8 and Philo, Gig. 30; Mut. Nom. 211 and Som. II.8. He thinks Paul takes the metaphor from Hellenistic Judaism.

[35]Noted by George T. Montague, Growth in Christ (Fribourg, Switzerland: St. Paul's Press, 1961) 235, who says "The Christian community not only belongs to God, but it is he who builds it up."

[36]Which is often done subtly. For example, in 1 Cor 8:13 he refers to his conduct in the question of eating. In 1 Cor 9:19-23 he explains his conduct in general terms obviously commending it to them, as is made

In 1 Cor 14 the church is the object of οἰκοδομέω in worship, as well as ethical conduct before outsiders. For example, in 1 Cor 14 Paul says that tongues have less value than prophecy precisely because the church is not built up (14:5, 12, which means "the other man," 14:17, cf. Rom 14:19), but only the speaker (14:4, the only Pauline reference to building up oneself). So the guiding principle for Christian worship is πάντα πρὸς οἰκοδομὴν γινέσθω (14:26), which is very similar to Paul's summary remark on eating sacrificial meat, Εἴτε οὖν ἐσθίετε εἴτε πίνετε εἴτε τι ποιεῖτε, πάντα εἰς δόξαν θεοῦ ποιεῖτε (10:31).

The similarities between 1 Cor 14 and 8 regarding οἰκοδομέω focus on how the brother is affected by one's actions. The object of οἰκοδομέω is never oneself, but the other man or the church. Because there is a mutual relationship between Christ and the church, serving the brother is service to Christ (Gal 6:2) and harm to the brother is harm to Christ (1 Cor 8:12). It is always *the brother in Christ* who is "built up" or "over-thrown."   Thus οἰκοδομέω has both soteriological and ecclesiological dimensions.[37]

The slogan of 1 Cor 8:1b—ἀγάπη οἰκοδομεῖ—sets forth succinctly and in a positive way the result of love, which is described negatively in 8:7-13 (cf. 10:23f., 31, 33). Building up the brother means placing no πρόσκομμα before the weak (8:9) lest the work of Christ be overturned (literally, "destroyed," ἀπόλλυται, cf. Rom 14:20, κατάλυε τὸ ἔργον τοῦ θεοῦ). In 10:23f. the same argument is found when Paul says the proper criterion of Christian conduct is not πάντα ἔξεστιν but πάντα οἰκοδομεῖ. The Christian is not to seek his own, ἀλλὰ τὸ τοῦ ἑτέρου, which is the same as being ἀπρόσκοποι to Jews, Greeks and τῇ ἐκκλησίᾳ τοῦ θεοῦ. Said negatively, Christians are admonished μηδεὶς τὸ ἑαυτοῦ ζη-τείτω (10:24), ἀλλὰ τὸ τῶν πολλῶν (10:33). The goal of this course of conduct is ἵνα σωθῶσιν (10:33, σωθῶσιν, is the reverse of ἀπολλύω in 8:11).

The same line of argument about οἰκοδομέω is found in Paul's later discussion in Romans 14. There too he argues that although πάντα μὲν καθαρά (14:20) the Christian must look away from himself seeking what advances the work of God. Guidance for Christian action is given nega-tively as τὸ μὴ τιθέναι πρόσκομμα τῷ ἀδελφῷ ἢ σκάνδαλον (14:13), even

---

explicit in 10:32-11:1.

[37]Vielhauer, OIKODOME, 96, ". . . es geht bei οἰκοδομεῖν nicht um Forderung und Gewinnung einzelner Menschen um den Bau der Kirche Gottes."

if ἐν κυρίῳ Ἰησοῦ one knows οὐδὲν κοινὸν δι᾽ ἑαυτοῦ. Thus abstaining from certain food for the sake of the brother (not to destroy him, 14:15, 16) is the same thing as κατὰ ἀγάπην περιπατεῖς (14:15).[38]

It has been mentioned that some commentators have suggested that the Corinthians felt the weaker brother was actually being "built up" through eating sacrificial meat. It has also been suggested that perhaps the Corinthians had used a slogan like ἡ γνῶσις οἰκοδομεῖ to defend their actions.[39] This possibility seems confirmed by 8:10 where οἰκοδομέω is used ironically.[40] The weak man acts as if he were strong—as if γνῶσιν ἔχων—which in truth he does not really have. His conscience contradicts this gnosis, in that it does not deny, but rather sanctions the existence of the idols.[41]

When the weak man follows the lead of the strong in eating ἐν εἰδωλείῳ he is not in fact "edified" but is destroyed (8:11). As Conzelmann observes, "with grim irony Paul points to the possible perverseness; you encourage him . . . to idol worship."[42] The consequence of this perverse edification is precisely[43] the destruction of the brother.

---

[38] Ibid., 98f. Paul stresses especially the work of building up his brother, as opposed to building up oneself. Parallels between the argument in 1 Cor 8 and Rom 14 are numerous: not placing a πρόσκομμα (Rom 14:13; 1 Cor 8:9); the criterion of ἀγάπη for one's actions (Rom 14:15; 1 Cor 8:1); not destroying (μὴ ἀπολύω, Rom 14:15; 1 Cor 8:11) the brother for whom Christ died (Rom 14:15, 1 Cor 8:11); and the summary not to do any eating which endangers the brother (Rom 14:21; 1 Cor 8:13).

For a recent study on the relationship between Romans 14 and 15 and 1 Corinthians, see Robert J. Karris, "Romans 14:1-15:3 and the Occasion of Romans," CBQ 35 (1973) 155-78.

[39] See Michel, "Οἶκος," 141 and Vielhauer, OIKODOME, 97. There is always a danger in this being "mirror exegesis," but there are some controls here: (1) Paul certainly does quote from the Corinthians' letter in this chapter. (2) Considering οἰκοδομέω as originating with the Corinthians appears to fit best with its use in 8:10.

[40] The use of irony is widely held: see Michel, "Οἶκος," 141; Vielhauer, OIKODOME, 94; Conzelmann, 1 Corinthians, 149; Lietzmann, Korinther, 39; Barrett, 1 Corinthians, 196; and many others.

This seems almost required, since Paul can hardly be supporting a conduct in which the weaker brother is destroyed by eating.

[41] Vielhauer, OIKODOME, 94.

[42] Conzelmann, 1 Corinthians, 149.

[43] Ibid., citing Blass-DeBrunner, Greek Grammar § 452(2).

The sentence in 8:11, ἀπόλλυται γὰρ ὁ ἀσθενῶν ἐν τῇ σῇ γνώσει, ὁ ἀδελφὸς δι'ὃν Χριστὸς ἀπέθανεν, is carefully constructed. It begins with the disastrous result of the weak man's eating: ἀπόλλυται, which is stressed by syntax.[44] Moreover, the one who is destroyed is ὁ ἀδελφὸς, "the brother," not just anybody. And "the brother" is further specified—the one for whom Christ (himself!) died.[45] This description prevents the strong from minimizing either the effect of his deed or the value of the brother who is lost.[46] In this way Paul shows the seriousness of a question which might appear very insignificant—what diet is permitted believers.

In summary, the Corinthians probably argued in their letter that, on the basis of Christian γνῶσις, they were seeking to encourage the reticent Christian, whose conscience was "weak," to join in pagan cult meals. They may have termed the imitation by the weak "οἰκοδομέω." Paul rejects this approach with three arguments.

First, the basis for real "building up" is not γνῶσις but ἀγάπη. Second, this supposed "edification" program (where the weak man sought to build up his conscience through imitation of the strong) was actually having disastrous consequences (8:11) and was really a sin against Christ (8:12). Third, the proper view of οἰκοδομέω is not one's personal advancement, whether of the weak or the strong, but of the church, including each person in Christ.[47] Thus in 8:1 when Paul says ἀγάπη οἰκοδομεῖ the implied object is τὸν ἀδελφόν or τὴν ἐκκλησίαν (cf. Rom 14:3).

3. *Knowing and being known.* In 1 Cor 8:1 Paul criticizes the Corinthians' γνῶσις by contrasting it with ἀγάπη, by pointing to the

---

[44]Ἀπολλύω is also used in 1 Cor 10:9, 10 to describe the slaying of the idolaters in the wilderness. It is a prefiguring of the fate of ultimate destruction, 2 Cor 4:3.

[45]Archibald Robertson and Alfred Plummer, *A Critical and Exegetical Commentary on the First Epistle of St. Paul to the Corinthians* (ICC; New York: Charles Scribner's Sons, 1911) 172.

[46]Conzelmann, *1 Corinthians*, 149, n. 34, says the strong simply disregard the weak.

[47]Thus Paul differs from the Corinthians on the issue of οἰκοδομεῖν in two ways: for Paul the proper basis of "building up" is ἀγάπη, not γνῶσις, and the Corinthians think of the individual as the locus for "building up," while Paul thinks of the other man or the church. Vielhauer, *OIKODOME*, 100, says, "Gegenstand der oikodome ist die Gemeinde, die im Nächsten als dem christlichen Bruder konkret wird." See also Furnish, *Love Command*, 112.

results of each. In 8:2, 3 he expresses doubts about γνῶσις as a way of relating to God. The text of 8:2, 3 is difficult. Zuntz says τι and τὸν θεόν should be omitted, reading: εἴ τις δοκεῖ ἐγνωκέναι, οὔπω ἔγνω καθὼς δεῖ γνῶναι, εἴ τις ἀγαπᾷ οὗτος ἔγνωσται.[48] In this reading Paul is contasting knowing and loving as opposite ways of relating to God.[49]

It is not clear what significance δοκεῖ has in the protasis of 8:2. It could mean, "if anyone believe himself to have γνῶσις" or "if anyone affects knowledge."[50] Paul uses εἴ τις with δοκέω five other times[51] and in each case the sense is "if anyone sets himself forth as one who . . ." which is consistent with three participial uses in Gal 2:2, 6, 9.[52] It is thus another lancet at the Corinthians' inflated self-estimate. The content of their presumed knowledge remains unstated, probably the γνῶσις to eat εἰδωλοθύτων.

---

[48]Günther Zuntz, *The Text of the Epistles* (London: Oxford University Press, 1953) 31. He follows the text of p. 46. He especially dislikes τὸν θεόν; it is "truly ruinous" as is the accompanying ὑπ' αὐτοῦ. Zuntz feels that Paul is using the *Kuntsprache* of the mystery religions.

[49]As Zuntz notes, 31f., τὸν θεόν is the object of ἀγαπάω in Rom 8:28, and thereby can be considered as Pauline. Calvin J. Roetzel, *Judgment in the Community* (Leiden: E. J. Brill, 1972) 159, notes the similarity of 8:3 to 16:22, especially in the protasis. In 16:22 of one does not love the Lord, he is anathematized, that is, "not known." In 8:3 if one loves the Lord he is recognized, i.e., "known." These are, Roetzel notes, the positive and negative forms of the same thought, although "one is from pre-Pauline Christian tradition and the other is a creation of Paul." Recently this phrase has been seen to reflect the gnostic theology of the knower and God; see especially, Schmithals, *Gnosticism*, 146-50. Barrett, *1 Corinthians*, 190f., says, "the language of mutual knowledge between God and man is gnostic in formulation, but it is the language alone that Paul borrows from gnostic sources; the content is the biblical doctrine of election and acceptance with God." Bultmann, "Γινώσκω," 709f., also says the operative idea is God's election. Bultmann's review of Dupont's *Gnosis* acknowledges the study has disproven the dependence on Hellenistic mysticism often asserted. Rudolf Bultmann, "Gnosis," *JTS* n.s. 3 (April 1952) 10-26.

[50]Georgi, "Corinthians," 182.

[51]1 Cor 3:18; 11:16; 14:37; Gal 6:3 and Phil 3:4.

[52]Similar is the participle in 10:12 which has the sense, "If anyone sets himself forth as one who stands." Other uses are 1 Cor 4:9 and 7:40 (of Paul himself) and 12:22, 23 and 2 Cor 12:19 which do not have a critical stance.

Paul says this affected knowledge is inadequate, for the "someone" does *not yet* (οὔπω) know as it is necessary to know. Paul only uses οὔπω three times: in Phil 3:13 it clearly refers to the eschaton (τὸ βραβεῖον τῆς ἄνω κλήσεως τοῦ θεοῦ); in 1 Cor 3:2 it may be an indefinite time, or perhaps is used ironically. Paul does not think that this γνῶσις is something to seek, as if he were urging more diligent striving.

That Paul is contrasting knowing and loving as ways of relating to God is confirmed in that he only speaks of Christians knowing God in one other place (Gal 4:9) where he quickly corrects himself, "rather you are known by God." Seeking to relate to God by knowing him is inherently wrong, for it remains a work of human striving. Knowledge by God,[53] by contrast, remains God's own work, his election of his own people, and this can be described as "knowing" them (see Gen 18:19; Ex 37:12; Amos 3:2; Hos 13:5).[54] It is neither mystical nor reflective (cf. 2 Tim 2:19).[55]

Paul generally speaks of God's love for man (e.g., Rom 8:37; 9:13, 25; 2 Cor 9:7 and Gal 2:20). But he does speak of men loving God in 1 Cor 2:9 and Rom 8:28. Romans 8:28 is especially instructive because the parallelism in that verse makes clear that "loving God" means "being elected by God." "We know that in everything God works for good with those *who love him, who are called* according to his purpose." Each of these passages, along with 1 Cor 8:3, speaks of God's election of his people (cf. Num 16:5). "In Paul's lexicon, then, 'those who love God' are the community of believers."[56]

In 1 Cor 8:2, 3 Paul continues his contrast of γνῶσις and ἀγάπη which he set forth initially as a response to the Corinthians' letter. Now

---

[53]The alternation of γινωσκεῖν and ἐπιγινώσκειν does not suggest a material difference, it is only rhetorical. See Bultmann, "Γινώσκω," 703. These cognates are also equivalent to 1 Cor 13:12.

[54]Bultmann, "Γινώσκεω," 698, n. 37. Jerome Murphy-O'Connor, "Freedom or the Ghetto (1 Cor VIII, 1-13; X, 23-XI, 1)," *RB* 85 (1978) 559, notes the shift from the present tense (ἀγαπᾷ) to the perfect (ἔγνωσται). He says the past tense suggests a particular time when God elected the believer.

[55]Earlier commentators had seen in v. 3, ἔγνωσται ὑπ᾿ αὐτοῦ evidence of Paul's dependence on the language of the mystery religions which spoke of the reciprocal knowing of the worshipper and his god. Lietzmann, *Korinther*, 37, cites Richard Reitzenstein, *Die hellenistischen Mysterienreligionen nach ihren Grundgedanken und Wirkungen* (Stuttgart: Teubner, 1927) 299 [English ed. 380-382], and Eduard Norden, *Agnostos Theos* (Leipzig and Berlin: Teubner, 1913) 287.

[56]Murphy-O'Connor, 560.

the contrast is not simply the resulting effects of each, but their conceptual base. The only γνῶσις that really counts is not the one achieved by believers, but the prior one of God's call. Thus the appropriate stance for Christians is not *knowing* God, but *being known*, which is seen in loving God—and this always means through the neighbor.[57] It is possible because God has first loved mankind and so enables them to love others.[58]

C. Is Love the Limit of Knowledge?

A comprehensive examination of 8:1-3 calls into question the frequent observation that Paul is saying here that γνῶσις is a good thing, but it must always be limited and tempered by love.[59] Rather it is the case that Paul contrasts knowing and loving as standpoints before God. The appropriate response to God's elective love/knowledge is not knowing him but loving him (through the brother) which in the particular case at hand means not tempting him to eat ἐν εἰδωλείῳ.

This contrast between knowing and loving in 1 Cor 8:1-3 is confirmed by looking at chapter 13.[60] There are several instructive parallels. First, in both 8:1-3 and 13 the "finite" limits of γνῶσις are stated. In 8:2 the gnostics do *not yet* (οὔπω) know. When will they? In 13:12 true

[57]Furnish, *Theology and Ethics*, 203.

[58]Heinz-Dietrich Wendland, *Die Briefe an die Korinther* (NTD 7; Göttingen: Vandenhoeck & Ruprecht, 1936) 67. Schlatter, *Korintherbriefe*, 99; Héring, *First Epistle*, 67, says, "Love for God is therefore the sign of election and the only token of true gnosis. . . ."

[59]Wendland, *Korinther*; 67, for example, says "Paulus erkennt diesen Masstab an . . . aber er hebt zugleich die Gefahr hervor. . . . Darum muss die Liebe mit der Erkenntnis vereinigt werden und diese begrenzen. . . .

Similarly, Vielhauer, *OIKODOME*, 93. Much of the basis for such a positive evaluation of γνῶσις in Paul is the assumption that in 8:1 Paul includes himself with those who know. But this depends on where the limits of the quotation from the Corinthians are set.

To decide that Paul is contrasting γνῶσις with ἀγάπη here in 1 Corinthians does not preclude his positive use of the word γνῶσις elsewhere. In the present debate the content and function of γνῶσις has been defined by the particular theology of the Corinthian opponents.

[60]Vielhauer, *OIKODOME*, 93, notes but does not elaborate on this connection, as does Hans von Soden, "Sakrament und Ethik bei Paulus," *Marburger Theologische Studien* I (Gotha: Leopold Klutz, 131) 7.

knowledge is a feature of the eschaton; present knowing, even as Christians, is ἐν αἰνίγματι. Second, in 8:1-3 and in 13:13 even Christian γνῶσις is seen as relatively inferior *vis a vis* ἀγάπη.[61] It is love which will abide the consummation of all things, and therefore love is the greater. It is the presence of eternity. Third, 1 Cor 13:4 recalls the observation of 8:1-3 when Paul says that ἀγάπη οὐ φυσιοῦται.

I conclude that in 8:1-3 Paul evaluates the relative merits of love and knowledge in a special question, which is generalized in chapter 13. In 8:2, 3 he is saying that one who seeks to establish a relationship with God on the basis of knowledge about God has failed to understand two crucial things, First, the γνῶσις that really counts is God's election. Second, the response to this "being known" is to love God, which means to act in love to others, since God is always the *indirect* recipient of Christian love.

As Schrage points out, Paul's comand to love usually has as its object the other person (ἕτερος Rom 13:8; 1 Cor 10:24;14:17; 15:5) or the neighbor (πλησίον Rom 13:9f.; 15:2) or one another (ἀλλήλους Rom 13:8; Gal 5:13; 1 Thess 3:12; 4:9; 2 Thess 1:3). This shows that the "neighbor" is not a mental abstraction, but the person in the concrete situation facing the believer.[62]

1 CORINTHIANS 8:4-7
CONFESSION AND CONSCIENCE

Paul begins chapter 8 with a quotation from the letter of the Corinthians. He then refutes it by a slogan of his own in 8:2 and a principle about one's relationship to God in 8:3. In 1 Cor 8:4 he resumes quoting from the Corinthians' inquiry. The introductory words, Περὶ τῆς βρώσεως οὖν τῶν εἰδωλοθύτων return to the topic announces in 8:1 and indeed closely resemble that verse.[63] Several issues are raised in these

---

[61]This is a relativizing evaluation. Paul does not oppose γνῶσις as sin, but as less valuable. Similarly he does not oppose the use of tongues as evil, but as less serviceable—because of the effect on the other man!

[62]Wolfgang Schrage, *Die konkreten Einzelgebote in der paulinischen Paränese* (Gütersloh: Gütersloher Verlagshaus, 1961) 252.

[63]Βρῶσις actually makes the inquiry more specific, it is the *eating* of the εἰδωλόθυτον which is the issue. Cf. *Aboda Zara* I.4 which deals with the purchase and selling of such meat. Paul only uses βρῶσις two other times: Rom 14:17 "the kingdom of God is not *eating* and drinking" and in 2 Cor 9:10 a quotation from Isa 55:10.

verses, the initial one being what is quoted from the Corinthians' letter
and how does Paul reply to their words. Second, and related to the first,
what is the role of the creed (apparently) quoted in v. 6? Third, what is
the offense of the Corinthians which injures the weak? Finally, what is
the meaning of conscience (συνείδησις) in 8:7 and how are some Christians ἀσθενής in conscience?

A. Possible Quotations in 8:4-7

The probability that in 1 Cor 8:1 Paul quotes from a Corinthian
letter has already been argued. Many interpreters have suggested that 8:4
also contains such a quotation: ὅτι οὐδὲν εἴδωλον ἐν κόσμῳ, καὶ ὅτι
οὐδεὶς θεὸς εἰ μὴ εἷς.[64] Although most interpreters have limited the
quote to verse 4, a longer quotation has been suggested by others. Hurd
notes that the somewhat polytheistic section of 8:5, 6 has been considered
such a quotation from the Corinthians' letter.[65]

Hurd himself does not think the quotation extends beyond v. 4. He
suspects those scholars who do attribute vv. 5 and 6 to the Corinthians are
guided by one of two motives. The first is "a hesitancy among some commentators to admit that Paul, like Jesus, could have believed in the real
existence of a variety of spiritual powers, some of them good but most of
them evil." A second motive, according to Hurd, is that some interpreters
are uncomfortable with the idea of cosmic mediation by Christ found in v.
6. "Thus in a paradoxical way the verse is alternatively too primitive and
naive, or too sophisticated and mature for Paul."[66] But with neither of
these motives, one can still hold that vv. 5 and 6 are best understood as
coming from Corinth.

---

[64]Barrett, *1 Corinthians*, 197, and Conzelmann, *1 Corinthians*,
142f. Schlatter, *Korintherbriefe*, 100, says that this is the ground of the
church's freedom to eat idol meat.
[65]Hurd, 121. Wilhelm Bousset, "Der erste Brief an die Korinther,"
*Die Schriften des Neuen Testaments neu Übersetz und für die Gegenwart
erklärt* (eds. Wilhelm Bousset and Wilhelm Heitmuller; Göttingen: Vandenhoeck & Ruprecht, 1918) 2.111, and Lock, 67, consider the words ὥσπερ
εἰσὶν θεοὶ πολλοὶ καὶ κύριοι πολλοί to be from Paul.
[66]Hurd, 121f. Karl Barth, *The Resurrection of the Dead* (London:
Hodder and Stoughton, 1933) 39, suggests that these arguments came from
the "Pauline Corinthians" and then ultimately from Paul himself.

Most who consider 5 and 6 as Pauline take them to be Paul's qualification of and correction for the Corinthian slogan of 8:4.[67] The reason
is well stated by Conzelmann, "In v. 4 he acknowledged the rightness of
the Corinthians' thesis that the gods do not exist; he merely stated it to
be inadequate. Here, on the other hand, he qualifies his concession; there
'are' 'gods' and 'Lords.'"[68]

The fundamental confession of monotheism, εἷς θεός, is set forth
in 8:4. This confession Christians have inherited from Judaism.[69] From
this fundamental truth some in Corinth concluded οὐδὲν εἴδωλον ἐν
κόσμῳ. This confession is elaborated in v. 5 to take notice of the apparent being of many gods and Lords, and is set forth in a creedal formula in
v. 6. A closer examination of the creedal form shows that these verses,
too, may have originated with the Corinthians.

B. The Creedal Confession

Whether verses 5 and 6 belong to a quotation from the Corinthians'
letter may be illuminated by a closer look at verse 6 which contains a
creed.[70] The creedal character of this verse is seen in the balanced
phraseology of the succinct style: ἀλλ' ἡμῖν εἷς θεὸς, ὁ πατήρ, ἐξ οὗ
τὰ πάντα καὶ ἡμεῖς εἰς αὐτὸν καὶ εἷς κύριος Ἰησοῦς Χριστός δι'
οὗ τὰ πάντα καὶ ἡμεῖς δι' αὐτοῦ. This style, as well as the bipartite
form, has led many to regard this as a pre-Pauline creedal formula.[71]

---

[67]Thus Hurd, 121; Lietzmann, *Korinther*, 37; Barrett, *1 Corinthians*, 191-94 and Conzelmann, *1 Corinthians*, 143.

[68]Conzelmann, *1 Corinthians*, 143, says that Paul's apparent concession of the reality of idols shows his view of the "existential character
of knowledge; the Corinthian knowledge is not sufficient even in the
realm of objective statement."

[69]Ibid., 142. Bultmann, "Γινώσκω," 702. However, Greeks too
speculated and affirmed the oneness of God, especially Stoics. See Erik
Peterson, ΕΙΣ ΘΕΟΣ: *Epigraphische, formgeschichtliche und religions-
geschichtliche Untersuchungen* (FRLANT 41; Göttingen: Vandenhoeck &
Ruprecht, 1926). Hellenistic monotheism is beautifully set forth in
Marcus Aurelius, *Med.* 7:9.

[70]The creedal character of this verse is even confirmed by the
textual tradition. In some later manuscripts a third member is added: καὶ
εν πνευμα αγιον, εν ω τα παντα και ημεις εν αυτω. See Zuntz, 163.

[71]See R. A. Horsley, "The Background of the Confessional Formula
in 1 Cor 8:6," *ZNW* 69 (1978) 130-135. No distinction should be drawn
between διά and ἐκ, see C. F. D. Moule, *An Idiom Book of New*

The origin of the creedal formula and the theology it summarizes has been variously interpreted. It has been regarded as representing either Stoicism[72] or Hellenistic Judaism.[73] It was perhaps originally cosmological in function but is now used soteriologically. These questions are not decisive for the present investigation. What is striking is its present use in 1 Corinthians for, as Conzelmann notes, "In itself it is eminently suited to the Corinthian Christology."[74]

The context makes it difficult to believe that Paul initiated reference to the creed. In the argument of 1 Cor 8 about eating ἐν εἰδωλείῳ this confession better serves Paul's questioners who are arguing against any danger in idol meat. It is they who would say that regardless of the "so-called gods" nevertheless, "For we Christians at any rate, there is only one God, the Father . . . and one Lord, Jesus Christ. . . ."[75] They may have known Paul would (or should) agree to this creed and thus considered it a valuable defense of their views.

If the creed of v. 6 and its introductory words ἀλλ' ἡμῖν, as well as v. 4, are quoted from the Corinthians' letter, then the likelihood that the intervening verse 5 is also from their letter is increased. This is especially true since v. 5 is syntactically linked to v. 6. However, most scholars, including Conzelmann[76] and Barrett, take v. 5 to be Paul's

<hr>

Testament Greek (Cambridge: University Press, 1967) 72.

Barrett, *1 Corinthians*, 192, apparently considers the formula to be Paul's and "probably a formula Paul had used before, and not coined on the spur of the moment." Conzelmann, *1 Corinthians*, 144, n. 38, however, says that the creed "is not 'Pauline,' and it reaches far beyond the context."

[72]References are given by Conzelmann, *1 Corinthians*, 144, notes 44, 46 and 145, notes 48, 49.

[73]Recently the question of influences has been reviewed by Horsley, "Background of Confessional Formula."

[74]Conzelmann, *1 Corinthians*, 145. Also Horsley, "Background of Confessional Formula," 134ff.

[75]Conzelmann, *1 Corinthians*, 145. He continues, "For this reason Paul can also use it as a common basis on which to develop his thoughts."

[76]Conzelmann, *1 Corinthians*, 143, says that Paul here qualifies his assent in 8:4 that the gods do not exist. (Conzelmann thinks that Paul includes himself in οἴδαμεν.) No, "there 'are' 'gods' and 'lords.'" In this view Paul is not as "enlightened" as the Corinthians. He continues, 145, to say that with ἀλλ' ἡμῖν in 8:6 Paul implies that this is a question of judging and adopting an attitude, "but not at our own subjective discretion." However, if Paul is quoting the Corinthians' position in 8:6, it seems best to give ἀλλά its normal adversative meaning —"but."

attempt to establish the "being" of pagan gods and lords, while at the same time denying their divinity. Thus Paul is arguing these have a *de facto* status as gods: they are worshipped. Barrett concludes, "It would have been foolish to deny that the word *god* was in common use. . . ."[77]

Of course it is possible that these words are Paul's paraphrase of the Corinthians' view. In that case, it would still be true that the arguments represent their viewpoint (as perceived by Paul) and not Paul's own position. However, agreeing with Lock, it seems best to take v. 5 as also a quotation from the Corinthians. In this approach καὶ γὰρ εἴπερ introduces a qualified assent by the Corinthians to the many gods.[78] They term these gods of their pagan friends λεγόμενοι.[79] Paul's own qualification is the phrase: ὥσπερ εἰσὶν θεοὶ πολλοὶ καὶ κύριοι πολλοί.[80] Paul is in the awkward position of having to argue with some Christians (formerly pagans) for the reality of the pagan divinities.

Omitting the Pauline qualification of 5b, the Corinthians' defense is cogently set forth in 8:4-6. It is consistent and firmly rooted in Christian monotheistic confession.

> We know that there is no idol in the world and that there is no God but one. Although there are so-called gods, whether in heaven or on the earth, yet for Christians as we confess, there is one God, the Father, from whom come all things, and to whom we belong, and one Lord, Jesus Christ, through whom are all things, and even we ourselves!"

---

[77]Barrett, *1 Corinthians*, 192. Cf., Murphy-O'Connor, 561, who says that Paul agrees with the "strong" that the idols have no real existence but insists on their "subjective existence." "They were 'gods' for those who believed in them."

[78]Blass-DeBrunner, *Greek Grammar*, § 454(2), "The reality of the assumption is presupposed." This reference is given by Conzelmann, *1 Corinthians*, 143, n. 31 and by Barrett, *1 Corinthians*, 191; however they do not draw the same conclusions.

[79]Conzelmann, *1 Corinthians*, 143, says that this is Paul's criticism, "not only of pagan belief in the gods, but of the gods themselves." He notes similar wording in Gal 4:8. But it is not Paul who needs to deny the reality of the pagan gods, rather his opponents who use this unreality to permit their eating of ἐν εἰδωλείῳ. On whether Paul had a belief in the "being" of pagan beliefs, see the discussion about 10:19 on pages 188-192.

[80]Conzelmann, *1 Corinthians*, 143 notes that we should not distinguish too sharply between θεοὶ and κύριοι, since these words are influenced by the Christian creed subsequently quoted.

Actually, Barrett's summary of the argument of 1 Cor 8:4-6 is more suited to the Corinthians than Paul, when he says:

> The drive of his (Paul's) argument is towards the assertion that, whatever other spiritual or demonic beings there may be, *for us* [Barrett's emphasis] there is only one whom we recognize as God, whom we trust and obey in a unique sense as the source of life and redemption.[81]

In 1 Cor 8 and 10 Paul himself is seeking to establish the reality of the pagan gods and especially their possible influence on Christians (esp. 10:19ff.), however he may regard them.

C. The Offense of Eating

Regarding 1 Cor 8:4-6 as substantially the argument of the Corinthians, now set forth by Paul, both makes their actions more understandable and makes more trenchant Paul's own criticism in verse 7. The action of the Corinthians is described in 8:7; they are eating food ἐν εἰδωλείῳ. Similarly, the result of the weaker brothers' imitation is described in 8:7, ἡ συνείδησις αὐτῶν . . . μολύνεται.

After giving the Corinthian defense Paul begins his reply with the adversative, ἀλλά. He replies that οὐκ ἐν πᾶσιν ἡ γνῶσις. Many commentators have noted the formal contradiction with 8:1 which says πάντες γνῶσιν ἔχομεν. How seriously the apparent contradiction is to be regarded is variously estimated.

Héring suggests that Paul is speaking of two different types of γνῶσις, one shared by all, one given only to some.[82] Lietzmann says, "Der formalle widerspruch zwischen 1a und 7a entspringt nur der temperamentvollen Ausdrucksweise des Apostels."[83] Similarly, most other interpreters say that the contradiction is only formal, not material. Paul is said to share (8:1, οἴδαμεν = first person plural) the basically correct knowledge of the opponents about the unreality of other gods and the acceptability of εἰδωλοθύτον. He only warns the strong to remember the few whose συνείδησις is ἀσθενής.[84]

---

[81]Barrett, *1 Corinthians*, 192.

[82]Héring, *First Epistle*, 72. See above note 16.

[83]Lietzmann, *Korinther*, 38.

[84]Conzelmann, *1 Corinthians*, 146; Merk, *Handeln aus Glauben*, 122 says "Ihre richtige Erkenntnis, die Pls teilt (er schliesst sich in 8,8 vgl.

However the alleged contradiction dissolves entirely if one takes οἴδαμεν in 8:1 to be part of the Corinthians' slogan and not Paul's assent to it.   Then it is Paul's opponents who claimed οἴδαμεν ὅτι πάντες γνῶσιν ἔχομεν. Paul himself at this point is not committed. Then in 8:7 when Paul does say οὐκ ἐν πᾶσιν ἡ γνῶσις he is correcting their claim— in fact not all do have this knowledge. It is not stated whether he himself does or does not. Actually, whether Paul is included as sharing this knowl- edge is beside the point. He is concerned that some do not.

Little attention has been given to what is the γνῶσις not all share.[85] Since 8:6 is a traditional creedal formulation it seems probable that it would have been shared by all Christians. Perhaps the γνῶσις is what the Corinthians have said in 8:4 and 5, although the second part of v. 4, οὐδεὶς θεὸς εἰ μὴ εἷς would appear to be obvious to all Christians (and Jews). This leaves from v. 4 οὐδὲν εἴδωλον ἐν κόσμῳ and v. 5 (less the Pauline correction) as the probable content of the γνῶσις which is not in all. On the other hand, it may be that the γνῶσις "not in all" is only stated obliquely; it may refer to the denial of the "gods and Lords" and the consequent action of eating εἰδωλόθυτον.

It is implied in 8:1 that the opponents felt the weak shared their γνῶσις. They may have felt since the weak did share the knowledge of the one God they must also share the denial of the reality of the pagan gods—even if they were unable (or unwilling) to act on it.[86] Next Paul takes up both the reason why the weak do not share this knowledge (their conscience trained by past habit) and the tragic results when they proceed as if they do (they are defiled).

---

auch 8,4 in die 1. Pers. plural mit ein. . . ." Others who take this view include: Barrett, 1 Corinthians, 194; G. D. Fee, 23, "II Cor 6:14f. and Food Offered to Idols," NTS 23 (1977) 151; Von Soden, "Sakrament und Ethik," 5.
[85]Wendland, Korinther, 69, says that the gnosis of 8:4-6 must be possessed by the entire church.
[86]This would fit with an interpretation of 8:10 which holds that the gnostics sought to "build up" their weak brethren to eat. One need not insist they had evil motives, they might well feel they were helping the weak to mature. Barth, Resurrection, 40f. says that some Corinthians had not worked through to act upon their confession. Cf. Murphy-O'Connor, 545, 61.
Conzelmann, 1 Corinthians, 140, and Barrett, 1 Corinthians, 194, rightly stress the practical, rather than speculative, character of this γνῶσις.

D. The Weak in Conscience

Influenced by the parallel discussion in Romans 14 and 15, studies of 1 Cor 8 and 10 habitually refer to the "weak" and the "strong." In 1 Cor 8:7 a certain brother is said to have a conscience which is weak. The "strong" are never so designated—although it seems a logical contrast. Probably the "strong" simply are the majority of believers, and those of weak conscience are the few. Two important considerations in v. 7 are: What is the συνείδησις which is here mentioned, and what does it mean for that συνείδησις to be ἀσθενής?

1. *The Meaning of* Συνείδησις. Ἡ συνείδησις usually translated "conscience," the Latin equivalent, has received considerable attention by students of the New Testament.[87] Of the 30 times the word is used in the New Testament 15 are in indisputably Pauline letters.[88] This means that Paul is both the earliest and the most frequent user of the word in the New Testament. Of Paul's usages six are in 1 Cor 8 and 10. Therefore, although a detailed study of the word is not possible, a brief review of the meaning of συνείδησις will be useful for the study of this concept in 8:7.

Probably because συνείδησις is one of the terms which Paul employs which is virtually without precedent in the Old Testament,[89] many believe Paul derived it from Greek philosophy. Since the most influential moral philosophy of his day was Stoicism, it has been generally regarded as the source of Paul's concept of συνείδησις.[90]

More recently, however, the evidence for a Stoic influence on Paul's use of συνείδησις has been shown to be unconvincing.[91] C. A.

---

[87]A valuable recent survey is Jewett, *Paul's Anthropological Terms,* 402-420. Especially thorough are: C. A. Pierce, *Conscience in the New Testament* (SBT 1, 15; London: SCM Press, 1955) and Christian Maurer, "Σύνοιδα," *TDNT* 8, 898-919. The latter work gives a full bibliography of works in the last century.

[88]Including the verbal form in 1 Cor 4:4, they are: Rom 2:15; 9:1; 13:5; 1 Cor 8:7, 10, 12; 10:25, 27, 28, 29; 2 Cor 1:12, 4:2 and 5:11.

[89]Pierce, *Conscience,* 13. See also J. N. Sevenster, *Paul and Seneca* (NovT Sup. 4; Leiden: E. J. Brill, 1961).

[90]For examples, C. H. Dodd, *The Bible and the Greeks* (London: Hodder & Stoughton, 1935). W. L. Knox, *Some Hellenistic Elements in Primitive Christianity* (London: Oxford University, 1944) 32f.

[91]B. F. Harris, "ΣΥΝΕΙΔΗΣΙΣ (Conscience) in the Pauline writings," *WTJ* 24 (1962) 173-186. Pierce, *Conscience;* Jewett, *Paul's Anthropological Terms;* and W. D. Stacy, *The Pauline View of Man* (New York: MacMillan and Co., 1956).

Pierce has done an exhaustive study of the use of the word in secular writers, both Greek and Latin, and found it largely absent from Stoic authors.[92] He summarizes, "The assumption then of a Stoic origin for the Pauline συνείδησις rests on insufficient evidence and is inherently improbable."[93] Presently most consider the word to originate in popular philosophy of Paul's day.[94] Horsley, however, has argued as a more precise source the use in Hellenistic Judaism, as evidenced in Philo.[95]

Because the Pauline uses of συνείδησις are distributed as they are (all but three in 1 and 2 Corinthians; half in 1 Cor 8 and 10) the probable suggestion has been made that the term arose with the Corinthians in their letter to Paul. This has been argued by Maurer,[96] Pierce,[97] Davies,[98] Jewett,[99] and Horsley.[100] If, as is likely, this is the case, how the Corinthians used the term becomes the crucial question and how, if at all, Paul differs.

2. *The Meaning of Συνείδησις in 1 Cor 8.* There is a general agreement that the normal use of συνείδησις, both in and outside the

---

Sevenster, 93f., suggests that the universal aspect of conscience as is assumed in 2 Cor 4:2 and Rom 2:15 may show Stoic influence.

[92]Pierce, *Conscience,* 13f. Similarly, Maurer, 902; W. D. Davies, "Conscience," *IDB* 1, 671 and Morton Enslin, *The Ethics of St. Paul* (Apex Books; Nashville: Abingdon, 1962). Both Davies and Enslin note that it is the Latin authors (especially Seneca and Cicero) who frequently use the term *conscientia.*

[93]Pierce, *Conscience,* 15.

[94]Pierce, *Conscience,* 16. He refers to Norden, *Agnostos Theos,* 136. Similarly, Maurer, 902 and Stacey, *Pauline View of Man,* 210. M. E. Thrall, "The Pauline Use of ΣΥΝΕΙΔΗΣΙΣ," *NTS* 14 (1968) 125, says that Paul enlarges upon the popular use of the term because he takes it to be a Gentile corollary to the Mosaic Law of the Jews.

[95]Richard A. Horsley, "Consciousness and Freedom among the Corinthians; 1 Corinthians 8-10," *CBQ* 40 (1978) 574-89.

[96]Maurer, 586, says "he [Paul] picked up the terminology of συνείδησις from the enlightened Corinthians who were eating idol meat." So also Furnish, *Theology and Ethics,* 48.

[97]Pierce, *Conscience,* 16. "The inference is inevitable, that conscience was introduced into Christianity under pressure from Corinth." He notes that the term is absent from the parallel discussion in Romans 14. Also Horsley, "Consciousness," 588.

[98]Davies, "Conscience," 675, who also notes the absence of the word in Rom 14. So also Conzelmann, *1 Corinthians,* 147.

[99]Robert Jewett, "Conscience," *IDBS,* 173.

[100]Horsley, "Consciousness," 581f.

New Testament, is to refer to the universal human capacity to evaluate
one's own actions.[101] This means normally the conscience comes into
play regarding past actions.[102] However, some insist that the conscience
can have a future role.[103] Thrall says, "it remains probable that Paul did
think of conscience both as giving guidance for future conduct and also as
judging the actions of others."[104] Sevenster, also holding Paul knows of a
conscientia antecedens, says "It is clear from these passages (1 Cor 8 and
10) that according to Paul no one should ignore the voice of his own
conscience."[105]

The prominent role given to "conscience" in moral theology and
ethical philosophy may have served to suggest a more developed view of
συνείδησις than was the case either for Paul or the Corinthians. One
ought not to assume συνείδησις refers to a specific aspect of man as has
been commonly conceived in contemporary ethical thought. As Maurer
says,

> Paul does not venture on either theological systematization
> or psychological analysis. This συνείδησις is not to be de-
> fined as a power of religious or moral evaluation or the life
> which can be detached from man. It is man aware of himself
> in perception and acknowledgment, in willing and acting.[106]

---

[101]Furnish, *Theology and Ethics,* 229.

[102]It is commonly accepted that the past-orientation is primary,
but some accept a future-aimed function as well. Maurer, 904, states well
the consensus about the dominant usage, "Moral conscience is not primarily concerned with preparation for approaching decisions (*conscientia
antecedens*) but with assessing and condemning acts already committed
(*conscientia consequens*).

[103]Maurer, 916; Harris, 176; Sevenster, 96; and Thrall, "Pauline
Use of ΣΥΝΕΙΔΗΣΙΣ," 119. Against a future guidance role is Pierce, *Conscience.*

[104]Thrall, "Pauline Use of ΣΥΝΕΙΔΗΣΙΣ," 123.

[105]Sevenster, 98. "Hence for both of them [the weak and the
strong] the conscience speaks with authority." The primary function of
conscience is to pass judgment on actions. Paul, for example, invites
others to assess his actions (2 Cor 4:2), as he himself does (1 Cor 4:4). But
it is clear that this judgment, whether Paul's own or that of another, does
not have a universal validity—it can be wrong. Thus the weak may stain
their conscience in an action not wrong in itself and the strong cannot act
as they wish by appealing to a clear conscience. (1 Cor 10:25-28).

[106]Maurer, 914. See also 904, n. 20. "Most modern languages
transl. συνείδησις etc., by 'conscience' but we have to realize that the

Accordingly Maurer and others[107] have recalled the linguistic origin of συνείδησις as meaning, "to know with (myself)," that is, "to be aware." The verb form in 1 Cor 4:4 illustrates this. There σύνοιδα must mean, "I am aware." This is what Pierce had termed the non-moral usage.[108] Davies too agrees that in some places "the term συνείδησις may merely signify 'consciousness' or 'awareness.'"[109]

This may have been how the Corinthians used the term. Horsley is on the right track in concluding that in their religiosity and in Paul's usage in 1 Cor 8, "*syneidesis* clearly means one's inner consciousness or awareness, and not 'conscience' in the modern sense of the English word."[110] Thus as employed in the Corinthians' letter συνείδησις referred to their personal knowledge of "the way things are." "Conscious" of the truth about idols (8:4) and hence idol meat, they acted in freedom deriving from this knowledge. Those who were "weak" in συνείδησις were simply those who were "not knowing" (8:7) the truth about idols and idol meat.

3. *Who are the "weak" in conscience?* The Corinthians in their letter criticized the "consciousness" of some and termed some fellow Christians "weak." Hurd has argued that there was no "weak" group: "the really striking fact is that in 8:10-13 and 10:28, 29 the 'weaker brother' is completely hypothetical and indefinite."[111] Still, most interpreters have felt the weak in conscience were real, not hypothetical, and have sought to define them variously.

---

moral components, which decisively shape the modern concept, arose only secondarily in the history of the Gk. term."

[107]Maurer, 914, terms it "percipient and active self-awareness (Selbstbewusstein)." See Furnish, *Theology and Ethics*, 48.

[108]Pierce, *Conscience*, 21f.

[109]Davies, "Conscience," 675, refers specifically to 2 Cor 4:2; 5:11.

[110]Horsley, "Consciousness," 581. He comments, "the 'freedom of conscience' (or rather 'consciousness') far from being Paul's solution, was the real problem in the ethical difficulty created by the eating of idol-meat in Corinth." 586.

[111]Hurd, 125. This follows from Hurd's basic thesis that Paul is dealing with only one front at Corinth. "All in all, it appears that Paul created two hypothetical situations involving a pair of hypothetical 'weak' Christians simply as a way of dissuading the Corinthians from eating idol meat." He grants, "We may presume, as Paul presumed (8:7), that some Corinthians were less secure in their new faith than others. But nowhere is there evidence that they formed a group, or that their point of view had been communicated to Paul."

A few interpreters have identified the weak as Jewish Christians. For example, Adolf Schlatter says some Jewish Christians (freed from their Jewish upbringing) ate sacrificial food. But from their childhood they had been impressed that these foods were evil and to eat them a great sin, from which followed the fall of Achan (Joshua 7). So when they were verbally reminded that this food was εἰδωλόθυτον they discovered their consciences were not as liberated as they had supposed.[112]

T. W. Manson[113] also thinks that the crisis arose from Jewish sensitivities regarding anything connected with pagan cults. He suggests that the specific occasion was the visit of a Petrine embassy which tried to impose the Jerusalem council's (Acts 15) decision on Gentiles at Corinth. Paul's refusal to debate that Jerusalem compromise (which Manson felt Paul had once accepted) is an intentional snub at those who sought to impose it at Corinth. In this view the issue is pressed by Jewish Christians but did not arise from Jewish Christians in Corinth.

Thrall is not clear on the identity of the weak. She argues that the danger at Corinth is that some weaker brothers who had begun to eat any meat may revert to legalism when faced with the extreme conduct of the liberal Christians who are willing to eat ἐν εἰδωλείῳ (she makes much of such a legalism at Galatia). Since she thinks that the weak may be brought under the Law she could either refer to Jewish Christians or to Gentile Christians who have been persuaded to accept Judaism in part. She defines the weak as "people who are in general inclined to religious scrupulosity."[114]

Generally, however, most have not sought to explain the Corinthian struggles by reference to the Jew/Gentile question. 1 Cor 8:7 says the weak have been accustomed to eating εἰδωλόθυτον ἕως ἄρτι, and thus seems obviously to imply they are Gentiles.[115] Conzelmann is correct, "The 'weak' are neither Jewish Christians, nor any closed group at all. They do not represent a position. They are simply 'weak.'"[116] Their

---

[112]Schlatter, *Korintherbriefe*, 101.

[113]T. W. Manson, "The Corinthians Correspondence (1) and (2)," in *Studies in the Gospels and Epistles* (Philadelphia: Westminster Press, 1962) 200-203.

[114]Thrall, "The Meaning of ΣΥΝΕΙΔΗΣΙΣ" 471.

[115]Almost all interpreters point this out. Bultmann, "Gnosis," 20, reviewing Dupont's study says that the "weak" are not Jewish even in Romans 14. Barrett, *1 Corinthians*, 194, agrees that the "weak" in 1 Corinthians are not Jewish but thinks that they may be in Romans.

[116]Conzelmann, *1 Corinthians*, 147.

identity comes from their inability to participate in certain meals without being "stained."

As has become normal in dealing with 1 Cor 8, one must ask if here also the vocabulary has not been shaped by Paul's opponents. Did some at Corinth term other Christians who could not, or would not, participate in cult meals "weak"?

Certain indications point to such a situation. First, the word ἀσθενής and cognates occur predominantly in the Corinthian correspondence.[117] Second, the theology of the Corinthians stressed their power (ἐξουσία) and freedom (ἐλευθερία), and accordingly those who were "lacking" (ὑστερούμεθα, v. 8) were open to being labeled "without power" (ἀσθενής). Finally, in 1 Corinthians as a whole, and in 2 Corinthians as well, Paul specifically treats "weakness" as a theological problem— although he has a view opposite to that of the Corinthians.

While it is not provable, it is likely that the term ἀσθενής was applied to some Christians who were troubled by eating εἰδωλόθυτον by those who made much of so doing. Those who wrote to Paul probably raised the issue of συνείδησις and also probably originated the designation of some as ἀσθενής. The idea of ἡ συνείδησις ἀσθενής was a slur at those who refused to eat idol sacrifices, or who did so with troubled consciences. This means the real definition of the "weak" in Corinth is "those not having knowledge."

It is usually noted that Paul's purpose here is to protect the weak from abuse.[118] That is certainly true, but one must not overlook the seriousness with which he takes up the idea of "weakness." It is not just a concession, simply taking over a term from the Corinthians, but in the epistle he grounds "weakness" theologically, specifically Christologically.

---

[117]In 1 Corinthians ἀσθενής and cognates occur 13 times, 12 times in 2 Corinthians, and elsewhere 13 times (3 of which are in Romans 14, in some way dependent on 1 Cor 8 and 10).

[118]Conzelmann, *1 Corinthians*, 147, "The 'weakness' of some people's consciences creates a situation which neither the strong nor the weak can ignore." Similarly, von Soden, "Sakrament und Ethik," 4; Barrett, *1 Corinthians*, 194f., and Furnish, *Love Command*, 113.

In each of these studies the additional point is made that while Paul himself will protect the weak, he is not defending their theology. Concerning their scrupulosity, Barrett, *1 Corinthians*, 195, says "All this is foolish, and Paul does not defend it." (Neither, it should be noted, does he attack it!)

If those who insisted on eating sacrificial meat had intended to shame their brethren who did not eat by terming them "weak," they picked the wrong term. For Paul sees all of the gospel as flowing from a stance of weakness. Weakness is not something to be overcome but is the foundation of the gospel. God's mysterious plan was to choose the weak and poor and thus shame the powerful (1 Cor 1:25ff.). Paul's apostolic mission to Corinth was "in weakness" (1 Cor 2:2) and this was not "beginner's nervousness" but his abiding stance (2 Cor 10:10; 11:30; 12:5, 9, 10; Gal 4:13). Paul willingly became weak to gain the weak (1 Cor 9:22). If some have insulted him by labeling him "weak" he will gladly accept the reproach. (1 Cor 4:10).

According to Paul, weakness, whether in the gospel message, its preacher, or in Christians, is the working out of a *theologia crucis*. As the Lord became weak for us (2 Cor 13:3, 4) so our only legitimate boast is our weakness (2 Cor 12:10). This leads to pastoral concern for the less impressive members. Just as in the human body, so also in the ecclesiological body, the "weak" deserve special care and have special value (1 Cor 12:22).[119]

This positive evaluation of weakness by Paul may in part explain his impassioned defense of the weak in this question of eating sacrificial meat. He has thoroughly identified with them, as he says in 2 Cor 11:29, "Who is weak and I am not weak? Who is offended and I do not burn?"[120] The use of σκανδαλίζειν and ἀσθενής in 2 Cor 11:29 shows the close similarity in 1 Cor 8. Thus the word μολύνεται in 8:7 is explained by σκανδαλίζω in 8:13.

In summary, 1 Cor 8:4-7 is largely a continued setting forth from the defense of the Corinthians, perhaps from their letter to Paul. In 8:1-3 Paul had taken up the issue of γνῶσις οἰκοδομεῖ from their letter, and in

---

[119]It is not clear where Paul picked up the term ἀσθενής. It too may have originated with his opponents. But it suits admirably how Paul perceives the contrast of human striving and divine grace in the work of Christ, in the preaching of the gospel and in the composition and care of the church. Pierce, *Conscience*, 79-81, relates it to Jesus's teaching, recorded in Mark 9:42, which warns against endangering the "little ones."

[120]As Pierce, *Conscience*, 80, says, "St. Paul is in general on the side of the weak as his Master was, and in this particular matter endorses their attitude." As is discussed below, any interpretation of the weak conscience must take into account that Paul, unlike the opponents in Corinth, has no program for the conversion/education of the weak. He will later say in Rom 14:17, 18 such concerns are irrelevant.

4-6 the content of this γνῶσις is explored. Their knowledge is the freedom to eat sacrificial meats since the idols are not real—at least not for
Christians. The Corinthians see this position as firmly rooted in a common Christian confession. This means 8:4-6 is not a second argument but
a continuation of that in 8:1-3.

Paul has to argue that while the confession is true, nonetheless the
pagan gods do have existence (this point is taken up in a different way in
chapter 10). But here his real concern is the effect of the Corinthians'
actions on some brethren whose "consciousness" of the non-being of idols
is weak. Christians must be concerned about leading others into actions
in which they are defiled.

Having dealt with the Corinthians' defense, Paul now turns in 8:8-
13 to describe more particularly their actions and the result. In these
verses the actual situation at Corinth becomes clearer and so does Paul's
anguish over it.

1 CORINTHIANS 8:8-13
OFFENSE AND FALLING AWAY

A. Possible Quotations in 8:8-13

Already in chapter 8 probable quotations have been located from a
letter sent by the Corinthians to Paul. Therefore, it is not surprising that
another quotation is often suspected in 8:8-13. Hurd lists ten scholars
who consider 8:8 to be from the Corinthians.[121] This is only a few more
than those who affirm 8:5f. is a quotation.

Walter Lock suggested that the whole of verse 8 is a quotation
from the Corinthians' letter.[122] Jeremias's judgment is similar, although
he notes that the first part of the saying accords with Paul's own view:
Βρῶμα δὲ ἡμᾶς οὐ παραστήσει τῷ θεῷ[123] On the other hand, C. K.

---

[121]Hurd, 68. Prominent among those who consider 8:8 to be a
quotation are: George Findlay, "The Letter of the Corinthian Church to
St. Paul," Exp Ser. 6, Vol 1 (1900) 404; Grosheide, First Epistle, 194, and
Jeremias, "Briefzitate," 273. Hurd, who is quite inclined to finding such
quotations, does not consider 8:8 to be one. Rather he considers 8:8 to be
one of three Pauline corrections in 8:7-9, each of which begins with δε.
See Hurd, 123.

[122]Lock, 67; similarly, Murphy-O'Connor, 547.

[123]Jeremias, "Briefzitate," 273f.

Barrett thinks that only the first phrase is from the Corinthians and the remainder of the verse (beginning with οὔτε ἐὰν μὴ φάγωμεν) is Paul's correction of their slogan.[124]

It is less certain that 8:8 contains a quotation, but the first person plural, found in the earlier quotations, appears here also. However, the content of v. 8 does not really seem to fit the Corinthians' own position. As Barrett notes, βρῶμα δὲ ἡμᾶς οὐ παραστήσει τῷ θεῷ sounds more like Paul's own view (cf. Rom 14:17). Also the latter part of the verse, as it stands, reverses the argument of the strong, for whom it should be: οὔτε ἐὰν φάγωμεν ὑστερούμεθα, οὔτε ἐὰν μὴ φάγωμεν περισσεύομεν.[125] But that would alter the controversy into a debate about Jewish food laws which it is not.

If the text is taken as it stands and is considered to contain quotations from the Corinthians, their position seems to say this eating of meat is an ἀδιάφορον[126] They are saying that eating (sacrificial) meat will not be a factor in divine judgment and that not to eat does not cause one to excel, nor does eating diminish one before God. However, since they seek to "educate" the non-eating brothers whom they term "weak," it is unlikely that the Corinthians view their conduct only as an indifferent act.

Because of the dangerous subjectivity of locating citations in Pauline letters, attempts to isolate any such quotations must be tentative suggestions. However, because of the precedent quotes in 8:1 and 8:4-6 it is entirely reasonable to suspect such a quotation here. The first clause, βρῶμα δὲ ἡμᾶς οὐ παραστήσει τῷ θεῷ, sounds like a proverbial expression or a cliche. Only the ἡμᾶς would incline one to think it comes from the Corinthians, for the position expressed is Paul's own. Moreover, there is no reason to think that the Corinthians were especially concerned about the coming judgment.[127] As it stands it is a Pauline correction.

The second half of the verse as it now reads also does not seem to fit the Corinthian position.[128] However, by a single simple change the latter half of the verse would represent accurately the enlightened Corinthians' outlook. There is no objective way to determine if the οὔτε . . .

---

[124]Barrett, *1 Corinthians*, 195.

[125]Noted by Lietzmann, *Korinther*, 38f.

[126]Jeremias, "Briefzitate," 274.

[127]This is seen in 10:1-12, esp. 12, where Paul addresses directly their self-assuredness.

[128]There are many textual problems in the verse, but they do not alter a decision about possible quotation from the Corinthians. Zuntz, 161f. and 194.

οὖτε clauses represent the Corinthians' position or Paul's adaptation of it.[129] If the οὖτε beginning each clause is omitted as a Pauline alteration the slogan runs: ἐὰν μὴ φάγωμεν ὑστερούμεθα, ἐὰν φάγωμεν περισσεύομεν. That is substantially the Corinthians' position, eating idol meat is a positive gain, not to eat a real loss![130] The enlightened Christians feel a compulsion to exercise their ἐξουσία/ἐλευθερία in regard to sacrificial meat. They regard failure to do so by some as showing a real deficit.

In summary, verse 8 begins with a Pauline slogan that encapsulates the argument of Chapter 8 (and is paralleled in 8:13): "food does not present us to God."[131] He then corrects a citation from the Corinthians by adding οὖτε at the beginning of each clause. But the citation, if uncorrected, gives a clear indication of why the enlightened Corinthians have made such an issue of eating idol meat and why they embarked on a campaign of "edification" (v. 10) to change the weak.

B. The Basis and Use of Ἐξουσία

In 1 Cor 8:9, 10 it finally becomes clear exactly what course the enlightened Corinthians followed which had injured certain other Christians. Paul begins his reproof in verse 9 with the imperative warning βλέπετε.[132] The action of the enlightened is described in verse 10 in two opposite terms. Paul's word for their action was πρόσκομμα but they themselves probably termed it ἐξουσία.[133] The primary idea is "power

---

[129]Horsley, "Consciousness," 578, thinks that this formulation which suggests a conscious criticism of Jewish food laws shows the "enlightened" "resemble a type of enlightened Hellenistic Jews (or proselytes) who have discerned the implications of their knowledge that the gods supposedly represented by idols have no real existence."

[130]Elsewhere Paul urges "abounding" (περισσεύω) in love, see 1 Cor 14:2; Phil 1:9; 1 Thess 3:12; 4:10. Schmithals, Gnosticism, 230f., sees this as the demand of the Gnostic to exhibit his essential power over the world rulers. But this eating does not have to represent "a case of compulsive (gnostic) liberation" as Horsley fears (Horsley, "Consciousness," 587). It simply shows an attitude of religious achievement and superiority not limited to Gnostics.

[131]So Robertson and Plummer, 1 Corinthians, 170. It is conceivable that these words too were originally from the Corinthians, and Paul corrected their sentiment by adding οὐ.

[132]Found in 1 Cor 1:26; 3:6; 10:12, 18; 16:10.

[133]Among those suggesting that ἐξουσία was a term originating with the Corinthians are Barrett, 1 Corinthians, 195; Bultmann, "Gnosis,"

of choice" or "liberty of action," as is seen by its frequent use in legal documents.[134]

Three considerations suggest that the term ἐξουσία was first raised by the Corinthians. First, the word is not common in Paul.[135] Most usages occur in 1 Corinthians.[136] Second, when Paul discusses the question of diet in the parallel passage in Rom 14-15 he does not refer to ἐξουσία. Third, in 1 Cor 6:12 and 10:23 Paul quotes a Corinthian slogan πάντα ἔξεστιν, with obvious similarity to ἐξουσία in 1 Cor 8:9.[137] From these considerations it follows that in all likelihood the view of ἐξουσία as allowing/requiring eating sacrificial meat was first proposed by the Corinthians.

If the term ἐξουσία was first raised by the Corinthians, what was its meaning for them? Various attempts have sought to explain the Corinthians' "authority" by isolating the probable source for technical terms like ἐξουσία. The source has been identified as Paul himself, Gnosticism,

---

201; Horsley, "Consciousness," 578f. and Schmithals, Gnosticism, 230f. Conzelmann, 1 Corinthians, 109, notes 5 and 8, is not clear on this point.

[134]James H. Moulton and George Milligan, The Vocabulary of the Greek Testament (Grand Rapids: Wm. B. Eerdmans, 1930) 225.

[135]Outside the Corinthians correspondence ἐξουσία is used in Romans three times (9:21; 13:1, 3), once in 2 Thessalonians (3:9) and three times in Colossians (1:16; 2:10, 15). The Collosians references, if Pauline, are very specialized; they speak of "principalities and powers."

[136]In 1 Cor 7:37 the topic is self-control; in 11:10 the discussion is the significance of a veil, and in 15:24 the topic of Jesus' return of the Kingdom to God.

References to Paul's apostolic ἐξουσία are found in 9:4, 5, 6, 12, 18. The importance of this for understanding ἐξουσία in chapter 8 is discussed below, 273-274. Also important are very similar references in 2 Cor 10:8 and 13:10 where the apostolic ministry is characterized by οἰκοδομέω not καθαιρέω.

[137]The slogan Πάντα ἔξεστιν is widely recognized as originating from Corinth. Lietzmann, Korinther, 27; Barrett, 1 Corinthians, 195; Conzelmann, 1 Corinthians, 108; Vielhauer, OIKODOME, 95. Lietzmann raises the possibility that the slogan originated from Paul in debate with Judaizers. Robertson and Plummer, 1 Corinthians, 121f., also consider the slogan to be derived from Paul's preaching and (mis)used by the Corinthians in their letter to him.

In both 6:12 and 10:23 the slogan, πάντα ἔξεστιν, is corrected by οὐ πάντα συμφέρει. In 10:23 it occurs twice and the second time is corrected by οὐ πάντα οἰκοδομεῖ. In 1 Cor 8 the Corinthian ἐξουσία is evaluated by what "builds up."

Judaism, and popular Hellenistic philosophy, especially Stoicism. Each of these must be looked at briefly.

Schlatter is one of those who thinks the idea of Christian ἐξουσία originally served to defend a freedom from Jewish legalism. This had been communicated to the Corinthian church as a part of Paul's own gospel.[138] But along with this idea Paul had also communicated the command not to be involved in idol cults. Therefore the Corinthians are asking for some clarification of these two teachings.[139] Following the idea that ἐξουσία arises in a context of Jewish legal debate is Foerster who says that it reflects Rabbinic discussion on that which is permitted or forbidden.[140] Horsley also argues for a Jewish provenance, precisely Hellenistic Judaism as reflected in Philo.[141] Both Schlatter and Foerster, as well as others, have suggested Paul as the person who first introduced the concept into a Jewish-Christian debate.[142]

The suggestion that ἐξουσία originated as a technical term in Gnosticism has found considerable support. Perhaps the most influential proponent was Reitzenstein.[143] In this view he has been followed by Weiss,[144] Lietzmann,[145] Schlier,[146] Barrett,[147] Jewett,[148] and, of course, Schmithals.[149] It is an attractive suggestion because gnostics, as

---

[138]Schlatter, *Korintherbriefe,* 98.

[139]Ibid. This view does not take adequately into account the polemical stance of the Corinthians. Their question is not "May we?" but "Why can't we?"

[140]Werner Foerster, "'Εξουσία" *TDNT* 2, 570. He cites Rom 14:4 as a parallel view, perhaps deriving from Jesus's own teaching as given now in Mark 7:15. Foerster, however, thinks that the weak in Corinth were Jewish Christians who could not adjust to such freedom.

[141]Horsley, "Consciousness," 576f., suggests Stoic ideas refined by Hellenistic Judaism.

[142]Schlatter, *Korintherbriefe,* 98, and Foerster, "'Εξουσία" 570, say that the slogan's basis is "Paul's own teaching on freedom from the Law." This could be interpreted either Gnostically, as power, or as freedom in respect to the Law.

[143]In: Reitzenstein, *Hellenistic Mystery Religions,* 383f.

[144]Weiss, *Korintherbriefe,* 229, n. 4.

[145]Lietzmann, *Korinther,* 27.

[146]Heinrich Schlier, "'Ελεύθερος," *TDNT* 2, 501.

[147]Barrett, *1 Corinthians,* 144.

[148]Jewett, *Paul's Anthropological Terms,* 39.

[149]Schmithals, *Gnosticism,* 224-229, discusses gnostic ἐξουσία in connection with idol meat.

reflected in the later church fathers, are known to have flaunted their freedom from conventions.[150]

Although the suggestion that ἐξουσία comes from a gnostic community is not separable from the broader question of the rise of gnosticism (especially whether there was a gnosticism in Corinth), that problem is well beyond the present study's scope. However, it should be noted that it is not necessary to assume a gnostic milieu to account adequately for the Corinthian emphasis on "authority" or for their use of the word ἐξουσία.[151] One can account for the use of ἐξουσία in 1 Corinthians on the basis of popular Hellenistic philosophy, especially as taught by the Stoa. As Conzelmann observes,

> The language points to a previous history in Stoicism. Only the Stoics and Cynics provide material for comparison. The same origin is suggested by the catch word "συμφερεῖν," "to be for the best."[152]

The Stoic teacher Epictetus considered basic to true happiness and freedom the ability to distinguish between what is under one's authority to change and what is not. For "each man's master is the person who has authority over what the man wishes or does not wish."[153] Ideally the true Stoic is a perfectly free man, since he does not struggle against events.

This awareness gave the Stoic wise man great freedom. But he would be the most just of men, for "who has a keener sense of justice than he who is above the law; who a more rigorous self-control than he to

---

[150]Schmithals, *Gnosticism*, 228-245, gives a good summary of evidence on gnostic "freedom" available in church fathers.

[151]Bultmann, for example, who is basically favorably disposed to gnosticism as a formative influence in primitive Christianity, considers Dupont, *Gnosis*, to have successfully refuted Reitzenstein on the alleged gnostic origin of ἐξουσία as a technical term. Bultmann, "Gnosis," 20f.

Schmithals, *Gnosticism*, 230, acknowledges that ἐξουσία was a technical term in the Stoa, and "it would be theoretically possible that there is some Cynic influence here."

[152]Conzelmann, *1 Corinthians*, 108. Also, Murphy-O'Connor, 350. Both cite in support Dupont, *Gnosis*, 301-308.

[153]Epictetus, *Ench.* 14.2 (Loeb 2.494, 5). See also Foerster, "'Εξουσία," 563, and Schlier, "'Ελεύθερος," 493f.

whom all things are permissible?"[154] Diogenes is the great example of a
wise man, and he argued that since "all things belong to the gods" and "the
gods are friends to the wise and friends share all property in common,
therefore all things are the property of the wise."[155]

The authority of the Stoic is an aspect of his freedom. "So it
follows of necessity that . . . the wise are free (ἐλεύθερος) and allowed to
do as they wish."[156] Indeed, to do as one wills is the real definition of
what it means to be free,

> But surely we may put the matter briefly and declare that
> whoever has the power to do whatever he wishes (ἔξεστιν ὃ
> βούλεται πράττειν) is free (ἐλεύθερος) and whoever has not
> that power is a slave (ὅτῳ δὲ μὴ ἔξεστι, δοῦλος).[157]

These examples from Hellenistic popular philosophy do not show
that Stoicism is the source for the Corinthian boast of ἐξουσία and certainly do not imply a literary dependence (none of the citations is early
enough). They do suggest an attitude current in the period which can
account for similar terminology and outlook. Thus there is no necessity to
look to gnosticism to explain the Corinthians' appeal to ἐξουσία.

Whether ἐξουσία as used by the Corinthians was a term taken from
popular usage or one derived from their founder-apostle, for them it has

---

[154]Dio Chrysostom, *Orat.* 3.10, τίνι δὲ σωφροσύνης ἐγκρατεστέ-
ρας ἢ ὅτῳ πάντα ἔξεστι; note that πάντα ἔξεστι is equivalent to being
"above the law." Cf. 1 Cor 9:21. Philo, *Quod Omn Prob* 59 is very similar.
[155]Diogenes Laertius, 6.71f. (Loeb 2, 73f.). The last phrase is
πάντα ἄρα τῶν σοφῶν. See also 6.37f. and 7.125 where ἐξουσία is used.
[156]Dio Chrysostom, 14.17.
[157]Ibid. Cf. Epictetus, *Disc.* 4.1.1. Epictetus also insisted the free
man was under no one's authority, not even kings and tyrants, *Disc.*
3.24.70. In 1 Cor 10:23-29 Paul also interchanges ἐξουσία with ἐλευθερία. The equation may simply be obvious, but it was also made explicitly in Stoic thought. On ἐλευθερία in popular philosophy see Friedrich,
"Freiheit und Liebe," 81-98.

Schmithals, *Gnosticism*, 231, says that ἐξουσία = ἐλευθερία in
gnostic theology as well, and "the two concepts are interchangeable."

Epictetus, *Disc.* 3.22.94, says that the true cynic's conscience
(συνειδός) has the authority (ἐξουσίαν) to censure those who do wrong,
since it is clear.

one specific content, "the authority to eat any kind of food."[158] In 1 Cor
8:10 this even includes the right to eat sacrificial meat ἐν εἰδωλείῳ.[159]
The motive of this conduct by the Corinthian strong is not stated,
only the result. Perhaps they were simply not willing to give up pleasant
social relationships.[160] More likely, based on their ἐξουσία, perhaps they
insisted on employing their freedom to show their knowledge that no idols
means no idol meat.[161] Others have suggested that the strong were
simply insensitive, "they made use of their freedom without any consideration for the weak."[162] Robertson and Plummer give a suggestive picture:

---

[158]Barrett, *1 Corinthians*, 195. Also, based on 6.12, the authority
to go to the prostitute.
    [159]Εἰδωλείον is not a classical Greek word. It occurs five times in
the LXX. However, analogous terms like Σαραπείον and 'Απολλωνείον
are found in the papyri. See, for example, *P. Oxy.* 110. Such texts are
given by Robertson and Plummer, *First Corinthians*, 171 and Conzelmann,
1 Corinthians, 148, note 32.
    In the present study see p. 4f. on the association of cultic shrines
and dining rooms. Cultic dining rooms have been located in Corinth at the
shrine of Demeter and Kore on the side of Acrocorinth, also at the Askle-
pion, and in caves at nearby Isthmia. The latter are probably associated
with the worship of Poseidon.
    On cultic dining sites in Corinth see Cynthia Thompson, "Corinth,"
IDBSup, 180. Also the recent major study of Roman Corinth: James
Wiseman, "Corinth and Rome I: 228 B.C.—A.D. 267," *Aufstieg und Niedergang der römischen Welt* (eds. H. Temporini and W. Haase; Berlin:
Walter de Gruyter, 1979), 2.7.1, 469-472.
    Whether the activity referred to in 1 Cor 8 is the same as that
mentioned in 10:27 is discussed below, 237-240.
    [160]Von Soden, "Sakrament und Ethik," 6, observes: "An solchen
Mählern teilzunehmen, war für die alten Christen einfach ein Stück
Familien- und Gesellschaftsleben, und sich ihnen zu entziehen, mochte für
manchen das 'aus-der-Welt-gehen' bedeuten." Similarly, Margaret E.
Thrall, *I and II Corinthians* (Cambridge: University Press, 1965) 64 and
also Barrett, *1 Corinthians*, 196.
    [161]Barrett, "Things Sacrificed," 152. "The conclusions [of moral
indifferentism based on rationalism] drawn are valid in all circumstances,
or if others fail to draw them, that is their affair." Schlatter, *Korintherbriefe*, 103, draws a similar conclusion: "Er geneisst das Opferfleisch so
in aller Öffentlichkeit und stellt seine Freiheit mit keckem Trotz vor den
Augen aller aus."
    [162]Conzelmann, *1 Corinthians*, 149, note 34. He thinks that their
actions are built upon a speculative individualistic principle of each man

A Corinthian, in a spirit of bravado, to show his superior enlightenment and the wide scope of his Christian freedom, not only partakes of idol meats but does so at a sacrificial banquet within the precincts of the idol temple.[163]

But the more probable motive of those who ate ἐν εἰδωλείῳ is they were acting purposefully to educate (οἰκοδομεῖν) the weaker brother. This view takes οἰκοδομηθήσεται to be Paul's ironic, even sarcastic, use of the Corinthians' defense for their eating.[164] Jewett says that the conduct of those who ate was more than indifference to the weak: "These radicals had embarked on a campaign of ridicule and enticement, forcing those caught by the conscience lag to violate their consciences until they were free."[165]

It is not possible to be certain, but it seems likely that the Corinthian strong described the effect of their eating ἐν εἰδωλείῳ as οἰκοδομέω.[166] It is clear that their conduct arose from convictions, not carelessness, and 8:8 suggests that they considered eating a positive gain. Moreover, they write to Paul defensively; they are not asking for his view but defending their own conduct. For these reasons it is best to consider their motives to include setting a desirable and needed example for others to emulate.

C. The Effect on the Weak.

The situation is clear: some in Corinth are going to eat in temple dining halls.[167] The description of these Christians as τὸν ἔχοντα

acting for himself. Conzelmann rejects explicitly οἰκοδομέω as a Corinthian slogan, for the strong did not give a demonstration purposively.

[163]Robertson and Plummer, *First Corinthians,* 171. For Paul "this was *per se* idolatrous." Contrast Conzelmann, *1 Corinthians,* 148, "Paul declares: your conduct does not affect you; your inner freedom to go to these places is no problem."

[164]Weiss, *Korintherbriefe,* 230; Lietzmann, *Korinther,* 39; Parry, *1 Corinthians,* 133; Robertson and Plummer, *First Corinthians,* 171 give this as a possibility although not themselves endorsing it. Similarly von Soden, "Sakrament und Ethik," 5.

[165]Jewett, *Paul's Anthropological Terms,* 173f.

[166]On οἰκοδομέω, see above, 73, 75-77.

[167]Karris, 164, says the future conditional, "if" (ἐὰν)-clause in 8:10 serves to make Paul's teaching and principles concrete. Contrast Hurd, 150, who says this syntax proves the situation is hypothetical.

γνῶσιν appears a self-estimate, although perhaps one shared by the weak
brother who is awed by their conduct.[168] Whatever the motive of these
"knowledgeable" Christians, their actions have a serious effect on the
weak.

Οἰκοδομέω, a word taken from the Corinthians' defense, is used
ironically by Paul to describe the disastrous effect of the strong's program. The man of weak awareness is himself emboldened to eat in the
temple halls. He is "led to eating." But the weak man does not simply eat
meat, but τὰ εἰδωλόθυτα. Subsequently he is self-indicted.[169]

Most interpreters say the injury to the weak man's "conscience"
arises when in retrospect he evaluates his actions to have been wrong.[170]
It is possible, of course, that the pangs accompanied his eating, but he was
simply unable to resist pressure (implicit or explicit) to eat.[171] Either
way his "weak conscience" is the opposite of the current meaning: someone without scruples. Rather, the man is over-scrupulous. The weak does
not act *because* his conscience is weak, "as if weak conscience = weak
will, but *in spite of* his weak conscience."[172] The man of weak
conscience "indicates a person whose conscience is over-active,"[173] but
who follows the example of those enlightened Christians.

The tragic result of this "edification" of the weak man's emulation
of the strong is described in a striking fashion: ἀπόλλυται ὁ ἀσθενῶν ἐν

The omission of σε in P46, B and G serves to change Paul's words
from direct address to a general statement. See Lietzmann, *Korinther*,
39. Conzelmann, *1 Corinthians*, 148, n. 29, says that the σε belongs and
shows Paul's diatribe style.

[168]Robertson and Plummer, *First Corinthians*, 171.

[169]Furnish, *Love Command*, 114, observes "This is obviously an
extreme case" but still a real possibility given the variety of such opportunities and the ἐξουσία of those who have γνῶσις.
In 8:7 his conscience is said to be "stained" (μολύνεται, a rare
word in the New Testament, otherwise 2 Cor 7:1; Rev 3:4; 14:4).

[170]Furnish, *Love Command*, 114. Pierce, *Conscience*, 81f.
observes that thus it is a *conscienta consequens*.

[171]Davies, "Conscience," 675. Rudolph Bultmann, *The Theology of
the New Testament* (New York: Charles Scribner's Sons, 1951) 218-220,
shows how this case is parallel to Rom 14 and its discussion of the "weak
in faith." See also James Moffatt, *The First Epistle of Paul to the
Corinthians* (New York: Harper & Bros., n.d.) 118.

[172]Rightly, Thrall, *1 and 2 Corinthians*, 64f. Contra, Pierce,
Conscience, 80.

[173]Furnish, *Love Command*, 114, n. 67.

τῇ σῇ γνώσει. Ἀπολλύω is emphatic by its position at the first of the
sentence. It "must not be taken in a weakened sense as moral ruin; here
as elsewhere it means eternal damnation."[174] The results of the strong
man's action cannot be escaped or minimized. They have eternal significance—a process of damnation already begun.[175] In this fatal result the
strong man is indicted, for the brother is destroyed ἐν τῇ σῇ γνώσει.[176]
He cannot dismiss the result as being the fault of the other man's weakness. The blame lies with him who leads the weak man astray (cf. Matt
18:6).

The last part of verse 11 is very expressive in its structure, as
Robertson and Plummer note:

> The last clause could hardly be more forcible in its appeal,
> every word tells; "the brother," not a mere stranger; "for the
> sake of whom," precisely to rescue him from destruction;
> "Christ," no less than He; "died" no less than that.[177]

The weak man had previously been described as "some" (τινές 8:7)
or the "weak in conscience" (8:9, 11a), but now "both climactically and

---

[174]Conzelmann, 1 Corinthians, 149, n. 38, cites Rom 14:15 as
parallel.

Ἀπολλυεῖν is not a prominent word in Paul. Otherwise it is found
in 1 Cor 1:18, 19 of those who reject the gospel; 10:9, 10 of Israel's fate in
the wilderness; and 15:18 of the dead in Christ if there were no resurrection. In 2 Thess 2:10 it refers to eternal judgment. Other references
are: Rom 2:12; 14:15; 2 Cor 2:15; 4:3, 9.

There are an unusual number of textual variations at the beginning
of this clause. Zuntz, 201f., sees the original text as ἀπόλλυται γάρ. So
also, Conzelmann, 1 Corinthians, 149, n. 37, "The variants καί and οὖν
'and' and 'therefore,' were attempts to make things easier, when Paul's
question was no longer understood because his concept of conscience was
no longer understood. . . ." It is best to render with Blass-Debrunner
§ 452(2): "to be sure, just so." Cf. 1 Thess 2:20.

[175]Note ἀπόλλυται, present tense. "Paul sees him as even now
perishing." Leon Morris, The First Epistle of Paul to the Corinthians
(Grand Rapids, Mich: Wm. B. Eerdmans, 1958) 129. Gustav Stählin,
"Σκάνδαλον," TDNT 7, 355, points out that σκανδαλίσω is equivalent.

[176]"By reason of your knowledge." Conzelmann, 1 Corinthians, 149
n. 38.

[177]Robertson and Plummer, First Corinthians, 172, compare Rom
14:15b, ὑπὲρ οὗ Χριστὸς ἀπέθανεν.

emphatically—Paul refers to 'the brother' and 'the brethren.'"[178] The "strong" Corinthians cannot minimize the loss of those who are devastated by terming them "weak"; they are ἀδελφοί. To offend them is to counteract the purpose of Christ's work and destroy the community formed by it.[179]

This disastrous result of the strong man's ἐξουσία not only derives from him but is his responsibility. "Thus"—(οὕτως) by acting ἐν τῇ σῇ γνώσει—the strong is the agent of sin. He sins against his Christian brother. Thus the damage is not just to the weak one who is offended, but to the strong person who is involved in sinning.[180]

This is the only time Paul says one sins against his brother (but the verb is infrequent, only in Romans and 1 Corinthians). This sinning is also described as "wounding" (τύπτοντες, a hapax in Paul). It is to be equated with μολύνεται in 8:7.[181]

The result of the strong person's actions is not only sin against the brother but against the Lord himself. This "against Christ also" may mean Christ remains continually involved in all he has redeemed, or it may mean "Christ as present in the brother" (as in Matt 25:40, 45; Acts 26:14, 15).[182] In view of Paul's use of the "building up" imagery in the letter it is perhaps best to understand εἰς Χριστὸν as εἰς σῶμα τοῦ Χριστοῦ i.e., the church.[183]

---

[178]Furnish, *Love Command*, 114.

[179]Schlatter, *Korintherbriefe*, 104. "So wird der Wille Jesu durch die Freien zerbrochen."

[180]Morris, *First Epistle*, 129, and Schlatter, *Korintherbriefe*, 104, raise the synoptic warning against those who offend "the little ones" (Matt 18:6). See also Pierce, *Conscience*, 81.

[181]Pierce, *Conscience*, 81. Blass-Debrunner § 442(9), says that the καί is epexegetical. Robertson and Plummer, *First Corinthians*, 172, note that the present participle, τύπτοντες implies a continuing process, as does the weakness, ἀσθενοῦσαν.

The RSV translation of ἀσθενοῦσαν is perhaps too interpretive, "when it is weak." This may suggest a temporal condition which will be overcome in the future—which may have been what the strong suggested. The vague, "being weak" retains a useful ambiguity.

[182]Moffatt, *1 Corinthians*, 113. Similarly, Conzelmann, *1 Corinthians*, 149, "my brother represents to me the Lord himself; my conduct toward my brother affects Christ himself."

Furnish, *Love Command*, 114, rightly notes that this is basically a negative formulation of the New Testament teaching that one meets Christ in the neighbor. Cf. Rom 14:15, 18; Acts 9:4, 5.

[183]Murphy-O'Connor, 564, says here sin against "Christ" means against "body of Christ."

D. Paul's Conduct as a Pattern.

Up to now Paul has engaged the Corinthians' defense and criticized their actions. How one ought to act has been implied by the negative warnings. In 8:13 he gives an additional direction, which is positive, and sets himself forth as an example to follow.

Διόπερ is an uncommon word in the New Testament. It occurs only here, in 1 Cor 10:14 and in some witnesses to 1 Cor 14:13,[184] meaning "for just this reason." Here it begins Paul's conclusion to this first discussion of eating sacrificial meat and introduces his personal example which is elaborated in 1 Cor 9.

Paul sets forth as a general principle εἰ βρῶμα σκανδαλίζει τὸν ἀδελφόν μου, οὐ μὴ φάγω κρέα εἰς τὸν αἰῶνα ἵνα μὴ τὸν ἀδελφόν μου σκανδαλίσω. This is a general principle, but obviously modeled upon the existing situation at Corinth. Continuing a point made sharply in 8:11, Paul insists the problem is one among *brothers:* How one must conduct his life if he is aware that a brother may be scandalized by his actions.

The verb σκανδαλίζω is a rare word in Paul. It otherwise occurs only in 2 Cor 11:29, [185] and in some texts of Rom 14:21.[186] The noun form, σκάνδαλον is only slightly more common in Paul.[187] Indeed, these words are not frequently found in Greek. Originally σκάνδαλον meant a trigger for an animal trap, and it is seldom used metaphorically in Greek

---

[184]Bauer, ed. Gingrich and Danker, *Greek-English Lexicon,* 198. Moule, *Idiom Book,* 164.

[185]In 2 Cor 11:29 Paul asks rhetorically: τίς ἀσθενεῖ, καὶ οὐκ ἀσθενῶ; τίς σκανδαλίζεται, καὶ οὐκ ἐγὼ πυροῦμαι; Note the verbal connections with 1 Cor 8, where σκανδαλίζω is also connected to ἀσθενής. Moreover, in both passages Paul is using himself as an example.

[186]The Nestle text of Rom 14:21 reads: καλὸν τὸ μὴ φαγεῖν κρέα μηδὲ πιεῖν οἶνον μηδὲ ἐν ᾧ ὁ ἀδελφός σου προσκόπτει.

In some manuscripts (Textus Receptus, B, D, Gpl, latsy^h sa; W) the verse continues ἢ σκανδαλίζεται ἢ ἀσθενεῖ. This may be assimilation to 1 Cor 8:13.

In Rom 14:21 Paul gives his instructions in hortatory style, but the similarities with 1 Cor 8:13 are numerous: μὴ φαγεῖν, κρέα (the only Pauline usages), ἀδελφός and σκανδαλίζεται, if it belongs to the text of Rom 14:21.

[187]Rom 9:33; 11:9; 14:13; 16:17; 1 Cor 1:23 and Gal 5:11. The first two are Old Testament quotes. Rom 14:13 parallels the discussion in 1 Cor 8, and Rom 16:17 describes church discipline.

literature.[188] In the LXX, however, it is used as a metaphor, and this is probably the source of Christian usage.[189] In the LXX it refers especially to the results of idolatry (Judg 2:3; 8:27; Josh 23:13; Ps 105:36; Deut 7:16). Psalms 68:23 has some similarities with 1 Cor 8; "Their meal [the wicked] will be for them a snare (εἰς παγίδα) and their sacrificial meals a trap (εἰς σκάνδαλον)."

Both from the LXX usage and other New Testament uses (especially in Matthew) it is clear that σκάνδαλον means far more than "offense in our modern sense of the term; it means here, as it did on the lips of Jesus, something that makes a man lose his footing."[190]

Why does Paul set forth his principle in such general terms in 8:13? Robertson and Plummer suggest that he is describing a conditional policy,

If the apostle knows of definite cases in which his eating food will lead to others being encouraged to violate the dictates of conscience, then certainly he will never eat meat so long as there is real danger of this (10:28, 29). But if he knows of no such danger he will use his Christian freedom and eat without scruple (10:25-27).[191]

---

[188]Stählin, "Σκάνδαλον," 339-343, rehearses the history of the word. Henry G. Liddell and Robert Scott, A Greek-English Lexicon 9th ed. (Oxford: Clarendon Press, 1940) give two non-biblical examples, both from the papyri.

[189]Stählin, "Σκάνδαλον," 334 notes that the word is missing in Philo, Josephus and the Epistle of Aristeas.

[190]Moffatt, 1 Corinthians, 113. This is why the sin against the brother is so grave; his Christian faith is thereby endangered. Schrage, Einzelgebote, 243, n. 20, says that 8:13 shows Paul's knowledge of a Jesus logion such as is now found in Matt 18:6.

Paul also knows a σκάνδαλον which is unavoidable and intrinsic to the gospel message (Rom 9:33; 11:9; 1 Cor 1:23 and Gal 5:11). But like the "offense" of 1 Cor 8, the result is the same, a man is separated from Christ. The seriousness of the "offense" is the same, but one is avoidable.

[191]Robertson and Plummer, First Corinthians, 173. They add, "He does not, of course, mean that the whole practice of Christians is to be regulated with a view to the possible scrupulousness of the narrow-minded." Yet that seems to be what he says in 10:31-33. Similarly, Grosheide, 1 Corinthians, 197.

Certainly Paul is not arguing for a Christian vegetarianism. That, too, would make the kingdom a matter of eating and drinking, rather than peace and joy in the Spirit (Rom 14:17).

However, Barrett says that Paul is simply setting forth his own course. He adds, "Paul does not dictate to others (an interesting sidelight on his understanding of his ministry)."[192] This is hardly the case, for Paul has just warned that ignoring the weak man is a sin against Christ! Surely this claim demands obedience from those with "knowledge." Moreover, even his own example is given to guide the conduct of others (11:1 explicitly, see 286-291 on the imitation of Paul theme).[193] Paul is not just stating his proposed course and letting others choose theirs.

Others have felt that Paul is not setting out a policy in general terms, but stating an extreme to which Christians ought to go if need demanded.[194] It has been suggested that Paul is replying to a Corinthian objection that to abstain from sacrificial meat would mean to give up all meat (cf. 5:9-11). If that is so, Paul accepts the conclusion.[195] Adolf Schlatter has strikingly and succinctly described this view:

> Nicht nur auf das Opferfleisch, sondern auf alles Fleisch verzichtet Paulus, nicht nur für ein paar Tage, sondern ganz und gar, wenn aus dem, was er isst, eine Gefahr für die Brüder wird, weil sein Beispiel ihnen den Mut zur Versündigung verschafft.[196]

CONCLUSIONS

A. The Corinthians' Conduct and Their Justification

The study of 1 Corinthians 8 has made clear that the Corinthians in their letter raised the question about eating sacrificial meat in a defensive manner. In no way was their conduct accidental. They had reached

---

[192]Barrett, *1 Corinthians*, 197.

[193]See Furnish, *Theology and Ethics*, 218-223, for a good summary.

[194]Lietzmann, *Korinther*, 39, says "Aus Rücksicht auf meinen Bruder lieber zuviel als zu wenig zu tun!" See also Conzelmann, *1 Corinthians*, 150.

[195]Von Soden, "Sakrament und Ethik," ff. See also, Hurd, 225f.

[196]Schlatter, *Korintherbriefe*, 105. Note οὐ μὴ with φάγω for emphatic denial. A close parallel is found in P Oxy 199: οὐ μὴ φάγω, οὐ μὴ πεινῶ. See also Nigel Turner, *Syntax* Vol 3 of James Hope Moulton, *A Grammar of New Testament Greek* (Edinburgh: T & T Clark, 1963) 96.

their own determination about eating and communicated it to Paul along with their justification of their actions.[197] Their defenses are set forth within the chapter either in Paul's paraphrase of their letter or, as seems likely, in quotations taken from the letter.

The defense of the Corinthians is grounded theoretically in knowledge. Specifically the knowledge is of the oneness of God, as exemplified in a Christian confession which they cite, and the consequent denial of the reality of idols. They argue if there is only one God and one Lord—at least for Christians—then it follows logically that meat from animals sacrificed to idols and even the dining rooms of pagan temples are not tainted through their association with these idols. They believe that this is a truth known by all Christians (8:1).

Based on this knowledge, the Corinthians think that they have the ἐξουσία to eat at temple shrines. The word ἐξουσία means both "power" and "right" or "freedom." Both ideas are probably present in the Corinthians' defense. Because of their Christian knowledge they have the power to eat such food without suffering harm, and this legitimates their right to do so.

Finally, the Corinthians believe that acting on their knowledge and exercising their Christian right in this manner is a means of emboldening more reticent believers to act in a similar manner on the same knowledge. Their course of conduct they term "building up" those whose awareness in this matter is weak.

It is not stated how they regarded the occasions when their education policy resulted in the loss of those who were weak in conscience. Perhaps they simply disregarded these as unfortunate cases, or perhaps their individualism led them to regard each person's case as his or her own responsibility. For whatever reason, they were unwilling to restrict their actions.

---

[197]This comes out in the Corinthian position as set out in 8:1, 4 (5, 6), 8. Findlay, "Letter of the Corinthians," 404f., gives a useful reconstruction of their letter based on these verses. His treatment is weaker in that he does not allow for the defensive, even polemical, stance of the Corinthians in their inquiry.

A similar reconstruction based on these verses is given by Barrett, *1 Corinthians,* 197, although he does not include vv. 5, 6 in the Corinthian inquiry. But in describing those verses he considers quotations he notes: "there is a clear, compelling sequence of thought. . . ."

B. Paul's Reply

Paul takes up the question of Christians eating idol meat in 1 Corinthians 8-10. In his initial response in chapter 8 the discussion is determined by the way in which the Corinthians have defended their right to eat in temple dining halls. Failure to recognize how the Corinthians' inquiry has shaped Paul's reply has led to two common errors in interpretation.

First, failure to see in vv. 1, 4 (5, 6) and 8 the setting forth of the Corinthians' position has resulted in dividing Paul's response into his real beliefs about the eating and the accommodation he feels constricted to by others. According to this view Paul agrees with the Corinthians about the harmless character of the meat and Christian participation but limits their participation because of the possible effects on the brothers.[198] If allowance is made for the role of the Corinthians' inquiry one need not follow the path of having Paul agree with the Corinthian position in theory although refusing to allow them to act on it.

Second, the differences in approach in chapter 8 and 10:1-22 have been mistakenly attributed to a post-Pauline redactor. It is not the content of the two sections but their juxtaposition which has been regarded as troublesome. However, recognizing the influence on Paul's argument in chapter 8 adequately accounts for the shift in approach.

Some scholars have asked why Paul raises the norms of "building up" and "consider your brother" if shortly afterward he will prohibit the eating in temple halls (10:14-22) and will warn of the danger of being destroyed by God (10:1-13). Again attention to the crucial influence of the Corinthians' arguments reduces this tension often alleged between the various sections of 1 Cor 8-10. In chapter 8, Paul begins as he does because of the way the Corinthians had made their points. In chapter 10, Paul works more from his own agenda.

---

[198]This is finally the view of Barrett, "Things Sacrificed," 152: "We find Paul's fundamental criticism of a position which in many respects he was prepared to uphold: ἀγάπη must take precedence to γνῶσις (1 Cor 7:1-3; 13:2, 8, 9, 12f.) and my neighbor's conscience is always more important than my own."

A similar interpretation is given by Grosheide, *1 Corinthians*, 244, "Paul, like every other Christian, may do what he likes to do, he is free in his conscience and he does not need to abstain from any food. This is the Christian liberty in theory; which must be distinguished from its practice."

The fact that Paul's response is occasioned by the arguments of the Corinthians does not lessen its importance. As will be seen, there is a fundamental agreement in his arguments in chapter 8 and chapter 10.

In 1 Cor 8 Paul sets forth four basic arguments: (1) a critique of "rights" (ἐξουσία) on the basis of love, (2) a reminder of the necessity of considering the other person, (3) the importance of the communal dimension of Christian life, and (4) Paul's own conduct as exemplary.

1. *Love and Freedom.* As has been argued in the exegesis, the Corinthians stressed both their "rights" or "freedom" (ἐξουσία) and their knowledge (γνῶσις) in defending their eating at pagan sacrificial meals. Based on their γνῶσις they are confident in their ἐξουσία to eat. Paul first of all denies that γνῶσις is a safe criterion for decisions. "Knowledge" is not what counts, but "love" (8:1). The reason is that knowledge leads individuals to become "puffed up," whereas love leads to building up the community of faith.

A second criticism of knowledge as a basis for Christian action is that the only knowledge which counts is God's knowledge (= election) of those in Christ (8:2, 3). Christians who rely on "seeming to know" (8:2) something are not yet (οὔπω 8:2) rightly aware of the proper stance before God in the present age. The right attitude of believers is love (ἀγάπη). Love for God is what is decisive (cf. Rom 13:9, 10; Gal 5:13, 14).

Just as the Corinthians have misunderstood the role of knowledge, so also they are mistaken about Christian freedom. They understand freedom to be the right of each person to act on his own knowledge. Because faith gives this freedom, they ought to exercise it in actions. In the case of idol meat, this means one ought to eat.

Freedom (ἐλευθερία) was a major concern for Greek philosophers.[199] Although in 1 Cor 8 the term employed is ἐξουσία it is to be understood as virtually synonymous with ἐλευθερία. This is clear in 1 Cor 10:23, 29 where Paul interchanges the two words. In 1 Cor 9:1 he uses ἐλευθερία in continuing the discussion of "rights" which he began in chapter 8 with ἐξουσία.

Originally ἐλευθερία was a political term; it was that which distinguished the citizen from the slave.[200] But with the passing of the Greek

---

[199]See 382ff. The Jewish authors Philo and Josephus were also concerned about ἐλευθερία. See K. H. Rengstorf, *A Complete Concordance of Flavius Josephus* (Leiden: Brill, 1975) 2, 75ff.

[200]S. Scott Bartchy, ΜΑΛΛΟΝ ΧΡΗΣΑΙ: *First Century Slavery and the Interpretation of 1 Corinthians 7:21* (SBLDS 11; Missoula, MT: Scholars Press, 1973) 66f.

city-state in the Hellenistic period, ἐλευθερία adds to its political meaning and acquires a philosophical focus.[201] Particularly in the popular
philosophies a guiding rule for conduct is what makes one ἀκώλυτον . . .
καὶ αὐτεξούσιον."[202] With this heritage of a passion for freedom,
understood as self-determination, it is not surprising that some Corinthians perceived Christianity as personal liberation.[203]

In view of the prominent place of "freedom" in Greek philosophy
and popular authors, it is strange that the terms are so seldom used in the
New Testament. Paul is often considered the champion of freedom in the
New Testament because he makes more of the idea of freedom than any
other New Testament author. However, it is easy to overestimate the
place of "freedom" in Paul's theology.[204] Actually he does not discuss
freedom very often.[205] He uses the word ἐλευθερία to describe the

---

Also see the excellent article by Schlier, "Ἐλεύθερος'" which
discusses the development of the concept of freedom in Greek politics and
philosophy.

[201]Schlier, "'Ἐλεύθερος," 495f. He notes ἐλευθερία is especially
prominent in Cynic philosophy. "The cynic is the one who stands out as
ἐλεύθερος, ἐλευθερωτής, ἐλευθεριάζων . . . who not only loves freedom,
but prefers it to all else."

[202]Ibid., 494. Furnish, Love Command, 98, notes that pagan
philosophers would not have endorsed the suggestion that service is
freedom. He cites Epictetus, Disc. 4.7.16, 17; Plato, Gorg. 491E and
Aristotle, Metaph. 1.2.

[203]It should be remembered that popular philosophy grounded this
freedom in knowledge. Stoics even produced an epistemology of how one
purified himself from false δόγματα. See Schlier, "'Ἐλεύθερος," 494.

Moreover, Paul himself did preach a Christian "freedom" (e.g., Gal
5:1; 2 Cor 3:17) which to some may have been perceived as his endorse-
ment of a "freedom theology." Nevertheless, Friedrich, "Freiheit und
Liebe," 91, is right that freedom is not the content of the Pauline message, but the message realizes freedom for those who hear and receive
it. Paul, then, does not propagandize freedom, rather he makes it possible
through his gospel.

[204]As for example in the recent work by Peter Richardson, Paul's
Ethic of Freedom (Philadelphia: Westminster Press, 1979).

[205]Outside of Paul's letters, ἐλευθερία occurs only in James and 1
and 2 Peter in the New Testament. The cognate, ἐλεύθερος is found in
Matt 17:26; John 8:33, 36; 1 Pet 2:16; Rev 6:15; 13:16 and 19:18. The verb
occurs in John 8:32, 36.

Of course, simply counting uses of ἐλευθερία cannot be decisive,
for other words—such as δοῦλος, the opposite idea—may point to the

social distinction between slave and free man (1 Cor 7:21, 22; Gal 3:28; Col 3:11). In a theological sense the word is used to describe release from the Mosaic legal system (Rom 8:2; Gal 2:4; 4:22, 23, 26, 30, 31; 5:1) and from the power of sin (Rom 6:18, 22).

Thus when Paul speaks of freedom metaphorically it is not a liberation from the restraints of interpersonal relationships. Rather it is from the Law and its wages, death. Freedom is from an existence which, because of sin, leads through the law to death.[206]

While Paul praises freedom as a Christian blessing, his understanding of freedom is very different from that of self-determination as preached in popular philosophy of his day. The major difference is that Paul does not understand freedom individualistically. "It is not in isolation, but in life with others that the Christian attains freedom."[207]

Several scholars have suggested that in 1 Cor 8 Paul admits the fullness of Christian ἐξουσία except that it must be limited by love.[208]

___

same reality. However, (1) the word ἐλευθερία itself was a prominent topic of Hellenistic debate and Paul is surprisingly little interested, (2) Paul's metaphorical use of δοῦλος describes sin, not constraint.

Friedrich, "Freiheit und Liebe," 91, notes that nowhere is the freedom of Christians so characteristically brought to expression as in 1 Cor 3:21f., although the word "freedom" is not used there.

[206]Schlier, "'Ελεύθερος" 496. This freedom is achieved vicariously in Christ's death and is appropriated by faith and baptism.

[207]Ibid., 500. Friedrich, "Freiheit und Liebe," 93, says that freedom is not a private matter, rather one is free when he looks more to the interests of others. This distinguishes Christian freedom from pseudo-pneumatic libertinism which is only egoism.

Furnish, Theology and Ethics, 177: "He [the Christian] has been given freedom for a specific reason: 'in order that [he] might belong to another' (εἰς τὸ γενέσθαι ὑμᾶς ἑτέρῳ). That 'other' is Christ 'who has been raised from the dead.'"

[208]Vielhauer, OIKODOME, 95, says that ἐξουσία, even as ἐλευθερία, must be sacrificed for the love of the brother. Schmithals, Gnosticism, 231, comments regarding the slogan, πάντα μοι ἔξεστιν "Paul apparently affirms the slogan as such; but ... he also wants to see it limited by love." Similarly, Fee, "II Cor 6:17—7:1," 152, "this 'ἐξουσία of yours' must be subject to love." Friedrich, "Freiheit und Liebe," 81.

Other examples of this viewpoint are numerous: von Soden, "Sakrament und Ethik," 5; Merk, Handeln aus Glauben, 123, "Das σκανδαλίζειν ist ein ἁμαρτάνειν εἰς Χριστόν (8:12), und geschieht dort, wo die ἐξουσία des Gnostikers nicht durch die Liebe begrenzt ist." Karl Barth, Resurrection, 54f: "He makes the eating of that meat a matter of conscience, a regrettable restriction, certainly."

This is often based on the questionable assumption that Paul affirms the
Corinthian slogans which he quoted in 8:1 and 8:4-6. But as has been
shown Paul really quotes those words to refute them, not to affirm them.
This is explicit in 8:7 where Paul reminds the Corinthians οὐκ ἐν πᾶσιν ἡ
γνῶσις. The view that Paul prefers freedom of action, but that he will
temper it with love, gives priority to freedom. It assumes that for Paul,
as for the Corinthians and Hellenistic philosophy generally (and most
modern Christians), freedom is the greatest good, even if it must be
limited from time to time.

The outlook that prioritizes freedom, even if it will limit that in
various situations, makes love the "second-best" good. This viewpoint
may be influential in that many modern interpreters are puzzled that Paul
begins to restrain Christian participation in eating with a discussion of
love, although he later says outright: φεύγετε ἀπὸ τῆς εἰδωλολατρίας.
If he is ultimately going to restrict such eating, why does he go through
the topic of considering the brother? On this approach the fundamental
question is how one's freedom will be allowed or restricted. If it is ultimately restricted, why discuss other considerations? But Paul himself,
who prioritizes love, not freedom, feels the greater consideration is how
love may be expressed in the specific question of eating idol meat.

It seems best not to think of Paul as holding freedom to be the
greatest good for Christians, although limiting its exercise by love.
Although ἀγάπη only occurs in 8:1, it is really Paul's first consideration.
The greatest good is love which is given concrete shape in the freedom
not to eat if a brother is endangered or if Christ himself is wronged (8:11;
10:21). Christians correctly understand freedom only if they first understand that Christian freedom is the freedom to express love.[209] As
Friedrich says, love and freedom are indissolubly bound to one another. In
the practice of love, freedom shows itself. Love therefore is not a crimp-
ing and limiting of freedom, but rather an act and test of it.[210]

---

[209]Von Soden, "Sakrament und Ethik," 6, says: "Es handelt sich um
den Konflikt zwischen der ἐξουσία und der ἀγάπη oder besser das richtige
Verständnis der ersten aus der letzteren."
[210]Friedrich, "Freiheit und Liebe," 97f. He gives an excellent
ananlysis when he says, 96: "Wenn die grösste Knechtschaft in dem
Verfallensein an sich selbt besteht und die grösste Freiheit im Dasein für
den anderen sich dokumentiert, dann ist Freiheit nichts anderes als
Praktizierung der Liebe." Similarly, Heinz-Dietrich Wendland, Ethik des
Neuen Testaments: eine Einführung (NTD 4; Göttingen: Vandenhoeck &
Ruprecht, 1970) 56, observes: ". . . die christliche Freiheit ist keine
Freiheit zum Sündigen, sondern die Freiheit zur Liebe (Gal 5:13ff.), zum
Dienst am Nächsten, zu allen guten Werken."

It is not decisive whether love is first and freedom derives from it, or whether freedom (understood as God's enabling grace) is first and from it comes love.[211] But it is decisive that freedom and love are not competing but coordinate aspects of Christian faith. Christian ἐξουσία is not limited to or qualified by love but is fulfilled in it.[212] Indeed, as Conzelmann points out, Paul is not concerned to define a general concept of freedom. "This definition of freedom in historic terms distinguishes Paul from Greek philosophical ethics and from Gnostics. . . . His remarks have a definite aim; they are meant for the strong."[213]

2. *Consideration of the Other Person.* Paul stresses love, not knowledge, as the ground of Christian conduct, and on this basis he derives a practical norm for Christian ethics: consider the effect of your actions on others. It is of the character of love that it has primary regard for others (13:5; Rom 14:15). It is in considering others that love takes concrete shape, for it asks in each situation how one's conduct will affect the other person.

In 1 Cor 8 consideration of others means: (1) being aware of their weakness and lack of knowledge (8:7) and therefore (2) being sure that one's conduct does not place a stumbling block (8:9) or scandalize them (8:9). This would result in leading the other person to destruction (8:11). Consideration of the other person means no action can be approved or even considered "in itself," but always as it affects others.[214]

---

[211]Furnish, *Love Command*, 111f., ". . . it is often said that the love command is an important restriction of one's freedom. . . . but it is much more accurate to say that Paul regards love as an act of freedom. The man in Christ, claimed for service in the realm of grace, is for the first time really free to love."

[212]Furnish, *Love Command*, 115, says: "Freedom must be exercised in love, for, like the law, it is fulfilled as it serves the neighbor. Paul states this in another way in 1 Cor 10:24: 'Nobody should be looking for his own advantage, but everybody for the other man's' (*JB*). Thereby one is not *restricting* his own freedom, but *exercising* it in love."

In regard to 8:13, Friedrich, "Freiheit und Liebe," 95, is correct: "Die wahre Freiheit gibt ihm die Möglichkeit so zu handeln. Darum sieht er in seinem Verzicht nicht eine Beschränkung, sondern einen Akt der Freiheit."

[213]Conzelmann, *1 Corinthians*, 148.

[214]Walter, "Christusglaube," 428, n. 30, observes that Paul's criterion of the other man's conscience is apparently very difficult for Western society shaped by Neo-Kantanism. He refers specifically to Hans

It is not known how many of the Corinthians could be termed "weak." Paul addresses his remarks to the "strong" alone, and perhaps that is most of the church. But however few the weak, they may not be disregarded. Those who felt free by reason of their knowledge that there was only one God and the idols were nothing did not consider adequately the effects of eating on their brethren. Either they disregarded the effects on the others, or fully aware of the pangs of the weak, they followed a program of education. Either way they insisted on their privilege to eat ἐν εἰδωλείῳ.

Horsley has rightly stressed the individualistic approach of the strong as the reason they do not consider their brethren.

> For the Corinthians, therefore, the eating of idol meat and other matters were issues only in an internal personal sense, for one's individual consciousness, and not in a truly ethical, i.e., relational sense.[215]

This assessment both describes their passion for freedom and explains their conduct—each man made his own decision about eating. In typical Hellenistic fashion the Corinthians stress individual freedom as the greatest good. For that reason each is free to act on his "awareness" (a proper and appropriate translation of συνείδησις). But for Paul "such issues are ethical, that is, matters of relationships between people, not of one's own inner consciousness."[216]

As noted above in connection with 8:1, Paul insists on love, i.e., acting with regard first for the brother's needs (cf. 10:23, where Paul corrects the Corinthians' slogan πάντα ἔξεστιν with συμφέρω and οἰκοδομέω). It is characteristic of love that it considers the other person's needs and frailties (12:25, 26; 13:5). It puts no stumbling block in their way (8:9; Rom 14:13). Love does not offend him (8:13; Rom 14:13, 21). Rather, love supports the brother (13:7; cf. Gal 6:2).

It comes as something of a surprise, if 1 Cor 8 is examined closely, that Paul seems unconcerned about changing the weak, "strengthening" him. Indeed, many commentators have supplied what they assume Paul must have intended. For example, Robert Jewett says,

---

von Soden's and Rudolf Bultmann's treatments of conscience in reference to these verses. Yet one suspects Walter shows similar inclinations when he contrasts 1 Cor 8 with 10 by saying that in the former Paul sees no problem with cultic meals "an sich."

[215]Horsley, "Consciousness," 589.
[216]Ibid.

> To educate the conscience requires a gradual, indirect approach of exercising freedom while avoiding pangs (1 Cor 10:23-29). This may require temporary abnegation of freedom on the part of the "strong" to encourage the "weak" to avoid anything that would cause pangs of conscience. . . . This does not imply a permanent disavowal of freedom, because his [Paul's] own strategy was to free the "weak" to eat meat to the glory of God (1 Cor 10:31).[217]

None of this program of educating the weak out of his scruples is described in the text. The same approach is assumed and implied in suggestions that the attitude of the "weak" is "petty prejudice,"[218] or that their "scrupulosity rests on pure error," and "all this is foolish."[219] As noted above, this interpretation expresses itself in the frequent assumption that Paul himself is on the side of the strong,[220] (which he never says).

How is Paul's (apparent) disinterest in changing the weak to be accounted for? A complete answer must also take into consideration chapter 10. In this broader context it appears that regarding the eating of εἰδωλόθυτον involved two different occasions: the eating of the flesh

---

[217]Jewett, "Conscience," 174. However, 1 Cor 10:31 is not a proposal for education of the weak; it is a general hortatory word, as seen by the third phrase: εἴτε τι ποιεῖτε.

Other examples of students who think Paul plans to improve the "weak" are numerous. Stacy, *Pauline View of Man*, 208, says: "The weak conscience can either be enlightened till it reach maturity, or offended so that it loses power to form moral judgments." See also Schlatter, *Korintherbriefe*, 104, on 1 Cor 8:12. Murphy-O'Connor, 568.

Maurer, "Σύνοιδα," 915, says those who are weak, "have not yet won through to the liberating acknowledgment of the truth. . . ." This implies they may do so.

[218]Moffatt, *1 Corinthians*, 111.

[219]Barrett, *1 Corinthians*, 194f.

[220]Thrall, *1 and 2 Corinthians*, 62, "In principle he agrees with the more liberal members of the congregation." Almost verbally the same is Moffatt, *1 Corinthians*, 104.

Whether Paul numbers himself among the "strong" is related to how one resolves the possible quotations in 8:1 and 8:4 (see 1, 2, 17, 18). Rom 14:14 shows Paul considers kosher laws meaningless for Christians, but it says nothing about eating εἰδωλόθυτον.

On whether the same situation is under consideration in 8 and 10:27 see the discussion below, 237-240.

itself in private situations (10:25-28) and the other, eating such meat at cultic worship (ἐν εἰδωλείῳ. The major criticism in *both* cases was consideration of others, although the cultic occasions are also prohibited on other grounds, and the private situations conditionally approved.[221]

Paul's unconcern about changing the weak shows how deeply he feels that eating and not eating are not decisive for the kingdom of God (Rom 14:17).[222] It also shows Paul's insight that "each is called and able to believe in the position in which he finds himself."[223] The "neutrality of food does *not* mean neutrality of conduct,"[224] for all Christian conduct must take due regard for others and their belief.[225]

If the present analysis of the quotations in 1 Cor 8 is basically sound Paul does not include himself among those having γνῶσις, he does not agree that οὐδὲν εἴδωλον ἐν κόσμῳ, and he certainly does not favor eating ἐν εἰδωλείῳ. Yet he does not in 1 Cor 8 attack this eating explicitly as εἰδωλολατρία (as he will in 10:14ff.). Rather, he begins with the most important consideration flowing from love: act with regard to the other person.

3. *The Communal Dimension of Christian Ethics.* Although he elaborates it more in 1 Cor 10, already in chapter 8 Paul points to the

---

[221]Hurd, 148, "The only limitations Paul set on their freedom was that they (i) must not offend a weaker brother and (ii) must not commit an act of idolatry."

Whether Paul is inconsistent or mistaken in considering the location of eating a determining factor is a problem of systematic theology. The first question is whether he did so, not whether he was justified in so doing. From 10:14, 20, 21 it appears that he did.

[222]Moffatt, *1 Corinthians*, 111. Schrage, *Einzelgebote*, 151, says that Paul regards both the viewpoints of the majority and of the weak as acceptable, although distinct, Christian lifestyles. He also points to Romans 14 to support this view.

[223]Conzelmann, *1 Corinthians*, 147.

[224]Ibid., 148.

[225]Harris, "Conscience," 182, says that conscience gives different Christians different judgments on such practical issues of living. "The law of love (vvl, 11f.) between Christians is therefore appealed to as the *overriding* dictate of conscience recognized by both weak and strong."

The same approach is evident in dealing with the spiritual gifts, i.e., how does it affect the brother? (See 1 Cor 12-14). It is different in that the spiritual gifts are not forbidden. However, it ought to be noted that with the regulations of 1 Cor 14 on restricting glossalalia, most of what the Corinthians prized about this gift are removed.

importance of Christian community as a guide in conduct. This corporate dimension is a major difference between Paul and the Corinthians who make individualistic decisions (cp. the case of incest in 1 Cor 5, inequalities in the Lord's Supper in 1 Cor 11, and divisiveness in the exercise of spiritual gifts in 1 Cor 12, 14). The communal dimension is integral to the norm of Christian love, since love is not a sentiment or inner attitude but conduct toward others. Similarly, the communal dimension involves the consideration of the other person, since in the question of eating meat it is the "weak" Christian whose faith is endangered.

Thus consideration of the community in one's acts includes the concrete case of how the brother is affected, but goes beyond in that it reminds Christians that both they and the brother are bound with others in the body of Christ, in a covenant relationship with God.

In 1 Cor 8 Paul sets forth the norm of considering the community in two ways. First, he says that all actions must be evaluated on the basis of whether they "build up" (οἰκοδομεῖν). As has been pointed out, Paul understands οἰκοδομέω in a corporate, not individualistic, sense. Second, the community aspect is present when Paul warns that injury to the *brother* is actually sin against Christ. Even the designation "brother" points to this communal relationship of those in Christ, but especially when the brother is further described as "the one for whom Christ died" (8:11).[226]

The community dimension shows that Paul's concern for the brother is not simply a different form of individualism—as if he were enjoining each individual to watch for the other. The concern for the other person is rooted in ecclesiology and Christology. It is Christology in that to wound the brother (8:12) is to sin against Christ himself: for Christians meet Christ in the brother. It is ecclesiology in that Paul's concern is for the church as a whole, what "builds up" the temple of God.

Paul's encouragement to "build up" in love (8:1) does not refer to "one's own moral edification but to his relationship with others and thus to the community of faith as a whole."[227] The ecclesiological focus of οἰκοδομή has been well established by Philipp Vielhauer, who observes

_____

[226]Murphy-O'Connor, 564. He suggests that the shift from the singular ὁ ἀδελφός in 8:11 to the plural τοὺς ἀδελφούς in 8:12 shows a shift to the comunity focus.

[227]Furnish, *Love Command*, 113, who cites Rom 15:12 and esp. 1 Cor 14:3, 4, 5, 12, 17, as well as chapter 13.

that in Paul the word οἰκοδομή loses every "I" designation, and if the
"building up" is characterized by τῆς εἰς ἀλλήλους, then with this every
individualistic misunderstanding is expressly turned away.[228] This means
that the object of the "building up" is the church, which makes the neighbor concrete as a Christian brother.[229]

4. *Paul's Conduct as Exemplary.* It is noteworthy that in 8:13
after Paul responds to the arguments of the Corinthians he illustrates the
demand to consider the other person by reference to himself. The appeal
to Paul's conduct in 10:31-11:1 concludes the treatment of sacrificial
meat in 1 Corinthians. A fuller discussion of this motif in guiding moral
decisions is delayed until the conclusion of the present study (286-291). At
this point it is to be noted: (1) The motif of Paul's conduct occurs often in
the discussion of sacrificial meat. In addition to 8:13 and 10:31-11:1,
there is also the longer discussion of chapter 9. (2) This means the motif
has an importance beyond the two specific references in regard to sacrificial meat in 8 and 10. (3) The recurrence of the appeal to Paul's conduct
indicates the integrity of the discussion of 1 Cor 8-10.

---

[228]Vielhauer, *OIKODOME,* 99. His reference to τῆς εἰς ἀλλήλους
is to the parallel discussion in Rom 14:19.
[229]Ibid., 100.

1 CORINTHIANS 10:1-13:
WARNINGS FROM ISRAEL'S HISTORY

INTRODUCTION

A. Problems

The section 1 Corinthians 10:1-13 is related to 10:14-42 by content. Both discuss the Lord's Supper and idolatry. However, the style of 10:1-13 is very distinct from 1 Cor 8 and 9 and from 10:14ff. In 10:1-13 the discussion centers on Old Testament events which are set forth as exemplary for the Corinthians' Christian life. The interpretation of this pericope involves determining its subject and its function in the setting 1 Cor 8-10.

1. *The subject of the pericope.* The first problem of interpretation is finding the subject matter which is the focus of this section. Some scholars have seen in this passage a pattern of early Christian hermeneutics. Obviously Paul is concerned in the section with the meaning of the history of Israel for the Christian age. Yet it is highly debated whether his method is properly termed allegorical, typological, midrashic, or some other. Apart from designations such as these, is the appeal to Israel's history the focus, the main subject, of the pericope, or is the biblical interpretation in service of another purpose?

Other scholars have seen in 10:1-13 a Pauline refutation of an exaggerated sacramentalism in Corinth. The hyper-sacramentalism of the Corinthians, these scholars argue, has led to their sense of overconfidence which is manifested not only in eating sacrificial meat but in other ways as well. They are willing to have intercourse with prostitutes, they deny the resurrection, and they believe their language is that of angels. The specifics of this interpretation will be examined in this chapter, but here the question is whether this alleged sacramentalism is the focus of the passage.

A third approach sees this passage still basically concerned with the issue of idolatry, already raised in chapter 8 and continued in 10:14-11:1. The exegesis will show the value of this line of interpretation.

2. *The function of the pericope.* The second problem, closely related to the first, is deciding on the function of these verses in their present context. This question is related also to the problem of integrity. However, even some scholars who hold to the integrity of 1 Corinthians consider 10:1-13 to be something of an aside or excursus in which Paul basically leaves the topic of idol meat. Others have suggested that these verses form a transition from Paul's "apologia" in 1 Cor 9 to the resumption of the topic at hand in 10:14-11:1. Finally, these verses have been viewed as directly important for the discussion of idol meat. Like the question of the subject of these verses, the question of their function must wait for a closer exegetical examination.

B. Structure

The organization of 1 Cor 10:1-13 will be investigated more fully and argued with details in the exegesis. However, it may be useful to give a brief analysis of the passage's structure at the beginning.

This section may be divided into two major parts: 10:1-5 which sets forth an exposition of Israel's experiences and 10:6-13 where admonitions to the Corinthians are made based on these biblical precedents. The second unit, vv. 6-13, may also be divided into 6-10, specific admonitions introduced with an explanation of the relevance of these Old Testament events (v. 6). The relevance of the biblical examples is repeated (v. 11) and introduces a concluding word of both warning and promise (12, 13).[1]

C. Paul's Use of the Old Testament

This section, 1 Cor 10:1-13, has received considerable attention by scholars interested in primitive Christian hermeneutics. Much of their studies have revolved around locating categories and formal rules of interpretation.[2] For the purpose of the present study it is not necessary

---

[1]This pattern is noted by Lietzmann, *Korinther*, 47. He says this repetition in 6-10 and 11-13 is a characteristic style of Paul. He cites as similar: Rom 1:24 = 26 = 28; 5:12 = 18, 19; 5:15 = 16 = 18 = 21; 6:1 = 15.

[2]Of the many works examining 1 Cor 10:1-13 for Paul's hermeneutical approach see: Myles M. Bourke, "The Eucharist and Wisdom in First Corinthians," *Studiorum Paulinorum Congressus Internationalis Catholicus*

to decide on these technical issues about Paul's use of the Old Testament. His purpose for using these biblical stories was not to establish a typological model for Old Testament interpretation,[3] but to use these examples for hortatory remarks directed to the Corinthians. He stresses the similarity of the Old Testament event with the Corinthian situation because this fits his parenetic purposes.[4] For our purposes it is the function of Paul's use of the Exodus stories in 1 Cor 10:1-13 which is important.

1 CORINTHIANS 10:1-5:
THE EXAMPLE OF ISRAEL

The organization of this section of 1 Corinthians is easily determined. First, grammatically, 10:1-4 is a single, long period in Greek. Its relation to verse 5 is made clear with the sharp adversative ἀλλά, which begins 10:5. This shows the point of the initial description of Israel's life in the wilderness: namely that most of the people of God failed in their pilgrimage.

Another indication of the relation of 10:1-4 to 10:5 is the stylistic repetition of πάντες which occurs five times in vv. 1-4, followed by the unexpected and decisive twist of 10:5: οὐκ ἐν τοῖς πλείοσιν αὐτῶν εὐδόκησεν ὁ θεός.

The separation of 10:1-5 from 10:6ff. is suggested because in 10:6 the history of Israel is taken up explicitly as exemplary for Christians. While in 10:1-5 the situation of Israel as the people of God is documented, in 10:6 Paul begins to make explicit how the danger of Corinthian "idolatry" is similar to the sin of Israel in the Exodus.

Paul begins 10:1 with a phrase, οὐ θέλω ὑμᾶς ἀγνοεῖν, which he uses elsewhere five times (in Rom 1:13; 11:25; 1 Cor 12:1; 2 Cor 1:8 and

---

1961 (*Analecta Biblica*, 17, 18) 2, 267-81. Also Leonhard Goppelt, "Paul and Heilsgeschichte," *Int* 21 (1967) 315-26.

[3]On the category of typology see: Leonhard Goppelt, "Τύπος," *TDNT* 8 (1972) 246-60 with an extensive bibliography; Elisabeth Achtemeier, "Typology," *IDBS* (1976) 926f.
More extensive is Leonhard Goppelt, *Typos: Die typologische Deutung des Alten Testaments im Neuen* (BFTh, 2, 43; Gütersloh: Bertelsmann, 1939).

[4]Rightly, Barrett, *1 Corinthians*, 227 and Conzelmann, *1 Corinthians*, 168. Even Goppelt, "Τύπος," 251, notes that this is Paul's immediate concern.

1 Thess 4:13). This is not simply an appeal to the reasoning abilities of
the Corinthians to follow his arguments.[5] Paul uses this formula to
introduce ideas he does not expect his readers to understand previously.
This is clear in Rom 1:13; 11:26[6] (it introduces a "mystery") 2 Cor 1:8 and
1 Thess 4:13. Only in 1 Cor 12:1 might it be used differently (i.e., in
irony).

There is no way to determine how much of the Old Testament
history and writings Paul's Corinthian hearers might have known. It is
even uncertain how much Paul may have thought they knew. He certainly
uses scripture himself to illustrate and to substantiate his arguments, but
how familiar such appeals would have been to the Corinthians cannot be
known. For this reason, Conzelmann's reasonable conjecture must remain
uncertain. He says Paul's "typological" (his term) exposition shows that he
assumes the biblical material is known. "The new element which Paul has
to offer is the *interpretation* introduced by οὐ θέλω ὑμᾶς ἀγνοεῖν."[7]

Whether the new element is the scriptural account itself or Paul's
own application of that account, Paul begins with an exposition of Israel's
experiences in the Exodus. It is mildly surprising that he begins "our
fathers."[8] The use of *"our* fathers" may be a subtle way to connect the
Old Testament events with the church at Corinth.[9] Or Paul may be

---

[5]Contra Robert M. Grant, "Hellenistic Elements in 1 Corinthians,"
Early Christian Origins (ed. Allen Wikgren; Chicago: Quadrangle Books,
1961) 60f. Grant thinks an appeal to the Corinthians' rationality also is
evidenced by the use of οὐκ οἴδατε in several places and by the appeal to
"judge for yourselves" (10:15; 11:13, on 10:15 see below 273).

[6]This is somewhat obscured in Rom 11:25 by the RSV translation, "I
want you to understand."

[7]Conzelmann, *1 Corinthians*, 165. This may be true. What is clear
is Paul's own method places a high premium on the Old Testament events
and interpretation.

[8]This term is somewhat improper, strictly speaking, when addressing a basically Gentile church. Barrett, *1 Corinthians*, 220, terms it
"surprising." However, it is really consistent with other Pauline thought.
He speaks of the church as the "true Israel" (Gal 6:16, cf. Rom 11:17-21)
and of Abraham as the "father of all the faithful" (Rom 4:12-17).
Robertson and Plummer, *1 Corinthians*, 199, note that Clement of
Rome (*Cor* 60) uses τοῖς πατράσιν ἡμῶν in the same sense. This reference proves that a Gentile church could thoroughly adopt such terminology.

[9]Conzelmann, *1 Corinthians*, 165, says that it fits Paul's
typological exposition.

unconsciously connecting the history of God's people both under Moses and Christ.

Paul's examples, set forth in vv. 1-4, suggest Jewish equivalents of baptism and the Lord's Supper. However, the function of these examples is not to explain or interpret Christian rites but to warn of the possibility of God's judgment, even upon his own people.

A. Paul's Use of the Exodus Blessings

It is beyond the scope of the present study to examine the many ways Paul employs the Old Testament in his teaching.[10] In fact, in vv. 1-4 Paul may not have specific Old Testament texts in mind. His allusions to these events are general and several Old Testament passages could be considered as sources.[11] This makes it unlikely that Paul here is using an existing Jewish Exodus midrash,[12] or even that his form of biblical exposition is best termed midrash.[13]

It must be remembered that Paul does not receive the Old Testament texts uninterpreted. Many scholars have pointed to similarities

---

[10]Among other studies, see: E. Earle Ellis, *Paul's Use of the Old Testament* (Edinburgh: Oliver and Boyd, 1957) Otto Michel, *Paulus und seine Bibel (BfChTh* 18; Gütersloh: C. Bertelsmann, 1929) and Joseph Bonsirven, *Exegese rabbinique et exegese Paulinienne (Bibliotheque de theologie historique;* Paris: Beauchesne et ses fils, 1936).

A brief, helpful overview is found in Furnish, *Theology and Ethics,* 28-34.

[11]This possibility is generally overlooked in discussions of 10:1-10. Various scholars cite texts they assume Paul has in mind, but often these are different texts. Conzelmann, for example, *1 Corinthians,* 165, says the cloud comes from Exod 13:21; the sea from Exod 14:21f.; the manna from Exod 16:4, 14-18; the well from Exod 17:6; Num 20:7-13; and the apostasy from Exod 32:6. All these are possibilities but not the only ones.

[12]Considered by Barrett, *1 Corinthians,* 220, but not endorsed by him. This view is accepted, however, by Richard Longenecker, *Biblical Exegesis in the Apostolic Period* (Grand Rapids: Wm. B. Eerdmans Co., 1975) 118f.

Conzelmann, *1 Corinthians,* 165, does think that the section was composed before its use in this epistle.

[13]It is so regarded by E. E. Ellis, "How the New Testament Uses the Old," *New Testament Interpretation* (ed. I. Howard Marshall; Grand Rapids: Wm. B. Eerdmans, 1977) 207.

between Paul's words and passages in Philo and in Rabbinic writings. But the process of reinterpretation of Israel's history takes place already within the Old Testament itself. The events are interpreted when they are first written down in the books of Exodus and Numbers. Then these same events are reinterpreted by other biblical writers. For example, the manna tradition recorded in Exod 16:4, 35 is reinterpreted in Deut 8:3; the divinely provided well of Exod 17:6 (or Num 20:7-13) is interpreted by Ps 105:41 and 114:8 before either Philo or the rabbis refer to it.

Paul says in 10:6 that "these things" (those described in 10:1-5) occurred as "examples" (τύποι) for Christians. Nevertheless it is not made explicit how the events recounted in 10:1-4 are comparable to the similar ones of the Christian era. Käsemann says, "the whole trend of the passage is designed to present not mere similarity between, but the identity of, the Old and New saving events."[14] But Conzelmann disagrees,

> It should be noted that his thought moves back to the Old Testament from the present datum, baptism, and certainly does not vice versa derive and interpret baptism from the Old Testament. Paul does not seek a point-for-point correspondence. . . .[15]

In the first four verses of 1 Cor 10 Paul enumerates five experiences of the fathers in the Exodus: (1) they were all under the cloud, (2) they all passed through the sea, (3) they were all baptized into Moses, (4) they all ate the same "spiritual" food, and (5) they all drank the same spiritual drink. The first two experiences are clearly incorporated in the third, "all were baptized into Moses in the cloud and in the sea." Paul sets forth here parallels in old Israel to the Christian practice of baptism and Lord's Supper. These events are often termed "sacraments," of course,

---

[14]Ernst Käsemann, "The Pauline Doctrine of the Lord's Supper," *Essays on New Testament Themes (SBT* I, 41; London: SCM Press, 1964) 114. He continues, "Only the establishment of the identity between past and present saving events gives force to the parenesis which follows and enables the important conclusion to be drawn that even sacraments do not guarantee salvation."

This interpretation places too much stress on the (alleged) hyper-sacramentalism of the Corinthians. Moreover, it does not take sufficient account of the real focus of the passage (i.e., idolatry) nor of the very general character of the examples enumerated.

[15]Conzelmann, *1 Corinthians,* 166.

and this may be convenient for discussion purposes. However, the problematic character of "sacramental" thought in both Hellenistic religion and in 1 Cor 8-10 is frequently noted in this study and ought to be kept in mind here.

1. *Baptized into Moses (10:1, 2)*. The Old Testament clearly sees Israel's passing through the sea and the accompanying cloud as divine activity (Exod 13:21; Ps 105:39; Wis 10:17; 19:7),[16] but the Old Testament itself does not even imply that Israel was baptized into Moses. Nor is there sufficient evidence to suggest this was a view current in Judaism of Paul's day.[17] Rather, Paul moves backward from his Christian experience and *from it* interprets the Exodus events, not vice versa.[18] In fact, strictly speaking, the analogy is faulty, for Israel was not covered with water but rather passed through dry land.[19]

Accepting that Paul begins with Christian baptism and moves by analogy back to Moses best accounts for the phrase "into Moses." The expression was created to resemble the experience of Christians being baptized "into Christ" (Rom 6:3; Gal 3:27).[20]

---

[16]Lietzmann, *Korinther*, 44, thinks that Paul here refers to Exod 13:21, but Kümmel in the revision's appendix, 180, thinks that Paul has in mind Ps 105:39.

Conzelmann, *1 Corinthians*, 165, cites Midr. Exod 13:21 (30a) and 14:16 (36c) also Tg. Yer. Exod 13:20-22 for Rabbinic allusions to the crossing of the sea. Philo, *Vit. Mos.* 1.166, says that inside the cloud was "an unseen angel," a forerunner on whom the eyes of Moses were not permitted to look.

[17]In spite of the attempt by Goodenough, *Jewish Symbols*. See especially 10:135ff. where he argues that the mural from the Dura Europas synagogue shows a baptism into Moses.

[18]Conzelmann, *1 Corinthians*, 166, ". . . he is satisfied with the exemplary character of the history of Israel in one specific respect: apparently the cloud is the sign of the divine presence, and to this the Spirit in baptism corresponds." See Lietzmann, *Korinther*, 45 and Barrett, *1 Corinthians*, 221. A. Bandstra, "Interpretation of 1 Cor 10:1-11," *Calvin Theological Journal* 6 (1971) 7, rightly says, "Paul interprets the exodus events in light of what has happened in Christ in the end-time."

[19]Wendland, *Korinther*, 29.

[20]There is a textual confusion on the verb βαπτίζω. The textual readings are fairly evenly distributed between the middle voice ἐβαπτίσαντο (B K L P p46) and the passive ἐβαπτίσθησαν (ℵ A C D E F G).

Robertson and Plummer, *1 Corinthians*, 200 and Zuntz, 234, believe the change to passive is later, reflecting Christian practice being imposed

There is no reason to think that Paul believed this baptism "into Moses" was a "forerunner and type of the Messiah."[21] Nor does this baptism imply "union with Moses."[22] In spite of attempts to see Paul here as giving a "sacramental" significance to the Old Testament experiences, that is really going beyond his point.

Paul need not have consciously considered if these experiences were sacraments or only illustrations,[23] because his interest was not in the Old Testament marks of salvation themselves, but in the danger that the people of God could void their election.[24] All Israel had experienced God's saving work in the cloud and the sea, under Moses' leadership—yet ("however," ἀλλά, v. 5) most did not see the promise of their election completed.

2. *Eating spiritual food and drinking spiritual drink (10:3-4a).* Following the analogy of the sea and baptism, Paul recalls a second experience of the Exodus generation which sets forth a parallel to Christian experience. For this reason he recounts both acts, eating and drinking (probably based on Exod 16:4, 35; 17:6; Num 20:7-11, but possibly Ps 105:41 or Ps 114:8).[25]

As with the baptism into Moses, it has also been argued that Paul considers the miraculous food and drink of the Exodus as "sacraments." The reasons for seeing them as sacraments are basically two: the adjective "spiritual" (πνευματικόν)[26] before food and drink and the statement

---

on top of the Jewish method of self-immersion. But Blass-DeBrunner, § 317, favor the passive. Conzelmann, *1 Corinthians,* 164, n. 1, says that it is probable that in Paul's day the language has lost the precision of voice and one cannot determine practice from verb form. However, since the analogy is Paul's and since Israel's practice is not under discussion, the point is really moot.

[21]Käsemann, "Pauline Doctrine," 114.

[22]Robertson and Plummer, *1 Corinthians,* 200.

[23]Conzelmann, *1 Corinthians,* 165f.

[24]Rightly, Paul Neuenzeit, *Das Herrenmahl: Studien zur paulinische Eucharistieauffassung (SANT* 1; Munich: Kosel, 1960) 47, observes that the structure of Pauline typology shows that the Old Testament baptism is not being equated with Christian experience.

[25]Conzelmann, *1 Corinthians,* 166.

[26]E. G. Selwyn, *The First Epistle of St. Peter* (London: Macmillan & Co., 1946) 281ff. argues the proper translation of πνευματικός is "sacramental." He thinks the word as a religious term is of Christian coinage.

of 10:4, ἡ πέτρα ἦν ὁ Χριστός. Because these points have been prominent in the exegesis of the chapter, each must be examined more closely.
The first question is the correct interpretation to give πνευματικόν. The word has been understood to mean "food and drink which
convey πνεῦμα." Käsemann has sought to document this in Hellenistic
metaphysics, as well as in Gnostic speculation.[27] Robert Jewett sees a
realistic sacramentalism in Gnosticism as the key to the passage; the
pneumatic meal assured the Gnostic of his salvation. "The sacrament was
the 'medicine of immortality.'"[28]

A different, less "realistic" view is that the word πνευματικόν
means that God's Spirit effects a special relationship with God through
the provision of this food, yet no "spiritual substance" was conveyed in the
manna or the water. In this view, "spiritual" means coming from God's
sphere and conveying divine power as opposed to ordinary food and
drink.[29] Grosheide states this view well:

> Here "spiritual" implies that the manna and the miraculous
> water were not of the natural order of things. In Paul's
> letters all manifestations of the grace of God in this sinful
> world are spiritual (pneumatic) since they are manifestations
> of the Holy Spirit.[30]

---

[27]Käsemann, "Pauline Doctrine," 113. Käsemann thinks that it is
πνεῦμα material which is conveyed to the believer in the sacraments,
whether old or new. In this experience the believer physically receives
Christ (as Spirit) and is incorporated into his body, whether in the old or
new age. Conzelmann, 1 Corinthians, 166, n. 23, also favors a realistic
sense and based on Did 10:3 suggests that it was well-known.
Goppelt, "Πόμα," TDNT 6 (1968) 146, n. 17, says that Käsemann
"overhellenizes" the apostle's concept of πνεῦμα and in fact contradicts
Paul's own view of the role of the Old Testament community in salvation
history.
[28]Jewett, Paul's Anthropological Terms, 38f. Unlike Käsemann,
Jewett thinks that the Gnostics' understanding of the Lord's Supper led
them to reject the bodily presence of Christ in the sacrament. The differences between Jewett and Käsemann, however, in their interpretations
of the Corinthian theology are slight.
[29]Eduard Schweizer, "Πνεῦμα," TDNT 6 (1968) 437. He explicitly
rejects the view of Käsemann that the elements are bearers of πνεῦμα.
[30]Grosheide, 1 Corinthians, 220f. Similarly, Schlatter, Korintherbriefe, 121, says that the food and drink were spiritual in that they were
provided miraculously by God's creative work, and all of God's creative

132   Idol Meat in Corinth

C. K. Barrett also favors such a view, based on other Pauline uses of πνευματικός. "The word . . . is usually employed by Paul to denote something (or person) that is the bearer of the Holy Spirit (9:11; 12:1; 14:1; 15:44, 45; Rom 1:11; 7:14; 15:27)."[31] Yet in these other Pauline references it really appears that no single pattern of usage emerges. The word πνευματικός is often used in contrast to "human" (ἀνθρωπίνης, 1 Cor 2:13, 14) and "fleshy" (σάρκινος, 1 Cor 3:1; 9:11; Rom 7:14) as well as by itself. To consider the Corinthians "pneumatics" need not imply some form of Gnosticism, since Paul uses the word πνευματικός not only in criticism of the Corinthians (2:13-15; 3:1) but also of the Galatians (6:1).

A third understanding of πνευματικός, not too different from the second, sees the word to mean "miraculous" or "supernatural" food and drink.[32] It had a supernatural origin.[33] This view stresses the source of the food and drink, rather than its special qualities differing from ordinary food.[34]

A major consideration for understanding Paul's words about the food and drink provided in the wilderness is how to interpret the words in 10:4b, ἡ πέτρα δὲ ἦν ὁ Χριστός. This is important not only because the verse equates Christ and the Rock, but also because the use of πνευματικῆς to describe the rock must be considered in defining the same word in 10:3, 4 where it describes the food and drink. The repetition of πνευματικός cannot be unintended.[35]

---

work in the world happens by the Spirit.
Also see Bandstra, "Interpretation," 9f., who says that in Paul "spiritual" denotes "that which comes from God's sphere and gives divine power. . . ."
[31]Barrett, 1 Corinthians, 222. Similarly, Goppelt, "Πόμα," 146.
[32]Héring, First Epistle, 86, cites as examples Ps 17:24, 25 and the references to "bread from heaven" and "bread of angels."
[33]Robertson and Plummer, 1 Corinthians, 200, cites Ps 128:28 and Wis 16:20. They give an alternative interpretation that πνευματικόν means "allegorical," and that it prefigured the Christian communion. Barrett, 1 Corinthians, 222, also mentions this suggestion and thinks it may be present in addition to the meaning "bears the Spirit." Similarly, William F. Orr and James A. Walther, 1 Corinthians, (AB 32; Garden City: Doubleday, 1976) 245.
[34]Robertson and Plummer, 1 Corinthians, 200.
[35]Von Soden, "Sakrament und Ethik," 26, rightly says that the food and drink of 10:3, 4 are "spiritual" in the same sense as the rock mentioned immediately afterwards. They are miraculous phenomena, revela-

B. The Rock Was Christ (10:4-6)

There have been many attempts to explain Paul's words, "the Rock was Christ," by examining parallel expressions in Judaism. I note briefly some of these parallels alleged in Rabbinic writings, in Philo and in the Apocrypha.

There are several references in Rabbinic literature to the rock which provided water and the water which followed the Exodus generation. Different things are said about the rock and the well. In Targum Onkelos on Num 21:17, the well is said to have followed Moses and the people over mountains and hills, and in fact ran to the door of each tent.[36] Similar is Midrash Sifre on Num 11:21.[37]

The well was given for the merit of Miriam, Moses's sister, and hence is called "Miriam's well."[38] That such stories about the well enjoyed popular interest is probably indicated by traditions in the Christian era that the well could still be seen in the sea,[39] and that its waters were healing.[40] There is even some suggestion of the eschatological significance to the well. In Midr. Eccl. 19:1, where the topic is that the End Time will be like the first time, it is said:

> As the former redeemer made a well to rise, so will the latter redeemer bring up water, as it is stated, *and a fountain shall come forth of the house of the Lord, and shall water the valley of Shittim* (Joel 4:18).[41]

---

tory phenomena, promissory phenomena, intended to convey an event effected by God.

[36] J. W. Etheridge, *The Targums of Onkelos* (New York: KTAV reprint, 1968) 142f. This reference is taken from Longenecker, 119.

[37] See also b. Sabb. 35a, where it is called a movable well. See also Midr. Num. Rab. 19:25f. Ellis, *Paul's Use of the Old Testament*, 66f., gives several Rabbinic references.

[38] b. Sabb. 35a; b. Ta'an 9a (thus when Miriam died the well disappeared). According to Midr. Exod. Rab. 25:7 Israel was permitted to drink from the well because they had accepted God's statutes and ordinances.

[39] b. Sabb. 35a.

[40] Midr. Eccl. Rab., 5:85. The same stories are found in Midr. Lev. Rab. 22:4; Midr. Num. Rab. 18:22. In each passage it is called Miriam's well.

[41] Midr. Eccl. Rab., 1:9. Also pertinent is what precedes this citation: "As the former redeemer caused manna to descend, as it is stated, Behold I will cause to rain bread from heaven for you (Exod 16:4)

Philo himself certainly was not a source of Paul's ideas about the rock and the travelling well. Nevertheless, several scholars have suggested that the Hellenistic Judaism which Philo stands within and illustrates may have provided important precedents for Paul.[42]

Bandstra has examined thoroughly the allusions in Philo which seem to be parallel to Paul's words. He says Philo identified the rock with the wisdom of God (*Quod det. pot.* 115f) and also says this wisdom is a fountain, or manna, which is the divine word (λόγον θεῖον).[43] Philo identifies the well of Num 21:16 with wisdom.[44]

From these references which equate the rock, the well, and manna with the wisdom of God, Bandstra feels it is only a small step to equating the rock and the well with Christ, "the wisdom of God." The pre-existent Christ was "as much the source of the spiritual food and drink of the

---

so will the latter redeemer cause manna to descend, as it is stated, May he be as a rich cornfield in the land (Ps 72:16)." bPesha. 54a says the well and the manna are two of the ten things which God created on the eve of the first Sabbath. This could be indicative of an eschatological significance to the manna and the well.

Other rabbinic references are found in Hermann L. Strack and Paul Billerbeck, *Kommentar zum Neuen Testament aus Talmud und Midrasch* (3d; München: Beck, 1924ff.) 3.400f.

[42]For example, Barrett, *1 Corinthians*, 223, says, "In Philo's allegorical interpretation of the law, the miraculous food and drink (or source of drink) are taken to mean the word and wisdom of God, which themselves are at least partially hypostatized beings. By adapting these identifications Paul interprets Christ in terms of the wisdom of Hellenistic Judaism."

[43]Philo, *Det. Pot. Ins.* 115-118. Cp. *Leg. All.* 2.86. Referring to God's presence in the wilderness (understood as an allegory of the soul's journey) Philo says: "For the flinty rock is the wisdom of God, which he marks off highest and chiefest from his powers, and from which are satisfied the thirsty souls that love God. And when they have been given water to drink, they are also filled with the manna [interpreted as the word of God]."

[44]*Som.* 2:271 and *Sobr.* 112. In both cases the reference is to the singing at the well (Num 21:17) and the well in response swelling up. In *Somniis* the application is made that, like the well, knowledge is deep and often hidden, but when found waters the field of reason. See also *Rer. Div. Her.* 205.

Israelites as he is the one present in the Lord's Supper at Corinth (1 Cor 10:16-21; 11:17-34)."[45]

E. R. Goodenough, like Bandstra, emphasizes the references in Philo as examples of a Hellenistic Judaism which in turn did influence Paul. He thinks that Philo not only has his allegorical interpretations, but a real cultus, in which a sacramental understanding has been formed under the influence of pagan mysticism.[46]

In addition to Philo, Goodenough insists that additional evidence for influence of Hellenistic Judaism which developed images used by Paul can be found in the murals from the Dura synagogue. The center panel on the west wall of the Dura synagogue shows a beehive-shaped rock pouring forth water like a fountain with streams running to the tents of Israel.[47] Goodenough thinks that this mural illustrates Philo's thought of Wisdom as the source of water = grace.[48] This shows that Philo's ideas are not unique curiosities held only by him.

This may be so, although the mural does not, perhaps could not, equate the Rock with the divine σοφία or λόγος as does Philo. Goodenough says in summary, "Behind the verses in 1 Corinthians lies a hellenistic Jewish tradition which Paul has Christianized only by making the rock and its flow not sophia or the logos, but Christ."[49]

Since both Philo and certain Jewish wisdom writings come from Hellenistic Judaism, they are not competing examples, but complementary.[50] Philo really inherits a Jewish wisdom-speculation and develops

---

[45]Bandstra, "Interpretation," 14. He thinks that Paul means to say "Christ himself, the pre-existent Christ, was present with the Israelites in their wilderness journey." He cites as confirmatory 1 Cor 8:6, where Christ, like Wisdom, is the mediator of creation.

[46]Goodenough, *Jewish Symbols*, 6.197-217, summarizes the Philonic evidence. Hans Dieter Betz, "The Mithras Inscriptions of Santa Prisca and the New Testament," *NT* 10 (1968) 66f., says both Paul and Philo are influenced by mystery cult ideas here.

[47]This panel is reproduced in Goodenough, *Jewish Symbols*, 11, plate 12. A similar description of the rock is Midr. Num. Rab. 1:2.

[48]Goodenough, *Jewish Symbols*, 10.134f.; 12:171.

[49]E. R. Goodenough and A. T. Kraabel, "Paul and the Hellenization of Christianity," *Religions in Antiquity*, ed. Jacob Neusner, (*Supplements to Numen*, 14; Leiden: E. J. Brill, 1968) 59.

[50]Thus many commentators cite both Philo and Wisdom as parallel to Paul's illustration about the rock and water. See Robertson and Plummer, *1 Corinthians*, 201, citing Wis 11:4 and Philo *Det. Pot. Ins.* 116f. Similarly, Knox, *Church of the Gentiles*, 122f.

it. Some writers have stressed the wisdom literature, rather than Philo, in interpreting Paul's description of Christ as the rock.[51]

Bourke thinks *Wisdom* shows that before Philo and Paul a connection had already been made between the wisdom of God and the miraculous provisions of the Exodus. He finds this in Wis 10:17 and 11:4, as well as Sir 15:3, "She [wisdom] will feed him [the man who fears the Lord] with the bread of understanding and give him the water of wisdom to drink." (See also Sir 24:15-21.)[52] Bourke sees Philo, *Leg. alleg.* 2.86 and 1 Cor 11:1-4 as independent interpreters of this wisdom idea.[53] He even thinks that Paul has a literary dependence on Wisdom.[54]

1. *Paul's development of existing ideas.* Only in the case of the wisdom literature can one argue reasonably that Paul was in direct dependence on a known, written, post-biblical source. The Rabbinic haggadah has some similar expressions; however, they cannot be dated securely in Paul's time.[55] Of course, the Rabbinic arguments themselves may have been available to Paul in oral form. Certainly there are Old Testament passages which provide suggestive parallels.[56]

----

[51]See, among others, Bourke, "Eucharist and Wisdom," 367-381.

[52]Ibid., 377. Bourke thinks that the idea of "rock" is a Pauline adaptation of the Old Testament terminology which applied to YHWH the designation rock or stone.

[53]Ibid., 367f. He finds especially important the passages which speak of Wisdom as the means of God's creating work. The move then to Christ as the creating agent is a short step (2 Cor 5:17; Gal 6:15; 1 Cor 8:6). He cites, page 371, the pre-Pauline hymn in Col 1:15 to prove the equation was made early in Christian thought.

Additional support for a wisdom background is found in Paul's designation of Christ as the "wisdom of God" (1 Cor 1:17-2:5) and that designation in turn leads to identifying acts of wisdom and the work of Christ.

Knox, *Church of the Gentiles*, 122f., suggests that these concepts were mediated to Paul through Hellenistic synagogues.

[54]Bourke, "Eucharist and Wisdom," 172.

[55]Bandstra, "Interpretation," 11, who notes also that in the Rabbinic discussions the rock is associated with water, not both food and drink as in Paul.

[56]E. E. Ellis, "A Note on First Corinthians 10:4," *JBL* 56 (1957) 55f. cites Pss 77:20; 104:41; 113:8 and Isa 48:21 as likely sources for Paul's exposition (and Rabbinic as well). He thinks especially striking the phrase "spiritual following rock." Ellis explicitly doubts influences from Rabbinic ideas.

In view of these very different attempts to explain Paul's words by parallels in other writings, one is encouraged to try another path. A better approach is to see Paul (and wisdom, and Philo, and the Rabbis) as working in a general way with traditional legends in Judaism.[57] The Rabbinic, Philonic, and even the Wisdom traditions then serve to illustrate these legends, but none are the "origin" of Paul's thoughts in a concrete way.

Cullmann has rightly noted the development of the Rock legend and the miracle of the well in numerous Old Testament passages (Deut 8:15; 32:13; Isa 48:21; Neh 9:15; Job 29:6; Pss 78:15-20; 81:16; 105:41; 114:18, in addition to the Exodus references).[58] Thus already within the Old Testament the rock has a special exemplary importance as part of God's work.

It is not possible to determine which single biblical passage, or even a series of passages,[59] was crucial for Paul's exposition.[60] Paul, unlike the rabbinic materials, does not quote the passage he is using (with the exception of Exod 32:6). His method indicates he is thinking of the story itself, contained in several passages. Paul is primarily interested in the thought as a whole.[61]

Moreover, it is neither necessary nor wise to restrict Paul to reflection on Old Testament texts (even including those of Wisdom). The

---

[57] Geza Vermes, *Scripture and Tradition in Judaism (Studia Post Biblica* 4; Leiden: E. J. Brill, 1961) is a suggestive study that shows how haggadah cannot be isolated to Rabbinic literature but is found in various Jewish and Christian sources, beginning with the Old Testament itself, but including the apocrypha, writings from Qumran, Philo and even Josephus.

[58] Oscar Cullmann, "Πέτρα," *TDNT* 6 (1968) 97.

[59] Ellis, *Paul's Use of the Old Testament,* 69f., says Pss 77:20, 105:41; 113:8 and Isa 48:21 LXX particularly influenced Paul and the Rabbinic writers.

[60] Bandstra, "Interpretation," 13, thinks Deut 32 "may well have been in Paul's mind." Of course it may, or other passages may, or many may. Robertson and Plummer, *1 Corinthians,* rightly observe, "The origin of the allusion is interesting, but not of great importance."

[61] Martin Dibelius, *Die Geisterwelt im Glauben des Paulus* (Göttingen: Vandenhoeck & Ruprecht, 1909) 44, conjectures that this method may be the reason for the discrepancy in the number of those slain (24,000 in the Old Testament and 23,000 in 1 Cor 10).

number and variety of expositions about the rock and the well in Rabbinic
literature, wisdom literature, Philo and elsewhere (e.g., Ps-Philo, *Biblical
Antiquities* 10:7) indicate that this topic was "in the air." Paul's exposition stands within a tradition of haggadic and homiletic development.[62]

2. *How was Christ the rock?* With such disagreement on the
sources of Paul's account of the manna and the well, it is not surprising
that there is also disagreement on how he intends to equate Christ and the
rock in 10:4b. It seems clear that Paul uses the manna and the well in
conscious parallel to the Christian communion. Does he then intend ἡ
πέτρα ἦν ὁ Χριστός to be understood "realistically" (so that the Rock in
Moses's day was really Christ) or "symbolically" (the rock stands for
Christ)? Many contemporary interpreters favor the former view.

Lietzmann says that Paul is seeking to show the Rock of Horeb was
nothing other than the pre-existent Christ himself.[63] Similarly, Conzelmann thinks Paul's words "mean real pre-existence, not merely symbolic
significance."[64] Hanson, too, says "Paul here means that the rock really
was Christ," and he finds this confirmed by the verb choice, ἦν.[65] But no
one is more emphatic about the realism of the equation than Ernst Käsemann, who insists Paul's whole argument of 10:1-13 stands or falls on "the
establishment of the identity between past and present saving events."[66]

However, others do not favor a realistic equation of Christ and the
rock, but rather see these as parallel, not identical, experiences.
Barrett[67] and Walter[68] see the common feature in that the same God's
saving activity was manifested both in Moses's day and in the Christian
era. Others say that the equation was typological: as the spiritual water
and food symbolized the Lord's Supper, so the rock symbolized Christ

---

[62]Conzelmann, *1 Corinthians*, 166f., Ellis, "Note on 1 Cor 10," 54.
Both note how hard it is to isolate the various facets of the legend in the
first century.

[63]Lietzmann, *Korinther*, 44f.

[64]Conzelmann, *1 Corinthians*, 166f., feels that this is clear because
Paul is giving Christ the role in the Exodus events which Jewish traditions
had accorded wisdom.

[65]R. P. C. Hanson, *Allegory and Event* (Richmond: John Knox,
1959) 79. Similarly, Robertson and Plummer, *1 Corinthians*, 201, think the
ἦν shows Paul is thinking of a real event.

[66]Käsemann, "Pauline Doctrine," 114.

[67]Barrett, *1 Corinthians*, 222.

[68]Walter, "Christusglaube," 431.

himself.[69] Cullmann denies Paul directly equates the rock with Christ
(neither, he says, does Philo directly equate the Logos with the rock), "as
though the latter took the form of the rock." But it is the same Christ,
acting in saving history, who is behind both the Old and New saving
events.[70]

One reason for the debate whether Paul means "the rock was
Christ" to be understood realistically or symbolically is that the answer to
this question is vitally related to locating the *subject* of 10:1-13 and its
function in 1 Cor 8-10.

Most of those who insist on a "realistic" (to use perhaps meaningful, although anachronistic, terminology) view think that Paul here is
arguing with the Corinthians over their incorrect sacramentalism. It is
argued by von Soden[71] and Käsemann[72] that the Corinthian "gnostics" see
participation in the Lord's Supper as a magical protection against any
possibility of losing God's favor. The Spirit, who is conveyed to believers
in the sacrament (this is the meaning of πνευματικόν), is a means and
insurance of their state as "spiritual men." The Ignatian phrase "medicine
of immortality" is borrowed to describe the sacramentalism of the Corinthians.[73]

The argument proceeds: Paul is opposing the thoroughgoing sacramentalism of the Corinthian enthusiasts by appealing to the example of
the fathers in the wilderness who also had "baptism" and "communion" yet
who were lost. Paul must prove Israel's sacraments were no less powerful
than the Christian ones to insure the Corinthians see that they too are in
danger (lest the Corinthians reply, "Certainly they were lost, their sacraments were not as strong as ours"). For this reason Paul develops the

---

[69]Bourke, "Eucharist and Wisdom," 373, "the entire passage is
typological, pointing to the Christian reality, and there is no reason to
suppose that Paul departed from the typological sense of the whole when
he called the rock 'Christ.'" Similarly, Neuenzeit, *Herrenmahl*, 52, and
Wendland, *Korinther*, 79.

[70]Cullmann, "Πέτρα," 97.

[71]Von Soden, "Sakrament und Ethik."

[72]Käsemann, "Pauline Doctrine," 113-119, is the most emphatic
treatment of this "sacramentalist" view of the Corinthian enthusiasts.
However, similar if less thoroughgoing positions are taken by: Wendland,
Korinther, 78; Conzelmann, *1 Corinthians*, 166, n. 23; and Günther Born-
kamm, "Lord's Supper and Church in Paul," *Early Christian Experience*
(New York: Harper and Row, 1969) 127-30.

[73]Supra, 131.

discussion of 1-4 by describing the food and drink in the wilderness as "spiritual" and even equates Christ and the rock. Paul insists Israel's sacraments were as powerful as the Christian ones; indeed, they are identical.[74]

In spite of the coherent features of this very popular reconstruction, it does have serious difficulties. (1) A major difficulty is the common identification of the Corinthians as gnostics or proto-gnostics. A full critique of the gnostic hypothesis in interpreting Corinthian theology is outside the limits of the present study. However, it has been observed elsewhere that the hypothesis, often treated as proven, of gnosticism at Corinth is very debatable.[75]

(2) Moreover, even if one grants the identification of certain Corinthians as gnostics, it remains questionable whether they had a highly sacramental view of the Lord's Supper, which Paul is criticizing here. That the Corinthians were "sacramentalists" is strongly denied by Walter Schmithals, the most vigorous proponent of a prominent gnostic movement in Corinth.[76] Schmithals is particularly refuting the "sacramentalism" thesis as developed by Bornkamm,[77] but he also mentions and rejects similar presentations by von Soden and Käsemann.[78]

(3) Although there is some uncertainty about the meaning of the words τύπος and τυπικῶς,[79] their use here by Paul to describe his argument from the Exodus tradition is best taken to mean "exemplary" or even "prefiguring," but not "identically." It is true that Paul sees a real similarity in the Exodus events and Christian practices, but he does not equate

---

[74]Käsemann, "Pauline Doctrine," 114.

[75]On the question of gnosticism at Corinth see supra, 72f.

[76]Schmithals, *Gnosticism*, 393-95. These few pages are a trenchant critique of the "sacramental-enthusiasm" hypothesis. One cannot simply insist that a presumption of security must rest on a heightened sacramentalism. The Old Testament history, on which Paul calls in these verses, often complains of Israel's presumption of God's gracious favor. A classic statement from the Old Testament is Jeremiah's complaint of Israelites who chant "This is the temple of the Lord" (Jer 7:4) to prove their security.

Yet surely Israel's presumption and (mistaken) sense of overconfidence cannot be termed "gnostic." Religious presumption is possible on many grounds.

[77]Bornkamm, "Lord's Supper and Church," 123-60.

[78]Von Soden, "Sakrament und Ethik," and Käsemann, "Pauline Doctrine."

[79]Supra, 128f. Also Goppelt, "Πόμα," 146.

them. The use of the words τύπος and τυπικῶς cannot be used to justify equating Christ and the rock, at least not in a way which suggests that the rock had the same signficance for Israel as Christ does for the new Israel.

(4) Paul's description of the wilderness food and drink as πνευματικός does not require one to believe that he saw these elements as realistic sacraments. As noted above, πνευματικός only means "coming from God; wrought by the Spirit."[80] This terminology may well have been drawn from descriptions of the Christian eucharist.[81] Just as in the "baptism" of Moses, so also in the wilderness provisions, Paul begins with the Christian experience and then moves back to interpret the Old Testament experiences.[82]

(5) Finally, the context of 1 Cor 8-10 (especially what follows in 10:14-11:1) and the specific interpretation which Paul gives in 10:6-11 show that the concern of his argument is not sacramentalism (either to refute a Corinthian understanding or to set forth his own view), but the danger of idolatry. Just as it is a mistake to see 10:16, 17 as Paul's "doctrine" of the Lord's Supper (although surely aspects of his eucharistic understandings are implied),[83] so too it is wrong to see 10:1-4 as designed to set forth a correction of the Corinthian sacrament. The reshaped haggadic elements of 10:1-11 are employed in warning the Corinthians that their involvement in idolatry may cost them God's pleasure and bring subsequent loss of salvation. This is made explicit in 10:14 where Paul draws the conclusion of his argument in 10:1-13, "Therefore, flee idolatry!"[84]

---

[80]Bandstra, "Interpretation," 9f., Conzelmann, 1 Corinthians, 166, n. 23. Goppelt, "Πόμα," 146, even suggests that the designation πνευματικός reflects the designation of the Lord's Supper used in the Pauline congregations. Both Conzelmann and Goppelt cite Did 10:3 as showing such a designation was otherwise known in early Christianity.

[81]Wendland, Korinther, 79, says that the expressions "spiritual food" and "spiritual drink" are modeled upon the Lord's Supper.

[82]Bourke, "Eucharist and Wisdom," 373, insightfully cites as supporting an approach of reading the Old Testament events through the Christian fulfillment Paul's own words in 2 Cor 3:4-18. He also suggests that 2 Cor 3:17, ὁ δὲ κύριος τὸ πνεῦμα ἐστίν, is analogous to Paul's terming the manna and the water from the rock πνευματικόν.

[83]See 205-209 in the present study.

[84]Orr and Walther, I Corinthians, 244, divide the chapter at 10:15. While this is not convincing, it does point out that 10:14 is closely related to 10:1-13. One of the great disadvantages of dealing with these chapters as separate units (i.e., 8; 10:1-13; 10:14-22 and 10:23-11:1) as is done of

Adolf Schlatter gives a good summary evaluation of 10:1-4. He says that the example of the Exodus people of God shows that they too received God's acts of salvation and were redeemed, but they did not reach their goal. Just so the church has seen and experienced the sending of Christ, his resurrection, but they are still "on the way."[85]

C. Their Tragic Fate (10:5)

Paul's conclusion about the Exodus generation's experiences is abrupt and unexpected. "But with the most of them, God was not pleased" (ἀλλ' οὐκ ἐν τοῖς πλείοσιν αὐτῶν εὐδόκησεν ὁ θεός). The severity of God's displeasure is graphically depicted, "for they were strewn about in the desert."[86]

The poignant understatement, οὐκ ἐν τοῖς πλείοσιν αὐτῶν, was set up by the repetition (five times) of πάντες in vv.1-4. Paul makes this theological point with this stylistic method.[87] All the host received the divine blessing of deliverance and sustenance, but few were saved. (If, indeed, the Corinthians knew the Old Testament story, the analogy is even more striking, because the "few" were, in fact, two!)[88]

---

necessity in commentaries, is that one may subconsciously fail to appreciate their interrelatedness.

Conzelmann, *1 Corinthians*, 165, however, describes 10:1-13 as "a self-contained scribal discourse" which "appears to be totally foreign to its context." He also, 170, explicitly denies a serious connection with 10:14, saying "Formally speaking, the movement of thought is loose." Yet Paul (if one accepts the integrity of the letter) explicitly links the warning of v. 14 (Διόπερ) with what precedes.

[85]Schlatter, *Korintherbriefe*, 120.

[86]Robertson and Plummer, *1 Corinthians*, 202.

[87]Generally noted, e.g., Conzelmann, *1 Corinthians*, 165, 167; Robertson and Plummer, *1 Corinthians*, 199. Héring, *First Epistle*, 86, suggests that the pronoun τὸ αὐτό which preceded βρῶμα and πόμα in 10:3, 4 is also a stylistic way to stress the universal experience of all the wilderness generation (both the rejected majority and the saved minority).

Moule, *Idiom Book*, 108, notes that πολλοί here in the comparative degree simply means "the majority." Similarly, Blass-Debrunner, § 244(3).

[88]Robertson and Plummer, *1 Corinthians*, 202. They also note that the contrast here between the many who are lost and the two who are saved is analogous to Paul's description of his striving in 9:27f. Grosheide, *1 Corinthians*, 222, rightly notes that Paul is not concerned here about the personal salvation of either the Exodus generation or the Corinthians.

The reference to God's displeasure (οὐκ εὐδόκησεν) is not to a divine unhappiness but to the forfeiture of election. It is expressly the withdrawal of the election of most of the people.[89] The evidence of this loss is then given (γάρ),[90] "for" they were destroyed in the desert.

I CORINTHIANS 10:6-10:
THE WARNING IS FOR US

Although Paul continues his appeal to the fate of Israel and its significance for the Corinthians, a shift in the argument is clear at v. 6. Paul moves to direct, rather than indirect, application both in form (now using hortatory subjunctives and imperatives) and by designation of these events as "examples" (τύποι) for Christians. 10:6-10 is a more detailed elaboration of how Israel's experiences are exemplary.[91] The transgressions enumerated in vv. 7-10 are stylistically framed by vv. 6 and 11 which designate these as typical.[92]

Although some have considered "craving evil things" as the first in a list of sins at Corinth,[93] it should be regarded as a general complaint, which is then specified in the four warnings which follow (idolatry, fornication, testing the Lord, and grumbling).[94] However, the distinction

---

The horizon is the corporate people of God.

[89]G. Schrenk, "Εὐδοκέω," TDNT 2, 740f. Also Conzelmann, 1 Corinthians, 167. This is normally the meaning of εὐδοκέω in Paul when God is the subject. See 1 Cor 1:21; Phil 2:13; and especially Gal 1:15.

[90]Robertson and Plummer, 1 Corinthians, 202, note: "The γάρ introduced a justification of the previous statement. God cannot have been well pleased with them, for κατέστρωσεν αὐτοὺς ἐν τῇ ἐρήμῳ (Num 14:16)." It should be noted that this original wording in Numbers is somewhat sharper, for the active verb makes clear that God slew them in the desert.

[91]Lietzmann, Korinther, 47; Bandstra, "Interpretation," 14f. Harold Sahlin, "The New Exodus of Salvation According to St. Paul," The Root of the Vine (ed. Anton Fridrichsen; New York: Philosophical Library, 1953) 84, notes that the Passover rite in Judaism emphasized the contemporary relevance of the past salvation.

[92]Walter, "Christusglaube," 431.

[93]Thrall, 1 Corinthians, 74; Héring, First Epistle, 90f. and (apparently) Schlatter, Korintherbriefe, 122.

[94]Barrett, 1 Corinthians, 244; Conzelmann, 1 Corinthians, 167; Robertson and Plummer, 1 Corinthians, 203, say ἐπιθυμία κακῶν is the genus and the sins of 10:7-10 are the species.

between genus and species is not crucial, for we will see that the four sins which illustrate "craving evil things" are general too, not a catalogue of specific problems in Corinth.

A. Desiring Evil Things

"Desiring evil" (ἐπιθυμητὰς κακῶν) may come from the example of Israel's rebellion in Numbers 11:4-34; although the phrase itself does not occur there, the idea is present.[95] Moreover, the events recorded in Numbers do suggest some comparison, not only regarding the "craving" but also regarding eating and God's angry punishment. Yet here also Paul may only have drawn on the Old Testament in a general way and one need not seek to locate a specific biblical text.

More important for interpreting the passage are the other Pauline uses of ἐπιθυμία. Although Paul can use this term in a positive sense (e.g., 1 Thess 2:17), he characteristically is negative about "desiring." Three passages which refer to ἐπιθυμία are especially important: Rom 7:7ff.; 13:8-10; Gal 5:16-24.

In Romans 7:7 Paul encapsulates the purpose of the Mosaic law by saying it was to expose "coveting." He selects as representative (or perhaps inclusive) of the commandments the prohibition, "Thou shalt not covet." This is stated generally, for it does not have a direct object stating what is coveted.[96] The general character of this prohibition is also clear from 7:8, where sin is said to bring about "all kinds of covetousness" (πᾶσαν ἐπιθυμίαν).

Paul similarly interprets the intent of the law in Rom 13:9-10. Here he lists four specific prohibitions (adultery, murder, theft and coveting) and concludes summarily, "and other commandments." Again, coveting is without an object. These commandments are not intended to be ranked or to be exhaustive (as if other commands were less important for Christians), but only to illustrate life which is not acceptable to God. Set

---

[95]Several commentators point to Num 11:4-6. For example, Héring, *First Epistle*, 90. Also see Friedrich Büchsel, "θυμός," *TDNT* 3 (1965) 171.

[96]Exod 20:17 and Deut 5:21, which Paul probably has in mind, go on to specify prohibited objects. Conzelmann, *1 Corinthians*, 167, n. 32, points to the connection of 1 Cor 10:6 and Rom 7:7. Büchsel, 169f., notes in the LXX too, ἐπιθυμία is used without a direct object to mean "sin." He also notes, 173, that 4 Macc 2:6 describes the will of God as "not desiring," similar to Rom 7:7 and 13:9.

in contrast to these is that which God requires, "love one another."[97]
Commenting on 1 Cor 10:6ff., von Soden rightly observes that ἐπιθυμία is
the opposite of ἀγάπη both for Israel and for the Corinthians.[98]

In Gal 5:16-24 another important reference to "coveting" is found.
Paul contrasts walking by the Spirit (Gal 5:16, cf. 25) with the "desires of
the flesh" (5:16f.). The ἐπιθυμία of the flesh stands for all that opposes
God and his Spirit. This ἐπιθυμίαν σαρκός is manifest in particular deeds
(τὰ ἔργα τῆς σαρκός) among which are πορνεία and εἰδωλολατρίας (both
found in 1 Cor 10:6-10). Those who belong to Christ (should) have
crucified the flesh and with it its ἐπιθυμία.[99] It should be noted that in
Gal 5:25. 26 which follows this general statement Paul also uses hortatory
subjunctives seeking particular conduct from the Galatians (structurally
similar to 1 Cor 10:6-10).

From this brief examination of Paul's other discussions of ἐπιθυμία
four implications are found for understanding 1 Cor 10:6. First, the other
Pauline references suggest that ἐπιθυμία is a cover term for all rebellion
against God which may be manifested in many varied ways. This is seen
in the absence of direct objects for "to covet," and also in the clustering
of offenses around the reference to "craving" (Rom 13:8-10; Gal 5:16ff.).

Second, these varied sins (or to use Paul's term, "works of the
flesh") suggest that not all the sins enumerated must be thought to have
been prominent among his readers. One need not think that the Romans
were especially troubled with adultery, theft and killing. In fact, the one
specific demand Paul gives in Rom 13:8-10 is "love the neighbor," and that
too is not a single issue. Nor must one think the Galatians were particularly involved in the list of vices in 5:19-21.[100] In relation to 1 Cor 10:6-

---

[97]On this verse and its importance in understanding Paul's inter-
pretation of the command to love the neighbor, see Furnish, *Love
Command*, 108ff. See also C. E. B. Cranfield, *The Epistle to the Romans*
(ICC; Edinburgh: T. & T. Clark, 1979) 2.676f.

[98]Von Soden, "Sakrament und Ethik," 8.

[99]Also in Rom 1:24 where Paul gives the results of the pagan
world's idolatry which has become "void in reasoning" (1:21) and then
exchanged the glory of God for idols (1:23). He concludes, διὸ παρέδωκεν
αὐτοὺς ὁ θεὸς ἐν ταῖς ἐπιθυμίαις τῶν καρδιῶν αὐτῶν. Here in Rom 1
also, ἐπιθυμία is used in a general way, and it also is related to the problem of idolatry.

[100]Noted by Furnish, *Love Command*, 99, who says that these
verses give "some practical and timely implications." The implications
continue in chapter 6. He does not relate Gal 5 and 6 to 1 Cor 10.

10 this observation suggests that the four sins listed in 7-10 need not have been prominent at Corinth (as if one should think Paul knew of occasions there of "testing the Lord" or "murmuring").[101]

Third, two sins do occur in other discussions of ἐπιθυμία which are also known to be problems at Corinth: εἰδωλολατρία and πορνεία. These sins are found in the Galatian "vice list" and in Rom 1:24ff., in Paul's description of pagan sins which flow from rebellion. It is possible that the connection of πορνεία and εἰδωλολατρία in 10:7, 8 does arise from concrete problems in Corinth.[102] But equally the connection may come from a common Jewish religious polemic,[103] or these two sins may simply be general examples of sins which result from "desiring."[104]

Fourth, the consistent factor which appears in these verses explicitly and also relates to the context of chapters 8 and 10 is really idolatry. Moreover, when Paul summarizes the import of this discussion of the Old Testament the warning is about idolatry; Διόπερ . . . φεύγετε ἀπὸ τῆς εἰδωλολατρίας (10:14). Therefore Paul's real concern in the whole discussion of 10:1-10 is the problem of idolatry, other sins are incidental.

---

[101]Ibid., 98. His discussion of "vice lists" and their function in Paul's letters is important. Furnish, *Theology and Ethics,* 84ff.

On the character of Paul's vice lists, see also Enslin, *Ethics of Paul,* 161f. Siegfried Wibbing, *Die Tugend- und Lasterkataloge im Neuen Testament* (BZNW 25; Berlin: A. Töpelmann, 1959) 81ff.

[102]Schlatter, *Korintherbriefe,* 122, suggests for example the lust for the old life of idol worship and intercourse with the prostitutes always available in pagan cities. Similarly, Wendland, *Korinther,* 79; Jewett, *Paul's Anthropological Terms,* 258.

[103]See especially Barrett, "Things Sacrificed," 138-53. Note that in 1 Cor 12:2 the phrase "dumb idols" which recalls a Jewish polemic against pagan gods as being mute, cf. Wis 13:10ff. Similarly 1 Cor 10:19 describes the idols as "nothings," another idea suggested in Jewish apologetics.

[104]A connection between πορνεία and ἐπιθυμία also occurs in 1 Thess 5:1-8. This too is a general parenesis, but not therefore simply rhetoric. See Furnish, *Theology and Ethics,* 85f.

B. Four Examples of Desiring Evil Things

The four examples of ἐπιθυμία κακῶν in 10:7-10 are set forth in a very stylized way:

μηδὲ εἰδωλολάτρια γίνεσθε,   καθώς τινες αὐτῶν
μηδὲ πορνεύωμεν   καθώς τινες αὐτῶν
μηδὲ ἐκπειράζωμεν τὸν κύριον[105]   καθώς τινες αὐτῶν
μηδὲ γογγύζετε[106]   καθώς τινες αὐτῶν

These admonitions vary in an A-B-B-A pattern between imperative and subjunctive. This pattern, and the formulaic μηδέ + verb, balanced by καθώς τινες αὐτῶν[107] shows a rhetorical concern, which agrees with the assessment of these enumerated sins as conventional, not concrete.

1. *Do not be idolators.* Paul's first example of ἐπιθυμία and the one most important or Corinth, since it is the primary concern of this exposition, is εἰδωλολατρία. Although the example comes from the Exodus experience, the idolatry that Paul really is concerned about at Corinth is that which results from the community's involvement with pagan cult meals. This Paul goes on to discuss in 10:14-22.[108]

---

[105]The textual tradition varies here. Evidence is rather evenly divided between τὸν κύριον and τὸν Χριστόν as objects of ἐκπειράζωμεν. See Zuntz, 126f.

[106]Although some good textual basis is available for γογγύζωμεν rather than γογγύζετε the stronger evidence favors the imperative and thus the A-B-B-A pattern.

[107]It has been suggested that the fourfold τινες αὐτῶν is a way to say "some" of the Exodus generation perished in each of four punishments, rather than all at once. Dibelius, *Geisterwelt*, 43f. Grosheide, *1 Corinthians*, 223, suggests that the "some" is to convey that just as not all Israelites worshipped the golden calf, so not all the Corinthians ate in idol shrines. Note that the repetition of τινες balances stylistically the repetition of πάντες in 10:2-4.

[108]Robertson and Plummer, *1 Corinthians*, 203, say that εἰδωλολατρία is "the most important of the special instances, because of its close connexion with the Corinthian question." Paul is warning the strong (cf. 8:10) that their sitting in an εἰδωλείῳ does amount to taking part in idolatrous rites, and "the danger of actual idolatry is not so imaginary as the Corinthians in their enlightened emancipation supposed."

Most commentators note the special relevance of 10:7 to the Corinthian church. Grosheide, *1 Corinthians*, 219, is unique in thinking

The Old Testament support which Paul cites against idolatry is a specific passage, in contrast to the other references here which are allusions. He quotes Exod 32:6 in substantial agreement with the LXX.[109] This is an appropriate citation because it does involve idolatry (the golden calf) and sacrifice (the people offered burnt offerings and brought peace offerings). Their worship and subsequent meal together constituted idolatry.[110] This is precisely the situation at Corinth for those who partake of pagan worship and meals.[111]

The relevance of the words φαγεῖν καὶ πεῖν from the LXX, Exod 32:6, is obvious. They recall participation in cult meals which the Corinthians have claimed is harmless. But the words ἀνέστησαν παίζειν are more difficult.[112] Some Rabbinic interpreters suggest that the word "play" (צחק) in Exod 32:6 means idolatry and/or erotic dancing. The connection between idol worship, dance and sexual play was real in some pagan religions and was of special concern to Jewish writers.[113]

---

that this verse is addressed to the "weak" urging them not to follow the lead of the strong and participate in such meals. For the weak it will be idolatrous, since they think it is.

[109] The LXX has πιεῖν rather than πεῖν.

[110] H. W. Bartsch, "Der korinthische Missbrauch des Abendsmahls," *Entmythologisierende Auslegung* (Theologische Forschung 26; Hamburg-Bergstadt: H. Reich, 1962) 174, suggests that Paul cites this verse rather than many other Old Testament passages about idolatry precisely for its connection of "eating and drinking" with "idolatry." Similarly, Wendland, *Korinther*, 80.

Bandstra, "Interpretation," suggests that Paul here assumes the Old Testament story is known because idols are not mentioned in the quotation. He concludes that here at least the context for the Old Testament reference is important for Paul's argument. He cites C. H. Dodd, *According to the Scriptures* (Digswell Place: James Nisbet, 1952).

[111] Rightly, Kümmel in the appendix to Lietzmann, *Korinther*, 181. He says that Paul's designation of these meals as "idolatry" is in apparent contradiction to 8:4, 8.

[112] Παίζειν occurs only here in the New Testament.

[113] Ellis, *Paul's Use of the Old Testament*, 55, says "to play" (παίζειν the Hebrew is צחק) is considered in Rabbinic literature to mean "idolatry," a view Paul shares. Midr. Exod. Rab. 1:1 interprets this as idolatry. The Hebrew צחק in Gen 26:8 is clearly sexual play. In Exod 32:19 the golden calf and dancing are connected, as noted by Robertson and Plummer, *1 Corinthians*, 204. They note a similar event in 2 Sam 6:14.

Barrett, *1 Corinthians*, 225, says that παίζειν could mean either

2. *Let us not commit fornication.* The second specific warning, μηδὲ πορνεύωμεν, is understandable from the context of Exod 32:6 (which Paul has just quoted), especially if παίζειν is a euphemism for sexual misconduct. But also there was a close connection of idolatry and immorality in paganism (especially as seen in Jewish religious polemics). Finally, since fornication at Corinth is discussed elsewhere in the letter as well, this warning could also be related to the Corinthian situation and occasioned by it. It is difficult to determine how much influence each of these three considerations may have had.

Commentators often argue that this warning against fornication was occasioned by Corinthian conduct. This would seem to be supported by an examination of word usage in Paul; all but three uses of this word group (πόρνη) are found in 1 Corinthians[114] and the only other verbal use by Paul in 1 Cor 6:18. In addition, Paul does discuss two specific cases of πορνεία in 1 Corinthians: in 5:1-11 there is the difficult case of the "man living with his father's wife" and in 6:12-20 the problem seems to be the Corinthians are justifying their involvement with prostitutes on the ground, "all things are lawful for me." It has even been argued that the association of idolatry and immorality here in 10:7, 8 arises from a pagan worship which featured cultic meals and cultic prostitution.[115]

"amorous play" or idolatry. He favors the latter since fornication is mentioned explicitly in the next clause. Conzelmann, *1 Corinthians*, 167, says: "Παίζειν 'play,' can mean to dance, scil., in the cult, idolatry." Most Greek cults featured dance in the worship.

[114]Πορνεία: 1 Cor 5:1; 6:13, 18; 7:2; 2 Cor 12:21; Gal 5:19; 1 Thess 4:3 (and Col 3:5). πόρνη 1 Cor 6:15, 16. πόρνος 1 Cor 5:9, 10, 11; 6:9. πορνεύω 1 Cor 6:18; 10:18.

[115]Grosheide, *1 Corinthians*, 224: "Fornication was one of the special sins of the Corinthians. Often fornication follows upon debauchery of a sacrificial repast." Also Jewett, *Paul's Anthropological Terms*, 258, says that the Corinthians "joined themselves freely to the temple prostitutes after the temple meals." On the other extreme, Hurd, 86ff. argues that the connection is only hypothetical and arises in Paul's mind. One has the impression that scholarly emphasis on the prominence of πορνεία at Corinth is influenced by the common characterization—in both ancient and modern times—of "wicked Corinth," especially the purported "sacred prostitutes" of Aphrodite on Acrocorinth. This alleged religious prostitution at Corinth has been thoroughly examined by Hans Conzelmann and shown to be derived from anti-Corinthian propaganda in antiquity. See Hans Conzelmann, "Kornith und die Mädchen der Aphrodite," *Nachrichten von der Akademie der Wissenschaften in Göttingen 8*

The Old Testament basis for Paul's second warning is usually considered to be Num 25, because of the phrase ἔπεσαν μιᾷ ἡμέρᾳ εἴκοσι τρεῖς χιλιάδες.[116] Yet 1 Cor 10:8 is clearly not a quotation but an allusion. Num 25:1 says, "While Israel dwelt in Shittim the people began to play the harlot with the daughters of Moab. These invited the people to the sacrifices of their gods, and the people ate, and bowed down to their gods."[117] This connection of idolatry and adultery is widespread in Jewish religious polemic, including within the Old Testament itself. Later Jewish writers also connect idolatry and fornication, the latter being the consequence of the former.[118]

This second warning, then, can be argued to have in mind a specific problem among the Corinthians. But at least in the present context (chs. 8 to 10) that is not made explicit. There is a danger of "over-exegeting" the text here when one concludes: "fornication was one of the special sins of the Corinthians."[119] 1 Cor 10:8 may be only a general admonition, resulting from the inner-relatedness of idolatry and immorality in Jewish thought, or even specifically in the Old Testament with which Paul is here dealing. This is not to deny that Paul is concerned with πορνεία among the Corinthians elsewhere in the letter, e.g., 5:1-11; 6:12-20.[120]

A development of Paul's discussion then might run: the Corinthians

---

(1967-68) 247-61. A convenient summary is in his *1 Corinthians*, 12, especially note 97.

[116]There is no certain way to explain Paul's slight divergence in count (23,000 as contrasted with the 24,000 in Num 25:9). Perhaps it is easiest to say Paul just remembered wrongly. This is a minor, but still noteworthy indication that Paul's method here is to refer to Old Testament events, rather than exact Old Testament passages.

[117]Robertson and Plummer, *1 Corinthians*, 204. In view of the relevance of the events of Baal-Peor to the situation of idolatry in Corinth, it is actually surprising Paul makes as little of this as he does.

[118]Wis 14:12; T. Reu. 4:6; Philo, *Vit. mos.* 1:302. The latter reference says the Israelite whom Phineas slew with a Midianite woman was acting "boldly and shamelessly." Philo says this man was "offering sacrifice and visiting a harlot." Both the actions and the attitudes are similar to what Paul criticizes in Corinth. See also note 92 above and Barrett, "Things Sacrificed," cited there for additional references.

[119]Grosheide, *1 Corinthians*, 224. Other commentators also say that Paul is attacking a real practice in Corinth.

[120]That there was a problem with πορνεία at Corinth and that Paul opposed it are obvious and not doubted. What is not obvious is that in the present passage it is more than an aside.

participated in pagan religious meals, which Paul considered idolatry. To persuade them to avoid such participation, Paul appeals to examples and allusions (or citations, 10:7) from the Old Testament history. These Old Testament events connect idolatry and adultery (as does Jewish thought contemporary with Paul, with which he was no doubt well familiar). Thus Paul's warning about adultery is drawn from his scriptural sources (not problems at Corinth). That this is a plausible explanation is seen by examining the next two prohibitions, which can only vaguely be related to Corinthian practices.

3. *Let us not test the Lord.* The third specific admonition in 10:9 is μηδὲ ἐκπειράζωμεν τὸν κύριον.[121] Various Old Testament texts have been suggested as behind this warning, including Num 21:5f. and Ps 77:18, καὶ ἐξεπείρασαν τὸν θεὸν ἐν ταῖς καρδίαις αὐτῶν. Again, it is probable that Paul does not have a specific text in mind.

There are also attempts to locate some concrete occasions of "tempting the Lord" in Corinth, including their spiritual pride,[122] their fornication,[123] idolatry,[124] sense of spiritual "innoculation,"[125] or (surely most original) the unwillingness of the "weak" to mature to strong convic-

---

[121]The textual tradition on the object of ἐκπειράζωμεν varies between τὸν κύριον and τὸν Χριστόν. Zuntz, 126f., favors Χριστόν since to have changed from κύριον would have been to create an unnecessary difficulty. He finds especially convincing the use of Χριστόν in Marcion's text, since this contradicts Marcion's program.

Lietzmann, *Korinther*, 47, thinks τὸν κύριον was original; τὸν θεόν (A) a correction to the LXX Ps 77:18, and τὸν Χριστόν a later Christianizing interpretation.

It ought to be recalled that often in citing Old Testament passages κύριον is understood to mean Χριστόν, not YHWH. Bousset, *Kyrios Christos*, 149f., notes that this equation was already made in pre-Pauline Christianity.

[122]Conzelmann, *1 Corinthians*, 168, suggests this but does not really favor a certain problem in Corinth. Héring, *First Epistle*, 91, considers and rejects the suggestion.

[123]Robertson and Plummer, *1 Corinthians*, 205, mention the possible connection of 10:9 with 10:8 but term it "rather fanciful."

[124]Barrett, *1 Corinthians*, 225f. He notes that Ps 77:18 was in Paul's mind, there the testing of the Lord is the challenge to provide food in the wilderness. Similarly, Fee, "II Cor 6:14f.," 160.

[125]Weiss, *Korintherbrief*, 253.

tions.[126] This wide variety of attempts to find a concrete occasion in Corinth which Paul is correcting suggests that this approach is suspect.

It is better to see 10:9 as a general hortatory admonition, with no specific cases in mind.[127] Robertson and Plummer say this well: "It is doubtful whether the apostle is thinking of anything more definite than the general frailty and faultiness of the Corinthian Christians."[128] Paul here is influenced by rhetorical style and perhaps spurred on by recalling the example of Israel in the wilderness. This interpretation accords with the evaluation of 10:8 suggesting πορνεία is general parenesis and is confirmed by 10:10.

4. *Do not grumble.* The final warning of 10:10, μηδὲ γογγύζετε, is even more difficult to relate to any known problem at Corinth, or even to any certain Old Testament passage. Among those Old Testament passages suggested as possible sources are: Num 14:2, 36; 16:41-49; Ps 106:25-27.[129] However, a more reasonable explanation is that Paul speaks generally of the Exodus experiences, perhaps combining several events and texts. Conzelmann rightly notes, "Between πειράζειν, 'tempting,' and 'grumbling' . . . no clear-cut distinction is to be made."[130]

The only clue to a specific Old Testament event might be if one could decide where Paul gets his reference to "the destroyer" (τοῦ ὀλοθρευτοῦ). This exact word does not occur in the LXX, and similar expressions (2 Sam 24:16; 1 Chron 21:15; Exod 12:23; Wis 18:20-25)[131] do not deal with the murmuring of the people. It seems impossible to determine with confidence who is being designated "the destroyer."[132]

---

[126]Héring, *First Epistle*, 91. In view of 8:9-13 this is impossible, for there Paul opposed the attempts of the strong to persuade their weak brethren.

[127]Conzelmann, *1 Corinthians*, 168 notes this general style, even if he seeks a concrete case to explain Paul's warning.

[128]Robertson and Plummer, *1 Corinthians*, 205.

[129]Ibid., 206. They think Paul must be referring to the rebellion of Korah in Num 16, "for we know of no other case in which the murmurers were punished with death." Grosheide, *1 Corinthians*, 224f., favors the case of the returning spies (Num 14), "slightly."

[130]Conzelmann, *1 Corinthians*, 168.

[131]Barrett, *1 Corinthians*, 226.

[132]Robertson and Plummer, *1 Corinthians*, 206f.; Wendland, *Korinther*, 80, suggest that it is either the "angel of death" (Exod 12) or Satan. Dibelius, *Geisterwelt*, 44f., says that the Old Testament usually refers either to God's wrath or the manifestations of that wrath in the punishing angel (Enoch 62:11; 63:1; 66:1). But he thinks here (based on 1 Cor 5) it is

Just as no concrete Old Testament passage is being used, so too it
is probable that no specific occasion at Corinth is being corrected. There
is no reason to think Paul is addressing the grumbling (past or expected) of
the strong except in a most general way.[133] This is not to say that Paul
does not expect some Corinthian opposition to his strictures, for the
whole letter has a defensive tone to it.[134] Barrett is on the right track
when he observes, "Paul seems here to be driven forward by the momen-
tum of his Old Testament material; there is nothing to suggest that com-
plaining was a special failing of the Corinthians."[135]

I CORINTHIANS 10:11-13:
LET US THEREFORE TAKE HEED

Paul's argument from the Old Testament events is concluded in vv.
11-13. In 10:11 he explains how these exemplary events described in 1-10
are to be understood by the Corinthians. The introductory "thus" (ὥστε) of
v. 12 shows that this sentence is the major point of the discussion. The
real concern of the pericope is focused in this warning. It is uncertain
whether 10:13 is best regarded as continuing the warning of 10:12, or
offering a concluding word of encouragement to the Corinthians, or both.

Satan. For a summary of the Rabbinic speculation see Strack-Billerbeck,
3.412f., also Johannes Schneider, "Ὀλεθρεύω," TDNT 5, 169f.
    [133]Robertson and Plummer, 1 Corinthians, 206, are very specula-
tive when they suggest that Paul is warning any who may be murmuring
against his demand of discipline against the incestuous man (1 Cor 5) and
his severe rebukes in the letter.
    However, it may be the choice of ἀπολλύναι is meant to recall 8:11
and the destruction of the brother. Conzelmann, 1 Corinthians, 168, n.
35, asks (but does not answer) "Does the return to direct address (imperative) imply an intentional dig at the bravado of the strong?"
    [134]This tone fits Hurd's thesis that Paul is under attack for his
theological shift to a more conservative stance on certain key topics, in
accord with the apostolic decree of Acts 15. Grosheide, 1 Corinthians,
224f., is more modest in saying: "What is at stake is that the attitude of
the Corinthians was like that of the murmuring forefathers." If we do not
insist on specific complaints, this is a reasonable assessment.
    [135]Barrett, 1 Corinthians, 226. This observation also holds for the
warnings of 10:8, 9: μηδὲ πορνεύωμεν and μηδὲ ἐκπειράζωμεν.

A. These Biblical Events Are Significant for Us

Despite the textual uncertainty,[136] the substance of 10:11 is
certain, if the exact wording is not. Having rehearsed the experiences of
the Exodus generation in receiving divine favor (1-4), divine judgment (5)
and in committing sins of rebellion (6-10), Paul makes explicit the relevance to the Corinthian church. "These things happened to them from
time to time (συνέβαινεν, imperfect tense) but were recorded (ἐγράφη
aorist) to place caution in our minds."[137] Although these experiences
have already issued in judgment for the Exodus people, they have become
warning examples for the Corinthians whose fate is still open.[138] In spite
of the mention of the Exodus "sacraments," it is still unnecessary and
unhelpful to see these warnings as directed against a magical view of the
Christian sacraments.[139]

The Christian church (ἡμῶν) for whom these biblical examples are
important is further described as those εἰς οὓς τὰ τέλη τῶν αἰώνων
κατήντηκεν. There are several meanings suggested for this phrase. Some
take it to refer to a series of world epochs.[140] Occasionally the phrase is
taken to refer to the end of the old order and the beginning of the Last

---

[136]Major readings are ταῦτα δε, ταῦτα δὲ πάντα, and πάντα δὲ
ταῦτα. There is also textual disagreement on τυπικῶς with some
significant texts reading τύποι. It is unnecessary to follow Zuntz and
delete both τυπικῶς and τύποι.

[137]Robertson and Plummer, 1 Corinthians, 207. Note the verb
changes. Νουθεσίαν is a hapax in Paul. Eph 6:4 gives the proper sense,
"instruction."

[138]Barrett, 1 Corinthians, 22; Merk, Handeln aus Glauben, 128.
Schrage, Einzelgebote, 229, says that Paul understood the Old Testament
to be primarily for Christians, the true children of Abraham (cf. Rom
4:23f.; 15:4; 1 Cor 10:11).

[139]As is often done. For example, Barrett, 1 Corinthians, 220.
But see above 139-141 and note 76.

[140]Robertson and Plummer, 1 Corinthians, 207, "The 'ages' are the
successive periods in the history of humanity." They suggest, alternatively, that it could refer to the fact that previous ages are ended and Christians stand in the final one.
Also Grosheide, 1 Corinthians, 226, who thinks that this refers to
two cultural epochs, Jewish and Greek. Similarly, Barrett, 1 Corinthians,
227, paraphrases, "We are those who are confronted by the ends of the
past ages of history."

days.[141] Conzelmann's view is best, that Paul does indeed take over apocalyptic terminology of world epochs (such as is found in 4 Ezra 6:7-10; Eth. Enoch 91:12-17, 93) but does not develop the apocalyptic picture. He is uninterested in the chronological schema but only concerned to point out that Christians are in the last eschatological period.[142]

Other Pauline uses do not solve the question. Generally Paul uses αἰῶνες either in a doxology (Rom 1:25; 9:5; 11:36; 16:27; Gal 1:5; Phil 4:20) or in the singular number to describe the present (evil) age (Rom 12:2; 1 Cor 1:20; 2:6-8; 3:18; 2 Cor 4:4).

However, the general meaning is clear. Christians are in a unique position, in which the written record of Israel's fate ought to spur them to greater resolves and striving.

B. The Point Is, Don't Presume on Your Call

The point of the entire pericope is clearly and concisely stated in 10:12: ὥστε ὁ δοκῶν ἑστάναι βλεπέτω μὴ πέσῃ. The introductory word, ὥστε, indicates the conclusive character of this sentence.[143] The history of Israel was recounted to show that God's people may not sin safely, presuming upon their election. It is possible to think that the Corinthians'

---

[141]For example, Schlatter, *Korintherbriefe*, 122f., notes that this accords with a common biblical expectation that temptations and trials would increase in the last days. Similarly, Héring, *First Epistle*, 89, and Weiss, *Korintherbriefe*, 254.

[142]Conzelmann, *1 Corinthians*, 165. Paul does know periods in history of salvation and he does believe Christians are in the final period. He does not designate these periods as αἰῶνες See 168, n. 44.

Barrett, *1 Corinthians*, 227, says that the division of history into two decisive epochs which overlap may be an accurate account of Paul's eschatology, but that he is not stating that here.

Barnabas Lindars, *New Testament Apologetic* (Philadelphia: Westminster Press, 1961) 247, says that Paul employs these speculative, apocalyptic ideas for the need of his readers in their situation. This need, he says, led Paul to modify the apocalyptic concept of an end-time testing into the daily temptations of spiritual life. Turner, *Syntax*, 114f., warns against assuming the plural αἰῶνων must refer to "two ages," for the plural may be a Semiticism (cf. T. Lev. 14:1).

[143]The word ὥστε is used to indicate consequences or conclusions derived from an argument. Liddell and Scott, *Greek-English Lexicon*, 2040. Bauer, ed. Gingrich and Danker, *Greek-English Lexicon*, 908.

presumption may have included a belief in the great power of the sacraments,[144] but their presumption need not be based on that. Basically it is
grounded in their status as believers. However, Paul is not as concerned
with refuting the grounds of their presumption as he is with exposing its
basic error, and especially restraining the Corinthians from exercising
their sense of security in idolatry.

It is possible but not certain that the designation ὁ δοκῶν contains
an implicit rebuke to the conceit of the strong. This would agree with the
phrase in 8:2, "the one thinking himself to know" (see pp. 78-79, 81).
Alternatively, to label such a person ὁ δοκῶν may be a way of distinguishing between his own estimate of himself and the harsh reality that he is in
real danger.

Although 10:12 sounds like a general maxim, the reference to
"standing" (ἑστάναι) is significant not just rhetorical. Christians may be
described as those in "good standing" with God. Their standing is based on
God's grace (Rom 5:2; 14:4) which is received in faith (Rom 11:20; 2 Cor
1:24) through the preaching of the gospel message (1 Cor 15:1). This
standing of Christians is thus derivative and dependent on God's work,
since men cannot provide their own secure standing before him (Rom
10:3). The Corinthians were in danger of forgetting that their standing is
not indelible but depends on a continuing faithfulness to God.[145]

Paul often uses βλέπω in hortatory passages. He did so earlier in
8:9. Here in 10:12 the Corinthians are to "watch out" lest they fall (μὴ
πέσῃ). "Falling," like "stumbling" (σκάνδαλον see 162f. on 8:13), is more
serious than one might first think. In 10:12, as in 3:10, 16:10 and Rom

---

[144]See supra 139f. Against seeing here an attack on a Corinthian
sacramentalism, see Robertson and Plummer, 1 Corinthians, 208.
[145]Cf. Rom 11:22. Conzelmann's suggestion, 1 Corinthians, 168,
n. 43, that "stand" means having oneself under control may catch the
importance of striving in faith for which Paul is here arguing. He rightly
notes that Paul is not denying the possibility of an assurance of salvation,
but stressing the need of "applying oneself to the proffered salvation."
Robertson and Plummer, 1 Corinthians, 208, say: "The apostle does not
question the man's opinion of his condition; he takes the security for
granted; but there is danger in feeling secure, for this leads to carelessness." This may be true, but goes beyond what the text says. Paul is not
concerned here with protecting the believer's security, but with warning
of its limits.

11:10, βλέπω has an eschatological connotation.[146] It is clear from Rom 11:11, 12 that "falling" means the loss of salvation, not just occasional slips.[147] In this way the experience of Israel in 1 Cor 10:5 is a pertinent warning to the Corinthians—God's grace can be forfeited.

Rom 14:4 is similar to 1 Cor 10:12, except that the point is made in the opposite direction. There too Paul says that Christians can stand or fall, and that the Lord's action is decisive in this. But in Rom 14:4 the focus is on the Lord's ability to secure his people—weak or strong. In contrast, in 1 Cor 10:12, the point is that one may not presume upon his standing before God, since the Lord remains in control of the final outcome. Of course, in both cases Paul is not writing abstractly of salvation and condemnation, but in the one case (Rom 14:4) encouraging believers, and in the other (1 Cor 10:12) warning them about their conduct.

C. Comfort or Continued Warning?

It is difficult to decide if 10:13 is a word of warning or of comfort. It appears anticlimactic after the strong warning of 10:12. It also appears to interrupt the explicit warning in 10:12 which is continued in 10:14. As a result, 10:13 has been regarded both as a parenthetical word of comfort and also as a continued warning.[148] If the context is taken as decisive, then 10:13 is probably a warning, which certainly accords with 10:13a. Yet the verse as a whole, especially the latter half, seems more comfort. Both interpretations may be considered more closely.

"Testing" or "trial" (πειρασμός means both) is not a prominent theme in Paul. The noun form is used twice (Gal 4:14 in addition to the present 1 Cor 10:13) and the verb five other times, once in 1 Cor 10:9. Paul ascribes πειρασμός to Satan (1 Cor 7:5) or "the tempter" (1 Thess 3:5) and even to Paul's own personal condition (Gal 4:14). However, Paul also encourages his readers to "examine" (same verb) themselves (2 Cor

---

[146]Roetzel, Judgment, 172.

[147]Ibid. He says "Πέσῃ in 10:12 means more than falling into sin or unbelief; it refers to the danger of falling out of grace (Gal 5:4) or into eschatological ruin (Rom 11:22)."

[148]Barrett, 1 Corinthians, 219 says that it is a warning. "No testing has fallen upon you but what is the common lot of men. They need not therefore claim that they themselves (or their prophylactics) have proven exceptionally resistant." Similarly, Schlatter, Korintherbriefe, 123, and Robertson and Plummer, 1 Corinthians, 208.

13:5) and to be aware of their danger (Gal 6:1). As Conzelmann observes, whether Paul means "trial" or "temptation" here depends altogether on what one means by each word.[149]

No specific occasion of testing is mentioned, nor does the adjective ἀνθρώπινος make clear what the πειρασμός may be. The word ἀνθρώπινος means "human," but it is unlikely that Paul here is contrasting trials originating with men and those originating from God himself (or demons).[150] If Paul does have a specific problem in mind, it probably is cult meals of idols.[151]

In 10:13b the thought clearly is one of encouragement; God himself can be relied upon to aid his people in all temptation. The faithfulness of God is the only reliable source of faith (1 Cor 1:9; 2 Cor 1:18) as well as the sustainer of the faithful (1 Thess 5:24; 2 Thess 3:3).[152]

Although 10:13 may seem to imply that God is behind the testing, as well as the ἔκβασιν, this is not explicit. In fact, Paul is not speculating on the source of temptation but only concerned with showing the genuine danger of falling (10:12), already made manifest at Corinth in temptations.[153] The testing, whatever its nature, is obvious—it is the ἔκβασιν which must be established.

The word ἔκβασιν has been interpreted as either "a way out"[154] or "the conclusion."[155] If it is the former, as seems suggested by the context, the point is that God will provide the escape from all testing.[156] Conzelmann thinks that Paul has in mind the awaited eschatological

---

[149]Conzelmann, *1 Corinthians*, 169, n. 44.

[150]Already Lietzmann, *Korinther*, 47. Also Barrett, *1 Corinthians*, 229; Grosheide, *1 Corinthians*, 227, and Conzelmann, *1 Corinthians*, 169.

[151]Héring, *First Epistle*, 92; Lietzmann, *Korinther*, 47; Bartsch, "Korinthische Missbrauch," 175; Grosheide, *1 Corinthians*, 227, goes further to say that Paul means the sins enumerated in vv. 6-10; evil desiring, fornication and a "spirit of pride." This is clearly "over-exegeting" the text.

[152]Robertson and Plummer, *1 Corinthians*, 209.

[153]Conzelmann, *1 Corinthians*, 169. Also Kümmel, Lietzmann *Korinther*, appendix, 181.

[154]Lietzmann, *Korinther*, 47; Héring, *First Epistle*, 92.

[155]Weiss, *Korintherbrief*, 255.

[156]Von Soden, "Sakrament und Ethik," 12; Conzelmann, *1 Corinthians*, 169. Robertson and Plummer, *1 Corinthians*, 209, note that the definite article before ἔκβασιν implies a particular way out of every temptation. This may be right, but it is overdrawn to suggest "temptation and possibility of escape always go in pairs."

salvation which is the ἔκβασιν from all trials. "Paul does not say that God helps again and again, he is speaking of the one eschatological act of salvation."[157] Some who see the temptation specifically as allurement to idol meat connect the "way out" with v. 14, and the ἔκβασιν is φεύγετε.[158]

As to the question whether this is a comfort or continued warning, no certain answer can be given. Each approach has its advantages and disadvantages.[159] It is better to regard this verse cautiously as a word of comfort. The comforting word does not arise from the Corinthians' despair but from Paul himself as he concludes his very stringent warnings taken from the Old Testament (10:1-10).[160]

CONCLUSIONS

After a detailed examination of 1 Cor 10:1-13 we can return to the important questions raised at the beginning of the chapter: the subject of this pericope and its function in the overall argument.

A. The Subject of the Passage

Regarding the subject of this section, recent studies have stressed either Paul's hermeneutical method or his concern with refuting Corinthian sacramentalism. The present study has shown that these are not the primary concerns of Paul in the passage. A brief review of these options, however, is useful.

1. *Alleged Corinthian sacramentalism.* Today the view is prominent that in 10:1-13 Paul is exposing the mistaken assumptions held by the

---

157Conzelmann, *1 Corinthians*, 169.

158Barrett, *1 Corinthians*, 229. Von Soden, "Sakrament und Ethik," 12, says two escapes are being considered: one for the strong—flee idol worship (10:14ff.) and one for the weak—do not fear all meat (10:25f.). The present study concludes the weak are not being addressed in these chapters.

159Héring, *First Epistle*, 91, says that a word of comfort seems to contradict a word of warning in 10:12. His solution is that Paul is addressing different groups within the Corinthian church. Similarly, Robertson and Plummer, *1 Corinthians*, 208.

160Von Soden, "Sakrament und Ethik," 11; Grosheide, *1 Corinthians*, 227; Schlatter, *Korintherbriefe*, 123; Conzelmann, *1 Corinthians*, 169.

Corinthians about the indelible power of the sacraments.[161] In this view
it is argued that the Corinthians consider the sacraments of baptism and
the Lord's Supper to have immunized· them from any possible loss of
salvation. They are confident that they "stand" well before God (10:12). It
is frequently argued that the Corinthians' overdeveloped sacramentalism
is also the basis of their willingness to have intercourse with prostitutes
as well as to participate in idol meals. Accordingly, Paul is said here to
be correcting their tendency to make the Christian sacraments a magic
charm.[162]

However, as we have seen, the focus of Paul's argument is not to
correct the sacramentalism of the Corinthians but to warn them of the
real danger of idolatry. His major concern in these verses is the possibility of apostasy by their involvement with idols (10:12, cf. 10:14).
Certainly Paul refers (implicitly!) to the Christian rites of baptism and
Lord's Supper by drawing attention to Israel's baptism in the sea and
divinely provided food and drink. However, even in referring back to the
Exodus experiences, the focus remains the sins—and ultimate loss—of the
Exodus people.

It may be that the Corinthians were overconfident of their Christian security in part because of their baptism and their participation in
the eucharist. They may have held as "high" a view of these sacraments
as they clearly did of Christian wisdom and the Spirit. However, since
Paul's subject in these verses is the danger of idolatry, it is still somewhat
misleading to refer to the section as organized around "sacrament and
ethic."

2. *Hermeneutical concerns.* Paul's hermeneutical methods in 10:1-
13 are of interest not only in their methodology but because he explicitly
says (10:11) that Israel's experiences were "written down for us." It is not
crucial for the present investigation to have formal categories of interpretation for Paul's exposition. Indeed, recent work has suggested that
such categories were still developing in Paul's time,[163] and he is probably
more flexible than restriction to set categories would suggest. With
proper limitations and discretion it may be possible to mine this passage

---

[161]Among others: Barrett, *1 Corinthians,* 224; Bornkamm, "Lord's
Supper and Church," 128f.; Conzelmann, *1 Corinthians,* 167; von Soden,
"Sakrament und Ethik;" Wendland, *Korinther,* 78; Héring, *First Epistle,* 84.

[162]Von Soden, "Sakrament und Ethik," 8.

[163]For example, see Achtemeier, "Typology," 926f. This means
attempts to classify and restrict the passage's use of the Old Testament
to formal categories are unfruitful.

for insight into Paul's use of the Old Testament and into early Christian hermeneutics. Yet the focus of the passage is not the elaboration of means of biblical interpretation but the desire to dissuade Corinthian Christians from their involvement with idolatry.

3. *The subject of 10:1-13: Take heed!* The real subject of 10:1-13 is the danger of idolatry. This is clear in Paul's concluding warning of 10:14, "Wherefore . . . flee idolatry!" This warning goes at least as much with 10:1-13 as with 10:15-21, for really 10:1-22 is united in theme. 10:14 is explicitly grounded in the prior verses' argument. Within 10:1-13 Paul makes his conclusion obvious in 10:12. "Therefore, let the one who thinks he stands watch out lest he fall!" This "falling" looks back to the description of Israel's tragic fate in the desert, but in Paul's concern the concrete danger is Corinthian involvement with idols.

A third evidence of the real subject of the passage is the general character of the sins enumerated. This speaks against attempts to find a point-by-point correspondence with the Old Testament events. It also warns against overly stressing the "sacraments" of Israel. Paul uses these allusions to illustrate the basic attitude of sinful rebellion (ἐπιθυμία). The sins enumerated in 10:7-10 are illustrations of this rebellion. The real object of the danger facing the Corinthians is found in the broader context of 1 Corinthians 8-10, although the reference to idolatry in 10:7 is especially pertinent.

B. The Function of the Passage

A second important question about the section 10:1-13 is its function in its present context. We have already suggested that the context is important for determining the subject of the passage, since the danger of idolatry is made explicit in 10:14. However, other studies have concluded that 10:1-13 is not integral to its context but a digression or excursus dealing with a different topic.[164] This assessment was bound to come if one takes the subject of 10:1-13 to be either sacramentalism or an explanation of biblical interpretation.

The following evidence shows that 10:1-13 is related to its context. First, the connection with 9:24-27 is obvious: both passages warn of the

---

[164]Conzelmann, *1 Corinthians,* 165. He suggests that this section was composed before the writing of the epistle.

possibility of forfeiting one's salvation and therefore the need for effort and self-discipline.[165]

Second, 10:1-13 is grammatically linked to 10:14ff. by διόπερ.[166] Also connecting 10:1-13 with 10:14ff. is the topic of idols, raised in chapter 8, and continued in 10:7 and 10:14, 19. It must be remembered that the topic of idolatry is very limited in Paul, and over half of the references occur in 1 Cor 8-10. Another connection of ideas between 10:1-13 and 10:14ff. is the concern with sacrifice, including that of Israel.

These connections establish that 10:1-13 is related to its context, especially with 10:14-22. It is important to Paul's discussion of eating sacrificial meat. If 10:1-13 seems a digression, it is only because in form it is biblical exposition. The subject matter remains Christian participation in sacrificial meals.[167] Wuellner has argued that such "digressions" were a rhetorical convention of Paul's culture and were considered to be vital to the argument, not interruptions.[168] Accordingly, as Walter has noted, the Nestle paragraph division which separates 10:-13 from 10:14-22 is unfortunate.[169]

These verses serve to introduce an authoritative warning about the dangers of sacrificial meals. In chapter 9 Paul has used his own conduct to impress the need for Christians to forego certain liberties they feel are theirs. This expands on chapter 8's argument. But in 9:24ff. he turns to warn of dangers of losing one's salvation. In 10:1-13 he gives this authoritative grounding in scripture.

---

[165]Barrett, *1 Corinthians*, 218. Grammatically, this is established by γάρ in 10:1. See Schrage, *Einzelgebote*, 31f., on Paul's belief in a need for struggle in Christian living.
[166]Conzelmann, *1 Corinthians*, 165, says that in spite of this: "the connection with the context is loose." Similarly, Lietzmann, *Korinther*, 44. On the contrary, the overall problem of the danger of idols is found in both 10:1-13 and 10:14-22.
[167]Barrett, *1 Corinthians*, 219f. Unconvincing is Grosheide's suggestion, *1 Corinthians*, 216f., that in chapters 8 and 9 the strong are addressed and in chapter 10 Paul is speaking to weak believers. For this reason, he terms vv. 1-12 "a transition."
[168]Wilhelm Wuellner, "Greek Rhetoric and Pauline Argumentation," *Early Christian Literature and the Classical Intellectual Tradition* (ed. Wm. R. Schoedel and Robert L. Wilken; Paris: Editions Beauchesne, 1979) 177-88.
[169]Walter, "Christusglaube," 430. Similarly, Wendland, *Korinther*, 80. The United Bible Societies text combines 10:1-13 and 10:14-22 under the heading "Warning against idolatry."

It has already been seen that chapter 8 takes its shape because there Paul takes up and refutes the Corinthians' views. But here in 10:1-13 Paul argues for his own reasons. The differences in style, and even emphasis, can be explained on that basis. Here Paul documents the danger of apostasy in Scripture and will proceed in 10:14-22 to warn from contemporary examples. Both are arguments of his own choosing. The seemingly misplaced word of encouragement in 10:13 reveals Paul's personal involvement with his arguments.

1 CORINTHIANS 10:14-22
EATING AND ALLEGIANCE

INTRODUCTION

1 Corinthians 10:14-22 is a definable section within the larger argument of chapter 10 (and the still larger unit of chapters 8-10).[1] It is distinguished from 10:1-13 both by the change in form and in method—no longer is there a use of the Old Testament. Διόπερ links grammatically vv. 14ff. with what precedes it in chapter 10.[2] It both indicates a shift to a new stage of the argument and shows a relationship of this new stage to what has preceded it.

Where to end this section beginning with 10:14 is less certain. The topic of sacrificial meat continues past 10:21, and v. 22 could serve as well to introduce what follows as to conclude vv. 14-21. However, the use of quotations from the Corinthians' letter beginning in v. 23 would suggest, formally, that v. 22 belongs with vv. 14-21.

A. Problems

We begin by noting what issues are discussed in 10:14-21. First, the subject addressed, εἰδωλολατρίας, is announced in the imperatival admonition of 10:14. What follows are arguments about this topic. This

---

[1]See pp. 268-275 and the studies cited there regarding the unity of 1 Corinthians.

[2]See Bauer, ed. Gingrich and Danker, *Greek-English Lexicon*, 198. They note that this contraction is fairly uncommon. Note also that Weiss, *Korintherbriefe*, 256, and Conzelmann, *1 Corinthians*, 170, connect διόπερ only with 10:14ff. which follows, not with what precedes.

means that neither Paul's description of the Christian communion in 10:16, 17 nor that of pagan meals in 19-21 is focal. It is not these meals he sets out to explain but the danger of idolatry.

Second, the answer given in these verses to the problem of εἰδωλο-λατρία is closely connected to κοινωνία. Paul sets forth three examples of κοινωνία, the Christian communion, the Jewish fellowship, and the pagan cultus. This means a reasonable interpretation of 1 Cor 10:14-21 involves finding Paul's understanding of the term κοινωνία in these verses.

Third, as one instance of κοινωνία Paul points to the Lord's Supper by quoting an early Christian tradition. One must ask about the pre-Pauline traditions and about the Pauline interpretation of the Christian meal. How does he understand the Lord's Supper, and what is the significance of referring to it here?

Fourth, one must ask about the Pauline representation of the pagan and Jewish meals. How important are these meals in his argument? This involves both what the meals were[3] and how Paul describes them here.[4] A subsidiary question in the case of the pagan meals is how "demons" (δαιμόνιοι) are involved.

B. Structure

Paul's argument in 1 Cor 10:14-22 is organized in this way:

In v. 14, he interrupts his reasoned persuasion with an apodictic plea: φεύγετε ἀπὸ τῆς εἰδωλολατρίας. This imperative shows the urgency of Paul's concern.[5] He appeals to the Corinthians to consider and

---

[3]See Part I, Sacrifice, Cultic Meals and Associations in Hellenistic Life, esp. 17-21.

[4]The two questions are not necessarily the same. Svere Aalen, "Das Abendmahl als Opfermahl im Neuen Testament," NovT 6 (1963) 128-143, rightly notes that one must distinguish three questions dealing with pagan meals: (1) Paul's own understanding of pagan cult meals, (2) his theological interpretation of such meals, and (3) the analogies between such meals and the Christian meal.

[5]A similar warning is in 6:18, φεύγετε τὴν πορνείαν, noted by Barrett, 1 Corinthians, 230. Jewett, Paul's Anthropological Terms, 258, feels that this shows a connection of cult meals and prostitution in Corinth. Or this may be due to the common connection of idolatry, fornication and forbidden meat in the Jewish mind (as is implied in 1 Cor 10:7). See Harold W. Attridge, The Interpretation of Biblical History in

follow his reasons for prohibiting their association in pagan cult meals. Then in the remainder of the section he presents an argument about the nature and obligations of communal life.

In 10:16-21 Paul's argument consists of three examples of cultic associations which he terms κοινωνία. These examples are of Christians (16, 17), Jews (18), and pagans (19-21). The pagan meal, the problem being treated in this section of 1 Corinthians, is described as a threat. Although based on unreal deities, it is a real κοινωνία, even if based on demons.

Verse 22 could be limited strictly to summarizing vv. 19-21 but seems best taken as a summary statement looking all the way back to v. 14. The basic thought is, if you do not flee idolatry, you are provoking the Lord.

THE MEANING OF ΚΟΙΝΩΝΙΑ

In 1 Cor 10:16-21 the chief consideration for Christians regarding possible eating of sacrificial meals is κοινωνία. Paul sets out three examples of κοινωνία, all related to cultic meals. Therefore it is crucial for an understanding of these meals to find out about the word κοινωνία in this passage. To understand the word we must consider both the common meaning of the word (and its cognates) in Greek and also the specific intentions of Paul's letters.

What does the word κοινωνία basically mean?[6] What special meanings does Paul assume and use here? Is there a cultic use of these words behind Paul's selection and use of them?

In the history of interpretation of 1 Cor 10:16-21, considerable attention has been focused on the meaning of κοινωνία in 10:16, 17. There Christians are described as having κοινωνία with the body and blood of Christ. Some have interpreted these verses to mean "participation" and

---

the *Antiquitates Judaicae of Flavius Josephus* (HDR 7; Missoula: Scholars Press, 1976) 126-140.   Also Barrett, "Things Sacrificed," 138-53. Certainly since 1 Cor 6:18 and 10:14 are the only Pauline uses of the word, it is likely that there is some connection.

[6]The use of the Greek word κοινωνία in this chapter is intended to avoid prejudicing interpretation by translation. "Fellowship," "association," "participation" and similar words are all legitimate translations. However, some are so freighted that one may be led to assume too quickly their present-day meanings in the Pauline writings. This is the case

have understood Christians to have a part/share of Christ in the eucharist. How this is the case is understood in several ways, which will be examined below.

Others have stressed the associative character of κοινωνία. Then it is the "association" with other believers which is the key component in Christian κοινωνία. In this view it is the relationship among the participants which is most important.

The interpretation of pagan cult meals has also been a key factor in understanding what κοινωνία means in 1 Cor 10. Where these pagan meals have been understood sacramentally the tendency has been also to see the Christian meal (by parallel) as a sacramental partaking of Christ. For the understanding of 1 Cor 10:14-21, therefore, it is important to begin with an investigation of the non-Christian usage of κοινωνία.

A. Representative Uses of Κοινωνία in Greek Sources.

In the present study it is both impossible and unnecessary to examine comprehensively the uses and meanings of κοινωνία and κοινωνεῖν in Greek writing. There is sufficient agreement in major studies of the word group to show that a wide range of concepts was referred to by these words.[7] These words are used to describe business partnerships, various associations, joint enterprises, social relationships, marriage, and the sexual relationship. In other references κοινωνία points to the common political life of citizens and, in Stoicism especially, to the common life of "world citizens."

The basic sense of κοινωνία seems to be a relationship in which two or more individuals have a joint interest in something or someone. Thus one usually finds the person with whom and/or the thing in which κοινωνία exists. However, the word can be used absolutely. Although various students have suggested a necessary "inner relationship"[8] or

---

especially with the translation "communion," although the word *communio* is used several times to translate the Greek in the Latin version.

[7] See Hauck, "Κοινωνέω" *TDNT* 3, 798-809. Heinrich Seesemann, *Der Begriff* ΚΟΙΝΩΝΙΑ im Neuen Testament (BZNW 14; Giessen: Alfred Töpelmann, 1933). Bauer, ed. Gingrich and Danker, *Greek-English Lexicon*, 438f.

[8] Hauck, "Κοινωνία," 797.

"intimate friendship"[9] the wide-ranging use—from conjugal relations to business pacts—warns against such a necessary implication of intimacy.[10]

Without undertaking even to give examples of each of these varied uses of κοιν-stem words, perhaps a few citations will illustrate the variety of possible meanings.

There certainly are uses of κοινωνία and cognates which imply intimacy. Diogenes Laertius repeats Zeno's comment on φιλία saying that true friendship means "a common use of all that has to do with life" (κοινωνίαν τινὰ εἶναι τῶν κατὰ τὸν βίον).[11] Similar is Plato's dictum, "Friends have all things in common" (κοινὰ γὰρ τὰ τῶν φίλων).[12] Also Aristotle says:

> in every partnership (κοινωνία) we find mutual rights of some sort, and also friendly feelings; one notes that shipmates and fellow soldiers speak of each other as "my friend," (φίλους) and so in fact do the partners in any joint undertaking (ταῖς ἄλλαις κοινωνίαις).[13]

Aristotle assumes and enlarges upon a political understanding of κοινωνία[14] which need not suggest intimacy. Epictetus uses these words to denote human society,[15] and indeed considers it a natural characteristic of humanity.[16] He even extends the concept of a natural κοινωνία to include the relationship between men and gods, based on reason.[17]

But such references should not lead one to assume a friendly, intimate relationship, nor that a natural affinity is normally implied by

---

[9] George V. Jourdan, "KOINΩNIA in 1 Corinthians 10:16," *JBL* 67 (1948) 111.

[10] Examples of these varied usages may be found in the works cited in note 7.

[11] Diogenes Laertius, 7.124.

[12] Plato, *Phaedr.* 279c.

[13] Aristotle, *Eth. Nic.* 8.9.1, 1159.30. He quotes the proverb: κοινὰ τὰ φίλων.

[14] Aristotle, *Eth. Nic.* 8.9.4, 5, 1160a.10 says that all associations are components of the state.

[15] *Diss.* 2.21.5; 3.22.77, 78.

[16] See *Diss.* 2.20.6-14 where he attacks Epicurus for denying this common fellowship of mankind. The Epicureans favored a withdrawal from public affairs as the most beneficial life.

[17] *Diss.* 1.9.5.

κοινωνία. The word can refer also to very dispassionate matters. In a papyrus petition to a regional administrator an Egyptian woman declares she is not responsible for her deceased brother's debts since she had no involvement (κοινωνία) in his affairs.[18]

Κοινωνία, of course, is only one of a number of Greek words expressing the idea of sharing. It does seem usually to have included implication of *participation* in something in *association* with others. But the emphasis can fall on either aspect, even to the practical exclusion of the other.[19] It can, but need not, express an emotional involvement or bond.[20]

Certain references to a κοινωνία which exists between men and the gods are especially important to the present study. These are of two basic kinds: a κοινωνία which exists *per se* (ontologically, so to speak) and a κοινωνία established in sacrifice and accompanying events.

A. D. Nock rightly observed that some philosophers spoke of an essential κοινωνία between gods and men. This was especially found in the Stoics, as one would expect.[21] Dio Chrysostom says the truly happy city is one in tune with the gods, "the partnership of god with god."[22] What Dio says of the κοινωνία between gods and the city Epictetus says of the relationship between the gods and the true Stoic.[23] Cicero gives beautiful expression to the Stoic doctrine of the pervading logos which unites not only gods and men but the "whole universe as one commonwealth of which both gods and men are members."[24]

---

[18] *P. Ryl.*, 117. J. DeM. Johnson, Victor Martin and Arthur S. Hunt. *Catalogue of the Greek Papyri in the John Rylands Library* (Manchester: University Press, 1915) II, 103.
[19] J. Y. Campbell, "Κοινωνία and its Cognates in the NT," *JBL* 51 (1932) 352-380, reprinted in his *Three New Testament Studies* (Leiden: E. J. Brill, 1965) 1-28 (in this, page 5).
[20] An inward involvement is stressed by Jourdan, "ΚΟΙΝΩΝΙΑ," 111, and Hauck, "Κοινωνεῖν," 797. It is doubted by S. Currie, "Koinonia in Christian Literature to 200 A.D." (unpublished Ph.D. dissertation, Emory University, Atlanta, 1962) 9.
[21] A. D. Nock, "Cult of Heroes," 583.
[22] Dio Chrysostom, 36.23. The phrase is: τῶν θεῶν πρὸς ἀλλήλους κοινωνίαν.
[23] Epictetus, *Diss.* 2.19.27.
[24] Cicero, *Leg.* 1.7.23. See also *De Nat. Deo.* 2.62 (*communis*). For other examples of the philosophical idea of ontological κοινωνία between gods and men see Hauck, "Κοινωνεῖν," 800. Nock, "Cult of Heroes," 583,

Perhaps more important for the present study are various references to a κοινωνία which comes to expression or existence in sacrifice. Such κοινωνία is described in sacral events both in early and late authors, as well as in inscriptions and sacred laws. These substantiate Paul's assumption in 1 Cor 10:19f. of a connection between κοινωνία and sacrifice.

Plato says in his *Symposium:* "all sacrifices and ceremonies controlled by divination, namely all means of communion (κοινωνία) between gods and men, are only concerned with either the preservation or cure of love." It is clear that in some way he relates κοινωνία to sacrifice here.[25]

Plato is an example of the antiquity of κοινωνία in contexts of sacral practices, but more important for the understanding of 1 Cor 10 are inscriptions from the Hellenistic period. As illustrative of the fact that in "popular polytheism the sacrificial meal then becomes a communion of the deity with men" in which "the gods arrange and conduct sacrificial meals." Hauck cites Dittenberger SIG³ 1106.6f. The full text should be read, but the phrase which he cites is: ἐπιμελέσθων δὲ αὐτῶν τοὶ τῶν ἱερῶν κοινωνεῦντες ... (Trans: "Let those who share in the sacred affairs take care of them [the descendants of the cult founders]).[26] A similar inscription is found in SIG³ 647.50.[27]

Other inscriptional evidence could be given[28] which would also

gives four examples of philosophers who describe a κοινωνία related to sacrifice. They are Dion of Prussia, 3.97; Aristides, *To Sarapis,* 26, 28; Philo, *Spec. Leg.,* 1.221 and Porphyry, *De philosophia ex orac.,* found in Eusibius, *P. E.* 4.9.7.
   [25]Plato, *Symp.* 10.C, ταῦτα δ' ἐστὶν ἡ περὶ θεούς τε καὶ ἀνθρώπους πρὸς ἀλλήλους κοινωνία.
   [26]Dittenberger, *SIG³* 3.259f. See also SIG³ 330.248, where κοινωνεῖν is used with ἱεροῦ to mean "associated with the sanctuary and festivals."
   [27]Dittenberger, *SIG³* 2.208f., κοινωνεόντω δὲ οἱ Μεδεῶνιοι τᾶν θυσιᾶν τᾶν ἐν Στίρι πασᾶν, καὶ τοὶ τοὶ Στίριοι τᾶν ἐν Μεδεῶνι πασᾶν. The meaning of κοινωνέω as "to share" in these texts is confirmed by the use of μετέχω as an equivalent. See SIG³ 1023.18-23; 1106.145; and esp. 167.41, and an inscription from Magnesia, 44.17-20. It is found in Otto Kern, *Die Inschriften von Magnesia am Mäander* (Berlin: W. Spemann, 1900) 34.
   [28]Kern, *Inschriften,* numbers 54, 89. Also Hauck, "Κοινωνέω," 799f.; Moulton-Milligan, 350-51; and SIG³ 4.423.

show that in Hellenistic cult life κοινωνία and κοινωνεῖν were familiar terms. These inscriptions, many from sacred regulations, confirm that these words basically refer to "association" among the participants. Various literary figures also use κοινωνία in speaking of sacrificial associations. Demosthenes says that Athens by statute allotted a share (κοινωνοὺς πεποίησθε) of libations in all public services at every temple.[29] In *Electra* Euripides says of sacrifice that one is "bid to the feast" (δαιτὶ κοινωνὸν καλεῖ).[30] Plutarch also mentions κοινωνία in relation to sacrifice.[31] He implies a relationship of κοινωνία to meals after sacrifice which is especially instructive.

Plutarch says that when he was holding office he favored conducting these meals so that each participant received an equal share. But some complained that this innovation was hostile to sociability (ἀκοινώνητον) and was more like military rations. They favored returning to the older model of Pindar when each participant ate and drank as he wished, as in the halcyon days when "about the noble table heroes often met all sharing everything with each other" (τῷ κοινωνεῖν ἁπάντων ἀλλήλοις).[32] This passage from Plutarch suggests these meals considered κοινωνία primarily as the friendly association of the participants following the sacrifice. There is no indication of a sacramental understanding of κοινωνία.

There are also references in literature which describe explicitly a κοινωνία between the sacrificers and the gods, although these are not as numerous as one would think based on the prominence of "sacramental" interpretations of Hellenistic cult meals. Many of the references cited as proving a sacramental communion (not just association) between men and the gods only permit, at most, such an implication to be drawn.

Aelius Aristides is perhaps the most famous and also the most likely reference to prove that a special sacramental relationship is established in sacrifice and termed κοινωνία. Concerning his patron god, Sarapis, Aelius Aristides says,

men share in a special way the truest communion in the

---

[29]Demonsthenes, *De falsa legatione*, 280f. Cf. 190, where the presidents of Athens unite in sacrificial service.
[30]Euripides, *El.* 637-39.
[31]Plutarch, *Thes.* 23.3.
[32]Plutarch, *Quaest. Conv.* 10.64F-643A.

sacrifices to this god alone, as they invite (him) to the altar and appoint him as guest and host.[33]

We cannot examine Aristides in detail, but we note here: (1) the uniqueness of this alleged communion concept in Aristides—if granted—should not be assumed normative in other authors, and (2) Aristides's attachment to Sarapis is certainly atypical of Hellenistic devotees.[34] Still, it may be that Aristides does provide an example of a special use of κοινωνία stressing a deep involvement, for which "communion" may be a preferred translation.

Julian, *Oration* V. 176 is also sometimes cited to prove "communion" as an appropriate translation for κοινωνία. He writes (concerning sacrificing of fish), "that is not the custom in the sacrifices which we honor most highly, in which alone the gods deign to join us and share our table. . . ."[35] As the translation cited shows, no implication of communion is necessary. Moreover, in addition to the lateness of Julian, A. D. Nock notes that in this passage κοινωνεῖν is better translated "give a share," so the gods are the source, not the recipients of the meal.[36]

These examples are illustrative of κοινωνία and its cognates, used in contexts dealing with sacral concerns. The passage from Plato shows the antiquity of such a usage, and that from Julian shows its perseverance. The combination of literary and inscriptional citations shows how widely κοινωνία was employed. These citations and others not given at least show that the use of κοινωνία in describing cultic meals was well known in Hellenistic society.

However these passages also show that it is unnecessary to assume

---

[33]Aelius Aristides, *Sarapis* VIII. The great influence of interpretation on translation (and vice versa) is well illustrated in E. Bevan's rendering of this passage as "it is only in sacrifice offered to this God that men are in a special way communicants, that there is communion in the true sense." E. R. Bevan, *Later Greek Religion* (Boston: Beacon Press, 1950) 71f.

[34]Behr, *Aelius Aristides*. Aristides himself seems to have been a very unusual person. An inveterate hypochondriac, Aristides when he felt cured by a devout attachment to Sarapis (not expressed in sacrifice) and so hymned his savior in prayers and dedicated his rhetorical career to him. On Sarapis Hymn, see A. Höfler, *Der Sarapis-hymnus des Ailios Aristides* (Berlin: W. Kohlhammer, 1935) 95f.

[35]Julian, *Or.* 176, . . . τοιαῦτα θύματα, ἀλλ' οὐκ ἐν ταῖς τιμητηρίοις, ὧν μόνων κοινωνεῖν ἄξιου καὶ τραπεζοῦν θεοῖς.

[36]Nock, "Cult of Heroes," 597f.

that the word group implies sentiments presently associated with what
Christians term "Holy Communion." When found in cultic laws the word
may only mean "associate together."[37] Even those passages which speak
of κοινωνία between gods and men ought not be assumed to describe
"communion." The Aristides passage alone seems to perhaps suggest a
deep relationship between god and worshipper.

The point is, κοινωνία and its cognates must not be colored in
advance with sacramentalism because they are in texts dealing with cultic
sacrifices and/or meals. These words simply describe a relationship
between two or more people (or things) sharing with a third person (or
thing). It is really begging the question to assume the presence of these
words in cultic speech implies sacramentalism. These lexical studies may
show that κοινωνία was used in sacral contexts but do not assure us of
Paul's meaning.

B. Jewish Sources

There are three important Jewish sources to consider in establishing
the contours of meaning for κοινωνία as found in Greek-speaking Judaism
(of which Paul, of course, is a part). These sources are: The Septuagint,
Philo, and Josephus. Although the use of κοινωνία in any of these does
not prove a similar use in Paul, they do provide some possibilities to
consider in looking at the Pauline epistles.

1. *The Septuagint.* Of the three Jewish sources considered here
only the LXX could seriously be considered to have influenced Paul's
writing, and for that reason it deserves first mention.

Perhaps the first thing to be noted is the paucity of use of κοινω-
stem words in the LXX. Κοινωνός occurs only five times,[38] κοινωνέω
four times,[39] and κοινωνία only once.[40] In none of these instances is the
relationship of men to God being described.[41]

---

[37]Ibid.
[38]IV Kgs 17:11; Esth 8:3; Prov 28:24; Mal 2:14 and Isa 1:23.
[39]κοινωνεῖν; II Chr 20:3, 5; Job 34:8; Prov 1:11; Eccl 9:4.
[40]κοινωνία: Lev 6:2 (5:21).
[41]Hauck, "Κοινωνεῖν" 801f., emphasizes the significance of this:
"Neither *haber* nor κοινων- is used for the relation to God, as so often in
the Greek word." Hauck finds this somewhat astonishing since "there can
be little doubt that in ancient Israel sacrifice, or the sacrificial meal, was
widely regarded as a sacred fellowship between God and man." He concludes, 801f., "conscious theology is hesitant to express what participants
in the feast know by experience."

However, in 4 Kgs 17:11 Israel's sin of idolatry is referred to with the phrase ἐποίησαν κοινωνούς. Campbell comments that this phrase "is clearly due to a mistake of some kind, since it neither translates the Hebrew nor gives any other satisfactory sense."[42] An inadequacy for translating the Hebrew may be granted, but good sense can be made from the LXX text itself.

The passage 4 Kgs 17:7-41 rehearses the reasons for the conquest of Israel by Assyria. The reasons enumerated include: Israel's building high places (v. 9), erecting Asherim (v. 10), serving idols (v. 12), burning incense on the high places, and ἐποίησαν κοινωνούς καὶ ἐχάραξαν τοῦ παροργίσαι τὸν κύριον (v. 11). I suggest the phrase ἐποίησαν κοινωνούς refers to "making allies with" or a similar idea of establishing covenant relationship with the gods of the pagans who were already in the land.[43]

Apart from this passage in 4 Kgs 17:11ff. there is little unusual in the LXX uses of the κοινων-stem words. They are used to describe an agreement between kings (2 Chronicles 20:35), the marriage relationship (Mal 2:14) and especially partners in evil works (Job 34:8; Prov 1:11; 28:24; Isa 1:23).[44]

---

[42]Campbell, "Κοινωνία," 7. The Hebrew is: וַיְעַשׂוּ דְּבָרִים.

[43]This explanation agrees with the observation of Stuart Currie that κοινωνία refers to the covenant relationship which was integral with ḥesed. See pp. 45-49. Also in 4 Kgs 17:35 the transgressions enumerated are a violation of the covenant which God made with Israel which demanded they worship no other gods. Israel had violated the covenant with God by making alliance with the gods of other nations (worshipping their idols). This contrast has importance for Paul's covenant relationship while in one body with Christ. To do this is to provoke the Lord (cmp. 1 Cor 10:24 with 4 Kgs 17:11).

One also ought to note Malachi 2:14 where God complains that the people of Israel are "faithless to one another, profaning the covenant of our fathers." Judah, espoused to YHWH, has become faithless and is married to the daughter of a foreign god. It is as when a man divorces his first wife although "she is your companion and your wife by covenant" (LXX, αὐτὴ κοινωνός σου καὶ γυνὴ διαθήκης σου).

In the Malachi passage two points deserve note: (1) the parallel between human divorce which breaks covenant and Judah's faithlessness to YHWH which breaks covenant. (2) In verse 14 there is an implicit equation of διαθήκη with κοινωνός.

[44]Prov 28:24 is not concerned with a covenant of idolatry, but the expression οὗτος κοινωνός ἐστιν ἀνδρὸς ἀσεβοῦς would be appropriate for Paul's own warning.

In the Old Testament Apocrypha additional uses are found of
κοινωνέω,[45] κοινωνός,[46] and κοινωνία.[47] These follow the customary
uses to refer to friendship (Sirach 6:10; 41:18; 13:2), association (Sirach
13:1; 2 Macc 5:20), or common life (2 Macc 14:25; 3 Macc 4:6).[48]

In summary, the LXX usage of these words does not seem different
from the common Greek uses. Several students have remarked that the
failure of the LXX to use these words to describe a relationship between
God and man is noteworthy, since this is in contrast to customary Hellenistic usage.[49] However, this can be explained by noting that the Hebrew
Old Testament which is being translated does not use haber to describe
such a relationship with the true God, but only with false gods.[50] In this
regard 4 Kgs 17:11ff. may offer some insight for the interpretation of
1 Cor 10:16f. Otherwise it is unlikely that the LXX use of κοινωνία can
be used to explain Paul's phrasing in 1 Cor 10:16-22.[51]

2. *Philo*. Philo has been cited as a Jewish writer who breaks with
the LXX precedent and turns instead to the Greek thought-world.[52] It is

---

[45]Wis 6:23; Sir 13:1, 2, 17; 2 Macc 5:20; 14:25; 3 Macc 2:31; 4:11
and 4 Macc 7:6.

[46]Sir 6:10; 41:18; 42:3.

[47]Wis 8:18; 3 Macc 4:6.

[48]Campbell, "Κοινωνία," 7f., notes that there is no departure
from classical usage, except that perhaps the dative of the person occurs
more often.

[49]Hauck, "Κοινωνεῖν," 801; Jourdan, "KOINΩNIA, 112; Bartsch,
"korinthische Missbrauch," 176.

[50]Hauck, "Κοινωνεῖν," 800ff., and Bartsch, "korinthische
Missbrauch," 177. For example, Hos 4:17 where haber is translated by
μέτοχος in the LXX. Similarly, Isa 44:11.

[51]I follow here an argument and conclusion set forth by Stuart
Currie in the dissertation cited in note 20. He rejects the view set forth
by Jourdan, "KOINΩNIA," 112, that "Josephus, and the writers of the New
Testament too, doubtless following the example of the LXX, retained for
κοινωνός the meaning of 'partner' (in life and work) which had belonged to
haber."

It is not at all obvious that the NT writers, at least Paul, "follow"
the LXX, since there is no distinctive LXX use of κοινωνία. Moreover,
as Currie notes, the LXX does not equate haber and κοινωνία, for it also
translates haber with μέτοχος.

[52]For recent studies seeking to show similarities between Philo and
1 Corinthians see Richard A. Horsley, "Consciousness," 574-89. Ibid.,
"Wisdom of Words and Words of Wisdom in Corinth," *CBQ* 39 (1977) 224-
239. Ibid., "Pneumatikos vs. Psychikos: Distinctions of Spiritual Status
among the Corinthians," *HTR* 69 (1976) 269-88.

alleged that he does use κοινωνία to speak of the relationship between men and God. This tendency has been cited as proof of Philo's "helleniza-tion."[53]

Certainly some similarities between Philo and other writers of the period can be shown. For example, Philo, speaking of Moses's special privilege as the "Priest of God," quotes the Greek proverb, κοινὰ τὰ φιλῶν.[54] He also writes like a Stoic philosopher when he describes the harmony between men and the rational universe.[55] Four specific references in Philo are often noted: *Vit. Mos.* 1.156-58; *Flacc.* 136ff.; *Spec. Leg.* 1.131 and 221.

In the *Vit. Mos.* Philo says that God judged Moses worthy to be a partner (κοινωνός) of God's own possessions, i.e., the world. In this way it is evident that Moses was a "friend of God" and shared God's possessions. Thereby, too, Moses has partnership (κοινωνίας) with God and is even called God.[56] Here we have non-Pauline evidence that a Jewish writer could speak of men as κοινωνοί of God.

A second important reference is Philo's *Flacc.* 136f. where he describes pagan clubs in his city of Alexandria which are termed σύνοδοι καὶ κλίναι by the local citizens. These clubs (θίασοι) have a fellowship (κοινωνίας) based on strong drink and carousing rather than sound prin-

---

[53]Philo's usage is "quite distinctive" and "so different from Old Testament usage" that they are "undoubtedly influenced by corresponding expressions in Hellenism." Hauck, "Κοινωνεῖν," 803: "Philo first could also speak of a κοινωνία between God and men." Bartsch, "korinthische Missbrauch," 177. Therefore Philo's usage, stated bluntly, "unJewish." Aalen, "Opfermahl," 138.

Perhaps qualification ought to be made about terming Philo "un-Jewish" since he certainly is a Jew. The consensus is basically sound: alongside the more common meanings for κοινωνία, Philo has some atypical among Jewish writers.

[54]Philo, *Vit. Mos.*, 1.156. This phrase was already proverbial by Zeno's time and perhaps even by Plato's. See notes 10, 11.

[55]ὡς γὰρ ἥλιος ἁπάντων ἐστὶ φῶς τῶν ὄψεις ἐχόντων, οὕτω καὶ ὁ σοφὸς τῶν ὅσοι λογικῆς κεκοινωνήκασι φύσεως. *Som.* 1.176.

[56]*Vit. Mos.*, 1.156. It should be noted that in the passage Philo uses μετέχος of Moses's relationship to God as well as κοινωνός.

ciples.[57] This accords with what we have observed in studying cultic
meals, pp. 49-62.

The two passages in *Spec. Leg.* show the relationship of κοινωνία
in a setting of Jewish worship. In 1.131 the priests are said to have a
supreme honor in that they share with God in the thank-offering rendered
to him. As Aalen points out, this actually illustrates Paul's own description of priestly service and blessing in 1 Cor 9:13.[58] It is not said, however, that this sharing produced a personal relationship between the
priests and God, or that it mediated a divine presence to them.

In *Spec. Leg.* 1.221 Philo says that the sacrificial meats are not to
be hoarded but that they are free and open to all who have need, for they
are now the property not of him *by* whom but of him *to* whom the victim
has been sacrificed. "Who has made the convivial company of those who
carry out the sacrifice partners (κοινωνόν) of the altar whose board they
share."[59]

But these references do not prove that "God eats and drinks together with his worshippers,"[60] as is often alleged about pagan cults.
Certainly Philo is not saying that in such meals worshippers partake of
their God.[61] *Spec. Leg.* 1.221 speaks not of the relationship of the individuals to God, but of their relationship to each other. God, having received the sacrifice, turns over his animal gift to his worshippers who are
to have free shares. The point is that the officials of the cult are to
consider God himself as the host, not themselves. They are to distribute
the food equitably to God's guests, who are collectively termed κοινωνοί.[62]

Philo is useful to show that the use of the term κοινωνία for

[57]This illustrates from a non-Christian writer the criticism of
pagan θίασοι as disreputable. It may also serve to illumine the various
invitations to κλίναι of gods, found in the papyri. In Colson's notes in the
Loeb edition he comments, "The present passage suggests that the religious side (of these associations) was often left very much in the background," 536f.

[58]Aalen, "Abendmahl," 176f.

[59]Philo, *Spec. Leg.* 1.221.

[60]Hauck, "κοινωνεῖν," 803, says in the reference, *Spec. Leg.*
1.221, "Thus Philo speaks of a close fellowship between the righteous and
God in the cultus, esp. in the sacrificial meal."

[61]Correctly Aalen, "Opfermahl," 137. He says, "The term is much
more oriented to the sacrifice, esp. the altar."

[62]Currie, "Koinonia," 44-45.

participants in the Greek cultus has been taken over into Judaism. *Spec.
Leg.* 1.221 may be illuminating for a study of 1 Cor 11:23ff. and the
problem of the selfish abuse of the common meal associated with the
Lord's Supper.

But Philo cannot be taken as proof that κοινωνία was used to
describe a "close fellowship" between God and worshippers in a cultic
meal, as is often urged. Nor is it clear that Philo illustrates a usage of
this word group that may be considered to have influenced Paul.

3. *Josephus.* The frequency of the occurrence of κοινωνία and its
cognates in Josephus is striking. In the Rengstorf index κοινωνία is found
33 times.[63] Like the LXX, Josephus uses these words to refer to accom-
plices in evil deeds.[64] Agreeing with common Greek usage, he employs
them to refer to business relationships,[65] family kinship,[66] and especially
to having a share in the ruling of a nation.[67] The most prominent, and not
unprecedented, usage of κοινωνία in Josephus is to describe sexual relationships, both marriage[68] and sexual union.[69]

There are some uses of κοινωνία and cognates in Josephus which
seem to bear directly on the proper understanding of Paul's writing.
These are references which use these words to refer to dietary practice,[70] religious exclusivism,[71] sacrifice,[72] and the Jewish people as a

---

[63]Rengstorf, *Concordance to Flavius Josephus* 2, 512. The verb
occurs 40 times, the noun 26.

[64]*Bell* 1.498; 2.253, 7, 47, 60, 257. *Ant* 2.154; 6.237; 19.32.

[65]*Ant* 2.62.

[66]*Ant* 4.236; 1.315; 7.162; 11.341. *Ap* 2.31.

[67]*Bell* 1.72, 423; *Ant* 11.278; 13.303; 16.195; 17.115.

[68]*Ant* 18.361; 20.18.

[69]Of men and women, *Ant* 1.35; 2.52; 4.257; 11.307; 15.86, 228;
16.226. Similarly, Plutarch, *Con. Praec.* 48.145D. Josephus also refers to
animals, *Ant* 1.32 and even homosexuality, *Ant* 16.231. It may be, as
Jourdan, "KOINΩNIA," says that *Ap* 1.35 refers to comradeship. But one
may suspect that it is sexual intimacy, both because of a similar use in *Ap*
2.198 and because the context is a discussion of the accuracy of Jewish
priestly genealogies.

[70]*Ap* 2.174; *Ant* 6.346.

[71]*Ap* 2.174, 258; *Ant* 4.228.

[72]*Ap* 2.196, 208; 146, 196, 281. This passage describes what Paul
assumes in 1 Cor 9:13. Josephus says Moses ordained that the priests,
their families and servants should participate (κοινωνεῖν) in a portion
from the sacrifice.

special people.[73] These references are also instructive in that these ideas often occur together in a particular passage. In describing the work of Moses, Josephus says Moses

... left nothing, however insignificant, to the discretion of the individual. [including] What meat a man should abstain from, and what he may enjoy; with what persons he should associate (περὶ τῶν κοινωνησόντων τῆς διαίτης)....[74]

In another passage Josephus links dietary practices with the demarcation between Jews and Samaritans in the time after Alexander the Great's kingdom was divided. When anyone in Jerusalem was "accused of eating unclean food (κοινοφαγία) or violating the Sabbath or committing any other such sin, he would flee to the Schechemites, saying that he had been unjustly expelled."[75]

Josephus uses κοινωνία also to refer to the exclusivism among Jews and their reticence to be involved with other peoples. He accepts the common ancient charge that Jews refused to accept people with different conceptions of God and declined "to associate with those who have chosen to adopt a different mode of life."[76] Commenting on the Law of Deut 22:9f. (Lev 19:19) against "mismating" he says "nature delighteth not in the conjunction of things dissimilar,"[77] and goes on to say that this principle is to prevent a similar practice among men.

A similar allusion to Jewish self-identity is suggested in those references which describe the sense of community among Jews. He says that the three annual festivals from Deuteronomy are designed to promote mutual affections. "For it is good that they should not be ignorant of one another, being members of the same race and partners in the

---

[73] Ant 4.75; Ap 2.196.
[74] Ap 2.174. Note here the combining of dietary requirements and proper associations.
[75] Ant 11.346. κοινοφαγία is a *hapax legomenon* in Josephus.
[76] Ap 2.258, μηδὲ κοινωνεῖν ἐθέλομεν τοῖς καθ' ἑτέραν συνήθειαν βίου ζῆν προαιρουμένοις. Josephus's reply is that such exclusivism is not peculiar to Jews, but Greeks practice it, too.
[77] Ant 4.228, οὐ γὰρ τῇ τῶν ἀνομοίων κοινωνία χαίρειν τὴν φύσιν.

same institutions."[78] Likewise, the varied Mosaic laws are praised because "these and many similar regulations are the ties which bind us together."[79]

Finally, these motifs just discussed occur in connection with sacrifice in a reference where Joesphus contrasts the cult sacrifice of Israel with those of others.

> Our sacrifices are not occasions for drunken self-indulgence—such practices are abhorrent to God—but for sobriety. At these sacrifices prayer for the welfare of the community (κοινῆς) must take precedence of those for ourselves; for we are born for fellowship (κοινωνία), and he who sets its claims above his private interests is specially acceptable to God.[80]

From this passage we see that Josephus could use κοινωνία to describe the relationship between individuals found in their worship of a common God. The cult itself is then a demonstration of this κοινωνία because within it the interests of the community are placed above those of individuals. This may not be the same as the theological understanding of covenant found in the Old Testament, but it does show an awareness of mutual obligation related to worship of Israel's God, and is termed κοινωνία.[81] In this respect it is very similar to Paul's understanding in 1 Cor 10.

---

[78] Ant 4.204; καλὸν γὰρ εἶναι μὴ ἀγνοεῖν ἀλλήλους ὁμοφύλους τε ὄντας καὶ τῶν αὐτῶν κοινωνοῦντας ἐπιτηδευμάτων. In Ant 1.315 a variant reading describes the relationship between Laban and Jacob as κοινωνίας. Laban rebukes Jacob for acting δὲ οὔτε τῆς μητρὸς τῆς σαυτοῦ καὶ κοινωνίας ἧς ἔχεις πρὸς ἐμὲ συγγενείας. Here κοινωνία can refer to the family relationship created by the marriage or to a compact between Jacob and Laban—probably both.

[79] Ap 2.208, ταῦτα καὶ πολλὰ τούτοις ὅμοια τὴν πρὸς ἀλλήλους ἡμῶν συνέχει κοινωνίαν.

[80] Ap 2.196f. In Ant 3.258 the nation is called a "general community" (κοινωνίας).

[81] See Attridge, 71-91, dealing with the concept of self-identity as God's people.

1 CORINTHIANS 10:14-20:
THREE EXAMPLES OF ΚΟΙΝΩΝΙΑ

A. Introducing the Argument

As noted earlier in this chapter, the purpose of 10:14, 15 in the structure of 10:14-21 is to introduce a reasoned argument against Christian participation in pagan cultic meals. In 1 Cor 8 Paul answered a defense of eating conveyed to him from the Corinthians. However, in 10:1-13 he turned to present his own argument, based on an exposition of the salvation history. Then in 10:14-21 Paul presents a second argument, this time based upon the significance of religious meals. These two arguments are grammatically related by διόπερ. Thus the sections 10:1-13 and 14-21 both present reasons for avoiding the danger which Paul sees in pagan cult meals.

The designation of the Corinthians as ἀγαπητοί in 10:14 accords with his use of that word elsewhere. It is a term of genuine affection. Most commonly it occurs either with "my" (1 Cor 4:14; 15:58; Phil 2:12; 4:1; 1 Thess 2:8) or when a certain person is designated (Rom 16:5, 8, 9; 1 Cor 4:17; Phlm 16).[82] The designation here suggests that Paul's concern that the Corinthians heed his instruction is motivated by genuine interest in them.

The imperatival warning, φεύγετε ἀπὸ τῆς εἰδωλολατρίας,[83] shows the intensity of Paul's feelings about participation in these pagan meals. He will continue to give his reasoned approach, but his initial word is sharp and urgent: φεύγετε.

Many writers follow Weiss in noting the parallel use of φεύγειν in 1 Cor 6:18 (φεύγετε τὴν πορνείαν).[84] In 10:13 Paul spoke of a divinely

---

[82]Other occurrences are: Rom 1:7; 11:28 referring to God's elective work (cf. the designation of Jews in Matt 3:17; 16:5) and 2 Cor 7:1; 12:19, which refer to the Corinthians as a whole but without the possessive μοῦ.

[83]Conzelmann, *1 Corinthians*, 171, n. 9, notes that φεύγετε is a standard term in parenesis.

[84]Weiss, *Korintherbriefe*, 256. Weiss suggests that ἀπό may add emphasis to the imperative, φεύγετε. Robertson and Plummer, *1 Corinthians*, 211, doubt this.

A connection between idolatry and immoral sex is made in 10:7, 8. Perhaps this explains the similarity in the two injunctions in 6:18 and 10:14. Certainly since these are the only Pauline uses of φεύγειν it is

provided ἔκβασιν from temptation. Here it is set forth as the way to
avoid idolatry, "flee."[85]

Paul begins a transition to reasoning again in 10:15 where he appeals to the Corinthians to consider and accept his reasons for avoiding
these cultic associations. He begins, ὡς φρονίμοις λέγω.[86] Some
scholars suggest that φρονίμοις is used here ironically, "I speak as to
reasonable men—although such is not the case."[87] Yet since Paul does
continue to give a rational presentation, and because he does address
them genuinely as "beloved," it is probably better not to find irony in
φρονίμοις.[88]

Accordingly, it seems clear that Paul is honestly inviting the
Corinthians to evaluate his arguments. "You yourselves, judge what I
say."[89] This is not to say that Paul has doubts concerning the correctness
of his position and is looking for an objective evaluation.[90] He was not

---

probable that there is some connection between the two warnings, at least
in Paul's own fears.

[85]Robertson and Plummer, 1 Corinthians, 211, "They must not try
how near they can go, but how far they can fly." (They cite Tertullian, De
Cor. 10: Fugite idolatriam: omnem unique et totam.) Héring, First Epistle,
93, says that here ἀπό has "almost a locative sense: flee pagan temples
where you might fall into idolatry."

[86]Weiss, Korintherbriefe, 256, fn. suggests that λέγω relates only
to what follows it, not to what precedes in 10:1-13.

[87]Barrett, 1 Corinthians, 230, concludes: "sensible men can surely
not fail to see the point." He regards this as a continuing of the rebuke of
the Corinthians "knowledgable" self-esteem begun in 8:1-6. Similarly,
Weiss, Korintherbriefe, 256, and Robertson and Plummer, 1 Corinthians,
211, feel no sarcasm is involved. Although the latter do say, "yet there is
perhaps a gentle rebuke in the compliment. They ought not to need any
argument. . . ."

[88]Conzelmann, 1 Corinthians, 171, n. 12.   Cf. Lietzmann,
Korinther, 47, and Wendland, Korinther, 80.

It ought to be noted that elsewhere Paul does use the word
φρόνιμος both positively (Phil 2:2-5; 3:15) and also negatively (Rom 8:6, 7;
12:16).

[89]Robertson and Plummer, 1 Corinthians, 211, note that the ὑμεῖς
is emphatic by position.

[90]Grosheide, 1 Corinthians, 230, is too democratic when he says
that Paul's intent for the Corinthians is: "They should decide for themselves whether it is possible for a Christian to eat sacrificial meat against
his conscience and at the same time sit at the Lord's Table." Paul, writing as a father to his children (ἀγαπητοί), admonishes rather than invites
reply.

expecting to be refuted or to have his arguments overturned. Barrett
rightly says that κρίνατε is not really a testimony to the power of human
reason in solving this question. Still it does suppose that the use of common sense will lead the Corinthians to see the rightness of Paul's position.[91] Schrage correctly observes that Paul writes his letters expecting
an understanding obedience from his readers.[92] He gives 1 Cor 10:15 as
evidence of this expectation.

Now the study must turn to 10:16-20, the substantive center of
Paul's argument which is based on the κοινωνία of cultic meals. The
examination of non-biblical uses of κοιν-stem words has shown a wide
range of meanings for these terms. This variety suggests that the meaning of κοινωνία in 1 Cor 10 cannot be determined by lexical studies
alone. Rather, the context of 1 Corinthians, along with the other Pauline
usages, must be determinative. Therefore we now turn to consider the
use of the words in 1 Cor 10.

The first observation must be that Paul uses κοινωνία to describe
religious meals involving each of three groups: Christian, Jewish and
pagan. A satisfactory interpretation of κοινωνία in 1 Cor 10 should fit
each of the three references, since their repetition can scarcely be accidental. Because the meaning of Christian κοινωνία in 10:16 is the most
disputed, we will begin with the other two examples, seeking to shed light
on Christian κοινωνία from the other uses.

B. Κοινωνία τοῦ θυσιαστηρίου

In 1 Cor 10:18 Paul terms "natural Israel" κοινωνοὶ τοῦ θυσιαστηρίου. He does this to illustrate the relationship of Christians to the Lord,
already mentioned with the Lord's Supper as a κοινωνία. There are three
important considerations in 10:18 for the present study. First, what does
it mean to call Israel κοινωνοὶ τοῦ θυσιαστηρίου? Second, more specifically, what is meant by θυσιαστήριον? Is it, as some suggest, a circumlocution for the divine name? Or does it mean the altar upon which
sacrifice was placed? Or something else? Third, and dependent upon how

---

[91]Barrett, *1 Corinthians*, 231. He adds, "Perhaps Paul's point is
that (unlike some at Corinth) he is appealing not to (supposedly) inspired
discourse but to reasoned argument."

[92]Schrage, *Einzelgebote*, 113. He has a valuable discussion of the
role of argumentation in Paul's admonitions, see 109-115.

the second question is answered, is the genitive θυσιαστηρίου subjective or objective?

Beginning with the more specific question, what is referred to by θυσιαστήριον? Quite often it is said that this is a reverential euphemism for God.[93] Most authors holding this view cite the study by Hugo Gressmann.[94] Gressmann himself says that it is the divine numen which is referred to by the word.[95] Although the "numenous" interpretation has generally fallen from favor, Gressmann's equation of θυσιαστήριον with God is still widely held.

Gressmann's support is largely the assumption of a universal sacramentalism of eating the deity, and a specific reference to Philo, *Spec. Leg.* 1.221.[96] The Philo reference has been shown above (p. 178) to have a different meaning than Gressmann thought. There are other things which also refute Gressmann's interpretation.

First, the other New Testament references point away from equating θυσιαστήριον with God. Elsewhere Paul uses the word only twice. In Rom 11:3 he quotes 1 Sam 19:10, where the word must be translated "altar," not "God of the altar," since the enemies of Elijah cannot have destroyed his God. In 1 Cor 9:13 the translation "sacrifices upon the altar" seems obviously correct, for these are what fed the priests. The other New Testament uses also suggest the translation "altar," or "sacrifices upon the altar."[97]

---

[93]For example, Robertson and Plummer, *1 Corinthians*, 215, "They are in fellowship with the altar, and therefore with the unseen God, whose altar it is."

Also see Hauck, "κοινωνία," 805. Seesemann, *Begriff* ΚΟΙΝΩΝΙΑ, 52f.

[94]Hugo Gressmann, "Η ΚΟΙΝΩΝΙΑ ΤΩΝ ΔΑΙΜΟΝΙΩΝ," *ZNW* 20 (1921) 224-230.

[95]Ibid., 224.

[96]Gressmann, "ΚΟΙΝΩΝΙΑ," 95. Contrast Josephus, *Bell.* 5.229 where it is clearly the altar.

But Jourdan, "ΚΟΙΝΩΝΙΑ," 123, is right. "This passage only lends testimony to the practical obligations of that partnership among Israelites of which we read in Deut. 12." Campbell, "Κοινωνία," 24f., makes the same point with additional evidence.

[97]They are: Matt 5:23, 24; 23:18-20; Luke 1:11; 11:51; Heb 7:13; 13:10; Jas 2:21; Rev 6:9; 8:3. Of these only Matt 23:18 makes any sense understanding θυσιαστήριον as "God" (See Eduard Meyer, *Die Papyrusfund von Elephantine* [Leipzig: J. C. Hinrichs, 1912] 65), and even there "altar" makes good sense. Heb 13:10 may refer to the Lord's Supper, but

Second, in the LXX the word θυσιαστήριον is used over 500 times
to translate the Hebrew נזבח which means a place of sacrifice. Indeed
only four times does θυσιαστήριον translate a different word.[98] In none
of these places is it reasonable to think it means "God."

Third, in the 17 passages where Josephus uses θυσιαστήριον it is
always to refer to an altar. One of these contrasts the altar of God
(θυσιαστήριον) with those of pagan gods (βωμός).[99]

In summary, there is no convincing evidence that θυσιαστήριον
was used in Hellenistic Judaism as a circumlocution for the divine name.
Therefore in 1 Cor 10:18 the obvious translation remains the best, "altar"
or "sacrifice on the altar."[100]

Consequently, this means that the genitive is objective (of the
thing shared) not subjective (of the person sharing), as would be the case
if God were termed θυσιαστήριον. This interpretation has the advantage
of agreeing with the Hebrew understanding of a distance between God and
man which prohibits mortals from being ḥaberim of YHWH.[101]

If θυσιαστήριον does not refer to God himself, then the right
interpretation of κοινωνία in 10:18 must reflect this. Paul says of the

in any event surely does not mean "God," for Hebrews would not argue
Christians have a different God!

[98]2 Chr 14:5 בָּמָה ; Ps 83:12 נָאָה ; Hos 3:4 מַצֵּבָה ; 2 Esdr 7:17
הַצְרֵמ. Aalen, "Opfermahl," 124, says that θυσιαστήριον means exactly as
the Hebrew מַזְבֵּחַ, the place of sacrifice, or the sacrifice.

[99]Josephus, Ant 12.253. Aalen, "Opfermahl," contends that in
1 Cor 9:13 τὸ ἱερόν means "sacrifice," not temple and reflects a concept
of "eating from the altar."

[100]So Aalen, "Abendmahl," 133f.

[101]Ibid., 123. Also see Jourdan, "KOINΩNIA," 112-113.

Barrett, 1 Corinthians, 235, rightly denies any reference is made in
10:18 to a partnership with God; rather those who partake are sharing in
the sacrificial meal with one another. "In this material sense there was
joint participation in the benefits arising from the altar."

Conzelmann, 1 Corinthians, 172, calls the Jewish sacrifice a
communal meal "and this means communion with the god to whom the
sacrifice is made and to whom the altar belongs." What he means largely
depends on what is meant by the word communion.

Seesemann, Begriff KOINΩNIA, 52f. says that the meaning of
κοινωνοί in 10:18 is "Genossen Gottes" (tablemates of God, as is found in
Greek writers). He continues that the meal here leads one into a very
strong contact with the divinity, one which is not possible to achieve
otherwise.

Jews that they are κοινωνοί in the altar, or the sacrifice of the altar.
This can only mean that in the joint participation of sacrifice and accompanying rites the relationship of κοινωνία is established and sustained
among the worshippers; they are a cultic community.[102] This meal-
sacrifice may have been an occasion of joy,[103] but essentially it was an
expression of religious fraternity. Aalen has pointed out that the sacrifice and the eating belong together.[104] To eat of the sacrifice is to
participate in the sacrifice.[105] This is exactly what is said in 1 Cor
10:18, since it is "those who eat" (οἱ ἐσθίοντες) who are κοινωνοί.

In Israel's faith and practice the sacrifice served to seal the covenant relationship between YHWH and his people.[106] It also established a
relationship among the people who worship YHWH, as the story of Moses
sprinkling the people with the sacrificial blood (inter alia) suggests.[107] It
is this relationship to which Paul refers in 10:18. Jourdan therefore
misleads when he objects that the Jewish κοινωνία cannot be regarded as
parallel to the Christian and pagan cults, because Jews have no sacrament.[108]

Although Paul does not make the point explicitly here, one aspect
of Israel's κοινωνία pertinent to the Corinthian problem was its exclusive
character, set over against the pagan world. Paul may assume this aspect
of Israel's κοινωνία when in 10:21, 22 he warns the Corinthians that
violation of the exclusive loyalty which God expects may provoke the
Lord's (probably Christ's, but perhaps the Father's) jealousy.[109]

---

[102]Blass-Debrunner, *Greek Grammar*, 169.1, 2.
[103]Aalen, "Opfermahl," 141, argues that every sacrificial meal was
a feast of religious joy.
[104]Ibid., 136.
[105]Ibid., 135. He sees this association especially in the shedding of
blood, 140f.
[106]Old Testament precedents are found in Exod 24:4-11; Lev 2:3,
10; Deut 12:4-28, inter alia. Nikolaus Walter, "Christusglaube und
heidnische Religiosität in paulinischen Gemeinden," *NTS* 25 (1979) 434, n.
57, is right in concluding that although Paul is not teaching a specifically
"Israelite" view of sacrifice, he does assume the Old Testament belief
that man cannot have a personal fellowship with YHWH.
[107]Joachim Jeremias, *The Eucharistic Words of Jesus* (New York:
Scribner, 1966) 158, says that atonement was effected in the Jewish cult
meal according to Siphra Lev. 10:17.
[108]Jourdan, "KOINΩNIA," 122.
[109]Walter, "Christusglaube," 434, notes the exclusive character of
Jewish sacrificial gatherings.

The starting place for an understanding of the three examples of κοινωνία set out in 1 Cor 10:16-22 is a proper appreciation for the Jewish fellowship noted in 10:18. Israel as κοινωνοὶ τοῦ θυσιαστηρίου refers to their relationship as worshippers bound together in common sacrifice to YHWH. There is no implication of consuming the deity. This secure point serves as a guide for interpreting more uncertain instances of κοινωνία in 1 Cor 10: Christian and pagan. We turn now to the latter.

C. Κοινωνοὶ τῶν Δαιμονίων

Paul's rhetorical question in 10:19, τί οὖν φημι; marks another shift, this time to a third example of κοινωνία that formed around a pagan idol.[110] His questions anticipate possible objections to his opposing Christian participation in pagan cult meals. Some in Corinth might object to such a prohibition on the grounds that Paul himself had agreed already there is only one God and thus idols are not real gods (in 8:4, 6).[111]

The possible misunderstanding he raises rhetorically is that sacrificial meat itself is somehow tainted (εἰδωλόθυτόν τί ἐστιν;) or even that the idols themselves are real (εἴδωλόν τί ἐστιν;).[112] He may sense

---

[110]Bartsch, "korinthische Missbrauch," 177f., argues that in 10:19-21 the example remains the practice of Israel. He thus denies a shift at v. 19, for Israel remains the object of discussion. He finds some support in the textual tradition. In significant manuscripts τὰ ἔθνη is omitted, apparently correctly. See Zuntz, 95, who observes that the later specification is a correct, but unnecessary, elaboration of the original text. The belief that what is sacrificed is really offered to demons Paul could only say of pagan worship.

[111]But really both passages deny the "divinity" of the idols, and that such "gods" can pollute the meat offered to them. Robertson and Plummer, 1 Corinthians, 215, and Barrett, 1 Corinthians, 236.

The non-being of idols was also argued in 8:4. This is a common Jewish critique of idolatry beginning within the Old Testament. The same line of criticism is continued in later Christian writer: Justin, Apol. 5:1, 2; 12:5; 19:1; 21:6, 54; Clement of Alexandria, Protrep. 55:5; 62:4 and Athenagoras 26f.

[112]There are also textual problems in this verse. Some old and good manuscripts omit εἴδωλον τί ἐστιν. Barrett, 1 Corinthians, 236, suggests that this is due either to homoeoteleuton or because the implied denial of the existence of such idols was seen to conflict with vv. 20f. See Conzelmann, 1 Corinthians, 170, n. 4. Such a paradox is almost characteristic of the argument in these chapters.

(or know from their communication) that some Christians in Corinth will object that idols are "not anything."[113]

Having noted these possible objections, Paul turns explicitly to the case of pagan κοινωνία. "But (ἀλλά, a classical adversative use of this particle[114]) I do not want[115] you to be partners (κοινωνοί) of demons." This admonition signals the beginning of Paul's major point about κοινωνία. He prohibits Christians from becoming partners with their pagan friends in demonic idolatry (κοινωνοὺς τῶν δαιμονίων γίνεσθαι).[116]

How one becomes a κοινωνός is made specific in 10:21; it is by participation at their table. Paul only uses the word τράπεζα here and in Rom 11:9 (an Old Testament quote). But, as is described in Part I on cultic dining, the τράπεζα was a common and prominent feature of pagan worship.[117] It is likely that Paul here has employed the designation of the Christian cult as τράπεζα κυρίου in conscious antithesis to the pagan table, τράπεζα δαιμονίων.[118]

It is not clear precisely what the word δαιμονίων meant for

---

[113]The enclitic τι may mean "anything at all" as suggested by Lietzmann, *Korinther,* 48, who thinks Paul protects himself against misunderstanding. The manner of expression is highly pregnant, τι = a real sacrifice.

[114]Noted by Barrett, *1 Corinthians,* 236.

[115]The phrase οὐ θέλω ὑμᾶς is characteristic Pauline hortatory style. "I do not wish" is a correct translation, yet probably not sufficiently strong. Paul is not simply giving his preference but admonishing those already engaged in the practice.

Paul uses θέλω ὑμᾶς in exhortations in Rom 16:15; 1 Cor 7:32; 2 Cor 12:20 and in the phrase οὐ θέλω ὑμᾶς ἀγνόειν in Rom 1:13; 11:25; 1 Cor 10:1; 12:1; 2 Cor 1:8 and 1 Thess 4:13.

[116]Not "partners in the demons," as is sometimes held. The actual expression κοινωνία τῶν δαιμονίων is used in Porphyry, *De Abst.* 2.42, as quoted in Eusebius, *P.E.* 4.23. Cites by Lietzmann, *Korinther,* 49. Nock, *Early Gentile Christianity,* 82f., doubts Lietzmann's interpretation.

[117]See Part 1, "Sacrifice, Cult Meals."

[118]Adolf Deissmann, *Light From the Ancient East* (London: Hodder & Stoughton, 1927) 351, says that it is a case of independent parallelism. Paul's expression perhaps was influenced by the LXX of Malachi 1:7, 12 and Ezek 34:20 and 44:16.

Paul,[119] and that is not crucial for understanding the function of this passage. It is clear that the "demons" are in some way the recipients of what is sacrificed to idols (v. 19).

The important question is what did Paul mean by calling those who participated in the sacrificial cultus κοινωνοὺς δαιμονίων? Basically three meanings must be considered: (1) in eating from idol sacrifices the worshipper takes demons into himself, (2) at the sacrifice the worshipper becomes an associate of demons who are eating there too, or (3) the worshipper associates with other men in a cult devoted to demons, if unintentionally.

From what was discovered in the study of pagan cultic dining in Part I, and from what has just been seen about κοινωνία τοῦ θυσιαστηρίου it is clear that option (1) is mistaken. Neither in the pagan cult meals, nor certainly in the Jewish ones, do participants eat their god.[120]

The second interpretation currently is most prominent, i.e., those who partake of the pagan meals are partners along with the demons in the sacrifice.[121] This view is represented by Aalen who says: "Die Dämonen sind also Wirt und Partner beim Opferschmaus."[122]

A third interpretation also must be considered. It is not clear that Paul thinks of any personal relationship between the demons and the

---

[119]On the reality of demons in Paul, see Martin Dibelius, *Geisterwelt*.

Δαιμονίων occurs only here in Paul's letters. But considering demons as real forces (although not real gods) is in basic agreement with Paul's *Weltanschaung*. See G. B. Caird, *Principalities and Powers* (Oxford: Clarendon Press, 1956).

[120]Gressmann, "KOINΩNIA," 95, consistent with his view of verse 18, thinks that the worshippers take into themselves the demons. This is based on his view that in the sacrifice pagans felt themselves to be eating the god. Similarly, Lietzmann, *Korinther*, 49.

[121]For example, Bultmann, *TNT*, 148, says that the pagans are "partners (or communicants) with demons." W. G. Kümmel in the appendix for Lietzmann, *Korinther*, 11 ed., 182, expresses this sentiment. Some writers seem to hold both views one and two. See Seesemann, *Begriff* KOINΩNIA, 154f.

[122]Aalen, "Opfermahl," 132. Κοινωνία with the genitive of the person has as the natural translation "companion of the demons." Others holding similar views are Lietzmann, *Korinther*, 49; Barrett, *1 Corinthians*, 237. Perhaps also Moffatt, *1 Corinthians*, 138f.

worshippers;[123] it is rather that the partaking of the meal together
creates a communal relationship among the participants—they are κοι νω-
νοί—in a forbidden worship. As is observed by Campbell,

> It is therefore much easier to take τῶν δαιμονίων as an
> ordinary genitive of the thing shared—"I do not wish you to be
> partners (with one another and with your heathen fellow-
> worshippers) in demons," which is simply a striking way of
> saying, "I do not wish you to participate in demon-
> worship."[124]

In addition to avoiding the erroneous sacramentalistic view we
have criticized, this view has three positive merits. First, it agrees with
the interpretation of 10:18, where κοινωνία τοῦ θυσιαστηρίου means
share together with others in the sacrifices of the altar (not share the
altar, certainly not have a share of God!). Second, the focus remains on
the thing common to Paul's three illustrations—κοινωνία—rather than the
demons. Third, the comparison is not Christ and demons, but *cult meals*
of Christ and of demons, as was already announced with the opening
warning of 10:14, φεύγετε ἀπὸ τῆς εἰδωλολατρίας.

Therefore, in the prohibition of v. 20 Paul opposes Christians
associating with pagans in their worship. The reason given, that such
participation involves one with demons, is an old Jewish argument.[125]
However, it is not a fear of demons which Paul has foremost in his mind,
but that being involved in these cult meals involves one with a tacit

---

[123]Campbell, "Κοινωνία," 25, says that there is "no suggestion of
any partnership between the worshippers and the deity whom they worship. If that idea is expressed here, it comes unexpectedly, and remains
quite undeveloped." Similar is Grosheide, *1 Corinthians*, 236.

[124]Ibid. This is not the same as taking the expression to mean
"ingest demons," for δαιμονίων here is ellipsis for "demon worship, i.e.,
cultus."

[125]Moffatt, *1 Corinthians*, 136.   Similarly, Robertson and
Plummer, *1 Corinthians*, 213.

On pagan worship as offered to demons see: Isa 65:11; Dt 32:17;
Baruch 4:11; 1 Enoch 19:1; 99:7; Jub 1:11; 22:17; Pss 96:5; 106:37 and Rev
9:20. In psPhilo, *Biblical Antiquities*, 25 certain Jews model a perverse
worship after pagan cults and their idols are termed "the evil spirits of
the idols." M. R. James, *The Biblical Antiquities of Ps Philo* (London:
S. P. C. K., 1917) 150. The same idea of demons using idols as a "front" is
found in Athenagoras, *Emb.* 26, 27 and Barnabas 16:7.

recognition of supernatural powers opposed to God.[126] These occasions of worship, Christian and pagan, are mutually exclusive.[127] Just as one shows his master by whom he serves (Rom 6:16ff.), so also one shows his allegiance by the worship in which he participates.

D. Κοινωνία . . . τοῦ Χριστοῦ

Finally we turn to take up the first example of κοινωνία which Paul gives in the section 10:14-22—the κοινωνία τοῦ αἵματος/τοῦ σώματος τοῦ Χριστοῦ. We take the first example last because this Christian κοινωνία has been the subject of the most study and debate. Thus it seemed best to begin with the less controversial instances.

Many writers have noted that Paul is not setting forth his "eucharistic teaching" (if such categories are not anachronistic) in 10:16, 17.[128] Nonetheless, these few verses very often have been studied to derive just

---

[126]Campbell, "Κοινωνία," 22f. Nock, *Early Gentile Christianity,* 82, says: "Perhaps the easiest explanation is that St. Paul is transferring his interpretation of the Christian rite to them [pagan cults] to make as effective a contrast as possible." There is no doubt that Paul's knowledge of pagan worship is that of an "outsider." It was also shaped by a Jewish attitude of a covenant alliance of those who are involved in a cultus.

[127]As Wendland, *Korinther,* 82, says, both are contradictory, excluding each other. From this knowledge exists the entire series of ideas of this section. Only here is there an either/or, Christ stands over against the demons (cf. 2 Cor 6:15, 16).

Barth, *Resurrection,* 52f. says that it is these demonic powers which constitute the "meaning, the object, and the reality of pagan idolatry. Whatever its gods are called, paganism is the worship of devils. . . ." This, he notes, is objectively true, regardless of the subjective denial by the Corinthians who would deny that this was their intent.

[128]For example, Barrett, *1 Corinthians,* 231, says "The present allusion [to the Lord's Supper] is made for one purpose only, to reinforce Paul's warning against idolatry. . . ." But he continues, ". . . it does make possible a few inferences about the way in which the Supper was interpreted in Paul's time."

Weiss, *Earliest Christianity,* 648, says regarding the mention of the Lord's Supper in 10 and 11: "Paul in both passages employs his interpretation of the Supper only as a means to other ends: in 1 Cor 10, to warn against meats offered to idols; in 1 Cor 11 to censure the unfraternal conduct of various members of the church."

that from them.[129] The result has been that 10:16, 17 frequently have been isolated from their context, and the real theme of the pericope— εἰδωλολατρία—has been neglected. What was originally composed as hortatory material has been misconstrued in the press for eucharistic theology. One result has been that some have denied that the other examples of κοινωνία which Paul gives are intended as parallels.

Of course the importance of Paul's understanding of the Christian κοινωνία must not be minimized. It is likely that he does interpret pagan meals and the Jewish meals as well under the influence of his view of the Christian cult meal. His prohibition of pagan cult meals as unacceptable κοινωνία is related to his view of the exclusive character of Christian κοινωνία. Still the focus of the pericope is not Paul's eucharistic thought, but a prohibition of pagan meals which is grounded in three examples of κοινωνία.

In this section of our study we will investigate what Paul refers to as Christian κοινωνία. An important initial question arises about the traditional character of v. 16 which comes from pre-Pauline thought and its Pauline interpretation in v. 17. A subsidiary question is the meaning of σῶμα Χριστοῦ both in the tradition and in Paul's own thought. Finally, we must turn to inquire what κοινωνία means in describing the Lord's Supper and how this relates to other references to κοινωνία.

1. *Tradition and interpretation in 10:16, 17.* Verse 16 has been widely recognized as a piece of pre-Pauline Christian tradition in content and in wording as well.[130] There are at least three indications of its traditional character. First, there is the expression ποτήριον τῆς εὐλο- γίας. In Paul's letters ποτήριον only occurs in passages dealing with eucharistic tradition: 1 Cor 10:2; 11:26-28.[131] Moreover, the modifying

---

[129]There are many examples, two recent of which are: Käsemann, "Pauline Doctrine," and Bornkamm, "Lord's Supper and Church," 123-160.

[130]First, perhaps, by Weiss, *Korintherbrief,* 283. But also noted by most recent commentators: Conzelmann, *1 Corinthians,* 171, 200f.; Barrett, *1 Corinthians,* 233; Wendland, *Korinther,* 80f.; and Käsemann, "Pauline Doctrine," 110.

[131]Käsemann, "Pauline Doctrine," 109, and Conzelmann, *1 Corin- thians,* 171. Barrett, *1 Corinthians,* 231, cites similar expressions from *Joseph and Aseneth* (8:5, 9; 15:5; 16:6; 19:5). See also L. Goppelt, "Ποτή- ριον," *TDNT* 6 (1968) 153-58, who points to Rabbinic evidence for a "cup of blessing." Similarly, Jeremias, *Eucharistic Words,* 60, cites evidence from Strack-Billerbeck, 4, 628ff.

word εὐλογίας is a Hebraic expression; Paul himself normally uses εὐχαριστία.[132]

Second, the conjecture that Paul in v. 16 is summoning the Corinthians to recall something already known, not to accept new teaching, is supported by grammar.[133] The use of οὐ in the question commonly assumes a "yes" answer from the reader.[134]

Finally, confirmation of the traditional character of this verse is given one chapter later by Paul himself. In 1 Cor 11:23f. Paul reminds the Corinthians that he has received and handed on (παραλαμβάνω and παρέδωκα, each a *terminus technicus*) a teaching about the Lord's Supper as αἷμα/σῶμα τοῦ κυρίου.[135]

Many have sought to move behind the present Pauline text and reconstruct a pre-Pauline eucharistic theology from the traditional materials taken over by Paul.[136] For the present purposes only two additional

---

[132]Paul only uses εὐλογεῖν and εὐλογία nine times, and with a different connotation. He uses εὐχαρίστειν and εὐχαριστία 15 times, not including the "thanksgivings" in his letter.

In the LXX εὐχαριστεῖν appears only 12 times, all of which are in the Apocrypha. Εὐλογία is used extensively.

Goppelt, "Ποτήριον," 156, agrees with Lietzmann that the phrase τὸ ποτήριον τῆς εὐλογίας comes from Jewish tradition. He disagrees with Lietzmann's assessment that the modifying phrase ὃ εὐλογοῦμεν is pleonastic. "It differentiates the Christian cup of blessing from that of the Jews."

[133]Noted by Bartsch, "korinthische Missbrauch," 176. He thinks this appeal to a common tradition is part of Paul's reasonable approach.

[134]Blass-DeBrunner, *Greek Grammar*, §427: "both οὐ and μη are still used in the NT in questions as in classical; οὐ when an affirmative answer is expected, μη . . . when a negative one is expected."

[135]On the traditional character of this section see works cited in note 130. Also Bultmann, *TNT*, I, 150f. Bultmann thinks the "sacramental" understanding of the Christian meal was a product of a pre-Pauline Hellenistic Christianity.

Αἷμα τοῦ Χριστοῦ is a very rare concept in Paul. It occurs only here and 1 Cor 11:27 in this epistle (both passages dealing with the Lord's Supper). Otherwise it is found in Rom 5:9 and 3:25 (generally regarded as traditional).

[136]To investigate the eucharistic theology of Paul himself is beyond the scope of our study. The beginning point for modern discussion of the development of eucharistic theology in the church would be Hans Lietzmann's exhaustive *Mass and Lord's Supper* (Leiden: E. J. Brill, 1953ff.) which contains the relevant sources. Lietzmann's thesis is of two

points need to be observed about the traditional formula quoted in 10:16.
First, as noted by Käsemann, the word κοινωνία in the formula is also probably pre-Pauline.[137] This means that all theories which suggest that the concept of the Lord's Supper as κοινωνία is Paul's unique contribution to the discussion are mistaken. Paul is not seeking to teach the Corinthians a new truth about κοινωνία and the Lord's Supper. Rather, he is reminding them of what they have already received. He employs a well-known designation of the Christian meal to compare it with other cult meals.

Second, although Paul apparently quotes traditional phraseology in v. 16, it is likely that he has altered the order of the events. It has been noted that the order cup/bread differs not only from the order Paul himself gives in 11:23f. but also from the account of the Last Supper in Matthew and Mark. It could be that the order itself was not fixed in Paul's time and that therefore no significance attaches to the order.[138] It has also been suggested that Paul emphasizes the cup precisely by placing it first.[139]

More often this order is considered to be Paul's own conscious reversal of the traditional order (found in 11:23f.). He is believed to have done this to stress the bread word, which offered a better basis for his interest in the one σῶμα of the Christian community.[140] Paul's interpretation of the traditional words, found in v. 17, does equate ἄρτος and σῶμα.[141] Yet the remainder of the pericope is not concerned with divi-

---

primitive understandings of the Christian meal: one sacramental (reflecting a Hellenistic outlook) and one fellowship oriented (a Jewish outlook). To assess this thesis is quite beyond present limitations, but the question of a "sacramental" view in our passage will be discussed at various points in the present study.
See also Bornkamm, "Lord's Supper and Church," and Oscar Cullmann and F. J. Leenhard, *Essays on the Lord's Supper* (Ecumenical Studies in Worship, 1; Richmond: John Knox, 1953).
[137]Käsemann, "Pauline Doctrine," 109.
[138]Barrett, *1 Corinthians*, 233, suggests this as a possibility although he himself does not embrace it. He notes that this order does agree with that given in Luke 22:17 and *Didache* 9:2f.
[139]Robertson and Plummer, *1 Corinthians*, 213.
[140]For example, Käsemann, "Pauline Doctrine," 110; Wendland, *Korinther*, 81; Conzelmann, *1 Corinthians*, 171; Barrett, *1 Corinthians*, 233.
[141]Käsemann, "Pauline Doctrine," 110. For Käsemann it is of crucial importance to Paul's argument that behind the analogy of the body

siveness or cliques. Perhaps the body and the unity it suggests, while noted here, is not a focus of the present argument. Indeed this topic of unity from the one σῶμα is dropped, to be taken up again in chapter 11.

If 10:16 is largely taken over from earlier Christian tradition, v. 17 is of special importance since it is Paul's interpretation of the eucharistic words from v. 16.[142] Two points are important for our study from v. 17: the meaning of σῶμα and its role in Paul's argument and the use of μετέχειν. We examine the latter first.

It is too often overlooked that in Paul's own interpretation of the tradition he uses μετέχειν as equivalent to κοινωνεῖν. This ought to warn against interpretations of 1 Cor 10:16, 17 which stress a supposed distinction between κοινωνεῖν and μετέχειν.[143] Jourdan, for example, says that Paul preferred μετέχειν for the "visible act of participation" and that this distinction was made in every case between κοινωνός and μέτοχος, κοινωνεῖν and μετέχειν, κοινωνία and μετοχή.[144]

---

is the primitive myth of the First Man (the *Urmensch*). Paul's modification of the Christian tradition is on the trajectory of the Gnostic speculation about the *Urmensch*, now interpreted as the body of Christ. Käsemann's reconstruction is assessed and critiqued by Jewett, *Paul's Anthropological Terms*, 216-20, 256-64.

[142]Käsemann, "Pauline Doctrine," 110; Barrett, *1 Corinthians*, 233; Bultmann, *TNT*, 147; Conzelmann, *1 Corinthians*, 171. Dissenting is Moffatt, *1 Corinthians*, 134, who regards v. 17 as "one of his pregnant asides." Also Seesemann, *Begriff* KOINΩNIA, 44f., says v. 17 is a digression from the theme of vv. 16 and 18.

[143]Robertson and Plummer, *1 Corinthians*, 212, "'partake' is μετέχειν: κοινωνεῖν is 'to have a share in'; therefore κοινωνία is 'fellowship' rather than 'participation,' ... The difference between 'participation' and 'fellowship' or 'communion' is the difference between having a share and having the whole. In Holy Communion each recipient has a share of the bread and of the wine, but he has the whole of Christ." Compare Seesemann, *Begriff* KOINΩNIA, 43: "Ein derartiger Unterschied scheint hier zwischen den beiden Worten vorzuliegen: am Brot hat man nur teil (v. 17b), mit dem Blut bzw. Leib Christi verbindet man sich (v. 16)." This mistakenly assumes that Paul is interested in the component parts, rather than the whole.

Similarly mistaken are attempts to make distinctions based on the use of ἐκ with μετέχειν. See Robertson and Plummer, *1 Corinthians*, 214.

[144]Jourdan, "KOINΩNIA," 121, says that this "visible act of partici-

Paul's use of μετέχειν in parallel to κοινωνία prohibits making any "spiritual" distinction between these words. Actually, popular Greek also used the words as synonyms.[145] No theological conclusions should be drawn on the basis of such alleged distinctions between these words.

It is true that Paul does use the word μετέχειν for the act of eating the bread.[146] But this does not mean that the actual eating is less spiritual than would be the case if he had used κοινωνεῖν.[147] Κοινωνεῖν does imply the idea of association with others[148] and/or perhaps a "more permanent" relationship.[149] But the idea of an intimate or personal relationship with Christ is not implied by the word κοινωνία. On the basis of the use of this word in sacral contexts it is implied that the members of a cultic community had a necessary and important relationship.

The second significant issue in 10:17 for the present study is the concept of σῶμα. In the tradition quoted in v. 16 the bread was called κοινωνία τοῦ σώματος τοῦ Χριστοῦ. This is interpreted in v. 17 where εἷς ἄρτος = ἓν σῶμα οἱ πολλοί ἐσμεν. This shows that Paul received and employed the concept of σῶμα τοῦ Χριστοῦ in speaking of the Lord's Supper. Many exegetes have found in the concept of σῶμα the decisive

---

pation" is a sign of the "exalted level of spirituality" of the believers' relationship to Jesus Christ, termed κοινωνία.

[145]Moulton and Milligan, Vocabulary, 305f., 405f.; Hermann Hanse, "Μετέχω," TNDT 2 (1964) 831. Conzelmann, 1 Corinthians, 172. Walter, "Christusglaube," 433, n. 53. Cf. Heb 2:14.

Κοινωνεῖν and μετέχειν are used synonymously in P. Oxy. 1408.25-27, and Plutarch, Quaes. Conv. 10 (with similarities to Paul). Like κοινωνία and its cognates, μετέχω is used also in non-Christian writings to describe table fellowship both with friends (Philo, De Jos. 196 and Ps. Lucian, Cyn. 7) and also of cults (Philostratus, Vit. Soph. 2.15.1 and 1 Esdr 5:40), and marriage (Josephus, Ap. 1.31).

[146]Currie, Koinonia, 434. See 1 Cor 9:12; 10:17, 21, 30.

[147]For example, see L. S. Thornton, The Common Life in the Body of Christ (London: Dacre Press, 1942) 450. says: "to indicate the mysterious implications of this outward act. . . ."

[148]Campbell, "Κοινωνία," 233f., and Hanse "Μετέχω," 831. Seesemann, Begriff KOINΩNIA, 43, says that κοινωνεῖν is the broader term.

[149]Currie, Koinonia, 8.

consideration for understanding Paul's view of the eucharist, of the κοινωνία involved therein, and even of the entire passage 1 Cor 10:16-22.[150]

Present limitations preclude a full examination of the imagery of σῶμα τοῦ Χριστοῦ. However, there are a number of readily accessible studies where the phrase is thoroughly studied.[151] The major issues examined are: the origin of the image σῶμα τοῦ Χριστοῦ;[152] its meaning and function in pre-Pauline theology; the use of the concept here in 1 Cor 10:16, 17.

Most studies of the expression in 1 Corinthians have noted the pre-Pauline character of the phrase. When the sacramental understanding of pagan cult meals was regarded as highly influential on Christian eucharistic thought (especially in Paul's Gentile churches), the σῶμα τοῦ Χριστοῦ was believed to be a reference to a Christian sacramental ritual in which participants believed that they were consuming the body of Christ as their pagan neighbors believed that they were consuming their god.[153]

Oscar Cullmann has a similar interpretation to this except he thinks that Paul was the originator of this sacramental eucharistic theol-

---

[150]Especially Käsemann, "Pauline Doctrine."

[151]The most recent survey is Robert H. Gundry, ΣΩΜΑ in Biblical Theology (SNTSMS 29; Cambridge: University Press, 1976). Other modern discussions include: J. A. T. Robinson, The Body (SBT I, 5; London: SCM Press, 1952); Jewett, Paul's Anthropological Terms, 201-304 (which includes a good history of the research); and E. Schweizer, "Σῶμα" TDNT, VII, 1024-1093 (with a full bibliography).

Older but very influential works include Ernst Käsemann, Leib und Leib Christi (BHTh 9; Tübingen: J. C. B. Mohr [Paul Siebeck], 1933); and Thornton, Common Life.

[152]The study of J. A. T. Robinson gives a good, succinct analysis of the probable sources for the concept in Christian theology. For the present study it seems more profitable to stress Paul's own use of the phrase, rather than to trace possible "origins" of the phrase.

[153]Classically summarized by Hans Lietzmann in his excursus on 1 Corinthians 10:16, 17. (Korinther, 49-51). His detailed study of the development of this sacramental thought among Gentile Christians is in his massive Mass and Lord's Supper. He thinks that Paul shared this pre-Pauline concept of the σῶμα τοῦ Χριστοῦ in the eucharist.

ogy in primitive Christianity.[154]   Other scholars continue to hold to a
sacramental view of pre-Pauline eucharistic use of the idea σῶμα τοῦ
Χριστοῦ although they think that Paul himself did not share it.[155]

Most recent investigations of the σῶμα idea in this passage have
focused on 10:17, the Pauline interpretation of a traditional phrase. In his
very influential article, Käsemann argues that in 10:17 Paul expounds the
idea of σῶμα by using the Gnostic myth of the Redeemed-Redeemer. The
body of Christ thus refers to the identity of Christ with his own, conveyed
in the πνεῦμα by the eucharist. The real point of 10:16, 17 is the Lordship
of Christ.[156]

Jewett, although accepting the view that Paul is interacting with a
Gnostic theology, has rightly attacked Käsemann by noting that in 10:17
the discussion is not about Christ's lordship to believers but of their
relationship to one another.[157] His own view is that the phrase is used by
Paul to insist upon the significance of somatic ("bodily") life for Christians in response to the Gnostic depreciation of this aspect of humanity.[158]

It seems to me, however, that one must understand Paul's reference to the σῶμα Χριστοῦ from the larger context of 1 Corinthians 10,
rather than just considering vv. 16, 17 as has been done by Lietzmann,
Käsemann and even Jewett to some extent.

I do agree that 10:16 is pre-Pauline and had reference to the sacrificial death of Jesus on behalf of his followers. There is no reason, however, to think that this pre-Pauline tradition viewed the bread and wine of
the communion as vehicles for a sacramental presence of Christ. Rather

---

[154]Cullmann, *Essays on the Lord's Supper*, 17.

[155]Conzelmann, *1 Corinthians*, 172; Käsemann, "Pauline Doctrine,"
140; Jewett, *Paul's Anthropological Terms*, 289.

[156]Käsemann, "Pauline Doctrine," 111-114.   Present limitations
preclude this study dealing with the hotly-debated topic of the "Urmensch" and other Gnostic mythology in Paul. See Colpe, *Religionsge-
schichtliche-Schule* and H. M. Schenke, *Der Gott 'Mensch' in der Gnosis*
(Göttingen: Vandenhoeck & Ruprecht, 1962). Recently George MacRae,
"The Apocalypse of Adam," *IDBS* 9, 10, suggests that this Gnostic writing
proves a non- (pre?) Christian Redeemer figure.

[157]Jewett, *Paul's Anthropological Terms*, 257.   The well-known
advocate of "Gnosticism in Corinth," Schmithals, also rejects the idea of a
Gnostic sacramentalism in Corinth. See *Gnosticism in Corinth*, 393.

[158]Jewett, *Paul's Anthropological Terms*, 258f.

the death refers to the once-for-all death of Jesus under Pilate. The use of σῶμα Χριστοῦ in 11:23-25[159] also reflects pre-Pauline usage, and relates the body and blood of Christ to a sacrifice establishing a new covenant (καινὴ διαθήκη, 11:25). The comparison of these two passages suggests that these "words of institution" refer to Jesus's *death* which accomplished a new covenant between God and the Christian community.

From the use of the pre-Pauline tradition in 10:16 and 11:23-25 it seems that Paul took over the expression used to describe the sacrificial death of Christ which was the foundation of the new community of God. However, in the larger context of 10:14-22 this tradition is used to appeal to the Corinthians to avoid the worship in pagan cults. The connecting theme of the pericope is κοινωνία of participants in *cult meals* (Christian, Jewish and pagan). This means the eucharistic formula about the singular salvific death of Jesus is used to prove that Christians are members (κοινωνοί) in the singular community which derives from that death. Their common meal binds them to each other and at the same time prohibits any similar alliance—specifically, those at the shrines of idols.[160]

2. *Conclusions on* Κοινωνία τοῦ Χριστοῦ. The meaning of this phrase in 1 Cor 10:16, 17 remains to be specified.[161] The intent of the pre-Pauline tradition and the meaning of σῶμα Χριστοῦ in those traditions and in Paul's reinterpretation contribute to our understanding, but they do not settle the question: what does Paul intend by referring here to the

---

[159]See below, 205-207.

[160]Nock, *Early Gentile Christianity*, 70. Cullmann, *Essays on the Lord's Supper*, 18f. agrees about the meaning of these words in Jesus' use but thinks that this emphasis was altered in Hellenistic churches, as is seen in Paul's use, to a sacramental one.

Thus, like Jewett, I think that the passage is concerned with the horizontal relationship among believers. However, unlike Jewett, I do not think that the problem of divisiveness in the community at the Lord's table (the problem in ch. 11) is yet being considered.

[161]Conzelmann, *1 Corinthians*, 171, puts the alternatives: "Does κοινωνία then, mean 'communion' or 'participation'?" He continues, "For the answer, we have to take account of the word 'is,' and then of the commentary which Paul himself provides in v. 17. It becomes plain that the proposed alternative is not a real one. The starting point is certainly the meaning 'participation': the partaking of the meal confers . . . communion with the death of Christ." Conzelmann takes αἵματος and σώματος as objective genitives. He also says: "the thought is understandable from the idea that a sacred meal establishes communion with the god of the cult."

κοινωνία τοῦ Χριστοῦ? There are two basic approaches to the interpretation of this phrase. Some scholars take κοινωνία τοῦ Χριστοῦ to mean "participation in Christ" or "communion with Christ." This view often stresses a sacramental character of the eucharist. Others take the phrase to refer to the common association of believers, their "fellowship." Because the view taken of κοινωνία τοῦ Χριστοῦ has such importance for the interpretation of 1 Cor 10:14-21, these approaches must be considered.

a. Participation: Κοινωνία as the receiving of Christ. The sacramental interpretation stresses the relationship with Christ established in the Lord's Supper. The vertical (in spatial imagery) or divine relationship is emphasized. This is done either by taking κοινωνία to refer to the partaking of Christ's body in the eucharist or to a special relationship thereby established with him. Often these interpretations are combined. What is common to this view is the belief that the κοινωνία described is primarily between the individual believer and his Lord. Thus Moffatt says, "Participation in Christ (1:9) *primarily* (italics mine) denotes enjoying a share. . . ."[162] Elert says, "the κοινωνία of the participants with one another arises . . . from this . . . that each through the eating and drinking has κοινωνία with Christ."[163]

This sacramental interpretation was prominent in older studies which stressed the similarities between the Christian sacred meal and meals found in pagan cults.[164] In such interpretations it was customarily argued that in the pagan cults the deity was ingested in a numinous meal, and that this mode of conception was followed by Paul and other Hellenistic Christians. This view has the advantage of taking seriously the parallels which Paul obviously sets forth in vv. 19-20.

However, this line of interpretation has three basic flaws: First, it assumes a mistaken understanding of pagan cult meals, as has been shown in our Part I.[165] There is scant evidence that a sacramentalist view of

---

[162]Moffatt, *1 Corinthians*, 134.

[163]Werner Elert, *Eucharist and Church Fellowship in the First Four Centuries* (St. Louis: Concordia, 1966) 37.

[164]This interpretation by the *Religionsgeschichtliche Schule* is well exemplified in the Lietzmann commentary, *An die Korinther*.

The view that κοινωνία means having a part of the body and blood of Christ is set forth recently by Elert, *Eucharist*. Elert feels 10:16 particularly means this and cites for support the patristic tradition.

[165]See 45-64. Aalen, "Opfermahl," 142, succinctly and correctly comments: "Solche Gedank liegen dem exegetischen wie auch dem religionsgeschichtlich Zusammenhang des Abschnittes völlig fern."

cult meals was found in pagan worship. Second, the context of 1 Cor
10:16-21 speaks against such a view, for it can scarcely be held that Jews
thought they were eating their God. Third, this sacramentalist explanation does not account for the Pauline reference to the cup, for there is no
reason to think pagans or (especially) Jews believed they drank the blood
of their god.

A slightly different interpretation of 10:16, 17 says Christians, in
their cult meal, experience union with the Lord, although not in the
elements, the cup and bread. This interpretation also takes notice of the
religionsgeschichtliche parallels, but does not insist on Christ's actual
presence *in* the bread and cup. Hauck says,

> For Paul the bread and wine are vehicles of the presence of
> Christ, just as the Jewish altar is a pledge of the presence of
> God. Partaking of bread and wine is union (sharing) with the
> heavenly Christ. . . . κοινωνία is here expressive of an inner
> union.[166]

Hauck is not the only interpreter to see κοινωνία in 1 Cor 10:16 as
referring to a special (inward, spiritual, or mystical) union of the believer
with his Lord. Similar interpretations are given by Jourdan,[167]

----

[166]Hauck, "Κοινωνεῖν," 805. "Thus the nature of the Lord's Supper is expounded by Paul in terms of fellowship with the person of Christ,
namely, κοινωνία with his body and blood (v. 16)." Hauck says that Paul
does not speculate on "how this union takes place in the cultic meal." But
the fellowship between believers is derived from each one's common union
with Christ. He finds this concept of "spiritual communion with the Risen
Lord" confirmed in 1 Cor 1:9 (see pages 209-211 in the present study).

Others also consider the partaking of Christ is primary, and from
each one's partaking derives the fellowship among the partakers. For
example, Sevenster, 172, ". . . it is axiomatic that those who have experienced this fellowship with Christ are also in mutual fellowship with one
another." Cf. also Barrett, *1 Corinthians*, 235. Jourdan, "KOINΩNIA," 113,
says that Paul uses ἐν Χριστῷ εἶναι to indicate this inwardness.

[167]Jourdan, "KOINΩNIA," 111 and 123f.

Robinson,[168] Bultmann,[169] Seesemann,[170] von Soden,[171] and Behm.[172]
Probably the most influential current presentation of the view that
κοινωνία means partaking of the Lord is that of Käsemann. Käsemann's
interpretation, too, emphasizes strongly the religious milieu of Hellenism,
but he draws on gnosticism as the decisive influence rather than cultic
sacrifice.[173] He says:

> . . . [as] to the hotly debated question whether, according to
> Paul, the Lord's Supper conveys participation in the dying or
> in the exalted Lord . . . unequivocally in the latter sense.
> Because the Lord is the πνεῦμα and because in the sacrament
> the exalted Lord conveys, along with his gift, participation in
> himself as the Giver.[174]

Käsemann extends this reconstruction of Pauline christology as based on
gnostic mythology to his doctrine of baptism and to those Pauline references which speak of "Christ in us" or we "in Christ."[175]
One need not enter into an examination of the gnostic background
to raise serious objections to Käsemann's reconstruction.[176]
Jewett shares Käsemann's belief in a gnostic conflict as the correct situation for understanding 1 Cor 10 but still objects to taking

---

[168]Robinson, *The Body*, 65.
[169]Bultmann, *TNT*, 14. He distinguishes between two levels of
interpretation: the pre-Pauline Hellenistic church which understood the
communion in the sense of ingesting the deity (v. 16) and Paul who adds
the ecclesiological dimension of the "body of Christ." A similar point is
made by Bousset, *Kyrios Christos*, 159.
[170]Seesemann, *Begriff* ΚΟΙΝΩΝΙΑ, 51. He believes that 1 Cor 10:16
refers to the "'participation' in the present time. In the Lord's Supper,
which occurs again and again, the believer experiences repeatedly anew
the nearness of his Lord, he acquires an immediate participation in him."
[171]Von Soden, "Sakrament und Ethik," 8.
[172]Behm, "Κλάω," *TDNT* 3, 738f.
[173]"Pauline Doctrine."
[174]See his "Pauline Doctrine," 111.
[175]Ibid, 114f. Käsemann explains the means of the self-conveying
of the Lord within a Hellenistic metaphysic taken over by Gnostics
speculating on the *Urmensch*. Paul himself critiques the gnostic
metaphysic even as he uses their master image of the risen Lord, 118.
[176]Ibid., 114f.

κοινωνία to mean participation in the risen Lord. Jewett rightly argues
that Käsemann's interpretation does not adequately explain 10:17 which
does not speak of Christ's rule over the believers or his relation to them,
but rather of their relation to one another in the one body.[177] Jewett is
also correct in saying that Käsemann is attributing a view to Paul which
would better fit the (alleged) gnostic opponents, and that Paul's appeal to
the sacrament stresses "an exclusive horizontal somatic unity among the
participants of the sacraments."[178] However, Jewett is mistaken in
focusing on alleged internal divisions among the Corinthians. The concern
for inner-church unity is not focal.

   b. Fellowship: Κοινωνία as association. Sharply opposed to the
view which takes κοινωνία as a sacramental receiving of the Lord is one
which sees κοινωνία in 10:16 as referring to a fraternal association
modeled on Hellenistic associations. In this view κοινωνία is basically the
relationship among the believers.

   There are distinct advantages in interpreting κοινωνία as "association." First, it accords with the basic meaning of the word κοινωνία, "to
have in common," which implies, "with someone else."[179] Secondly, if we
understand the Lord's Supper to have taken place in the context of a meal,
in antiquity there was a recognized fraternal association established in
common meals.[180] Finally, this "association" interpretation finds confirmation in the fact that the various guilds of Hellenistic society were
basically fraternal in character and were often called κοινωνία.[181]

   The view that κοινωνία in 10:16 refers to an association of table

[177]Jewett, *Paul's Anthropological Terms*, 257f. He adds, "Nor does
v. 17 deal with the question of divinization through the sacrament" as
Käsemann urges based on extending the argument of 10:1ff. against a
gnostic "medicine of Immortality" view of the sacrament.
[178]Ibid., 280. In rejecting Käsemann's ecclesiological view Jewett
says, "It is something of an enigma that just at the point where the ecclesiastical σῶμα Χριστοῦ concept has been thought to appear in 1 Cor 10:17,
Paul introduces a new and self-contained argument based upon the
metaphor of the loaf."
[179]Contra Campbell, "Κοινωνία," 13f., who says that the idea of
associating with other persons is derivative and secondary. "The meaning
'to have to do with things' is considerably more common."
[180]Jeremias, *Eucharistic Words*, 154. Jeremias has in mind Jewish
meals, easpecially those of a ḥaburah. But the same table obligations are
known in the Greek world. See Weiss, *Earliest Christianity*, 641.
[181]See Part I, "Sacrifice, Cult Meals."

mates, albeit Christian ones, has been argued by Johannes Weiss[182] and Ernst von Dobschütz,[183] among others. Such a view is compatible with equating κοινωνία with "church," if we mean by that simply an association of people with similar interests.

The difficulty is that Paul obviously considers the church to have its basis and its dimensions beyond that of a human institution. He means to say more than that the Christian church is the "right" association (among other human associations). Rather, he means to say that it is qualitatively different from them.[184] This associative concept is helpful in understanding κοινωνία in relationship to the church, for the association is a constitutive part of the church,[185] but it alone is inadequate.

What is needed is a way of understanding κοινωνία which both gives adequate attention to the parallel cases Paul sets forth in 10:18-21 and yet allows for its distinctive Christian character. In order to understand Paul's view of the church as a κοινωνία we must pay attention to the genitive phrases τοῦ αἵματος/σώματος τοῦ Χριστοῦ which qualify it. Real assistance is provided by a consideration of Paul's parallel description of the Lord's Supper found in 1 Cor 11.

c. Κοινωνία as a covenant relationship. We have noted that 1 Cor 10:16 uses a traditional, pre-Pauline phraseology. The same can be said of

---

[182]Weiss, Korintherbrief, 258, and Earliest Christianity, 640ff. Weiss thinks that the original idea is that of table communion. Paul means to say: "When we bless the cup and break the bread is not Christ there with us?" He also thinks, however, that in 1 Cor 11:20-34 there is already a movement toward seeing Christ as the object of the meal as well as the participant of honor.

[183]Ernst von Dobschütz, "Sakrament und Symbol im Urchristentum," ThStKr 78 (1905) 11f. (cited by Seesemann, Begriff KOINΩNIA, 41) considers societas (guild society) to be a proper translation of κοινωνία.

[184]How so is related, of course, to Paul's christology and his ecclesiology.

[185]As Jewett, Paul's Anthropological Terms, 257, rightly points out, v. 17 which interprets v. 16, is concerned about the relationship among the participants themselves.

Wendland, Korinther, 81, says rightly that the body of Christ in 10:16 has two references: first it refers to the body of Christ given in death . . . second, it is the body which is formed from the many, the body of the church.

his other reference to the Lord's Supper in 1 Cor 11:24ff.[186] Noting the formal parallelism between 10:16 and 11:24, one may schematize:

ποτήριον = κοινωνία τοῦ αἵματος (1 Cor 10:16)
          = ἡ καινὴ διαθήκη ἐν τῷ ἐμῷ αἵματι (1 Cor 11:25)
ἄρτος   = κοινωνία τοῦ σώματος (1 Cor 10:16)
          = τὸ σῶμα τὸ ὑπὲρ ὑμῶν (1 Cor 11:24)

The parallelism shows that the terms κοινωνία τοῦ αἵματος and ἡ καινὴ διαθήκη ἐν τῷ ἐμῷ αἵματι are equivalent.[187] The references to the body and blood in 11:24 have obvious connections to the concept of a covenant, which was finalized by the slaughter of a sacrifice and the pouring out of its blood. The connection with covenant ideas is made explicit in 11:24 by the use of the term διαθήκη.[188]

Stuart Currie has pointed out that a difficulty for most interpretations of κοινωνία in 1 Cor 10:16 (either that it means participation in Christ, or association with other believers) is that Paul mentions both the cup and the bread.[189] If the point of the word κοινωνία here is either participation in the risen Christ, or unity of Christians, a reference to the bread is all that is required. The "bread word" alone is usually dealt with by commentators, who are most interested in the idea of σῶμα τοῦ Χριστοῦ. But Paul refers to both the bread and cup as body and blood,

---

[186]Jeremias, *Eucharistic Words,* 131; Käsemann, "Pauline Doctrine," 110; and Nock, *Early Gentile Christianity,* 69.

[187]As pointed out by Currie, *Koinonia,* 44.

[188]The word διαθήκη is not at all prominent in Paul. Four times it refers to the Old Testament covenant (Rom 9:4; 11:27; Gal 3:17 and 4:24). Once it refers to the idea of a legal agreement (Gal 3:15), and three times it is used in comparing the Old and New Covenants (2 Cor 3:6, 14).

Käsemann, "Pauline Doctrine," 119f., commenting on 11:24, says διαθήκη is taken from the legal sphere, so that it means "decree" or "ordinance." "God's eschatological ordinance must be proclaimed on earth, and this is exactly what the assembled Christian community does when it celebrates the Eucharist. . . . The account of the Last Supper is thus a formulation of 'holy law'."

Without entering into the larger issue of the prophetically proclaimed "sacred law" in the Pauline churches, it is probable that in 11:25 we have a traditional piece, not derived from such prophets, but which may go back to Jesus himself.

[189]Currie, *Koinonia,* 12, cites Seesemann, *Begriff* ΚΟΙΝΩΝΙΑ, 39.

because he is thinking of Christ's sacrifice which formed a community of allegiance to him. In sacrifice, whether pagan or Jewish, both the body and blood of the victim were involved. The sacrifice and meal following were fundamental to a worshipping community, a brotherhood, as was common in the ancient world.[190]

The view that the cup points to a cultic meal and the sacrifice preceding such also explains why Paul does not simply omit a reference to the cup when he quotes the tradition in 10:16. One could argue that Paul was compelled by the traditional formula to mention the cup (although he apparently alters the tradition's order and presumably could have omitted reference to the cup altogether). The reference to the blood/cup occurs because the idea of sacrifice is involved. Shedd suggests that Paul is here influenced by Isa 42:6 and 49:8 where the suffering servant is described as "a covenant for the nations."[191] The cup of the Lord is κοινωνία, "participation in Christ's death, i.e., committal to him who died for us."[192] Thus in 10:21 when Paul points to the exclusive character of the Christian meal it is not because of some magical conflict, but because the Christian and pagan meals represent differing communities of allegiance.[193]

While these references to the blood confirm the close association between the sacrificial death of Christ and the Christian meal, they need not imply that Christians considered the Lord's Supper itself to be a "sacrifice." The doctrines of the real presence and the mass are much later in the development of dogma, although both make use of the sacrificial terminology of these verses.[194]

---

[190]Currie, *Koinonia*, 46f., quotes Ludwig Köhler, *Old Testament Theology* (Philadelphia: Westminster, 1958) 182, who described the relationship of sacrifice, sacrificial meal, and brothers in the covenantal meal. Cf. Gottfried Quell, "Διαθήκη," *TDNT* 2 (1964) 121, makes a similar point based on Ex 24:9-11. Also Gerhard von Rad, *Old Testament Theology* (New York: Harper & Row, 1962) 1.254-257.

Gressmann, "KOINΩNIA," 230, notes that a common meal before the god was a simple form of treaty conclusion. He notes also that this was apart from any view of a sacramental communion through consuming the god. See also Thornton, *Common Life*, 326.

[191]Russell Philip Shedd, *Man in Community* (London: Epworth Press, 1958) 147.

[192]Goppelt, "Ποτήριον," 157.

[193]Ibid., 158.

[194]Jeremias, *Eucharistic Words*, 159. Neuenzeit, *Das Herrenmahl*, argues for a sacrificial understanding of the Lord's Supper, although he rejects dependence on the pagan theophagy to support this view.

In 1 Cor 10:16f. the only sacrifice in view is that of Jesus on the
cross. The Lord's Supper is a resulting κοινωνία in that "the Christian
through taking the wine in the cup, receives an interest in the death of
Christ,"[195] that is, its benefits. It was only a short step from the concept
of the covenant community formed by Christ's sacrificial death to terming this meal a sacrifice, as occurs elsewhere in early Christian
thought.[196]

The sacrificial death of Christ established a relationship between
God and man and among men in Christ. A covenant in the Old Testament
involved both a relationship with God as giver of the covenant and a
relationship among the people of God as the recipients of it. Among the
obligations imposed upon those who received the covenant was a certain
fidelity and a sense of increased responsibility toward other members of
the community. As sharers of the divine covenant they had a relationship
to each other. As Goppelt points out, church membership in the New
Testament is much more than an association of those with similar convictions into a visible crowd. Avowal of church membership, as described in
1 Cor 12 and Rom 12, is to serve other members.[197] It is this special
relationship with its mutual loyalties and obligations based on the status
as God's elect (1 Cor 1:9) which is termed in 1 Cor 10:17 κοινωνία.

Although 2 Cor 6:16ff. is highly suspect as being non-Pauline, it is
interesting to note certain similarities with 1 Cor 10:16.[198] In 2 Cor 6:16
the denial of "agreement" (συγκατάθεσις) between the temple of God and

---

See also Aalen, "Opfermahl," 142f., although he himself denies that
a sacramental understanding is found in pagan cults as was argued by
Lietzmann and others.

[195]Barrett, 1 Corinthians, 232f. For all his useful insights on this
passage, Aalen is finally mistaken when he concludes Christians in the
Lord's Supper consume a real sacrifice. Aalen, "Opfermahl," 142f.

[196]Barrett, 1 Corinthians, 232. Jeremias, Eucharistic Words, 112.
Nock, Early Gentile Christianity, 71, notes the later tendency to term the
eucharist a θυσία.

[197]Leonhard Goppelt, "Kirchengemeinschaft und Abendmahlsgemeinschaft nach dem Neuen Testament," Koinonia, ed. Friedrich
Hübner (Berlin: Lutherisches Verlagshaus, 1957) 26, notes the designation
of the early church pool of goods as κοινά (Acts 2:44; 4:32).

[198]J. Gnilka, "2 Cor vi.14-vii.1 in the light of the Qumran texts
and the Testaments of the Twelve Patriarchs," Paul and Qumran (J.
Murphy-O'Conner, ed.; Chicago: Priory Press, 1968), examines this
passage and concludes it is a pre-Pauline text from Jewish Essenes.

idols recalls Ex 23:32f., which tells Israel not to make covenant with the native inhabitants of Canaan or their gods (οὐ συγκαταθήσῃ αὐτοῖς καὶ τοῖς θεοῖς αὐτῶν διαθήκην) lest Israel be tempted to sin. In interpreting 1 Cor 10:16f., one should note the connection in 2 Cor 6:16 of συγ-καταθήσις and κοινωνία; the connection of συγκαταθήσις and διαθήκη in Ex 23:32 LXX and the warning of possible idolatry in both. This suggests that the concept of association (κοινωνία) in 1 Cor 10:16 belongs to a group of ideas which assume covenant obligations and that involvement with pagan associations leads one into idolatrous allegiances.

Therefore, in 1 Cor 10:16f. κοινωνία does not mean "participate in the Lord," either understood as the ingesting of Christ, or as being incorporated into a Risen Lord. Nor does it mean comradeship, the association among people of similar beliefs and sentiments. Rather, κοινωνία means the relationship established among members of a covenant and the obligations ensuing from it. In a word, it means ḥesed.[199]

d. Other Pauline Uses of Κοινωνία. It is not necessary to establish this interpretation of κοινωνία in each of the other Pauline usages. One can grant that the word is not used in a univocal sense by Paul and still defend the interpretation just argued. Yet a quick glance confirms that other references are not at all incompatible with the proposed interpretation.

One passage especially deserves consideration because it seems to use κοινωνία in a way very similar to 1 Cor 10:16, 17. That reference is 1 Cor 1:9, which reads in the Nestle text: πιστὸς ὁ θεός, δι' οὗ ἐκλήθητε εἰς κοινωνίαν τοῦ υἱοῦ αὐτοῦ 'Ιησοῦ Χριστοῦ τοῦ κυρίου ἡμῶν.

Seeseman, whose study of κοινωνία is the most thorough, takes 1:9 to confirm his interpretaion of κοινωνία in 10:16, i.e., "to have a share of

---

[199]Currie, Koinonia, 15f., 42. An important part of Currie's argument about the meaning of κοινωνία in Paul is that Paul is using the word to convey one aspect of covenantal obligation which was included in the Old Testament term ḥesed. Currie specifically denies that Paul is using κοινωνία to translate ḥesed, rather that both words, one in Paul's Bible and one in Paul's letters, point to a special relationship among members of God's people.

I do not propose to investigate Currie's lexical and linguistic evidence in this regard, nor is the English word "covenant" decisive in my interpretation. I do think Currie has located an important consideration for understanding the sense of allegiance which Paul assumes true for the Christian community, and which in 10:17 he terms κοινωνία.

Christ" (objective genitive). He feels that in 10:16 κοινωνία is used with
the objective genitive and this helps interpret 1:9 which is the more
uncommon "genitive of the person."[200] In both passages κοινωνία τοῦ
Χριστοῦ means "to have a share (*anteilhaben*) of Christ."[201] He says that
1:9 refers to participation in the Risen Lord in the present time, not just
the consummation, as Weiss suggests.[202] For Seesemann it is equivalent
to being ἐν Χριστῷ.[203]

A position opposite to Seesemann on 1:9 is that the phrase refers to
Christians being called into a Christian association.[204] Seesemann
rejects this, saying that κοινωνία cannot be taken as referring to a
societas, i.e., that God calls the believers into a society established on
Christ.[205]

Following the suggestion of Currie, the meaning of 1:9 is made

---

[200]Seesemann, *Begriff* KOINΩNIA, 103, n. 2.

[201]Ibid., 47-51. He feels that κοινωνία must be understood in the
sense of standing in a close relationship. He does not make explicit in
what way Christians participate in Christ, but he clearly understands
Χριστῷ as the Risen Lord, not the community.

Similarly, Hauck, "Κοινωνία," 804, says Christians "enter into a
spiritual communion with the risen Lord."

As Currie, *Koinonia*, 41, points out, the idea of having a part of
Christ is certainly refuted by 1 Cor 1:13, whose point is "Christ is not
parcelled out."

[202]Seesemann, *Begriff* KOINΩNIA 49f. (see Weiss, *Korintherbrief*,
11).

[203]Seesemann, *Begriff* KOINΩNIA, 49.

[204]Barrett, *1 Corinthians*, 39f., ". . . here the sense would be that
God has called you into the community—that is the church—of Jesus
Christ." But he continues, "As in the Pauline expression 'in Christ,' the
thought is that Christians share in the position of the exalted, eschatological Lord."

Conzelmann, *1 Corinthians*, 29, is not clear on this point. He
says: "It is not understood as an experience of mystical communion but in
terms of belonging to the Lord until his parousia." In a footnote he adds,
"Sacramental participation in the Lord (see 10:16) is not thought of in this
passage." However, earlier, 25, he had said in another note that instead
of "fellowship" one could translate "participation in."

[205]Seesemann, *Begriff* KOINΩNIA, 47f. He believes this idea completely unPauline. However, the Latin version does render *societas* in
1 Cor 1:9. Both Thornton, *Common Life*, 72-78, and Currie, *Koinonia*, 62,
call attention to Acts 2:42 where κοινωνία means "the life in common" of
the church.

clear by noting the parallel expression in 1 Thess 2:12: τοῦ θεοῦ τοῦ
καλοῦντος ὑμᾶς εἰς τὴν ἑαυτοῦ βασιλείαν καὶ δόξαν. In 1 Thessalonians the call is clearly present in time and refers not to friendly associations, but to life as a member of the kingdom of God.[206]

Thus 1 Cor 1:9 cannot be taken to prove that κοινωνία refers to
the believer's individual relationship with Christ. Therefore it cannot be
used to support a similar interpretation of 10:16. In both passages
κοινωνία refers to the community of believers brought into covenant
relationship with God in Christ.[207]

The other Pauline references to κοινωνία are also consistent with
the "alliance" interpretation of 1 Cor 10:16. For example, the Pauline
collection (Rom 15:26f.; 2 Cor 8:4; 9:13; cf. Phil 4:14; Gal 6:6), termed
κοινωνία, is much more than a relief work for the Jerusalem poor; it is
the tangible expression of the common alliance of Jews and Gentiles in
Christ, i.e., their covenant bond.[208]

This view of κοινωνία also fits those passages which speak of a
special relationship between Paul and other Christians.[209] Philemon,

---

[206]Currie, *Koinonia*, 41. He also notes, rightly, that both texts are
hortatory in character, "Paul exhorts the saints to live in a manner appropriate to the kingdom into which they have been brought by faith and
baptism, appropriate to that alliance which is theirs in Christ." Elsewhere
Paul often uses καλῶ to refer to God's call into the redemptive fellowship
which is Christ's. E.g., Rom 9:24; 14:17; Gal 1:6.

[207]To be understood similarly are 2 Cor 13:13,ἡ κοινωνία τοῦ
ἀγίου πνεύματος, and Phil 2:1, κοινωνία πνεύματος. See Currie,
Koinonia, 36-39.

[208]Currie, *Koinonia*, 29-36. See also Keith Nickle, *The Collection*
(SBT 1/48; London: SCM, 1966), on the religious significance of Paul's
collection, especially for the Jew-Gentile question.

Currie, *Koinonia*, 36, notes the collection is termed by other terms
which carry similar implications of relationships, attitudes and conduct
implied in the Hebrew word ḥesed. Specifically he mentions: ἀγάπη,
χάρις, and πίστις.

[209]See Currie, *Koinonia*, 48-55. These passages are: Gal 2:9;
2 Cor 8:23; Phil 1:5; 4:15 and Phlm 6; 17.

This line of interpretation of κοινωνία does not seem as suited to
Phil 3:10, and perhaps not to 2 Cor 6:14 (if the latter is Pauline). Currie,
Koinonia, 65f., thinks that if 2 Cor 6:14 is from Paul, "it would have to be
granted that here *koinonia* is used in a form and with a meaning not
otherwise found in his writing . . . clear evidence of the power of *koinonia*
to represent mere relationship, the connection of any two things which
have anything in common."

which draws heavily on commercial terminology, is no exception, although it has other motifs.

1 CORINTHIANS 10:21, 22:
A SUMMARY WARNING

In v. 21 Paul draws the conclusion of his treatment of κοινωνία arising in cultic meals. The prohibition of 10:21 is "unambiguous."[210] The meal of Christians is exclusive in its loyalty; it permits no other such involvement. Thus Paul begins 10:21, οὐ δύνασθε. Strictly speaking, of course, it was possible. Indeed, that such involvements were taking place had occasioned the Corinthians' letter and Paul's reply. But the seriousness of Paul's attitude on this topic comes out in that he deems participation in such meals not only wrong for Christians but really impossible.[211]

The balanced structure of 10:21 shows how much this is a question of stark alternatives (in Paul's mind). One must choose either to drink from the "cup of the Lord" or the "cup of demons"; to eat either at the "table of the Lord" or the "table of demons." The Corinthians may consider the pagan cult meals as social, non-worshipful occasions, but Paul insists their choice is clear: the Lord or demons. This verse shows that Paul did intend a comparison (really contrast) between the Christian meal and the pagan one, for each is termed τράπεζα and involvement in each is called μετέχειν. Paul takes both meal occasions to be religiously significant.[212]

However, G. D. Fee, "II Cor 6:14f.," has given an explanation which would support the covenant interpretation of κοινωνία in 2 Cor 6:14 as well. He says that the prohibition is not general, but has in mind precisely the pagan meal situations such as are treated in 1 Cor 10. Therefore 2 Cor 6:14 would also support the present suggested interpretation of κοινωνία as alliance or covenantal loyalty.

[210]Barrett, 1 Corinthians, 237.

[211]Robertson and Plummer, 1 Corinthians, 217, paraphrase: "It is morally impossible." Their additional observation is pertinent. "Only those who do not realize what the Supper is, or do not realize what an idol-feast is, could think of taking part in both."

[212]It should not be overlooked that here Paul uses μετέχειν to refer to taking part in both pagan and Christian meals, and that he uses κοινωνός in 10:20 to denote members of pagan communities. It is clear that no sharp distinction ought to be made between μετέχειν and κοινωνεῖν.

Paul assumes, and is arguing here for, the exclusive character of Christian affiliation. This exclusivism is rooted in the Jewish heritage of both Paul and the early Christian church. It is well illustrated in Judaism by the prominence of the *shema* (Ex 20:32) in worship and theology. Such exclusive loyalty demanded by religion, however, was uncommon in paganism. Even those who had a patron deity did not deny the existence and power of other gods. Moreover, in the Hellenistic period there was a trend to regard the various deities only as manifestations of the One. This Hellenistic syncretistic monotheism was surely well known in cosmopolitan Corinth, but the extent of its influence is hard to determine.[213] When faced with this pagan syncretism Paul would have regarded it as irreconcilably in contradiction to Christian belief.[214] It is consistent with Christian (and Jewish) monotheism that pagan deities were considered either to be "no gods" or "demons" or both.[215]

As Paul seeks to impress the need for Christian exclusivism and abstinence from pagan cultic meals, his argument in 10:20 claims that Christian κοινωνία precludes others which were expressed in such meals. This argument assumes the covenant, or allegiance, character of κοινωνία discussed above. It is an exclusivism which ultimately stems from Judaism. Christians are forbidden participation in pagan cult meals both because they thereby become involved with demonic "no gods" (10:20) and because their allegiance to Christ is exclusive.[216] Substantially this is

---

[213]Walter, "Christusglaube," 435f., stresses this Hellenistic syncretistic monotheism as the background to the conflict in 1 Corinthians. He is surely right that pagan Christians would hardly have abandoned attitudes and assumptions overnight when they became Christians. It is not possible, however, to know how conscious the Corinthian Christians were of this syncretism.
    [214]Walter, "Christusglaube," 430.
    [215]Conzelmann, *1 Corinthians*, 173. He rightly notes that this is consistent with 8:5 where the pagan deities are regarded as "nothings," as they are in 10:20.
    [216]G. D. Fee, "II Cor 6:14f.," 153. Fee also extends this argument about Christian exclusivism in religious meals to interpret 2 Cor 6:14-7:1. He thinks that the problem of Christian involvement in such pagan meals is the specific problem resulting in the admonition against "mixed mating" (and thereby seeks to show 2 Cor 6:14-7:1 as Pauline).
    Gnilka, "2 Cor vi.14-vii.1," 51, also examines 2 Cor 6:14-7:1 and the attitude of Christian exclusivism manifested there. He says that the quotations of Ezk 37:27 and Lev 26:11f. establish the close relationship between God and his people which is the basis for the summons (διό) to

the same point.

The rhetorical questions of 10:22, "Shall we provoke the Lord?" and "Are we stronger than he?" both assume negative answers. The questions add a strong note of warning to the reasoned argument of 10:16-20, which is summarized in 10:21. These strong warnings also recall 10:14 and the opening admonition, φεύγετε ἀπὸ τῆς εἰδωλολατρίας.

The LXX uses the idea of provoking the Lord (παραζηλοῦμεν τὸν κύριον)[217] in several places. Deuteronomy 32:21, which Paul actually quotes in Rom 10:19 and may allude to in Rom 11:11, 14, is also probably behind his question on 10:22, ἢ παραζηλοῦμεν τὸν κύριον;[218] The context in Deuteronomy makes this a very appropriate citation, for it is Moses in his last will and testament warning of apostasy. Through Moses' song in Deut 32:21 God says, "They have moved me to jealousy with no gods, and provoked me to anger with their vanities." The LXX reads, αὐτοὶ παρεζήλωσάν με ἐπ᾿ οὐ θεῷ παρώργισάν με ἐν τοῖς εἰδώλοις αὐτῶν. Therefore in the Greek Old Testament provoking the Lord was the worship of idols—"no gods."

In Deuteronomy, as in 1 Cor 10, the issue is the people of God being involved with "no gods" (1 Cor 10:20), which are idols (10:19). The context of Deut 32 has other similarities with 1 Cor 10. Deut 32:17 says God was provoked by the sacrifice to "no gods" which were demons (ἔθυσαν δαιμονίοις καὶ οὐ θεῷ). These were gods Israel "did not know." (Exclusive allegiance to YHWH is often expressed as "knowing" or "not knowing" in Deuteronomy.)

Paul's allusions to provoking the Lord draw on Deut 32:21 and are very apt for his own situation. But the same idea of idolatry as a provoking of God and a breaking of loyalty to him is found also in 1 Kgs 14:22f. (of Rehoboam's reign) and Psalm 78:58 (of Israel's idolatry upon entering

---

separate themselves from unclean things.

Whether 2 Cor 6:14-7:1 is Pauline is beyond the present study's scope. However, the passage does illustrate a similar argument of exclusive loyalty of Christians based on an exclusive relationship to God.

[217] Whether the "Lord" (κύριον) here is Christ or YHWH is perhaps debatable. In the LXX, of course, it was YHWH. But in view of 10:21 where κυρίου is certainly Christ, it probably is best to take it the same way in 10:22. It is not uncommon for Paul to make such a transposition when quoting the Old Testament.

[218] Walter, "Christusglaube," 430. Conzelmann, 1 Corinthians, 174.

Canaan). This Old Testament tradition is a better clue to understanding
the "provoking" which Paul warns about here than the frequently assumed
hyper-sacramentalism of the Corinthians.[219] While the Corinthians may
not have considered such pagan meals as "idolatry" (1 Cor 8:4-6 suggests
they did not), Paul considers them to be idolatrous and therefore a
provoking of the Lord.

Paul's second rhetorical question, μὴ ἰσχυρότεροι αὐτοῦ ἐσμεν;
also expects a negative response. The word stronger (ἰσχυρότεροι) does
not allude ironically to a special group in Corinth ("the strong")[220] but to
the concrete issue of participation in the pagan meals. The participation
is the attempt to act stronger than God. Paul uses these two questions to
conclude this phase of his argument about sacrificial meals.

CONCLUSIONS

A. The Significance of the Parallel Examples of Κοινωνία

One of the basic questions in interpreting 1 Cor 10:14-22 is how to
regard the examples of Jewish and pagan κοινωνία which Paul gives along
with the Christian meal. Scholars earlier in this century considered the
Christian meal to have been modeled upon a widespread Hellenistic sacramentalism and therefore stressed the similarities between these other
meals and the Christian meal. The Christian meal essentially was different from the pagan meal only in its patron.[221] In this line of interpretation the parallel examples of κοινωνία were considered very important,
indeed they were almost identical.

Aalen is probably correct in suggesting that this "sacramental" or
"theophagy" interpretation of 1 Corinthians was established originally

---

[219]For example, Käsemann, "Pauline Doctrine," 124f.   Also
unconvincing is Grosheide, 1 Corinthians, 237, who argues that those weak
Christians who partake of sacrificial meat against their consciences,
compelled by a mistaken sense of shame, provoked the Lord by not acting
in faith.

[220]Rightly Conzelmann, 1 Corinthians, 174; contra Barrett,
1 Corinthians, 238.

[221]For example, Reitzenstein, Hellenistic Mystery Religions, and
Heitmüller, Taufe und Abendmahl. See in the present study, 10-13.

with Lietzmann's commentary and his excursus: "Kultmahle."[222] The subsequent critical reassessment of the *religionsgeschichtliche Schule* which overthrew its dominance in New Testament theology also effectively ended the interpretive approach which stressed the similarities between the Christian and pagan meals. The radical assessment of this approach showed that the mystery religions actually had limited effect in Hellenistic life, and also that there were fundamental differences between the mysteries and Christian theology.[223]

As a result of the demise of the *religionsgeschichtliche* approach, the recent trend has been to minimize the significance of the parallel examples given in 1 Cor 10:18-20. Käsemann summarized the recent mood:

> The attempt to shed light on Paul's teaching on the Lord's Supper from its links with Hellenistic cult-meals has completely broken down, so far as the essential issues are concerned. In 1 Cor 10:19ff. Paul himself acknowledges this connexion and uses it for paraenetic and polemical purposes. Yet the existing analogies are limited to details which neither provide concrete historical proof that the connexion is one of dependence, nor permit us to expose adequately and in its full depth the conception implied in the Apostle's writings.[224]

---

[222]Aalen, "Opfermahl," 129. He notes that the recent trend is to avoid the theophagy issue by minimizing the importance of the parallel cases of κοινωνία or by stressing the idea of competing lords.

[223]A readily available example of this critique is found in W. R. Halliday, *The Pagan Background of Early Christianity* (London: Hodder and Stoughton, 1925) 312-318. He argues that apparently there are parallels between Christian and pagan cults, but little borrowing. See also the insightful study by Nock, *Early Gentile Christianity*, 76, "there is then, as far as we can see, nothing in this pagan meals which can well have contributed to the genesis of the Christian rite, still less to its central position and soteriological significance."

[224]Käsemann, "Pauline Doctrine," 108. It should be noted that Käsemann's agenda is not a study of Paul's argument on idol meat, but rather his eucharistic thought.

Similarly, Bornkamm, "Lord's Supper," and W. G. Kümmel's appendix to the 13th ed. of Lietzmann, *Korinther*.

Also Behm, "Κλάω," *TDNT* 3 (1965) 740, declares, "Paul is not thinking here [1 Cor 10:16-22] in terms of a religious analogy. He sees an absolute antithesis. . . . The absence of sacrificial ritual or thinking from Paul's treatment of the Lord's Supper is an indication of the essential difference between the Christian feast and supposed analogies.

Interestingly, both the older view which stressed Christian dependence on a pagan theophagy and the recent trend which minimizes influence of pagan cult practice on Christian theology have assumed the accuracy of the sacramentalist understanding of pagan meals.[225] Part One of the present study has shown this is an ill-founded assumption about pagan cult meals, certainly in the Hellenistic era.

The aversion to taking seriously the references to the pagan cult meals in 1 Cor 10:19f. is understandable in view of the extremes to which the *religionsgeschichtliche Schule* took the comparisons. However, it remains the case that in the context of his argument about εἰδωλολατρία Paul himself does set forth the pagan cult meal and compares it with the Christian meal (and the Jewish one) as examples of κοινωνία. A satisfactory interpretation of 1 Cor 10:14-21 must take account of Paul's appeal to the pagan analogies,[226] although it is true that he is not comparing them in either their theology or worship.[227] Paul disagrees with the Corinthians in that he considers the pagan meals as religiously significant, regardless of how they are regarded either by pagans or Christians.[228] Participating (μετέχειν) at the table of these demonic idols is idolatry and endangers, if not severs, Christian allegiance to the one God.

Characteristically overlooked in the discussion about the impor-

---

[225]See Walter, "Christusglaube," 431, esp. n. 46.

[226]Rightly, Aalen, "Opfermahl," 130, who says that recent study which has minimized the importance of pagan sacrificial meals has served to make the entire parallel appear either inexplicable or meaningless.

Conzelmann, *1 Corinthians*, 174, also acknowledges Paul's intentional comparison of the Lord's Supper with the pagan meals. So also Thornton, *Common Life*, 326, and even Schmithals, *Gnosticism*, 225.

[227]Ibid., 435. Walter says that although strictly speaking the Christian meal is not a sacrifice, Paul lets the analogies stand in order to argue for the exclusive character of the Lord's Supper.

Paul S. Minear, "Paul's Teaching on the Eucharist in First Corinthians," *Worship* 44 (1970) 87f., goes too far when he says that Paul is unconcerned about the sacrifice or the meat, but only the worship offered to demons. The Corinthians could have argued (rightly) that these temple meals were not generally regarded as worship.

[228]Von Soden, "Sakrament und Ethik," 18f., is wrong when he contrasts 1 Cor 8 with 10, by saying that in the former Paul did not consider the sacrifice offered to the gods real, but he does in the latter passage.

tance of the parallels is Paul's reference to Jewish meals in 10:18. Although not a major point, it is a real one, and shows that Paul intended that his comparisons be taken seriously. It is true that the Jewish and pagan meals as well as the Christian one are used for a parenetic purpose to discourage certain actions,[229] but all three examples of κοινωνία should be taken as related. The common points of comparison in each are: eating a cultic meal, sacrificial imagery, and a κοινωνία resulting from these cult meals.

B. Sacrifice and Κοινωνία

It is necessary for interpretation to stress once again the comparison actually made in 1 Cor 10:16-20 between the Lord's Supper, Jewish and pagan religious meals. This does not imply that Paul regards the Lord's Supper as a sacrifice, except in its origin in Christ's death.[230] Paul's teaching about the sacrificial death of Jesus pictures that as a single, unrepeatable event, although with lasting implications. Nor should one assume that those pagan meals with sacrifices were considered occasions of special sanctity.

What is decisive about the sacrifice of Jesus is that it created a new covenant between God and man (1 Cor 11:21) and a resulting community of faith. This messianic community, established in and on Jesus's death,[231] is both exemplified by and embodied in its memorial meal, the Lord's Supper. In 1 Cor 10:16f. the Lord's Supper is used to document the exclusive alliance among those who share in the cup and bread. This is clearly the same with the Jewish sacrifice and meal in 10:18, and it was how Paul perceived pagan meals (whether their cults did so or not). The meal of a religious community, whether Jewish, Christian or pagan, embodies the community. It is in this respect that the eucharist is comparable to other cultic meals, not with respect to its "elements" or its "sacrifice."

Because the Lord's Supper is grounded in Christ's sacrifice and because believers have their new relationship to God through Christ, κοινωνία refers to the common alliance among those who belong to

---

[229]Nock, *Early Gentile Christianity*, 128.
[230]Contra Aalen, "Opfermahl," 141.
[231]Cullmann, *Essays on the Lord's Supper*, 18f., also Nock, *Early Gentile Christianity*, 70, who says: "Jesus said in effect, 'I am the sacrificial victim whose blood is shed for you, the faithful, to seal a new covenant with God.'"

Christ. In 1 Cor 10:16, 17 κοινωνία does not describe a personal (intimate, mystical, etc.) relationship between individuals and the Lord. Those views of κοινωνία which stress the personal relationship with the Lord (Käsemann, Hauck, Seesemann, and others) in distinction from or preference to the relationship with other believers are incorrect.[232]

On the other hand, neither is it sufficient to regard the Lord's Supper as κοινωνία in the sense of merely a guild or association (although perhaps many Greeks naturally did regard it in this way). The κοινωνία which results from Christ's sacrifice is a mutual obligation and commitment to the Lord, as well as a promise of salvation.

Stuart Currie's summary is apt:

> Thus in the practice of Israel those who eat the sacrifice are severally God's guests and collectively κοινωνοί; and those who eat in pagan temples are demons' company. . . . Surely, Paul says, you may accept invitations to the home of unbelievers and eat whatever is set before you (1 Corinthians 10:25-27); but you may not become their κοινωνοί in sacred meals (10:20-22).[233]

This fraternal alliance and its accompanying responsibilities are asserted often by Paul in 1 Corinthians. The same consideration expresses itself in 1 Cor 8:9-13; 10:23f.; 11:22; 12:21-46, and especially in chapter 13.[234] It is an expression of Paul's ecclesiology. The church is the temple of God, the people of God. The association (κοινωνία) in the Lord's Supper both arises from and leads to the church association (κοινωνία).[235] This is made clear by 10:17 where the eucharistic tradition (10:16) is interpreted ecclesiologically.

Paul's view of the relationship which exists in religious bodies makes understandable his use of this relationship to establish the obligations Christians owe to other members of their κοινωνία (in 10:23-11:1).

---

[232]For example, Hauck, "Κοινωνία," 805, says "Thus the nature of the Lord's Supper is expounded by Paul in terms of fellowship with the person of Christ, namely, κοινωνία with his body and blood." Also Elert, *Eucharist,* 37, "The κοινωνία of the participants with one another arises much rather from this, and in the eucharist solely from this, that each through the eating and drinking has κοινωνία with Christ."
[233]Currie, *Koinonia,* 45.
[234]Ibid., 44.
[235]Goppelt, "Kirchengemeinschaft," 25.

These obligations recall the Old Testament's stress on the life of brotherly fidelity as a part of covenant loyalty (e.g., 2 Sam 9:1, 3; 10:2; Zech 7:9).[236] This theme of mutual obligation by members of the community comes out clearly in 1 Cor 11:22ff., where eating and drinking in the assembly without regard for the other members of God's church is to deny the Lord's sacrifice and risk destruction. The eucharistic table carries obligations to consider the good of the community before one's own good.[237]

C. Christian Exclusivism

The mutual obligation which Paul feels is inherent in the community of God explains why Christians must have regard for their brothers and sisters. It does not explain why they could not participate in other religious meals—if other Christians were not injured by this eating. Why is it that Paul concludes a discussion of κοινωνία by demanding that Christians avoid the "table of demons" (10:21, 22)?

It may be that Christians in Corinth felt that they could join in such meals even if idols were involved because they knew those idols were unreal (10:19, cf. 8:4-6).[238] It is also possible that these Christians felt those meals were not religiously significant.[239] Such an attitude is very understandable in view of the highly social nature and function of these meals in Hellenistic life (see pp. 47-55). Moreover, the Corinthians could,

---

[236]Currie, *Koinonia*, 22.

[237]Minear, "Paul's Teaching on the Eucharist," 88.

[238]I do not have in mind here the alleged flaunting of freedom from bodily life by gnostics, as is speculated by Schmithals, *Gnosticism in Corinth*, 226: "The demons have indeed been conquered. This needs to be demonstrated." Similarly, Jewett, *Paul's Anthropological Terms*, 258f.

Barrett, *1 Corinthians*, 237, rightly says, "The effect of the sacrifice lies not in the eating (as Kümmel points out, Paul does not think that the Corinthians will eat demons) but in personal relationships, and the consequences that flow from them."

[239]Moffatt, *1 Corinthians*, 141, says that the motivation may have been a desire to retain a public and social life in the city. "The religion of such cults was so bound up with civic and social life that many Christians hardly knew where they needed to draw the line. . . ."

perhaps did, quote Paul himself to the effect that diet itself was an
adiaphoron.[240]

However, Paul insists on Christian abstinence from such religious
meals. They are, in his view, idolatry (as he explicitly states in 10:14 to
begin this phase of the argument). Thus Paul essentially disagrees with
the Corinthians on the religious significance of the pagan meals.

Paul's exclusivism demands that the Corinthians not be involved in
meals associated with other religous communities. Historically the basis
for his demand is the Jewish heritage which he shares with the church.
Judaism, both in its writings and its practice, stressed the exclusivism of
the bond it had to the one God, and the demand to avoid other religious
entanglements.[241] The gulf set between Israel and the pagan world was
perhaps widest in matters which involved worship.[242] Paul requires of
the New Israel the same kind of separateness required of "Israel according
to the flesh." It is clear that Paul thinks of Christians as "the called of
God" (1 Cor 1:9) in a way parallel to the prior status of Judaism. His
point then is, "Unmöglich ist es, gleichzeitig in zwei entgegengesetzten
Gemeinschaftsverhältnissen zu stehen. Die Gemeinschaft mit Christus
und die Gemeinschaft der Dämonen schliessen einander aus."[243]

It is not that Paul is demanding simply a Christian retreat from a
pagan culture. "Indeed you then would have to come out of the world"
(1 Cor 5:10). Where Paul argues for a Christian exclusivism the issue is

---

[240]Paul says this explicitly in Rom 14:14, which the Corinthians, of
course, could not have read. Still it is reasonable that Paul had earlier
expressed this view, as he essentially does in 1 Cor 8 and 10:22-29.

[241]Walter, "Christusglaube," 434, recalls that Jews were widely
regarded with hatred and suspicion precisely for their exclusivism, they
were even termed "haters of mankind."

[242]Note the directions in *Abod. Zar.* 2:3 where Jewish commerce
with Gentiles in certain goods is forbidden if the goods could become
employed in pagan worship.

[243]Wendland, *Korinther*, 80f. See also Edwin Hatch, *The Influence
of Greek Ideas on Christianity* (New York: Harper, 1957) 182, who says:
"To be a Christian was to be a member of a community. The basis of the
community was not only a common belief, but also a common practice. It
was the task of the community as an organization to keep itself pure."

quite specific: Christians must not practicipate in the (quasi) religious meals of their pagan neighbors held at an idol shrine. His position allows for no compromise. Christians cannot eat from the table of demons without thereby becoming members of their κοινωνία.

In taking this position Paul is remaining true to his Jewish heritage with its idea of the one God with his one covenant people who owed exclusive allegiance to him and to each other. He strengthens this position by referring to the eucharistic tradition according to which the meal constitutes a tie with Christ's body and blood.

In 1 Cor 8 Paul began his treatment of the issue of Christian participation in pagan meals by answering arguments raised by the Corinthians. He gives his own arguments against eating such meals first in 1 Cor 10:1-13 where he shows the relevance of the salvation history to this question. Then in 10:14-22 Paul sets out his second line of argument, his understanding of the κοινωνία which inheres in such meals. This argument also reflects the Old Testament understanding of an exclusive loyalty in worship. Finally, in 10:23-11:1 Paul considers some implications from his position and his arguments, and then summarizes his discussion on the topic. We turn now to consider this last major section.

1 CORINTHIANS 10:23—11:1:
CONCLUSIONS AND SUMMARY

INTRODUCTION

A. Problems

Several important problems arise within this final section of Paul's discussion of sacrificial meat in 1 Corinthians. First, how do Paul's instructions here relate to his earlier discussion in chapter 8 and what immediately precedes in chapter 10?

Second, what actually is involved in the two specific cases discussed in 10:25-27—eating meat sold in the market and accepting dining invitations? Most troublesome is the situation described in 10:27. Is this an invitation to eat in a private home, at a temple dining facility, a public dining hall, or does it make any difference?

Third, what is the meaning and importance of the phrase μηδὲν ἀναχρίνοντες διὰ τὴν συνείδησιν which is Paul's explicit reply to the cases described in 10:25-27?

Finally, how are verses 10:28-11:1 related to the immediate context of 10:23-27 and the larger context of the discussion of sacrificial meat in 1 Corinthians?

B. Structure

The last segment of Paul's treatment of sacrificial food in 1 Corinthians is in 10:23-11:1. In these verses he both deals with specific cases of eating sacrificial meat and also expands the discussion to broader horizons. He considers two tangential, yet important, cases of eating idol meat beyond the previous issue of eating at cultic occasions. But Paul also broadens the discussion to include all eating and drinking, indeed all that one may do. It is this combination of generality and concreteness which gives an uneven appearance to this section.

The section can be structurally divided as follows:

10:23, 24   The Corinthians' basic position on Christian
                   conduct in regard to idol meat is summarized
                   (10:23) and Paul's basic response succinctly
                   stated (10:24).

10:25-27   Two special cases of permissible eating: meat
                   sold in the markets (10:25) and that served by a
                   host (10:27) are considered and both permitted.

10:28-30   Paul qualifies the permission to eat even in
                   these acceptable situations. In these cases, too,
                   one must consider possible danger to others.

10:31-11:1   Paul's ethical guidelines for eating are sum-
                   marized and enlarged to include all conduct by
                   Christians.   This is illustrated by Paul's own
                   conduct.

1 CORINTHIANS 10:23, 24:
THE ISSUE AND THE REPLY SUMMARIZED

Paul begins this last unit by quoting once again from the Corinthians' letter, a concise slogan, "All things are permitted" (πάντα
ἔξεστιν).[1] This slogan appears earlier in 1 Cor 6:12, in a discussion about
sexual morality, There too it is a Corinthian defense of their conduct.[2]
The application of such a slogan to the problem of Christians eating
certain meat is probably original with the Corinthian Christians. However, the discussion of what is "permissible" (ἔξεστιν) and in what circumstances is a traditional Greek ethical topic.[3]

The question of "what is permitted" in classical Greek thought
referred to what is permitted by a higher norm, especially the law. By

---

[1]This slogan, occurring four times in 1 Corinthians, should not be
considered as stating Paul's own position.

[2]Various studies have made close connections between the problem
discussed in 6:12—πορνεία—and that discussed in 10:23. The connection
between immorality and sacrifice to idols was strong in Jewish polemics.
On this association see Barrett, "Things Sacrificed," 138-53. Also in the
present work, 149-151.

[3]Foerster, "Εξεστιν," 560f., discusses the role of the term in
Hellenistic philosophy and its legal background.

extension, the phrase comes to mean any right or permission for individuals to do something. In the ethical discussion of the Hellenistic period
ἔξεστιν often means that there are no personal obstacles to an action,
the individual has "the inner power to do it."[4] For Stoics this right was
especially based in the idea of the "natural."[5] The Stoic wise man with
his keen sense of justice and rigorous self-control is "he to whom all
things are permissible."[6]

Since people are different, what was considered permissible to
individuals differed as well. Philosophers were especially concerned to
show that the wise man had freedom (ἐλευθερία) to act as he pleased; for
him all things were "permissible."[7] Since the topic of what is permitted
was a popular convention in Hellenistic intellectual life it is not surprising
to find it in Philo[8] and among gnostics[9] as well. This also suggests that
the Corinthian slogan need not have come from any identifiable source.

---

[4]Ibid., 561.
[5]Grant, "Hellenistic Elements," 62. See Dio Chrysostom, 32:51.
[6]Dio Chrysostom, 3:10.
[7]See 113-117 in the present study. Also below, note 11 for a
reference to Dio Chrysostom which connects ἔξεστιν, ἐλευθερία and
συμφέρειν.
[8]Horsley, "Consciousness," 580f. He refers specifically to *Omn.
Prob. Lib.* 21, 22, 41, 59-61. Whether Paul and/or the Corinthians had
received their terms mediated through Hellenistic Judaism is difficult to
ascertain. This is especially true with so common a philosophical term as
ἔξεστιν.
[9]Of course, Schmithals, *Gnosticism in Corinth,* 230, argues that the
slogan "everything is permissible" is Gnostic. He continues, "Now in
Gnosticism precisely as in the Stoa ἐξουσία is employed as a *terminus
technicus.*"
Schmithals argues that ἐξουσία has three basic meanings: (1) the
power, inward or outward, or capacity to do something, (2) the permission
or authorization to do something, and (3) used figuratively to signify the
powers themselves which have the power. He is somewhat confusing in
ascribing these uses. He says that the Stoa uses ἐξουσία in the first
sense, and Gnostics in the second. However, he continues to describe
Gnostic usage as the first meaning, and even denies the second meaning
for Gnostics, 231: "He [the Gnostic] does not have authorization or permission [the second usage] to act in a libertine fashion but the *essential*
capacity and ability to act thus."
It is argued elsewhere in the present work that there is no need to
insist upon a Gnostic theology for understanding ἐξουσία as used in 1 Cor
8-10. See 98-103.

As in 1 Cor 6:12, Paul states the slogan πάντα ἔξεστιν twice and each time qualifies it with adversative ("but" ἀλλά) clauses. The first qualification in 10:23 is ἀλλ' οὐ πάντα συμφέρει, exactly as is given in 6:12. Like ἔξεστιν, "profitable" (συμφέρειν) was also a commonplace in Hellenistic philosophy.[10]

Dio Chrysostom, for example, said Diogenes argued it was not permissible (οὐκ ἔξεστι) to do that which was mean and unseemly and unprofitable (ἀσύμφορα) but rather that the things which are just and profitable and good (δίκαια καὶ συμφέροντα καὶ ἀγαθά) are both proper and permissible to do (προσήκει καὶ ἔξεστιν).[11] Diogenes also was said to give as proverbial that there are no men for whom freedom is not profitable (ἐλευθερία μὴ συμφέρει).[12]

Thus like the Corinthian slogan, Paul's first qualification represents a commonplace, almost a cliche.[13] The meaning of Paul's reply of what is "profitable" must be taken from the context of these verses. Parry suggests that Paul means that not all things are profitable "to the persons themselves, who possess the freedom; this was the point developed in 9:24-10:13."[14] But while the question of what "profits" (συμφέρειν) in 6:12 did relate to the individual, here it is considered in a corporate

---

[10]Konrad Weiss, "Φέρω," TDNT 9 (1973) 70-72.

Lionel Pearson, Popular Ethics in Ancient Greece (Stanford: University Press, 1962) 20, observes that in the fifth century Socrates critically examined the common ethical contrast between what is just (τὸ δίκαιον) and what is expedient (τὸ συμφέρον).

[11]Dio Chrysostom, 14:16: τά μὲν φαῦλα καὶ ἄτοπα καὶ ἀσύμφορα οὐκ ἔξεστι πράττειν, τὰ δὲ δίκαια καὶ συμφέροντα καὶ ἀγαθὰ χρὴ φάναι ὅτι προσήκει τε καὶ ἔξεστιν;

[12]Dio Chrysostom, 32:51. The basis for this assertion is "freedom is by nature advantageous" (τὸ γὰρ πρᾶγμά ἐστι φύσει τοιοῦτον). Diogenes is agreeable to this position, which is found in the diatribe, but still insists that the wise man avoids that which is foolish even when completely free.

[13]Grant, "Hellenistic Elements," 61, notes that the slogan of the Corinthians and Paul's qualification both resemble common Stoic attitudes. He cites Musonius Rufus, frg. 31: οὐ πολὺν διάγουσι χρόνον οἳ πρὸς τοὺς ὑπηκόους ὑπὲρ ὧν ἂν πράττωσι μὴ τὸ καθῆκει μοι λέγειν μεμελετηκότες, ἀλλὰ τὸ ἔξεστι μοι. From C. Musonnius Rufus, Reliquiae (ed. O. Hense; Leipzig: Teubner, 1905) 122.

[14]Reginald St. John Parry, The First Epistle of Paul the Apostle to the Corinthians (Cambridge: University Press, 1926) 153.

dimension.[15] This is confirmed by the repetition of the slogan from Corinth and Paul's second reply, ἀλλ' οὐ πάντα οἰκοδομεῖ.[16] Paul's two replies to the same slogan interpret each other. It is also confirmed by 10:33 where he contrasts seeking one's own advantage (σύμφορον) with that of the many. Finally in 12:7 the principle Paul sets forth for using the gifts of the Spirit is that things be done πρὸς τὸ συμφέρον, and there clearly the argument is what aids the church as a whole, not individuals.[17]

Paul's second qualification of πάντα ἔξεστιν is ἀλλ' οὐ πάντα οἰκοδομεῖ, which resumes a central argument from chapter 8.[18] Conzelmann rightly observes: "οἰκοδομεῖν denotes first and foremost the building up of the community, not the edification of the individual. This becomes clear from its usage in chap 12 and 14."[19] In 1 Cor 8 where Paul first discusses οἰκοδομέω it is clearly the "edification" of the church, not the individual believer.[20] The criterion of οἰκοδομεῖ shows then how rightly to interpret συμφέρει. It is not what benefits the one who acts, but those who are affected by his actions, especially the church.

In 10:24 Paul begins to state the conclusions to be gathered from his restrictions of the Corinthian slogan by giving a general principle:

---

[15]Barrett, 1 Corinthians, 239. C. K. Barrett, The Second Epistle to the Corinthians (HNTC; New York: Harper & Row, 1973) 307, notes that συμφέρειν in Paul's usage refers to the good of the Christian community. He cites as evidence: 2 Cor 8:10 and 1 Cor 6:12; 12:7.

[16]Conzelmann, 1 Corinthians, 176, notes this parallelism and draws the same conclusion; i.e., that Paul's understanding of συμφέρειν is that it is those things which οἰκοδομεῖν. Also von Soden, "Sakrament und Ethik," 12, n. 2.

Vielhauer, OIKODOME, 95, thinks that the first qualification, "not everything is profitable," is to be understood subjectively (profitable for the person acting), while the second qualification, "not everything builds up," has a corporate concern. Similarly, Foerster, "Ἔξεστιν," 570.

[17]Furnish, Love Command, 94, n. 8, observes that the RSV translates 1 Cor 12:7 "for the common good," which agrees with the interpretation here followed. Even the instructions about marriage in 1 Cor 7 are for the benefit of the Christian community, not just those who may marry or divorce. Note in 7:35 Paul says his instructions are πρὸς τὸ ὑμῶν αὐτῶν σύμφερον.

[18]On the word οἰκοδομεῖν see above, 74-78.

[19]Conzelmann, 1 Corinthians, 176.

[20]Barrett, 1 Corinthians, 239, notes that this is put negatively in Rom 14:20, where one must not destroy the community by doing what one may deem permissible.

μηδεὶς τὸ ἑαυτοῦ ζητείτω ἀλλὰ τὸ τοῦ ἑτέρου.[21] As Johannes Weiss notes, this principle is essentially that of chapter 8, the loving regard for the other man.[22]

This same principle is set forth in Phil 2:4, μὴ τὰ ἑαυτῶν ἕκαστοι σκοποῦντες, ἀλλὰ καὶ τὰ ἑτέρων ἕκαστοι. In Phil 2:4 this principle, although formulated negatively, is grounded in having the mind of Christ (2:5). Thus, as in 1 Cor 8:11f., regard for the effect of one's actions on the brother is equated with regard for the Lord himself.

Paul himself follows this principle of seeking the good of others, rather than himself, as he says explicitly in 10:33, which is virtually a parallel to 10:24.[23] Moreover, he has already set forth this thesis in 8:13 and illustrated it with reference to himself in chapter 9. His personal adoption of such a rule for conduct is also found in 2 Cor 12:14: οὐ γὰρ ζητῶ τὰ ὑμῶν ἀλλὰ ὑμᾶς.[24] This course of seeking the other's good rather than one's own, which Paul both exemplifies and teaches, is simply the course of love, for ἡ ἀγάπη . . . οὐ ζητεῖ τὰ ἑαυτῆς (1 Cor 13:5).[25]

In summary, the basic principle for conduct set forth in 10:24 is drawn from the character of Christian love (1 Cor 13:5), modeled upon the normative work of Christ (Phil 2:4, 5, 20; Rom 15:2, 3), and seen in the life of Paul himself (1 Cor 8:13; 9; 2 Cor 12:14). Thus in 10:24 Paul gives a foundation for all Christian conduct, which he then applies in selected specifics in the verses which follow.

---

[21]Robertson and Plummer, 1 Corinthians, 220, say that this prohibition is relative. "Seeking one's own good is not always wrong, but it is less important than seeking the good of others, and when the two conflict it is one's own good that must give way."

Grosheide, 1 Corinthians, 240, also notes the general form of the principle but suggests that "no man" = no member of the congregation and "the neighbor" = everybody God puts at my side.

[22]Weiss, Korintherbriefe, 263.

[23]Vielhauer, OIKODOME, 95, points out that Paul's reply in 10:23 which calls for "building up" and "what is profitable" is essentially the same as 10:24, 31, 33. He also notes that this continues a theme from chapter 9.

[24]Note again the generalized form and the brachylogy.

[25]Noted by Weiss, Korintherbriefe, 263.

1 CORINTHIANS 10:25-27:
THE INJUNCTIONS TO EAT

A. 1 Cor 10:25: Meat Sold at Market

In 1 Cor 10:25, 26 Paul deals with the first of two specific cases of eating. He applies the principle of 10:24 in a concrete manner to the eating of meat sold in the market (ἐν μακέλλῳ). Paul's basic position is that Christians should eat whatever is sold at the market. His qualification, μηδὲν ἀνακρίνοντες διὰ τὴν συνείδησιν, considered below, is somewhat unclear.

Regardless of the origin of the term μακέλλον[26] well before imperial times it described a distinct facility of Hellenistic cities. Ned Nabers' thorough investigation of the architecture of the *macellum* shows a widespread use and a consistent form and function in Hellenistic and Imperial times.[27] In a Romanized colony such as Corinth was in Paul's time, it would be an expected feature.

There have been varying attempts by excavators to locate the *macellum* of Roman Corinth.[28] However, it is likely that there was more than one *macellum* in a city of Corinth's size. Moreover, it is possible

---

[26]The origin of the term is debated. A full discussion is found in Ned P. Nabers, "Macella: A Study in Roman Archaeology" (Ph.D. dissertation, Princeton, 1967) 65-76. See also Moulton-Milligan, *Vocabulary*, 386. Also A. Cameron, "Latin Words in the Greek Inscriptions of Asia Minor," *American Journal of Philology*, 52 (1931) 249f.

[27]Nabers, "Macella," is a thorough research into this feature of Hellenistic life. A briefer, but very valuable, discussion is Nabers, "The Architectural Variations of the Macellum," *Opuscula Romana*, 9.20 (1973) 173-76.

The standard New Testament study is Henry J. Cadbury, "The Macellum of Corinth," *JBL* 53 (1934) 134-41.

Rankin, *Role of* ΜΑΓΕΡΟΙ, has a valuable discussion of the social function of the Macellum and its role in locating cooks.

[28]See Cadbury "Macellum of Corinth." See also the recent study, James Wiseman, "Corinth and Rome," 526f.

The relevant inscriptions are found in A. B. West, *Corinth VIII.2: Latin Inscriptions 1896-1926* (Cambridge: University Press, 1931) nos. 124 and 125, and J. H. Kent, *Corinth VIII.3: The Inscriptions 1926-50* (Princeton: University Press, 1966) no. 321. A review of these is Ned Nabers, "A Note on *Corinth* VIII,2, 125," *AJA* 73 (1969) 73-74.

that Paul is speaking generally, as in the modern expression, "go to market," and has no specific location in mind.[29]

It is most striking that Paul proposes Christians eat whatever meat may be purchased from the market. It is widely accepted that virtually all meat sold in public markets had passed through some ritual worship and was therefore technically ἱερόθυτον.[30] This free conduct is a logical step from Paul's position, later stated explicitly in Rom 14:14f., that meat itself does not contaminate. It does contrast sharply with the careful investigations of market items required of Jews (e.g., as seen in *Abod. Zar.* 2:3).[31]

The last phrase of 10:25, μηδὲν ἀνακρίνοντες διὰ τὴν συνείδησιν, (which is repeated exactly in 10:27), has been understood in several

---

[29]Cadbury, "Macellum of Corinth," 136. Wiseman, "Corinth," 520f. also suggests that several markets probably were located in Corinth during the same period.

[30]Lietzmann, *Korinther*, 49f., is the usual source of this conjecture. However, Cadbury, "Macellum of Corinth," 141, says this was not strictly true of all meats. Conzelmann, *1 Corinthians,* 176, n. 12, notes Plutarch, *Quaest. Conv.* 729C, says that the Pythagoreans, whenever they ate meat, usually ate from sacrificial animals, which implies that non-sacrificial meat was available.

Nabers, "Macella," has some interesting observations about the goods sold in the *macellum*. He notes, 97, that the macellum was not an equivalent to our supermarket, "but rather more akin to a delicatessen, in the sense that expensive foods were for sale there that one would normally purchase only for special occasions." This suggests that the decision about purchase of meat would not be a common issue for Christians.

Nabers also comments, 103-104, on the *macellum* excavated at Pompeii in which were found a number of sheep skeletons in a pen. Based on this he conjectures, "it is probable that much, if not all, of the slaughtering of meat which was sold in a macellum took place on or near the premises." This practice would be virtually necessitated by the very limited means available to keep meat from spoiling. This would appear to support the contention that one could purchase meat from the *macellum* which had not been slain in religious sacrifice.

[31]Cited by Conzelmann, *1 Corinthians,* 176, n. 14 and also by Barrett, "Things Sacrificed," 146; Schlatter, *Korintherbriefe,* 97. All note that the ban, based on Deut 13:18, was applied not only to the idols themselves but to anything used in idol worship. Therefore it did not matter—to the Jew—that the sacrificial meat did not come directly from a pagan altar.

ways. The word "investigation" (ἀνάκρισις) was used in Greek juris-
prudence to describe the pre-trial investigation.[32] The word is rare in the
New Testament, being found only in Luke-Acts (with this technical, legal
sense) and in First Corinthians.[33] A rigid scrutiny of table goods was
required of observant Jews. Thus it is a radical statement when Paul here
instructs Christians not to be careful investigators, but to eat whatever is
sold in the market "without investigations." Barrett rightly says, "Paul is
nowhere more un-Jewish than in this μηδὲν ἀνακρίνοντες. His whole life
as a Pharisee had been essentially one of ἀνάκρισις, not least into
foods."[34]

Although it is clear that Paul instructs Christians not to investigate the market meat, it is unclear how the phrase διὰ τὴν συνείδησιν
in the instructions is to be understood. There are two general ways of
construing the phrase: (1) conscience does not demand further inquiry—it
is not involved, or (2) make no inquiries so that your conscience will have
no basis for pangs.[35] While each interpretation is grammatically possible,
there is a real and important difference in meaning. An acceptable
choice between the two must take into account not only this verse, but
the parallel expression in 10:27.

The second suggested interpretation, "do not make any inquiries so
that your conscience does not become involved," has several defenders.
Pierce says Paul's warning means, "If you were to discover that it was
idol-meat, after you had eaten it, then you would suffer conscience."[36] A

---

[32]Friedrich Büchsel, "Ανακρίνω," TDNT 3, 943.
[33]Ibid., 943. The Pauline uses, all in 1 Corinthians, are: 2:14, 15;
4:3, 4; 9:3; and 14:24.
[34]Barrett, "Things Sacrificed," 146. Elsewhere Barrett is more
blunt, in 1 Corinthians, 240, he writes, "Paul had in fact ceased to be a
practicing Jew."
[35]On the topic of συνείδησις see above, 89-92. There the possibility is discussed that this term originated with the Corinthians. However, this remains uncertain.
One might hope for some guidance from other Pauline uses of the
phrase, διὰ τὴν συνείδησιν. However, the other use of the expression is
in Rom 13:5, a more difficult and controversial passage than the present
one. Maurer, "Σύνοιδα," 915f., summarizes the prominent interpretations
of "because of conscience" in Rom 13.
[36]Pierce, Conscience, 76. He says the alternative interpretation,
"do not let your conscience force you to ask questions" is tendentious.
However, one suspects that Pierce's preference in interpretation is also
affected by his insistence that in the New Testament conscience always
concerns past actions.

similar interpretation is given by Robertson and Plummer,[37] Jewett,[38] Maurer,[39] Grosheide,[40] and (apparently) Wendland.[41]

Most scholars who favor the interpretation, "do not ask questions so that your conscience will not suffer," also argue that Paul here is addressing those Christians "weak" in their conscience.[42] Jewett goes so far as to suggest that the language διὰ τὴν συνείδησιν and ἀνακρίνειν originates from the weak in conscience in Corinth.[43] Indeed, if Paul's words mean, "what you don't know won't hurt you,"[44] these words only make sense when directed to the weak. The strong, as is seen in 8:10, emphatically are not troubled by eating sacrificial meat, for they are willing to eat ἐν εἰδωλείῳ.[45]

A major difficulty with this interpretation is that otherwise in 1 Cor 8-10 Paul speaks only to the "strong."[46] 1 Cor 10:24 must be directed to the "strong" (really just the majority) since it is an answer to

---

[37]Robertson and Plummer, *1 Corinthians*, 220. "For the sake of your conscience making no inquiry, asking no questions which might trouble conscience. It is not wise to seek difficulties."

[38]Jewett, *Paul's Anthropological Terms*, 458.

[39]Maurer, "Σύνοιδα," 915.

[40]Grosheide, *1 Corinthians*, 241.

[41]Wendland, *Korinther*, 83.

[42]Wendland, *Korinther*, 83, says that Paul rejects not only the arrogance of the strong, but also the anxiousness of the weak.

Similarly, Maurer, "Σύνοιδα," 915, says, "Hence the weak should take the Gospel promise of their acknowledgment by God more seriously than their own knowledge. That is to say, they must let their own συνείδησις be limited and liberated by this."

Also see Merk, *Handeln aus Glauben*, 128.

[43]Jewett, *Paul's Anthropological Terms*, 427, says for the weak it means "painful awareness of transgression." Weiss, *Korintherbriefe*, 264, also believes that Paul here uses a slogan from the weak.

[44]Jewett, *Paul's Anthropological Terms*, 428, deserves credit for this courageous, if unconvincing, proposal. It is unconvincing because the weak are not being addressed.

[45]See above 102-104. Thus Jewett is led to say that the word συνείδησις is used in two different ways by the differing factions in Corinth. Paul employs the understanding of the strong in 8:7, 10; that of the weak in 10:25ff. Jewett, *Paul's Anthropological Terms*, 437, 458.

[46]Hurd, 124f., 143, insists that the weak are purely hypothetical. That is going to an unnecessary extreme. The weak are simply not directly addressed in these chapters.

their slogan πάντα ἔξεστιν. Likewise, 10:28-33 is also clearly addressed to the strong, since they alone are likely to exercise their freedom to eat in spite of a warning about the idolatrous source of the food. If 10:25-27 were addressed to another group (the "weak") one would expect a clear indication of a change in addressees. Thus the context speaks against taking μηδὲν ἀνακρίνοντες διὰ τὴν συνείδησιν to be addressed to the weak, urging them not to ask for unnecessary difficulties in eating.

In addition to the argument from context, one must also consider 10:27, which uses precisely the same warning about conscience. It is not likely that a "weak" Christian would even accept a dining invitation from a pagan, knowing of the potential dietary problems. More unlikely still would be that once so informed he would need an admonition not to proceed to eat.

Being persuaded that the warning, μηδὲν ἀνακρίνοντες διὰ τὴν συνείδησιν, is not addressed to the weak, and thus that the meaning "ask no questions so as not to bother your conscience" is wrong, one must follow the other alternative. In this explanation, Paul is saying you may and should eat whatever is sold in the market and need not investigate it, for this is not a matter of conscience.

This interpretation also has several defenders. Conzelmann paraphrases, "it should not be imagined that conscience calls for further inquiries."[47] This means "the conscience is not involved at all."[48] This view is developed by von Soden,[49] and apparently is followed also by Barrett in his translation: "make no inquiries based on conscientious scruples."[50] Beyond avoiding the difficulties in the view just rejected, this interpretation has much to commend it.

First, it fits the overall context in which the strong are being admonished, including 10:24 and 10:28ff. It also accords with Paul's emphasis in 1 Cor 8-10 that the eating of meat itself is a matter of consideration of the brother (not the same emphasis as 10:21, the τραπέζης δαιμονίων).[51]

---

[47]Conzelmann, *1 Corinthians*, 177, citing von Soden, 15.

[48]Conzelmann, *1 Corinthians*, 176. He objects that if διὰ τὴν συνείδησιν is taken as "so as to give conscience no cause for complaint," the result is "then we have precisely the Jewish, legalistically oriented attitude" (177, n. 15).

[49]Von Soden, "Sakrament und Ethik," 13-15.

[50]Barrett, *1 Corinthians*, 240f.

[51]Hurd, 145, suggests that the Corinthians had raised the questions about shopping and dinner invitations in an ironic and hyperbolic response to Paul's recent strictures urging acceptance of the apostolic decree.

Second, as von Soden has rightly argued, for Paul "conscience" always involves the brother; "... das Gewissen niemals von Dingen, sondern von menschen beansprucht wird. Das Essen als solches konstituiert keinen Gewissensfall . . ."[52]

Third, as was noted earlier regarding 1 Cor 8:7, 10, Paul does not have a developed concept of "the conscience" as is commonly assumed in contemporary ethical thought.[53] The conscience is not, for Paul, an independent source for ethical or religious guidance, but more man's awareness of himself in his desires and deeds. Thus in 10:25 Paul is not thinking of a part of man that may be troubled later, but man's consciousness of his actions. Horsley is right that for Paul's concept of conscience the focus is the "situation and self-consciousness of one's neighbor."[54] So unless objection is raised by others (10:28f.) one need not think the eating of any meat sold involves conscience.

It is clear that in 10:25a Paul thinks that the eating of the meat sold in the market is not a dangerous thing. This is confirmed by what he later writes, "I know and am persuaded in the Lord Jesus that nothing is profane in itself" (Rom 14:14).[55] Since the "strong" in Corinth are emboldened to eat at an idol's temple it is likely that they shared this evaluation, and more so! It is unlikely that they would later reverse their evaluation if by inquiry they discovered a sacrificial origin for their food. Paul confirms their viewpoint *in this regard*, and even proceeds to give a scriptural justification.

B. 1 Cor 10:26: Eating with Thanksgiving

In 1 Cor 10:26 Paul apparently quotes Psalms 23:1 from the Septuagint, although one word, "for" (γάρ), is not in the Old Testament text.[56] The point of the quotation here in 1 Corinthians is that meat is from God and its uses or history does not pollute it or the one who eats it.[57] Whether Paul was aware of the tradition later codified in Rabbinic literature that this Psalm established the need for saying grace over meals seems uncertain. Lohse thinks that Paul knew this tradition based on:

---

[52]Von Soden, "Sakrament und Ethik," 14.

[53]See 276f.

[54]Horsley, "Consciousness," 587.

[55]The topic, of course, in Rom 14:14 is also eating.

[56]Eduard Lohse, "Zu 1 Cor 10.26, 31" ZNW 47 (1956) 277-80.

[57]Robertson and Plummer, *1 Corinthians*, 220. They note that this agrees with Mark 7:19 and Acts 10:16.

(1) the connection of the Psalm with meals in both Paul and the Rabbinic texts and (2) the demand "to do all things to God's glory" (10:31) is similar to Tos. Ber. 4.1.[58] For Paul what is established is that the policy of eating any meat sold in markets is justified in scripture. Therefore he sees the permission as based upon the doctrine of Creation, not simply a concession to some in Corinth.[59]

C. 1 Cor 10:27: Eating with Friends

In verse 27 Paul deals with a second specific case: the Christian who receives a private dinner invitation. There are several difficulties in interpreting this verse, including: (1) what precisely is the type of dining being discussed here? Is this meal in a private home; a social occasion at some public dining facility, most of which were related to cultic sites;[60] or is it a post-sacrificial meal at a pagan temple? (2) Involved in discerning what precise situation is being considered is how verse 28 is to be related to verse 27. Generally, verse 28 is taken to offer additional details related to the situation described in 10:27.[61] However, it will be argued below that this is mistaken. (3) Finally, 10:27 and its meaning are

---

[58]Lohse, 277f.

[59]Schrage, *Einzelgebote*, 214, says that here the Creator role of God becomes a norm for Christian conduct. Less convincing is his similar treatment of 1 Cor 8:6. There Paul is debating against an appeal to justify eating cult meals on the basis of God as Creator.

[60]Wisemann, "Corinth," 475f., describes the evidence which suggests the South Stoa was used as a "hotel and entertainment facility for Corinth." However, there is a question about whether this facility survived into the Christian era with such functions.

Recently Kathleen Wright, "A Tiberian Pottery Deposit from Corinth," *Hesperia,* 49 (1980) 135-77, has argued that the "Cellar Building" in the southwest corner of the forum area was "most likely ... a restaurant or tavern" (174). She bases this conclusion upon the amount and variety of pottery found in the area which indicate a dining facility, however with no indication or association with a known cult.

At least it is possible to believe there were non-cultic, public dining facilities.

[61]This is explicit in Conzelmann, *1 Corinthians*, 177, "A hypothetical case which is subsumed under the case of v. 27." But others too imply this by assuming the "informant" is either the host himself, another Christian guest (usually a weaker brother) or perhaps a pagan guest.

related to 10:14 and 21 as well as 8:7, whether the occasions assumed are
the same or different.

Unfortunately most studies of 1 Cor 10:23-11:1 pass very quickly
over verse 27 to go to the more difficult and interesting questions raised
in 10:28 and 29. The result is that the specific injunction of Paul, before
any qualifications, is neglected too often. As in the question of foodstuffs
sold in the public market, so also with dinner invitations, the basic rule is
very similar: πᾶν τὸ παρατιθέμενον ὑμῖν ἐσθίετε μηδὲν ἀνακρίνοντες
διὰ τὴν συνείδησιν.

It is not stated in the text itself to what dining occasion the Christian has been invited in the situation of 10:27. Despite the creative
attempt by J. M. Ford to argue that ἀπίστων refers to a Christian equivalent of the Jewish *am haaretz*,[62] it is surely a non-Christian pagan who
issues the dining invitation. The word "unbeliever" (ἀπίστος) is used by
Paul to refer to pagans in 1 Cor 6:6; 7:12, 15; 14:22-24; 2 Cor 4:4 and 6:15
(if the latter is Pauline).[63]

Dining invitations were a common feature of Hellenistic life, held
for all major occasions of life: birth, adolescence, political advancement,
marriage, death, as well as good entertainment. Taking part in such
meals was simply a part of family and community life for the early Christians, abstention from which would virtually require "going out of the
world," something Paul opposes in 1 Cor 5:10.[64]

The word καλεῖν, "to invite," is common in papyri dinner invitations,[65] although Paul uses it only here and in 1 Cor 15:9 to refer to
something other than God's election. There is nothing unusual about the

---

[62]J. M. Ford, "Hast Thou Tithed Thy Meal? and Is Thy Child
Kosher?," *JTS* 17 (1966) 157f.

[63]Fee, "II Cor 6:14f.," 157f.

[64]Von Soden, "Sakrament und Ethik," 6. Barrett notes, *1 Corinthians*, 241, that this implies social contact between believers and non-
believers continued. Similarly, Grosheide, *1 Corinthians*, 242.

A. A. T. Ehrhardt, "Social Problems in the Early Church: I. The
Sunday Joint of the Christian Housewife," *The Framework of the New
Testament Stories* (Manchester: University Press, 1964) 286, notes that to
prohibit such meat would not only make the Christians outcasts but also
make them conspicuous.

For the variety and character of dining occasions in Hellenistic
life, see the chapter on cultic dining, 17-64.

[65]For examples, P. Oxy. 747; 926; 927; 1214; 1486; 1487 and 2147.
However, ἐρωτάω is used just as frequently, and thus Héring, *First Epistle*,
98, is wrong to see in καλεῖν a technical term.

form, and the conjecture that Paul implies Christians "surely would not go" without an express invitation[66] is reading too much into the phrase. Similarly, there is no reason to follow the suggestion that by "if you wish" (θέλετε) Paul is giving a mild rebuke—"if you *really* want to go."[67] The syntax of εἰ with the indicative indicates a "real conditional" sentence[68] which one may paraphrase "whenever, from time to time" rather then "if ever it should happen." Clearly what is being considered here is a common feature of life in which Christians are permitted to share.

The character of the dining occasion to which a believer has been invited has been a topic of considerable speculation. One possibility is that this eating opportunity is the same as that of chapter 8:10 and of 10:14-21, namely a cultic banquet following a sacrifice held in one of the temples' dining facilities, some of which have been uncovered at Corinth.[69] The difficulty with this interpretation is that then in 10:27 Paul seems to permit such eating, if a brother is not offended, while in 10:14, 21 he forbids it. The tension which results between these two pericopes has been one of the reasons given to partition the letter.[70] In fact, most interpreters who consider the invitation of 10:27 to refer to a temple meal also do favor partition. This is not without exception, however.[71]

---

[66]Robertson and Plummer, *1 Corinthians*, 221. Similarly, Héring, *First Epistle*, 98.

[67]Already by Weiss, *Korintherbriefe*, 264. Also implied by Robertson and Plummer, *1 Corinthians*, 221; Schlatter, *Korinther*, 129.

Against any implied prohibition in θέλετε are both Conzelmann, *1 Corinthians*, 177, n. 19 and Barrett, *1 Corinthians*, 241. Barrett rightly observes, "the language is normal."

[68]See Blass-DeBrunner, *Greek Grammar*, §372.

[69]See the brief review in the present study's introduction, 4, and the bibliography there given.

[70]See the conclusions to the present study, 269-270, and Hurd, 42-46 and 131-142. As Hurd notes, it is significant that virtually all scholars who divide 1 Corinthians nevertheless do not see the discrepancies so great as to deny Paul wrote each section—although at different times perhaps.

Pierce, *Conscience*, 79, makes the unusual and unconvincing suggestion that Paul had cooled off from chapter 8 and thus begins to mitigate his own earlier strictures.

[71]For example, Hurd, 129, n. 2, considers that 10:27 refers to the same type of occasion as is assumed in 8:10 and 10:19-21. Yet Hurd has presented perhaps the most exhaustive case for integrity of the letter.

The second possibility, and the most popular view, is that 10:27 refers to a different type of dining occasion from those named in chapter 8 or in 10:21. Barrett,[72] Parry,[73] Thrall,[74] Wendland,[75] Robertson and Plummer,[76] and Lietzmann,[77] are among those who consider 10:27 to refer to an invitation to eat in a private home.

Something of a *via media* is a third suggestion that 10:27 refers to a quasi-religious, social meal held at a cult site, but not actually an occasion of worship. Von Soden recalls that many of the dining occasions held at such shrines were simply a part of ordinary life and were hardly more than sentimentally religious.[78] Therefore the way such meals were perceived by the participants really determined whether they were "worship." One must recall that in addition to sacrifices on holy days for the patron deity, sacrifices and meals were held at sanctuaries by family clans, national groups, various guilds and associations, public and private festivals.[79] All these meetings, including those held in private homes,[80]

On the other hand, Héring, who favors partition, says 10:27 discusses an invitation to a private home in contrast to 8:10 which is a temple meal. Héring, *First Epistle*, 98.

[72]Barrett, *1 Corinthians*, 241.

[73]Parry, *1 Corinthians*, 154, "this clearly refers to an invitation to a dinner held at the host's house, not to one held in a temple, which could not avoid coming under the condemnation already uttered (21-23)."

[74]Thrall, "Paul's Use of ΣΥΝΕΙΔΗΣΙΣ," 122.

[75]Wendland, *Korinther*, 83.

[76]Robertson and Plummer, *1 Corinthians*, 219.

[77]Lietzmann, *Korinther*, 51. Hurd, 129, n.2, mistakenly cites Lietzmann as one who considers the meals the same as those mentioned in 10:19f.

However, Lietzmann is explicit about 10:27, "Gewöhnliche Einladungen zu Tisch in ein heidnisches Haus dürfen angenommen werden, das steht im Belieben (θέλετε) des einzelnen, ohne dass ihr euch daraus 'ein Gewissen macht.' Aber natürlich nicht solche, wie die im Exkurs s. 49 abgedruckten, die ausdrücklich zur Tielnahme am Kultmahl auffordern, das ist schon 14-22 gesagt."

[78]Von Soden, "Sakrament und Ethik," 6.

[79]See 13-15.

[80]Conzelmann, *1 Corinthians*, 177, "Verse 27 brings a second case, an invitation to a meal, whether in a private house, or a temple." He notes that even family dining might be religiously solemnized, see 177, n. 17.

were potentially religious, and then would have to be avoided as Paul
instructs in 10:20f. Conzelmann capsulizes this interpretation thusly:

> But what is the relationship of this [case in 10:27] to vv. 20f?
> Apparently Paul is thinking there of direct cultic proceedings,
> here of social occasions which may acquire a cultic tendency,
> but do not have to do so.[81]

In view of the several suggestions which have been set forth, we
may make some general observations about the situation discussed in
10:27. However, from the outset it must be acknowledged that the
sketchy information provided precludes a certain identification.

First, it is clear that in 10:27 Paul permits (actually, stronger,
ἐσθίετε is imperative in form) eating of meat on this occasion. Second, it
is equally clear that in 10:20f. he forbids involvement in κοινωνία and
τραπέζης of δαιμονίων. The simplest solution of this tension would be
that these are different occasions, although different in unspecified ways
(probably locality or intent). It is difficult to imagine how a meal at a
cult shrine would be non-religious, yet the study of cultic dining has
demonstrated that the religious character of such meals was often obscured by the entertainment aspect.

The first explanation, that 10:20f. and 27 both refer to cultic meals
and therefore the tension must be accepted or resolved by partitioning the
letter—both more complicated and less convincing—is the least attractive. The partition approach is more complicated because in addition to
hypothesizing about the character of the meal (all explanations do this) it
also requires an additional hypothesis of the letter's original units and
their reconstruction guided by modern theories. It is less convincing, for
still the tension between Paul's outright prohibition in 10:20f. and his
explicit permission in 10:27 still exists, albeit in diminished form, unless
one takes the additional step to say Paul changed his views.[82]

In the second case of eating, 10:27, like the first of 10:25, Paul
encourages Christians to eat and to feel no need to scrutinize. Thus the

---

[81]Ibid.

[82]Hurd, 129, gives yet another solution by claiming the situation of
10:27 is a hypothetical straw man, used by Paul seeking to save face after
he had changed his own position as a result of the apostolic decree.

instructions for eating are the same in both situations.[83]   Paul does not
encourage nor forbid the eating, but only reminds[84] the Corinthians of
what is decisive for Christians in such situations.

1 CORINTHIANS 10:28-11:1
BASIC PRINCIPLES OF CONDUCT

A. 1 Cor 10:27b, 30:
The Claim of Other People's Consciences

In 1 Cor 10:28, 29a Paul presents a third casuistic admonition in
this discussion of eating. This example is not another occasion of possible
eating but rather an occasion when one must forego eating. If proper
grammatical style is being followed here, this possible event is somewhat
more unlikely and uncertain than that pictured in 10:27.[85]

The event described in 10:28, 29a is quite general, and as a result
various interwoven questions have to be considered which can only be
answered by implication and hypothesis. Who is the "someone" (τις) who
informs the Christian about the sacred character of the meat? What is
the motive of this informant? Who is the "other man" (τοῦ ἑτέρου) whose
conscience may be damaged, and in what way? Is he the same as the
informant?

Generally the informant (τὸν μηνύσαντα) is considered to be either
another Christian guest, a pagan guest, or the host himself. There are
some difficulties, although not insurmountable ones, with each identification. It is often argued that the informant must be a non-Christian
because of his use of the word ἱερόθυτον, the proper pagan designation of
sacrificial meat, whereas Paul and other Christians would use εἰδωλοθύτον.[86] But a gentile Christian could have used the proper term either out

---

[83]Contra Barrett, 1 Corinthians, 241, who says that in the case of
one's own meat purchases no need exists to consider others.

[84]Thus Grosheide, 1 Corinthians, 242, describes how the situation
might come about with either a pagan or a weak Christian.

[85]Robertson and Plummer, 1 Corinthians, 224, "The change from
εἰ to ἐάν is perhaps intentional, although the difference between the two
is less in late Greek than earlier." They cite in support Moulton,
Grammar, I.187.

[86]Lietzmann, Korinther, 51, who says that it is another pagan
participant. Bultmann, TNT, 220, suggests that it is the host himself.

of consideration of the host[87] or habit.[88] Therefore the use of ἱεροθύτον
cannot decide against the informer being a Christian.[89]

A difficulty in taking the informer to be a pagan is that it is hard
to see how the Christian's eating would adversely affect the pagan's conscience, since he would consider the meat harmless.[90] Yet it is conceivable that Paul fears lest the pagan who observes a Christian eating
ἱερόθυτον might either think Christianity was syncretistic, or the
Christian really is uncommitted in faith.[91]

If the informer is considered to be the host, as well as a pagan, a
greater difficulty is added. One must infer his motive for first inviting
the Christian, then informing him about the meat, for the motive is not
stated. A pagan host may have sought to embarrass the Christian,[92] or to
protect him.[93]

Because of these difficulties the informer is most often believed to
be another Christian guest, whose uneasiness about the food provided has
led him to investigate it.[94] This "weak" Christian, becoming aware of the
character of the meat, seeks to warn his fellow Christian. However,
Lietzmann observes that if the informant was a weak brother as well as
the person who is endangered by eating one would expect 10:27 to end καὶ

---

[87]Barrett, *1 Corinthians*, 242; Parry, *1 Corinthians*, 221.

[88]Robertson and Plummer, *1 Corinthians*, 221.

[89]Thus Grosheide, *1 Corinthians*, 242, describes how the situation
might come about with either a pagan or a weak Christian.

[90]Barrett, *1 Corinthians*, 242; Wendland, *Korinther*, 83; and Weiss,
Korintherbriefe, 265, all suggest that it is hard to conceive how a pagan
could be strengthened for the gospel by the Christian's abstaining. Rather
one would expect the Christian's exhibition of strength to show his
freedom from demons to the pagan.

Robertson and Plummer, *1 Corinthians*, 221, say "That a heathen
would do it out of malice, or amusement, or good-nature . . . is possible,
but *his* conscience would hardly come into consideration."

[91]Von Soden, "Sakrament und Ethik," 14.

[92]Wendland, *Korinther*, 83; Barrett, *1 Corinthians*, 24, and
Lietzmann, *Korinther*, 51, think that a pagan guest is seeking to
embarrass a Christian guest.

[93]Parry, *1 Corinthians*, 154, gives this as an option, although not
himself endorsing it.

[94]This is favored by: Barrett, *1 Corinthians*, 242; Robertson and
Plummer, *1 Corinthians*, 221; Parry, *1 Corinthians*, 154; Thrall, "Pauline
uses of ΣΥΝΕΙΔΗΣΙΣ," 172; Maurer, "Σύνοιδα," 915; and Jewett, *Paul's
Anthropological Terms*, 427.

τὴν συνείδησιν αὐτοῦ.[95]   Also, how is the conscience of the weak
Christian endangered? Is it because he may be led to imitate the stronger
brother in eating and later accuse himself of sin?[96] Or will he simply
think less of the brother who eats?

In summary, it is obvious that there is a considerable diversity of
views on 10:28, and most interpretations involve 10:27 as well. The
situation is unclear; neither the informant nor his motives are clear, and
finally it is unclear how and whose conscience is endangered. Perhaps
such confusion is unavoidable because of the sketchy information actually
given in the text. However, some of this confusion may result from the
tendency of most interpretations to take 10:28, 29a as an elaboration of
10:27. That is possible, but not necessary.

Most scholars take 10:28, 29a to give additional information on the
situation of 10:27, the Christian who is invited to eat by a friend.[97]
Conzelmann puts this succinctly in saying that 10:28 is "a hypothetical
case which is subsumed under the case of 10:27."[98] Accepting this position has led to several problems. For example, the idea that the host in
10:27 is also the informant of 10:28 is largely dependent on restricting
10:28 to the preceding verse. This is also true of the difficulties which
attend taking the host to be the informant; what is his motive for inviting,
then informing, the believer? How could a pagan's conscience be injured
by the Christian's eating? Finally, there is the grammatical infelicity in
taking "anyone" (τις) in 10:28 to refer to the informant of 10:27.[99]

Moreover, restricting 10:28 to 10:27 also causes some difficulties
even if the informant is taken to be a "weak" Christian. First, why is this
not spelled out as it was in 8:7, which one might expect if it is precisely
the weak brother who is troubled? Second, the difficulty with the shocked

[95]Lietzmann, *Korinther*, 51.

[96]This is a common interpretation. See Maurer, "Σύνοιδα," 915;
Pierce, *Conscience*, 78; von Soden, "Sakrament und Ethik," 14; Barrett,
1 Corinthians, 242. Jewett, *Paul's Anthropological Terms*, 428, argues
that this is an education plan by Paul to bring along the weak man in a
gradual way.

Thrall, "Pauline Use of ΣΥΝΕΙΔΗΣΙΣ," 123f., suggests the weaker
brother might condemn the one who eats, and thereby be guilty of judging
him (citing Rom 2:17, 18 for such a sin).

[97]For example, Wendland, *Korinther*, 83; Robertson and Plummer,
1 Corinthians, and Barrett, *1 Corinthians*, 241.

[98]Conzelmann, *1 Corinthians*, 177.

[99]Weiss, *Korintherbriefe*, 265.

weak Christian employing the term ἱερόθυτον rather than εἰδωλόθυτον, although not critical, is real. Third, if the occasion of eating in 10:27 is other than in a private home, one finds it difficult to believe "weak" Christians would have been present.[100]

Certainly none of the difficulties mentioned above is unanswerable, but their existence suggests that a new approach is needed for interpreting the passage. However, 10:28, 29a need not be restricted to verse 27 and its situation but can be regarded as a general warning, applicable to either the dinner invitation of 10:27 or the meat purchased in a market (10:25), or presumably other occasions.[101] In this view Paul has moved from specific cases (10:25, 27) to general admonitions. The search for the "someone" (τις) who objects to the eating of ἱερόθυτον becomes fruitless and unnecessary.

Since obviously 10:25 and 10:27 are parallel, there may be a tendency to regard 10:26 and 28 as parallel. But this is mistaken, for 10:26 is a *justification* for eating (in the case of 10:25, perhaps also 10:27), while 10:28 is a *prohibition* of eating (μὴ ἐσθίετε) in certain circumstances.

If 10:28, 29a is taken to be a general restriction of a permission to eat "without investigation," urged in both 10:25 and 27, then several implications follow. First, attempts to identify the informant as the host, or the weak brother, are useless. Accordingly, speculation about the motive of the informer is unnecessary.[102] Second, the uneasiness about the use of τις to identify the informant is removed.[103] If the possible objection is applicable to various cases of meat purchased and dinner invitations, the very general "someone" (τις) is most appropriate.[104]

But perhaps the most significant result of not restricting 10:28 to

---

[100]Noted by Barrett, *1 Corinthians*, 242. Lietzmann, *Korinther*, 51, sensing the difficulty, says that the weak brother is not present but will hear of the event later.

[101]Of the sources consulted, only von Soden, "Sakrament und Ethik," 14, suggested that possibly a variety of occasions are considered.

[102]It would be the case in these verses, as in many other Pauline parenetical admonitions, that the parenesis is applied to a concrete situation (in this case eating), but it is not restricted to the particular occasion. See Furnish, *Theology and Ethics*, 90-92, on the Pauline parenesis and concrete cases.

[103]Weiss, *Korintherbriefe*, 265, notes that the τις of 10:28 is awkward, if the person is the same as the person referred to by the τις in 10:27.

[104]Contra Hurd, 125.

verse 27 is that Paul's admonition to abstain from any meat overtly identified as ἱερόθυτον is consistently and uniformly applied.[105] One must
always forego eating when another person is thereby endangered. At no
time is eating right "in itself," but all eating and drinking—indeed, everything one does (10:31!), is subject to this criterion of consideration of the
other person.

Accordingly there are not three classes of situations in regard to
sacrificial meat (as enumerated by Robertson and Plummer, and assumed
by others):

(1)   Eating at sacrificial feasts. This is idolatry, and
absolutely forbidden.
(2)   Eating food bought in the shops, which may or may not
have an idolatrous history. This is unreservedly
allowed.
(3)   The intermediate case of food at non-ceremonial
feasts in private homes. If no attention is drawn to
the "history" of the food, this falls into class (2). But
if attention is pointedly called to the history of the
food, its eating is prohibited, not as per se idolatrous,
but because it places the eater in a false position, and
confuses the conscience of others.[106]

In fact, there are two classes of eating considered in 1 Cor 8 and
10: eating at the τραπέζα δαιμονίων and thus becoming κοινωνοὺς
δαιμονίων (10:14-21) which is forbidden outright. Second, other eating
which while permissible must always be qualified by consideration of the
other person—as indeed everything a Christian does is so qualified (10:31-
32).

In what particular way one may endanger others by eating food
they identify as ἱερόθυτον is not specified. This fits with the general
character of the warning of 10:28, 29a. Looking back to chapter 8 one
may reasonably suspect that it is primarily the Christian with a weak
conscience who may be led either to follow the lead of eating sacrificial
meat to his own harm, or perhaps he may condemn his brother who eats
freely.[107]

---

[105]See above, 110-112.
[106]Robertson and Plummer, 1 Corinthians, 219. Similarly, Conzelmann, 1 Corinthians, 177f.; Barrett, 1 Corinthians, 242.
[107]Thrall, "Pauline Use of ΣΥΝΕΙΔΗΣΙΣ," 122.

However, it also may be a pagan who is either confused or offended by a Christian eating and finds this conduct an occasion of stumbling (πρόσκομμα cf. 10:32) to faith in Christ.[108] In fact, either or both suggestions may be right, for the warning is stated generally.[109] This situation may be termed, as sometimes is done, a *status confessionis*, a clear *no* to the pagan cult and its false idol.[110] But that would refer only to an occasion when a pagan was the other person (ἑτέρου) offended, and Paul's principle is applicable to situations involving Christians too.

In summary, l Cor 10:28, 29a gives a qualification to all eating which is not expressly forbidden as idolatrous (as those are in 10:14-21). It upholds the principle that Christians are not obligated to anxious investigations either about the meat they purchase or that they receive from others. The rule of not seeking one's own good but the good of the other person (10:24) is asserted again when "someone," for an unknown reason, identifies the meat as sacred. This does not change the character of the meat or the meal, but does require Christians to act out of consideration of the "awareness" (συνείδησιν) of others.[111] It must be noted that the expression in 10:29, συνείδησιν . . . οὐχὶ τὴν ἑαυτοῦ ἀλλὰ τὴν τοῦ ἑτέρου, closely parallels that in 10:24, μηδεὶς τὸ ἑαυτοῦ ζητείτω ἀλλὰ τὸ τοῦ ἑτέρου. This interpretation upholds von Soden's insight that claims on Christian conscience are not made by things but by people.[112]

---

[108]Von Soden, "Sakrament und Ethik," 14.

[109]Harris, "Conscience," 182f., shows how both pagans and other Christians might be under consideration.

[110]Wendland, *Korinther*, 83. Conzelmann, *1 Corinthians*, 177f., suggests that the declaration, "τοῦτο ἱερόθυτον ἐστιν," makes the meal [he is thinking of v. 27] "in itself harmless—into a sacrificial meal. Participation in it is now participation in the cult, and thus an act both of confessing to the gods and also of establishing communion with them in the sense of vv. 14-21."

All this is conjecture; nothing is said of it in 10:28ff. Paul does not warn here of idolatry but of injury to the other person.

[111]Thus Wendland, *Korinther*, 83; Conzelmann, *1 Corinthians*, 178; von Soden, "Sakrament und Ethik," 14.

[112]Von Soden, "Sakrament und Ethik," 14.

Some interpreters have suggested that Paul is warning the Corinthians to consider, in addition to their host, the conscience of another person. Usually this is the conscience of a weak Christian, see Pierce, *Conscience*, 75, and Merk, *Handeln aus Glauben*, 129. But this needlessly multiplies the cast of characters and also is too dependent on assuming 10:28 is a continuation of the case in 10:27.

B. 1 Cor 10:29b, 30: A Reservation about Eating

C. K. Barrett has noted that 10:29b, ἱνατί γὰρ ἡ ἐλευθερία μου κρίνεται ὑπὸ ἄλλης συνειδήσεως; is "notoriously difficult."[113] Indeed, the two questions in 10:29b, 30 have been regarded as a later gloss of the text by a scribe who was offended by Paul's too restrictive position set forth in 28, 29a.[114]

Apart from the theory of interpolation, there have been three basic interpretations of these verses.[115] (1) The first view sees these phrases as the objection of strong Christians to the restrictions Paul has just set forth.[116] (2) A second interpretation sees them as addressed to the weak Christian, urging him not to take advantage of the strong Christian's forbearance.[117] (3) Finally, these questions are taken to be a further elaboration of Paul's reasons for restrained actions in eating. The latter viewpoint can be subdivided into two explanations.

The first explanation sees 10:29b, 30 as reinforcing 29a by explaining to the one asked to forego his eating privileges, that nonetheless he

---

The present study considers καὶ τὴν συνείδησιν at the end of 10:28 to refer to the informant, not a second person. It is epexegetical.

[113]Barrett, *1 Corinthians*, 242.

[114]Weiss, *Korintherbriefe*, 265f. gives stylistic and historical considerations leading him to accept this conclusion. This position is also shared by von Soden, "Sakrament und Ethik," 15f. Also Zuntz, 17. The interpolator is objecting that one does not have freedom if it must be sacrificed to the scruples of another man.

[115]These three positions follow the summary of Jewett, *Paul's Anthropological Terms*, 429. Barrett, *1 Corinthians*, 243, gives essentially the same options.

[116]Those who take the questions to be serious see them raised either by the Corinthians (so Friedrich, "Freiheit und Liebe," 87) or as a Pauline diatribe advancing what he feels the Corinthians will object. Those supporting the diatribe interpretation include: Lietzmann, *Korinther*, 51; Wendland, *Korinther*, 83f.; Merk, *Handeln aus Glauben*, 129 and Pierce, *Conscience*, 78.

[117]Grosheide, *1 Corinthians*, 244. Héring, *First Epistle*, 99, says, "the Apostle seeks to define limits for the respect due to the weak." Similarly, Richardson, *Paul's Ethic of Freedom*, 129, "It seems that weak Christians were using their weakness aggressively to keep others from doing what offended them." In view of 8:13, 9:19-23 and 10:24 it is difficult to accept such an interpretation.

has not really lost his freedom of conscience.[118] Against this view it must be said that it understands "conscience" too subjectively, and "renunciation is seen as a withdrawal into the realm of inner freedom."[119] The second explanation sees 10:29b, 30 as an additional argument for forbearance in eating, not by explaining 10:28, 29a, but by giving another reason.[120] This latter interpretation seems most likely and agrees with the present study's assessment of the purpose of 10:28, 29a—a general admonition to consider the brother.

It is difficult to consider 10:29a, 30 as a defensive response, either real or rhetorical, to Paul's strictures in 10:28, 29a for two reasons. First, one would expect not γάρ but either δέ or ἀλλά to introduce an adversative argument.[121] Second, if it is an objection given in diatribe style, it is most striking that Paul apparently gives no answer.[122]

However, if 10:29b, 30 is taken as a second general argument for foregoing one's eating privileges, then the γάρ is grammatically appropriate. Moreover, the opening word, ἱνατί fits well also. Robertson and Plummer observe that this word means, "for what object," not "by what right" (as it is frequently interpreted when these questions are regarded as objections on the part of the strong). Thus the question of 10:29b is

---

[118]Bultmann, *TNT*, 219. His point is that since one declines to eat for the benefit of the other man's conscience (10:29a) he thereby loses none of his own inner freedom of conscience—since his own conscience is not involved. Bultmann says, "If 'I' (Paul) supposed that I had to decline for the sake of my conscience, I would have submitted to another's judgment and surrendered my freedom. . . ."

Barrett, *1 Corinthians*, 243, quotes Bultmann approvingly and accepts a similar explanation. Similarly, Davies, "Conscience," 674. Grosheide, *1 Corinthians*, 243, agrees that such a conscience remains free, whether the person eats or does not eat.

[119]Conzelmann, *1 Corinthians*, 178, especially n. 25 for his correct criticism of modern subjectivistic understandings of "conscience."

[120]Jewett, *Paul's Anthropological Terms*, 429; Maurer, "Σύνοιδα," 915; Robertson and Plummer, *1 Corinthians*, 222f.

[121]Noted by Weiss, *Korintherbriefe*, 265.

[122]Lietzmann, *Korinther*, 52, who defends the diatribe interpretation, notes this difficulty. Wendland, *Korinther*, 83f., also defending the diatribe, must consider vv. 31-33 as an answer, yet concedes that the impression is that Paul passed over these questions entirely. Also Zuntz, 17, says a "refutation is looked for in vain." Von Soden, "Sakrament und Ethik," 16, thinks 10:31ff. is an answer to 10:29b, 30. Yet is does not appear to be a real answer.

really, "to what purpose should the exercise of my freedom be an occasion to be judged on account of another person's conscience?"[123]

The idea of freedom (ἐλευθερία, mentioned in 10:29) has already been discussed in connection with 1 Cor 8:9-13.[124] There it was pointed out that although Paul is remembered as the apostle of freedom, too often this is misunderstood as a liberation from restraints or the autonomy of the spiritual man.[125] But for Paul freedom (ἐλευθερία; ἐξουσία is virtually synonymous) is freedom to consider the brother. In the case of permissible eating, whether market supplies or as the guest of another, Christians have the freedom not to eat if the other man's conscience may be injured.

A similar and informative point about freedom is made by Paul in Gal 5:13. "You are summoned to freedom, brothers, only do not let your freedom become an opportunity for the flesh, rather [stated positively] through love serve one another." As in 1 Cor 10:29b, Christians are warned about the true purpose of freedom, i.e., to serve others. If the exercise of this freedom results in condemnations and blasphemies, it is not Christian freedom. For Christian freedom what is decisive is the brother.[126] This is precisely the theme set forth in 1 Cor 10:24 and 10:31-33, and also set out in 9:18-23 by Paul's example.

---

[123]Robertson and Plummer, *1 Corinthians*, 222, "What follows, [ἰνατί γὰρ] is really a characterization of the act of eating." Héring, *First Epistle*, 99, n. 52, says that here ἰνατί means "to what purpose?"
[124]See above 169-173.
[125]This common understanding of freedom is assumed in those interpretations of vv. 29b, 30 which regard them as objections of the strong against constraint from another person's conscience. It is not solely a modern definition of freedom. For example, Epictetus, *Diss.* 4.1.56 says:

"And does freedom seem to you to be something independent and self-governing [αὐτεξούσιαν καὶ αὐτόνομον]? Of course. When, therefore, it is in another's power to put hindrances in a man's way and subject him to compulsion say confidently that this man is not free."

Similarly, Aristotle, *Metaph.* 1.2.11 (982b), says "just as we call a man independent [ἐλεύθερος] who exists for himself and not for another. . . ."

One could say that the Corinthians appear to hold such a view of Christian freedom, but Paul does not share it.
[126]Vielhauer, *OIKODOME*, 95. He mistakenly argues that Christian "freedom" must be sacrificed for the love of the brother. That is to oppose freedom and love, rather than see them as complementary.

Paul's argument in 10:29b and 30 may be paraphrased for clarity: "Why should I as a Christian conscious of my freedom to eat or not eat exercise freedom by eating if I know another person's awareness will lead him to condemn me?"[127] The second question is a parallel statement of the same point: "How can I offer grace over food, knowing that I will be blasphemed for eating that over which I have said a blessing?"[128]

Paul does not say specifically how the one who eats becomes the object of defamation and condemnation. It could be that the weak Christian who sees another Christian eat is led to condemn him for such eating or, following the parallel in 1 Cor 8:9-13, that the weak Christian is led to imitate the one eating in freedom and subsequently blames the strong person for his anguished conscience.[129] Horsley aptly summarizes on this freedom:

> In his response to the problem posed by the "freedom of consciousness," Paul insists on the "real ethical question" at the interpersonal level. Both the structure and the substance of Paul's response makes the effect of one's behavior on others the criterion of ethics.[130]

Confirmation of the interpretation of 10:29b, 30 followed here is found in Rom 14:13-23 (especially 14:16) which is a later reworking of the principles set forth in 1 Corinthians.[131] In Rom 14 the "strong" are admonished not to let their conduct become a stumbling block or offense to their brother (14:13). Even if one knows and is persuaded of the

---

[127] This is the view of Robertson and Plummer, *1 Corinthians*, 222f.

[128] Ibid., 223. Note the linguistic parallelism of χάριτι and εὐχαριστῶ. See also von Soden, "Sakrament und Ethik," 18, who says that prayer over a meal which injures a brother is frivolous and fails to take God seriously.

[129] Jewett, *Paul's Anthropological Terms*, 430, observes that otherwise in 1 Corinthians the weak do not appear aggressive, and it is unlikely that they openly condemn those who eat boldly. Rather, when they feel the example of the brother eating has led them to eat and thus to sin, they hold him responsible. According to Paul in 1 Cor 8:11, 12, they are correct although in a way different than they think.

[130] Horsley, "Consciousness," 586.

[131] Karris, 155-78, is an exhaustive discussion which establishes the dependence of Rom 14, 15 on 1 Cor 8, 10. See in his article especially 165f., where a chart shows verbal parallels. Also see Furnish, *Love Command*, 115, n. 69.

acceptability of all foods, he must exercise that awareness in consideration of "that one for whom Christ died" (14:15). Failure to do so will lead
to the perverse result of being blasphemed for that which is good
(14:16).[132] The tragic result of "being blasphemed" is especially noteworthy, since 1 Cor 10:30 and Rom 14:16 are two of only four Pauline uses
of the word.[133] Also showing the relation of the discussion of Rom 14 to
that in 1 Cor 10:30 is the mention of "giving thanks" (εὐχαριστεῖν) in
Rom 14:6.[134] Von Soden captures the force of the argument in 10:30 by
asking how Christians could pray over their meal if thereby their
neighbor's conscience was shaken?[135]

C. 1 Cor 10:31-11:1: The Consideration of Others

The final segment of Paul's argument in 10:23-11:1 is found in
10:31-11:1. These four verses are general and summarizing in form; only
in 10:31 does the specific issue which has occasioned them appear (and
that in a very vague way, "whatever you eat"). These verses do summarize on the topic of eating sacrificial meat and give some guidance for
all Christian conduct.[136] Their unspecific form renders them susceptible
to being regarded as cliches when they are taken from the context.
Perhaps this accounts for the sparse consideration they have received in
most studies of 1 Cor 10.[137]

---

[132]Karris, 166, n. 50, argues convincingly that "the good" (τὸ
ἀγαθόν) in Rom 14:16 is equivalent to "your freedom to eat" in 1 Cor
10:29b. The abstract phrasing of Rom 14:16 he takes to be another proof
of the parenetical rather than specific character of Rom 14-15.

[133]Otherwise, Rom 2:24, 3:8. Βλασφημία does not occur in Paul.

[134]The word is common in Paul, especially in the introductory
"thanksgivings" to his letters but also elsewhere. In 1 Corinthians it is
also found in 14:16-18 referring to prayer in the spirit.

On the practice of saying thanks for meals, see Lohse, "Zu 1 Cor
10, 26, 31."

[135]Von Soden, "Sakrament und Ethik," 16.

[136]Carl J. Bjerkelund, Parakalō (Oslo: Universitetsforlaget, 1967)
144, says that 10:31-11:1 summarizes 8:1-10:15 and 10:23ff., although in
10:14-22 Paul appears to argue in a different manner.

[137]Lietzmann, Korinther, 52f., allots only one (long) sentence to
the four verses. Hurd, otherwise very thorough, give no discussion of
these verses, only noting their similarities to 9:19-27 in a chart, 130.
Barrett, 1 Corinthians, has less than two full pages (244-246) and
Conzelmann, 1 Corinthians, slightly over a page, 179f., on the passage.

Stylistically "therefore" (οὖν) in 10:31 ought to be considered either as resuming an argument or giving a conclusion.[138] Here it "gathers up the results of the long discussion, and introduces a comprehensive principle which covers this question and a great many other things."[139]

Taken in itself, 10:31 could be proverbial, but from the context of the letter it is clear that there is a specific content.[140] "Therefore, whether you eat or drink or whatever you do, let everything you do be to the glory of God."[141] The first part of the sentence generalizes the discussion beyond idol meat. The context shows that the principle is being applied to idol meat, but it is stated so as to suggest a much wider applicability. This extension of the principle of considering the brother in one's actions had already been set forth in 8:13 and 10:24 and will be elaborated in Rom 14.

A far-reaching principle is set forth in 10:31: "Let everything you do be to the glory of God" (πάντα εἰς δόξαν θεοῦ ποιεῖτε). "Everything" returns to pick up the initial slogan of 10:23, πάντα ἔξεστιν. Here Paul gives as a standard for "everything" the glory of God rather than what "builds up" as in 10:23. However, these phrases interpret each other. Lietzmann rightly notes that the Corinthians could have affirmed such a slogan too,[142] but they would have differed radically on its inter-

---

[138]Blass-DeBrunner, *Greek Grammar*, §451(1). However this precision is lost in much of biblical Greek, and οὖν may simply be equal to καί. See also Bauer, ed. Gingrich and Danker, *Greek-English Lexicon*, 597.

[139]Robertson and Plummer, *1 Corinthians*, 223. Conzelmann, *1 Corinthians*, 179, says that this is the "conclusion to be drawn from the now established possibility of freedom of action." That is true. However, it is more a conclusion based on the established responsibility to the brother. Schrage, *Einzelgebote*, 45f., rightly notes that Paul's ethical warnings move beyond their specific occasion.

[140]Barth, *Resurrection*, 59, warns against considering the meaning of this verse to be "the vexatious modern idea that the whole of life, including eating and drinking, must be and can be a service of God." Conzelmann, *1 Corinthians*, 179, says in itself v. 31 is a cliche. However, the context shows specifically that the brother is in view.

[141]Blass-DeBrunner, *Greek Grammar*, §480(1), notes in the phrase, τι ποιεῖτε ἀλλό is omitted by ellipsis. Also noted by Blass-DeBrunner §454(3) is the formula εἴτε . . . εἴτε which in the New Testament is used only by Paul and 1 Peter.

[142]Lietzmann, *Korinther*, 52.

pretation. They would have insisted that acting out one's Christian freedom and encouraging others to do so was to "give glory to God" who had granted this power.

The motif of "glorifying God" occurs frequently in Paul.[143] It is often found in doxologies (e.g., Rom 11:36; 16:27; Gal 1:5; Phil 4:20). Elsewhere Paul also describes activities, not just words, as being to the glory of God. For example, his mission work leads to the increase of God's glory (2 Cor 4:15, cf. Rom 3:7). The Pauline collection for the poor in Jerusalem, as an act of Christian brotherly love, will be to "the glory of God" (2 Cor 9:13). Beyond these passages there are four other passages which mention "to the glory of God" which are especially instructive for 1 Cor 10:31.

In Rom 15:6, 7 Paul concludes a long discussion of the obligations of the weak and strong Christians to each other. In summary he appeals, "Welcome one another, therefore, as Christ has welcomed you, *for the glory of God.*" (διὸ προσλαμβάνεσθε ἀλλήλους, καθὼς καὶ ὁ Χριστὸς προσελάβετο ὑμᾶς εἰς δόξαν τοῦ θεοῦ) Several similarities can be seen to 1 Cor 10.

First, the concern in Rom 14 about how one's diet affects others, concluded in Rom 15:1-7, is parallel in subject matter to 1 Cor 8-10. The topic is very similar, and Romans probably represents a re-working of material from 1 Corinthians.

Second, Rom 15:2 which generalizes on this topic is very similar to 1 Cor 10:24. Rom 15:2 says "Let each of us please his neighbor for his good, to edify him" (edify is οἰκοδομέω also found in 1 Cor 10:23).

Third, in both passages the appeal to act with regard and consideration for the other person is grounded in Christ. In Rom 15:3 Christ is set forth as an example of the proper conduct, "for Christ did not please himself. . . ." Similarly, in 1 Cor 11:1 the Corinthians are urged to "be imitators of me as I am of Christ." In both cases Christ's self-giving is regarded as exemplary in these matters.

In 1 Cor 6:20 the topic is not how one's eating affects other believers, as in Rom 14, 15 and 1 Cor 8, 10, but it is instructive to look at the use of "glory of God" in the verse. Although the problem in 1 Cor 6 is

[143]See the summary of this motif in George H. Boobyer, *"Thanksgiving" and the "Glory of God" in Paul* (Leipzig: Robert Noske, 1929).

Christian involvement with prostitutes,[144] Paul does quote a slogan taken from the Corinthian letter which he also quotes in 10:23 in connection with eating sacrificial meat. The use of the same slogan, πάντα ἔξεστιν shows the Corinthians saw the issues as similar.

In 1 Cor 6 one of the arguments used to persuade Christians to avoid sexual contact with prostitutes is "*glorify God* in your body: (1 Cor 6:20). The basic argument against such illicit relationships is that the "body" of Christians is not for their own disposal but "for the Lord" (6:13). Proper conduct in this area involves how one uses his body, just as it does in the issue of idol meat. If one heeds Paul's warning "Shun immorality" (φεύγετε τὴν πορνείαν, the similarity to 1 Cor 10:14, φεύγετε ἀπὸ τῆς εἰδωλολατρίας, is striking!) then he glorifies God in his body.

It should also be noted that in 1 Cor 6:12-20 the call to live a pure life is grounded in Christ: his death (6:20, "you were bought with a price") and his lordship (6:13-15). While imitation is not mentioned explicitly, as it is in 1 Cor 11:1, in both cases the appeal to glorify God by one's conduct is stated with an eye to Christology.

A third important reference to acting to the glory of God is Phil 1:11, where in a prayer Paul asks that the Philippians may be "filled with the fruits of righteousness which come through Jesus Christ, *to the glory and praise of God*" (εἰς δόξαν καὶ ἔπαινον θεοῦ). One verse earlier, 1:10, Paul also prayed they might "be pure and blameless for the day of Christ." "Blameless" here is ἀπρόσκοπος, and the only other Pauline use is 1 Cor 10:32, which also speaks of "giving glory to God."

Finally, Phil 2:11 which concludes the pre-Pauline hymn of 2:5-11 gives as a goal that "every tongue confess that Jesus Christ is Lord, *to the glory of God the Father*" (εἰς δόξαν θεοῦ πατρός). In the hymn itself this verse clearly refers to the conversion of people to Christ. Thus it is their confession—"Jesus Christ is Lord"—which is to the glory of God. That is to say, the hymn itself uses the glory of God in a context of doxology and missiology.

However, Paul uses this hymn for a slightly different purpose in his letter. As is clear in Phil 2:1-4, Paul's real concern here, as in 1 Cor 10, is about intra-Christian relations. He encourages the Philippians not to act selfishly but with regard for others. "Let each of you look not only to his own interests, but also to the interests of others" (μὴ τὰ ἑαυτῶν

---

[144]Hurd's suggestion that 1 Cor 6:12-20 is only a sham by Paul to prepare for the real topic of diet in 8, 10 is unconvincing. Paul spends real effort in 6:12-20 and obviously sees this as a genuine issue.

ἕκαστος σκοποῦντες, ἀλλὰ καὶ τὰ ἑτέρων). This appeal has both verbal
and substantive agreement with the appeal of 1 Cor 10:24, 21ff. Indeed
Phil 2:3f. would fit nicely into the argument of 1 Cor 10:31ff.

In considering Phil 2:11 it is also noteworthy that the appeal to
consider the other person's needs is grounded in an imitation of Christ
(Phil 2:5) as it is in 1 Cor 11:1. It is looking after the needs of the other
person which is "having the mind of Christ."

When these several uses of appeals to "the glory of God" in Rom
15:7; Phil 1:11, 2:11 and 1 Cor 6:20 are examined along with 1 Cor 10:31 a
certain outlook appears. Living "to the glory of God" is living with the
highest regard for the needs of other people, seeking not to offend them.
Such a life is directly grounded in the work of Christ, who is both the
pattern (1 Cor 11:1, Phil 2:4-11, Rom 15:3) and the abiding power of
Christian life.[145] This means living "to the glory of God," as Paul appeals
in 1 Cor 10:31 has a specific content, it is not just "in the name of
God."[146] As Barrett rightly observes:

> This verse puts positively what has hitherto been put nega-
> tively. I do not act to the glory of God if I give to an idol
> some of the honour due to God alone; nor if I cause scandal or
> ill-feeling in the church, or cause a fellow-Christian to fall
> from his faith.[147]

The next verse, 10:32, is both a continuation and a restating of
10:31. It makes clear what Paul means by acting to the glory of God; it is
being "without offense (ἀπρόσκοποι) to Jews and Greeks and the church of
God. Although the word here, ἀπρόσκοπος is very rare (only Phil 1:10, see
above), Paul does often speak of avoiding offenses (πρόσκομμα). In 1 Cor
8:9 he urges the Corinthians not to let the exercise of their rights become

---

[145]Schrage, *Einzelgebote*, 187, says that "to the honor of God" in
Paul is a motive more than a norm for conduct, although he grants one
may not distinguish sharply between these.

[146]Weiss, *Korintherbriefe*, 266. Thus Barth, *Resurrection*, 45, is
wrong when he concludes that Paul is saying, "We can eat, drink, and do
whatever else, all to the glory of God (x. 31), when we know, according to
viii. 5, that we are created in Him and by Him and by the Lord Jesus
Christ." 10:31 is not the giving of a permission but a warning.

[147]Barrett, *1 Corinthians*, 244. See also Merk, *Handeln aus
Glauben*, 129, who says that the acting for the glory of God occurs when I
am guided not by my advantage but by my neighbor's salvation.

an offense to those weak in conscience. Similar warnings are in Rom 14:13, 20, 21, where those who may wish to eat are warned not to offend the brother. Rom 14:21 is very similar not only to 1 Cor 10:31 but also 8:13, and each verse contains the idea of a stumbling block (although with different words). Other Pauline uses of πρόσκομμα are in Rom 9:32, 33 which describe the failure of Israel to accept Jesus as the Christ, thus fulfilling prophecies in Ps 118 and Isa 8:14; 28:11. There the idea of "stumbling block" is not related to Christian conduct, but those references do make clear that being "without offense" does not mean simply not irritating the brother, rather avoiding those deeds which threaten this faith commitment. This "stumbling block" is a very serious matter.

The same point is made with a similar wording in 2 Cor 6:3, where Paul says his own conduct was guided by the priniciple, "giving no offense in anything" (μηδεμίαν ἐν μηδενὶ διδόντες προσκοπήν). This verse has obvious similarities with 1 Cor 10:32ff. where Paul also sets forth his conduct as an example of being "without offense."

Christians should seek to conduct themselves without offense to "Jews and Greeks and to the church of God." The combination of "Jews and Greeks" is fairly common in Paul.[148] But in none of the other passages is the "church of God" also mentioned. In other passages "Jews and Greeks" means the totality of humankind, whether united in their opposition to God or their reception of the gospel. The phrase "Jews and Greeks" thus is inclusive of all people. From Paul's uses elsewhere one must conclude that the addition of "τῇ ἐκκλησίᾳ τοῦ θεοῦ" in 1 Cor 10:32 is purposeful, not just rhetorical. "The church of God" is added because in this question of eating sacrificial meat has arisen among members of the Corinthian church.[149]

While the admonition to be without offense to Jews, Greeks and to the church of God is formulated generally, the emphasis clearly is upon

---

[148]Rom 1:16; 2:9, 10; 3:9; 10:12; 1 Cor 1:22, 24; 12:13 and Gal 3:28. See also Rom 1:14, "Ἕλλησιν καὶ βαρβάροις" (a more Greek phrasing).

[149]Blass-DeBrunner, *Greek Grammar*, §444(2), say that the connections καὶ . . . καὶ . . . καὶ serve to retain the distinctions among the members enumerated, whereas τε καὶ used elsewhere by Paul aside the distinctions. See also Robertson and Plummer, *1 Corinthians*, 224, "These are three separate bodies; the third does not include the other two."

the last named group, "the church of God."[150] Specifically, Paul has in mind the church of God in Corinth (1:2), especially the weaker members.[151] Probably the use of "church" rather than "brethren" is a means to make the point more strongly; similarly the use of the added words τοῦ θεοῦ.[152] The obligation to the brother is stated by reference to the community of God, as earlier (8:12) it was stated by reference to Christ the Lord.

Finally (10:33) Paul resumes an earlier argument and refers to his own conduct as exemplary for the Corinthians. He had used himself as an example in 8:13 and extensively in chapter 9. What he is asking of the Corinthians he is willing to do himself. "Even as (καθὼς) I seek to please all men in everything."[153] Paul's goal is to embody this conduct himself and to encourage it in others. In interpreting 10:33 two things are important to note: First, how this verse takes up much of the argument in 10:23-32; Second the close ties to 1 Cor 9:20-22.

1 Cor 10:33 has several verbal similarities with the argument as developed in 10:23-32. (1) There is the same broad-based concern about all (πάντα) of one's conduct which Paul had criticized in 10:23 and redirected in 10:31. (2) Just as Paul had admonished the Corinthians not to seek one's own needs (10:24, μηδεὶς τὸ ἑαυτοῦ ζητείτω) so he himself has not sought his own needs (10:33, μὴ ζητῶν τὸ ἐμαυτοῦ). (3) Earlier Paul had criticized the Corinthian slogan πάντα ἔξεστιν by replying ἀλλ' οὐ πάντα συμφέρει (10:23); here he says he seeks the benefit (τὸ σύμφορον) of the many. What is profitable (τὸ σύμφορον) to Paul is the salvation of others, not the exercise of one's wishes.[154]

---

[150]Thus speculation on how Jews' or Gentiles' scruples may be affected is unnecessary. Doubtlessly if and when Paul felt that this was a danger (e.g., 1 Cor 9:19f.) he would stand by the principle formulated. But here the general principle is addressing a specific situation, namely offending the brother by one's eating. See Barrett, 1 Corinthians, 244f.

Schrage, Einzelgebote, 196f., goes beyond the intent of the passage when he says that 10:32 proves that Paul acknowledges and employs a pagan standard for Christians. That may be so but is not under consideration here.

[151]Weiss, Korintherbriefe, 266, and Robertson and Plummer, 1 Corinthians, 229.

[152]Parry, 1 Corinthians, 155.

[153]Barrett, 1 Corinthians, 245, is doubtlessly right in taking the present tense (ἀρέσκω) as "connatative." "Paul could hardly claim that he succeeded in his attempt!" One may add, especially at Corinth.

[154]Robertson and Plummer, 1 Corinthians, 225, say that while

Many have noted also the obvious relationship of 10:33 to 9:20-22.[155] In fact, these passages help interpret each other. Conzelmann is right in saying that the opportunistic sound of 10:33, πάντα πᾶσιν ἀρέσκω, recalls 9:20-22. Yet both statements are shown not to be opportunism but service, by the clause ἵνα σωθῶσιν (10:33, cf. 9:22).[156] The description of this conduct as "saving" others shows the real, eternal significance of this policy. Whether the "many" (τῶν πολλῶν) has a specific referent is unclear. Barrett suggests that it may mean "the majority" or, in the sense of Qumran, "the community."[157]

These summarizing clauses in 10:31-33 serve to interpret each other. Doing all things for God's glory (10:31) is explained as being without offense to Jews, Greeks and the church of God (10:32). This practice Paul himself seeks to follow (10:33a) by not seeking his own advantage but that of the many (10:33b).

The conduct of Paul described in 10:33 is explicitly set out as worthy of imitation in 11:1. The idea of Paul as an example is summarized elsewhere in the present study.[158] Here it is only to be noted: (1) that 11:1 clearly belongs with 10:33 and what precedes; that the chapter division here is mistaken, and (2) that the example of Paul's conduct in considering the other person concludes each of the key sections of his argument: chapters eight (v. 13), nine (esp. vv. 26, 27) and ten (vv. 31ff.).

CONCLUSIONS

The exegesis has shown that in 10:23-11:1 Paul really deals with two concerns. One is to give guidance in two specific cases in which Christians might encounter sacrificial meat. These are meat sold in the public markets and meat served by a host at a private gathering. Paul supports the Christian's freedom to eat in these occasions, yet he reminds

---

Paul's object is the saving of the other man, thereby he himself is also benefited. "He seeks his own salvation through the salvation of others. The unity of the Church as the Body of Christ is such that the spiritual gain of one member is to be sought in the spiritual gain of the whole."

[155]For example, Conzelmann, *1 Corinthians*, 179; Barrett, *1 Corinthians*, 246; Friedrich, "Freiheit und Liebe," 94f. Karris, 167.

[156]Conzelmann, *1 Corinthians*, 179.

[157]Barrett, *1 Corinthians*, 245.

[158]See 286-291.

his readers that one can never overlook the effect of one's actions on others.[159]

The second concern which Paul has here is to establish broad guidelines for Christian conduct. Conduct is to be examined by its effects on others, whether Jews, Greeks, or—as in this case—other Christians. This broader horizon begins with the issue of eating but enlarges to take in all of one's conduct. Here the basic principle is to consider other peoples' needs as most important.

A. Two Concrete Cases

The topic of sacrificial meat was raised initially by the Corinthians in a letter to Paul. Their question was apparently about participation in meals held in pagan shrines, which they deemed permissible based in their Christian knowledge. It is possible that in the course of their letter the Corinthians also raised questions about meat sold in the markets and that served at social gatherings. This could have been done either as genuine questions or in an attempt to make it appear ludicrous that one be asked to avoid cultic meats unless also required to avoid all meats.

On the other hand, Paul may have felt it necessary to explain that his prohibition of the "table of demons" was not destined to lead to a rigid anxiety about all diet or a ghetto stance toward public life.[160] Structurally, Paul returns in 10:23 to pick up a Corinthian slogan, πάντα ἔξεστιν, which he then qualifies. Then in 10:24 Paul sets forth a slogan (and a principle) of his own. Thus conceivably the two specific cases of 10:25, 27 could either be Paul's taking up of another point from the Corinthians' own argument, or these cases may be Paul's way of illustrating that his principles do not require withdrawal from society. One cannot determine with any certainty which of these possibilities is correct.

One aspect of these cases in 10:25-27 must be noted because it has been important for evaluating the unity of Paul's argument in 1 Cor 8 and 10. The question is whether different occasions of eating are considered in 10:27 from those previously mentioned in chapter 8 and 10:20, 21. Generally scholars who hold to the integrity of these chapters have argued

---

[159]Schrage, *Einzelgebote*, 47, observes that these are examples of Pauline exhortation which are prophylactic, anticipating possible difficulties. His term is "eventualmahnungs."

[160]Murphy-O'Connor, "Freedom or the Ghetto," 543-74.

that Paul is speaking of cultic meals in chapter 8 and 10:20f. but not in 10:27.[161]

Many scholars have suggested that 10:27 refers to an invitation to a private home of a pagan friend.[162] This is certainly possible and would allow one to distinguish between the cultic meal (10:20-22) and private meals on the basis of location. It is also possible that a private meal which is held at a temple dining room is meant.[163] Or again a meal held at a public restaurant may be in view.

Although the limited information available from 1 Corinthians precludes any certainty, it does seem probable that Paul envisions different situations on 10:20f. and 10:27. He is just as positive in his permission to eat in 10:27 as he is negative in 10:20, 21 in his refusal of permission. Barring some change of mind, one must assume that Paul in some way saw a qualitative difference in the two occasions of eating.

Walter is correct that in 10:41-21 Paul is concerned not with meat which may be ἱερόθυτον, but with εἰδωλολατρία (10:14). That is, eating in 10:20f. is an event which can only be understood as a conscious action. In this way the faith itself is at stake.[164] It may be, as Walter suggests, that in chapter 8 the situation is a meal held in a temple restaurant but not as an occasion of worship.[165]

One could conjecture that the initial question of the Corinthians

---

[161]See Hurd, 129, n. 2 for a list of those who believe different situations are involved. To this listing should now be added Conzelmann, *1 Corinthians*, 177, and Walter, "Christusglaube, 427f. Hurd himself and von Soden, "Sakrament und Ethik," 33, both doubt that different situations are being considered.

[162]Héring, *First Epistle,* 98. Also Gerd Theissen, "Starken und Schwachen in Korinth," *EvT* 35 (1975) 155.

[163]Von Soden, "Sakrament und Ethik," 33, rightly notes that the religious aspect of pagan cult meals was sharply attenuated in Paul's time. His perception of the basically social character of such meals is confirmed by the present study as well. This may have led the Corinthians to regard the cultic meals of idols as not qualitatively different from other social and fraternal meals, some of which were held in temple precincts.

[164]Walter, "Christusglaube," 427f.

[165]Ibid., 428f. In contrast, in 10:28 ἱερόθυτον is used. Walter notes that the βρώματα itself has no religious quality which forbids its being eaten (8:8; 10:26, cf. Rom 14:14). He does note one can ask whether Paul's distinction between genuine cultic acts (10:1-22) and semi-private dining at a temple restaurant (8) is meaningful.

(quoted and discussed in 1 Cor 8) has to do with non-cultic meals held in temple precincts. In this circumstance Paul warns that they must consider the weaker Christians. Then on his own initiative Paul warns in 10:1-22 against any meals which are cultic by intent. Finally, in 10:25-29 he mentions other occasions where meat may be eaten although again with due consideration for the situation of other people.

Someone may complain that such distinctions between these meals based on external circumstances creates an unacceptable casuistry.[166] However, one cannot rule out dogmatically based on philosophical assumptions a casuistic stance in some degree. Paul's treatment of marriage in 1 Cor 7 certainly can be called casuistry in the proper, not pejorative, sense.

One must remember that *all* interpretations of the dining occasions in 8 and 10 make a conjecture about the circumstances involved. One cannot foreclose the possibility that Paul, perhaps wrongly, did distinguish times and intent of eating opportunities at pagan precincts. Moreover, it is possible that Paul did not share the same views of these meals as did his readers in Corinth.[167]

The first case Paul considers in 10:25 is whether Christians need to investigate the origin and history of meat sold in public markets. The second case is whether Christians must refuse invitations from pagan friends or, if they accept them, scrutinize the menu. In both of these cases Paul's principle is the same, "No investigation is called for, this is not a matter which involves conscience. Eat!"

It is argued in the exegesis that in 10:28-30 Paul qualifies the explicit permission to eat which he gives in 10:25 and 27. Thus, vv. 28-30 form a transition from the concrete cases to the more general admonitions of 10:31-11:1. They remind Paul's readers that even though in these two cases of 10:25, 27, the one who eats need not consider his own awareness of the meat's history, but he must always consider the "awareness" (συνείδησις) of others. "Conscience" or "awareness" serves as a catchword connecting 10:28-30 with 10:27 and 10:25. The consideration of

---

[166]Von Soden, "Sakrament und Ethik," 32f., objects to sharply distinguishing the cultic meal from the fraternal meal because that makes eating no longer a question of conscience but of circumstance. That, he feels, bends Paul's directions too much toward a Talmudic, casuistic nomism.
Wendland, *Korinther*, 84, expresses similar reservations.
[167]Aalen, "Abendmahl," 129.

others is necessary when purchasing meat, when eating in private parties, indeed in all eating and drinking (10:31).

Paul does not identify the informant of 10:28 nor his motive for stating to the Christian τοῦτο ἱερόθυτον ἐστιν. The suggestion that this informant is another Christian, perhaps a "weaker" one, is most likely. That conjecture would best account for the two rhetorical questions in 10:29b and 30. It is unclear how a pagan would have his conscience damaged by observing a Christian eating ἱερόθυτον, nor how he would "blaspheme" the one who eats. The vivid contrast of "giving thanks" for food (10:30) which, when one partakes leads to blasphemy, shows how seriously Paul takes the criticism of others (Rom 14:17).

In summary, 10:25-27 gives two occasions when Paul supports Christians eating meat without making any effort to learn of its prior history. This confirms the observation that Paul is not concerned about the *meat* itself. The following qualifications (10:28-30) to these acceptable occasions remind Paul's readers that Christians always remain responsible for the well-being of others. No action can be evaluated "*an sich*." These latter verses also serve to mark a transition to the concluding words of 10:31-11:1 which generalize beyond the immediate problem of eating sacrificial meat in pagan shrines.

B. Principles for Christian Conduct

The four verses (10:31-11:1) which conclude Paul's argument regarding idol meat both summarize his answers to the specific question raised from the Corinthian letter and show the far-reaching applicability of these principles.[168] Paul's concern to be inclusive is seen both in the *form* of these arguments and by their *appearance* elsewhere in his writings.

These concluding verses are seen to be general by their form. 10:31 is obviously all-inclusive, "whether eating or drinking or *whatever you do* (εἴτε τι ποιεῖτε)." This is continued in the call to "do all things (πάντα) to the glory of God." Similarly, in 10:32, Christians are said to be obligated to all people (Jews and Greeks, "the church of God" is added to stress the concrete situation in Corinth). Finally, in 10:33 Paul says the Corinthians should imitate his attempt "to please everyone in everything." This is to "seek the advantage of the many."

The arguments which Paul employs here in the final section are also used in other situations, which shows that his instruction is not

---

[168]Schrage, *Einzelgebote,* 151, says that πᾶς, πάντα in these verses show Paul's wish to be inclusive.

limited to the specific topic of idol meat or limited specifically to the Corinthian situation. One example is the call to "glorify God." This appeal is used significantly in several other situations (1 Cor 6:20; Rom 15:6, 7; Phil 2:11.).

The reverse of glorifying God by one's conduct is to place a stumbling block before others. Therefore the person who wishes to glorify God will seek not to cause others to stumble (10:32, cf. Phil 1:10). By causing one's fellow believer to stumble (Rom 14:21) one "destroys" the work of God rather than glorifying it (Rom 14:20).

The principles which Paul sets forth in 10:31-11:1 are interrelated. They are: acting to the glory of God, not offending others, acting for the benefit of others rather than one's self. These are not distinct guidelines but rather interpret each other. The conduct of Paul is both an example to follow ("just as I seek to please everyone in everything") and a motive for action ("as I imitate Christ"). This is because Paul's apostolic work is modeled upon the gospel and is not to be understood apart from it.

C. The Relation of 10:23-11:1 to Its Context

It has been shown that in 10:23-11:1 Paul expands the discussion beyond the concrete situation which had occasioned the discussion of "sacrificial meat" in 1 Corinthians. The concrete occasion was a defensive letter from Corinth which affirmed Christian freedom to participate in meals held at pagan temples. These meals may have been explicitly related to worship of the pagan gods, or only quasi-religious meals held in their precincts. In this concluding segment of his argument Paul summarizes by setting forth in broad strokes the principles of Christian conduct he has been urging in chapters 8 and 10.

Because of the summarizing character of 10:23-11:1 its connection with what precedes is uneven. Paul begins this summary by quoting again a Corinthian slogan: πάντα ἔξεστιν This returns to the Corinthians' own argument—the authority or freedom which comes from faith. Thus 10:23-11:1 is clearly linked to the discussion of 1 Cor 8 (and 9) by the topic of Christian "rights" and stylistically by the use of slogans from the Corinthians.

Another link to 1 Cor 8 is established by the norm of what "builds up" (οἰκοδομεῖ) set out in 10:23 and earlier in 8:1, 10. Perhaps returning to the Corinthian slogans and to the question of what "builds up" versus what "is permitted" is a way to give symmetry to the argument.

The relation of 10:23-11:1 to 10:1-22 is not as obvious, partly because Paul has returned to those themes set out by the Corinthians and partly because the case of 10:14-21 is specific rather than general.

Nevertheless, there is a real connection between 10:23-11:1 and 10:14-21. The connection is that in both passages the decisive consideration for Christian conduct is what reflects rightly the Christian's obligation to the community of faith. This ecclesiological consideration is illustrated in 10:23-11:1 in three ways.

First, the concern in 10:23 about what "builds up" and what "benefits" is not focused on individuals but on the good of the community. Second, the appeal in 10:31 to consider the "church of God" is obviously an appeal to the community of faith. Third, Paul's use of the phrase "to the glory of God" has also been shown to be focused on conduct which is for the well-being of others in Christ.

It has been shown in the study of 10:14-21 that the recurring word κοινωνία refers to the relationship which exists among members of God's people. It is not a reference to each believer's sacramental relationship with Christ. Therefore, κοινωνία in 10:14-21 has a basically ecclesiological reference. This means it is mistaken to contrast a "sacramental" appeal in 10:1-22 with an "ethical" appeal in 10:23-11:1 (and chapter 8). While the concern is expressed by different arguments, the common theme of 10:1-22 and 10:23-11:1 (as well as 8:1-13) is the communal alliance of God's people.

The link between 10:23-11:1 and what immediately precedes in 10:14-22 is the obligation which exists within the community of faith. This essentially reflects the Old Testament covenantal theology which stressed the mutual responsibility of members of God's people. This also can be seen in 10:1-13 where the character of the obligation required of the faithful in the Old Testament is explicitly set out as a norm for Christian conduct.

Therefore, 10:23-11:1 relates to its context both as a summary of a fundamental principle for conduct within the Christian community and as an application of that principle to two specific situations which could involve sacrificial meat. That fundamental principle is stated succinctly in 10:24, "Let no one seek his own good, but the good of his neighbor."

This principle is also implied in the call to "build up" and "benefit" the church (10:23). It is behind the reference to the συνείδησις of others (10:28-29). The "conscience" of the brother is decisive for conduct, even if one's own conscience is not involved. The same principle of acting so as not to harm the other believer is also expressed in the appeal to act to the glory of God (10:31) which is the same as to "give no offense" (10:32). In this verse the ecclesiological motif is made explicit, "the church of God." Finally, this norm is illustrated by an appeal to Paul's own conduct, which is modeled upon the Lord's—in that the benefit of others is primary.

Conclusions

THE SIGNIFICANCE OF HELLENISTIC DINING FOR UNDERSTANDING 1 CORINTHIANS 8-10

The significance of cultic meals and dining occasions has already been summarized in Part I. Therefore there is no need to retrace those steps again. It is clear that how one understands the meals associated with sacrifice in Paul's Hellenistic society has great influence on the interpretation of 1 Corinthians 8-10. Scholars writing at the beginning of the present century, such as Hans Lietzmann, explained 1 Corinthians 8 and 10 (especially 10:14-21) by reference to parallels in pagan sacramentalism. More recently, the pagan parallels have been minimized and the interpretive key in Hellenism has become Gnosticism (Käsemann, Bornkamm, Jewett and Schmithals).

It is clear that in their question to Paul the Corinthians conveyed that they are in a pagan temple (ἐν εἰδωλείῳ, perhaps referring to the *temenos*). The examination of cult meals associated with sacrifices has suggested three possible occasions in which the Corinthian eating might have occurred.

Corinthian Christians may have participated in an occasion of formal worship to a pagan god. They may have done this because they had a certain bravado based on their Christian knowledge of the non-being of pagan gods and the reality of the one true God. Or it may have been that the Corinthians were willing to eat on worship-oriented occasions because even these were regarded more as social events than as homage to the god.

A second possibility is that the Corinthians were eating in quasi-religious gatherings held by various social or fraternal organizations to which they belonged (or to which their friends belonged). Such associations, formed on the basis of family ties, civic life, or occupation were nominally religious in that they had a patron deity and featured a sacrifice to him/her. Yet as has been seen, these associations were not religious groups per se, and it is very conceivable that the Corinthian Christians had no compunctions about taking part because they were quite aware of this.

Yet a third possibility is that the eating under consideration was a private meal given by a friend who had offered a personal sacrifice (e.g., to fulfill a vow, to celebrate a success, to attempt to avoid "bad luck"). This friend (or perhaps relative) might well have invited a Christian acquaintance to share the meal following sacrifice, perhaps in one of the dining rooms associated with temples.[1]

Since it is the case that pagan meals, certainly the great majority if not all, did not have sacramental significance (45-63) the motive of the Corinthians who partook is unlikely to have been to exhibit their innoculation by a Christian sacrament (either baptism or Lord's Supper). It may be the case that those who felt their "knowledge" (γνῶσις) or "awareness" (συνείδησις) superior may have exhibited their elitism in activities other Christians deemed suspect. However, the probability is that those who ate simply were unwilling to remove themselves from normal social life.[2] There were perhaps pressures, implicit and explicit, from friends and family which must have encouraged Christians to remain socially involved. Since such cult meals were regarded primarily as social occasions there was no obvious reason to abstain. In addition to the minimal religiousity most pagans attached to such meals, Christians had the additional motive of their faith. At least some Corinthian Christians felt that the gospel conveyed to them certain rights (ἐξουσία) which included the freedom to eat anything.

The Pauline response to the conduct of the Corinthians has been analyzed in the exegetical sections. Paul's theological interests are

---

[1]Xenophon, *Mem.* 2.9.4, recounts how a certain Criton tried to keep Archedemus in his favor by giving him gifts "and when he sacrificed, he invited him" (καὶ ὅποτε θύοι ἐκάλει).

[2]Theissen, "Starken und Schwachen," seeks to prove that the conflict over eating idol meat was essentially along social class lines. He argues also that Gnosticism was an upper-class movement, and this accords with his thesis that those who ate were elitists. I am unable to assess his sociological arguments. However, since he says that his is only one approach to use with historical reconstructions, not an alternative to it, it is conceivable that his conclusions would not adversely affect the present interpretation.

assessed below. It would appear that Paul supported his opposition to Christian participation in these pagan meals, even those only nominally religious, with two primary appeals.

First, he appealed to the nature of the Christian community which he understood to be constituted on the basis of an exclusive allegiance to the one God. Involvement with other gods, even on occasions not taken very seriously by the devotees, was impossible. The one God has one people, and they have one loyalty. If Paul shared with Hellenism the view that κοινωνία refers to an association, he disagreed on the character of that association and its implications for members of the community.

Paul's second appeal in support of his opposition to the Corinthians' proposed conduct is really derivative from the first. He appeals to the mutual obligations which belong to those who are members of God's people. In 1 Corinthians 8 and 10 this motive finds expression in the exhortation to be considerate of the situation of the other (weaker) members of the community.

THE ARGUMENT OF 1 CORINTHIANS 8-10

A. The Position of the Corinthians

In their letter to Paul some Corinthian Christians had asked whether it was permissible to eat ἐν εἰδωλείῳ. Although it is possible that this would have included a variety of sacrificial foods (cakes, vegetables, wine, etc.), in view of 8:12, 13 it is almost certain that the Corinthians were thinking specifically of flesh from sacrificial animals. Since meals frequently included meat derived from pagan sacrificial slaughter, it is understandable that the Corinthian Christians would be concerned to know whether they ought to be willing to take part in these.

It is not possible to reconstruct with certainty what specific dining occasions the Corinthians may have mentioned in their letter. Even the fact that they ate ἐν εἰδωλείῳ does not necessarily prove a worship occasion.

Because in their letter the Corinthians not only asked for Paul's view on their eating but also gave reasons to justify their participation, it is possible to reconstruct their position on this issue. They may have given their reasons because they anticipated criticism from Paul, or simply because they had themselves (as "wise" people) developed a rationale and expected Paul to share it. They ask not, "May we eat?" but "Why can't we eat?" Their questions do seem to have a defensive tone, but are they defensive toward Paul or toward other Christians in Corinth?

A reconstruction of the Corinthian defense drawn from 1 Corinthians 8 and 10 can be suggested. Their defense rests upon the common
Christian knowledge (8:1, "we all have knowledge") that idols are
meaningless because there is only one God (8:4). At least, they felt, this
knowledge is shared by all Christians, even if other persons acknowledge
"so-called gods" (λεγόμενοι θεοί, 8:5). This knowledge they documented
in an early Christian creed (8:6). The Corinthians may have felt that a
refusal to eat implied a deficiency (ὑστερούμεθα) for a Christian, while
willingness to eat suggested a higher level of awareness (περισσεύομεν,
8:8). Based on these reasons the Corinthians had concluded that in the
matter of eating sacrificial meat, "Everything is permitted" (10:23).[3]

These arguments of the Corinthians reveal not only their reasons
for eating sacrificial meat, but also the manner in which they ate.
Apparently they ate fully aware that other Christians were greatly dis-
tressed by their eating. Those who ate considered their eating to be
grounded in Christian "rights" (ἐξουσία). They regarded those who were
unwilling to eat as having deficient Christian awareness (συνείδησις
8:7). It is probable that those who ate labeled those who did not as "weak"
(ἀσθενής) and sought to edify (οἰκοδομεῖν) their weaker fellow believers
in imitation of their example.

B. The Integrity of Paul's Response to the Corinthians

The present study has argued that there is a unity to 1 Corinthians
8 and 10, both in content and structure, but the unity of this section has
been challenged by interpreters who believe that our canonical 1 Corinthians is composed of two or more originally separate letters to Corinth.[4]

---

[3]Among others, see Hurd, 115f. Barrett, *1 Corinthians*, 197, says,
"That is a clear, compelling sequence of thought, which is entirely in
accord with the mind of Jesus (Mark vii.15a)—apparently!" Barrett here
cites Jeremias, "Die Briefzitate in 1 Kor 8:1-13," 274.
Whether the Corinthians are arguing against a previous letter from
Paul, or even using arguments previously formed by Paul (as suggested by
Hurd, 128-131) is impossible to know. In the present study it is argued
that these arguments *as employed* in 1 Corinthians 8 come from the
Corinthians, regardless of their possible prior history.
[4]See Hurd's summary, 131-157. Also see Conzelmann, *1 Corinthians*, 137f., for a good, succinct review of the issues.
The other important considerations urged against integrity are
summarized by Barrett, *1 Corinthians*, 12-14, and Conzelmann, *1 Corin-*

Therefore if these chapters can be shown to belong together one important item in the case against the integrity of 1 Corinthians is removed.

    1. *The challenge to the integrity of 1 Corinthians 8-10.* According
to Hurd's survey, there is a basic consensus about the units isolated within
1 Corinthians 8 and 10 by those who question their integrity. Following
his discussion, we may designate 1 Corinthians 8 as "A," 10:1-22 as "B,"
and 10:23-11:1 as "C."[5] In its most basic form the argument against
integrity holds that Paul's attitudes toward the eating of sacrificial meat
is different in "B" from what is it in "AC."

    This difference has been described in various ways. (1) It has been
argued that in "AC" Paul is dealing with εἰδωλοθύτα, while in "B" he
treats εἰδωλολατρία. (2) Another way this difference has been put is that
in "AC" eating is a matter of conscience, while in "B" it is a question of
sacrament. (3) Or the difference has been described by saying that in
"AC" eating or not eating is regarded in itself as a matter of indifference,
while in "B" eating is held to be precluded for Christians. That is, Paul
regards the meat as dangerous in "B" but not in "AC." (4) Yet one other
objection alleges that in "A" pagan gods are regarded as "nothings" while
in "B" they are considered demons.[6]

    In virtually every case, this shift alleged between "AC" and "B" is
assigned to Paul himself. The point is made that in "AC" Paul takes the
side of the "strong" (a term coined by interpreters, but not used by Paul),
while in "B" he adopts the outlook of the "weak." Sometimes this shift has
been accounted for as the result of Paul's growing understanding of the

---

thians, 2-4. A presentation of reasons to partition the letter by one who
inclines against integrity can be found in Weiss, *Earliest Christianity*,
1.325-341.

    [5]Hurd, 45. In identifying these units as "A," "B," and "C" he is
following von Soden, "Sakrament und Ethik," 17f. Even though von Soden
holds to the integrity of the chapters, he isolates blocks of material
within the letter.

    [6]Conzelmann, *1 Corinthians*, 127, lists all these arguments. See
also Hurd, 133-35, and von Soden, "Sakrament und Ethik," 14. Hurd and
von Soden argue that in "AC" and "B" the simple act of eating is a matter
of indifference.

    Conzelmann, *1 Corinthians*, 173, rejects the objection which
contrasts Paul's treatment of pagan deities as "nothings" and as "demons"
on the grounds that both attitudes are found in pre-Pauline Judaism. "The
presupposition of vv. 19-20 is the same as that of 8:5: behind the gods
there lurk demons."

situation in Corinth.[7] Alternatively, it has been argued that Paul himself has changed his position on the question of eating sacrificial meat due to agreements reached with a different faction of the apostolic church.[8] Yet another view says that Paul's two different positions arise from a tension between what he believes to be true about Christian freedom ("AC") and what he feels is demanded by practical necessities in Corinth ("B").

2. *Points in support of the integrity of 1 Corinthians 8-10.* There are several things to be said in response to objections raised against the unity of 1 Corinthians 8-10. First, there are indications of unity in both the structure and the arguments within chapters 8 and 10. (The major themes developed in 8 and 10 are dealt with below, 276-296.) Second, the intervening chapter 9 can be shown to function well in its present location between chapters 8 and 10. Third, a consideration of Romans 14 and 15, in which the arguments of 1 Corinthians 8 and 10 are restated in a context where integrity is not doubted, shows the cohesion of the arguments as found in 1 Corinthians 8 and 10.

a. The distinctive functions of chapter 8, 10. Although it has been argued that the sections "A," "B," and "C" are not related,[9] the present investigation has shown that there is a unified structure to these chapters. It is important, first of all, to recognize the distinctive functions of chapters 8 and 10.

In 1 Corinthians 8 Paul takes up the question raised by the Corinthians (περὶ δὲ τῶν εἰδωλοθύτων) and begins his reply by answering their arguments. The structure of 1 Corinthians 8, as well as its content, is

---

[7]Schmithals, *Gnosticism in Corinth*, 227, says that these differences arose when the "sacramental" letter (B) raised new issues which required additional answers (AC). Weiss, *Earliest Christianity*, 1.325-329, says that Paul retreated from his initial stance (B) when the Corinthians showed the monastic life this would compel.

[8]Argued by Barrett, "Things Sacrificed," and earlier by T. W. Manson, "The Corinthian Correspondence (I)," 200-203.

[9]Of course this is true for those who partition the letter, but others too see little connection between the separate units. For example, Conzelmann, *1 Corinthians*, 165, terms 10:1-10, "a self-contained scribal discourse" and speculates that it was composed prior to the writing of this epistle. Later, 170, he comments on 10:14-22: "The train of thought in this section is self-contained. It stands out plainly from vv. 23ff." Finally, his evaluation of 10:23-11:1 is very similar, 175: "The thought of this section is self-contained. . . . There is no connection with the preceding section."

formed basically by Paul's method of replying to the Corinthians' arguments.

In 1 Corinthians 10, however (leaving aside for the moment the role of chapter 9), Paul is setting forth his own arguments. He develops his position here along three lines.

First, in 10:1-13 Paul argues against participation in sacrificial meals on the basis of Scripture. Specifically, he recounts Israel's wilderness experience in which their covenant disloyalty led to the divine punishment (10:1-5). Paul insists that these events, both Israel's flirtation with pagan cults and their punishment for doing so, have exemplary importance for the Corinthians, because they also are tempted to such involvement with pagan deities (10:6-13).

Paul's second argument against Christian participation in pagan cult meals is set forth in 10:14-22. As in 10:1-13 he argues that involvement with other gods, even those that are "nothing" (10:19, cf. 8:4), compromises Christian commitment and endangers Christian community. The argument in 10:14-22 does not involve a sacramental view of cultic dining, as is often alleged, but it emphasizes rather the exclusiveness of the claim the one God makes on his one people. Their allegiance (or covenant loyalty) to him is manifested in and witnessed by their community meal. Paul finds similar allegiance in the meals of other communities, Jewish and pagan. This communal allegiance and obligation he refers to by the word κοινωνία.

Finally, in 1 Corinthians 10:23-11:1 Paul considers two occasions of eating which do not imply allegiance to or respect for pagan gods. In each of these cases (10:25, 27) Christians are instructed to eat without making uncalled-for investigations. Yet even on these occasions, Christians must always consider other members of the church who may be threatened or offended by such eating. Then in a summarizing way Paul concludes that all eating, indeed all conduct, must be evaluated for its effect on others, especially other believers. Paul makes this point in several ways, including a reference to his own example (10:31-11:1).

b. The function of Chapter 9. A thorough consideration of 1 Corinthians 9 is not possible here. However, because of its central location, bounded by two chapters discussing sacrificial meat, brief notice must be made of its place within Paul's argument.

1 Corinthians 9 has been regarded by some as virtually unrelated to chapters 8 and 10. It has been viewed as an aside on Paul's apostleship

which interrupts the topic of idol meat.[10] This is almost inevitable when
the subject of chapter 9 is regarded as Paul's defense of his apostleship
against attacks by the Corinthians.[11] Although the conclusions of the
present investigation would hold even if one were to decide that 1 Corinthians 9 is only tangentially related to the arguments of chapters 8 and
10, certain points can be registered in favor of the view that chapter 9
actually contributes to the development of Paul's argument about sacrificial meat in chapters 8 and 10.

First, it can be maintained that Paul himself has incorporated the
material of chapter 9 into his overall argument in accord with a common
Hellenistic rhetorical device. Wuellner has shown that digressions may
actually be used to support an argument. With respect to the present
chapters in particular he concludes: "The digression of 1 Corinthians 9
represents a rhetorical convention and shows skillful planning and place-
ment."[12]

A similar structure is seen in 1 Corinthians 12-14 where chapter 13
has been placed in the midst of the discussion of spiritual gifts.[13] Indeed
there are several important parallels in these units. 1 Corinthians 12
treats the question of charismata in a general way as it takes up the
question initially. Then in chapter 13, an apparent digression on love,
Paul advances the argument by reference to himself (note the first person
pronouns) just as he does in chapter 9. Finally, chapter 14 deals with
more specific cases and concrete directions, just as 10:14-11:1 does with
regard to idol meat. It is noteworthy that in both 1 Corinthians 8-10 and
12-14 consideration of others and acting for their benefit is a major
concern.[14]

---

[10]Thus Barrett, *1 Corinthians,* 220, terms it a digression. Cf.
Schlier, "Ἐλεύθερος," 500f.

[11]Barrett, "Things Sacrificed," 150; Conzelmann, *1 Corinthians,*
152.

[12]Wuellner, "Greek Rhetoric," 177-188. His view is in strong
contrast to most treatments which regard chapter 9 as at best a detour in
the main argument.

[13]Christian Maurer, "Grund und Grenze apostolischer Freiheit,"
Antwort: Karl Barth zum siebzigsten Geburtstag (Zollikon-Zürich:
Evangelischer Verlag, 1956) 634.

[14]Johannes Munck, *Christ and Israel* (Philadelphia: Fortress, 1967)
78, argues that a similar organization is found in Romans 9-11, with 9:30-
10:21 being the heart of Paul's argument. He cites 1 Corinthians 8-10 and
12-14 as parallels.

Second, 1 Corinthians 9 has important material connections in
chapters 8 and 10.

For one thing, in chapter 9 as well as in chapters 8 and 10 Paul is
concerned about Christian rights (ἐξουσία, 9:4, 5, 6, 12, 18) and Christian
freedom (ἐλευθερία, 9:1, 14). This was a point raised by the Corinthians
and is addressed by Paul with reference to himself in chapter 9.[15] Paul
summons the Corinthians to follow his own path of foregoing his "rights"
for the benefit of others.[16] Christian life is not characterized by individual freedom but by a conduct which is responsible to the needs of
others. This is because Christians are not "self-ruled" but belong to
Christ (1 Cor 6:19, "You are not your own." Cf. Rom 6:3-12). Therefore,
as he urges the Corinthians, Paul too is at pains to put no obstacle
(ἐγκοπὴν 9:12 = πρόσκομμα 8:9).[17] He is in fact concerned to advance the
gospel (9:23; cf. 10:33), a concern which reflects Jesus's self-giving life
(cf. 11:1). This means that the conduct which Paul manifests and asks of
others is rooted in ἀγάπη (although the word does not occur in 1 Corinthians 9), "in love which seeks not its own, but the welfare of the
other."[18]

Another theme found in 1 Corinthians 9 is the warning against a
possible loss of one's relationship to God and a concomitant demand for
Christians to be self-disciplined (9:24-27). This has clear parallels in
1 Cor 10:1-13 and perhaps is set forth implicitly in 8:12 (the weak are in
danger of falling away from Christ, and those who eat "knowingly" would
be held accountable for their "sin against Christ").

Finally, and most significantly, chapter 9 presents the life of Paul
as an example for Christian conduct. This appeal to the normative character of his own conduct may be understood as but the development of the
point which is implicit in 8:13 and which is then summarized in the exhortation of 11:1. In 1 Corinthians 9 Paul calls attention to his own willingness to forego his apostolic rights (9:1-5), although he can certainly establish them (9:5-14). Paul clearly labors his point to substantiate his plea

---

[15]See supra 224-227. In 1 Corinthians 8-10 ἐξουσία and ἐλευθερία
are functional synonyms.

[16]Fee, "II Cor 6:14-7:1," 152.

[17]Grosheide, *1 Corinthians*, 200f.; Maurer, "Grund und Grenze,"
632.

[18]Günther Bornkamm, "The Missionary Stance of Paul in 1 Corinthians and in Acts," *Studies in Luke-Acts*, ed. L. E. Keck and J. Louis
Martyn (Nashville: Abingdon, 1966) 197.

that the Christian life is not one of privileges but of service. He identifies this as a fundamental concern in the conduct of his ministry (9:19-23).

Given these themes common to 1 Corinthians 8, 10 and chapter 9,
one may conclude that chapter 9 is integral to Paul's argument. This
chapter is neither an aside on the apostolic office nor a personal defense.
It advances Paul's argument about the obligation Christians have to consider the good of others first. In its context 1 Corinthians 9 is another
part of Paul's attempt to instruct the Corinthians in the matter of participation in pagan cultic meals.[19]

c. The significance of Romans 14 and 15. Romans 14 and 15
represent a later reworking of themes and arguments which Paul originally had developed in 1 Corinthians 8 and 10.[20] For the question of the
unity of 1 Corinthians 8 and 10 it is not decisive whether Romans was
addressed to a concrete problem[21] or is a more general warning not aimed
at difficulties Paul knew to exist in Rome.[22] It is the similarity of Paul's
arguments on similar topics in the two letters which helps to show the
integrity of 1 Corinthians 8-10.[23]

Prominent in both Romans 14, 15 and 1 Corinthians 8-10 is the
point that one should be considerate of the weaker Christian (1 Cor 8:11f.,
10:28f.; Rom 14:1f., 15:1). This is the path of love (1 Cor 8:1; Rom 14:15)
which is service to Christ (1 Cor 8:12 negatively; Rom 14:6, 7, 19) and
which serves to glorify God (1 Cor 10:31; Rom 15:6, 7, 9). To act otherwise is to be guilty of causing harm to one for whom Christ died (1 Cor
8:11; Rom 14:15).[24] Both in 1 Corinthians (10:1-12) and in Romans (14:10)
Paul reminds Christians that God will hold them accountable for their

---

[19]Horsley, "Consciousness," 578f., says: "Paul's autobiographical
argument concerning 'freedom' in chap 9, in which he further explains his
instructions of 8:13, is aimed directly at the 'freedom' and 'authority' of
the enlightened Corinthians."

[20]Hurd, 133f. Cf. Furnish, *Love Command*, 117, who demonstrates
that Romans 14, 15 recapitulate the whole of 1 Corinthians 8.

[21]As is argued by Paul S. Minear, *The Obedience of Faith* (SBT
2/19; London: SCM, 1971).

[22]See the detailed critique of Minear's presentation by Karris,
"Rom 14:4-15:3."

[23]Von Soden, "Sakrament und Ethik," 34.

[24]Furnish, *Love Command*, 117, notes that "walking in love" in
Rom 14:18 is designated to "serve Christ," a positive stating of what Paul
puts negatively in 1 Cor 8:12, where to not serve the brother is to sin
against Christ.

conduct and its effect on others. The result of the behavior which Paul positively urges in both Rom 14, 15 and in 1 Cor 8-10 is the strengthening of the Christian community, its "building up" (1 Cor 8:1, 10:23; Rom 14:19, 15:2).

There are some differences in the way Paul develops his argument in 1 Corinthians and in Romans. In Romans there is no consideration of possible idolatry, nor is there any reference to "freedom" (ἐλευθερίᾳ) or "rights" (ἐξουσία). Neither does Paul appeal to "consciousness" (συνείδη-σις) in Romans.[25] Apparently these motifs were raised by the Corinthians and did not interest Paul in developing his own argument. For the same reason Paul does not refer in Romans to religious meals, including the Lord's Supper.[26] But these differences should not be allowed to obscure the fundamental similarity of the concerns present in the two letters.

In summary the parallel treatment in Romans 14, 15 suggests a unity to Paul's arguments as presented in 1 Corinthians 8-10.[27] Those important points made in 1 Corinthians which are absent in Romans 14, 15 are to be explained by the way in which the problem was presented to Paul from Corinth. The reusing of arguments in Romans is evidence that Paul's ethical admonitions are not strictly limited to the actual situations in which they first took shape.[28]

There is a unity of argument and structure in 1 Corinthians 8-10 which shows that this portion of the letter has a thoughtful organization and development. This unity can be seen also in the cohesion of the theological themes which Paul employs.

THEOLOGICAL MOTIFS OF PAUL'S EXHORTATIONS

This study has documented in a particular case the accuracy of Victor Furnish's observation that while Paul does not present a critical or systematic ethical theory, he certainly does have ethical concerns which are based on theological convictions.[29] In the question of eating sacrificial meat, Paul addresses an issue which does involve the relationship

---

[25]Noted by Horsley, "Consciousness," 588.

[26]Vielhauer, OIKODOME, 98.

[27]Schrage, Einzelgebote, 125. He observes that the similarities in Rom 14, 15 and 1 Corinthians 8 and 10 have their real origin in Paul's theology.

[28]Ibid., 43.

[29]Furnish, Theology and Ethics, especially 208-216.

between theology and ethics. His reply to an inquiry from the Corinthian church gives not only his decisions about certain actions but also a reasoned criticism of the Corinthians' views and a reasoned defense of his directions.

This means that the question of whether, or under what circumstances, Christians are permitted to eat meat from animals involved in pagan religion is a question of theology and ethics. Even in this rather specific issue important theological motifs are raised which have far-reaching implications. In concluding this study it is appropriate to look at these motifs to see how they are used in 1 Cor 8-10 and elsewhere in Paul's writings.

A. Conscience

Although the "conscience" has played a prominent role in Western ethical theory,[30] it is not very prominent in the New Testament itself. Half of the New Testament's thirty occurrences of the term are in genuine Pauline writings, and all but three of these are in the Corinthian letters. It is argued in the exegesis (pp. 89-94) that Paul took the term from the Corinthians' letter to him. Every use of συνείδησις in 1 Corinthians comes in chapters 8 and 10 and the discussion about idol meat.

The study of συνείδησις in 1 Cor 8 and 10 suggested that the word "conscience" is still too often thought of as a "faculty" of persons.[31] In dealing with 1 Corinthians it is more helpful to translate συνείδησις with "awareness" or "consciousness" which both accords with the root meaning of the word, "to know with one's self," and the way the term was employed by the Corinthians (and Paul).[32]

When the Corinthians complained that some of their fellow Christians were "weak" in conscience they apparently meant that these people

---

[30] See the survey in Paul Lehmann, *Ethics in a Christian Context* (New York: Harper & Row, 1963) 286-366.

[31] A recent survey which reassesses the place of conscience in ethical thought and tries especially to put it on a firmer basis psychologically is Walter E. Conn, *Conscience: Development and Self-Transcendence* (Birmingham, Alabama: Religious Education Press, 1981).

[32] For this reason, Davies, "Conscience," 674, is mistaken in his attempt to distinguish between the weak brother's opinions and his conscience.

had a poor understanding of the implications of the Christian faith.[33] The Corinthian majority sought by example and argument to produce a greater "awareness" in these weaker members, to lead them to eat sacrificial meat without difficulty.[34]

Paul takes over this word from the Corinthians and employs it in correcting their understanding of the role of each individual's self-knowledge. He certainly has no theory of the "conscience" as a person's valid inner guide in ethical decisions.

Thus for Paul the decision whether to eat sacrificial meat cannot be decided by personal examination within the one who wishes to eat the meat. One cannot employ as a standard: "Let your conscience be your guide." Rather Paul's position requires, "Let your neighbor's conscience (= awareness) be your guide." Stacy's slogan, although attractive to modern people, "Every man's conscience is valid for him"[35] does not accurately reflect Paul's view. The idea that each individual's conscience is a reliable guide would be valid for those who are "seeking their own good." But Paul's emphasis is on the conscience of the other person, which is compatible with his wish to seek the good of others (10:24, 31; cf. 9:19-23). Paul is not asking how one may protect his innocence in his conduct but how he can serve others.

In summary, in 1 Corinthians 8 and 10 συνείδησις is not set forth as a significant motif, certainly not in the popular sense of an inner guide for moral decisions.[36] It is a term which Paul borrowed from the Corinthians, which he himself does not develop. For Paul the συνείδησις which is important is that of the other person. Therefore consideration of the conscience is equivalent to consideration of the good of the other person.[37] This motif, which is a Pauline interest, is considered below.

---

[33]Murphy-O'Connor, 549, "The attitude of the strong becomes comprehensible if we assume that they identified συνείδησις and νοῦς."

[34]Ibid. The Corinthians' approach makes sense "only on the assumption that a mind informed by correct knowledge would not suffer the pangs of conscience."

[35]Stacey, Pauline View of Man, 207.

[36]Schrage, Einzelgebote, 210, lists conscience as one of the norms or criteria of Paul's "creation faith." This description is called into question with the realization that almost all the Pauline references to συνείδησις in 1 Cor 8 and 10 are taken from the argument of Paul's inquirers.

[37]This means that Schrage, Einzelgebote, 154, is misleading when

B. Salvation History

Unlike conscience, the history of salvation is a significant motif in Paul's argument about sacrificial meat. It is most obvious in 1 Cor 10:1-11 where the Exodus experience of Israel is appealed to in exhorting the Corinthians. But this motif is present also in a lesser degree elsewhere in chapter 10 as well as in chapter 8.

The importance of God's past saving work among his people is set forth explicitly in 10:1-11. In the exegesis (159-163) it was argued that the reason Paul appeals to these Exodus events is that he considers them instructive about the problem of idolatry. Paul establishes the relevance of those biblical events to the Corinthians' question about eating idol meat in several ways.

(1) The description of the wilderness generation as "our" fathers, when writing to a Gentile church, is obviously intended to indicate that these events have bearing on the Corinthians' situation.

(2) Although it is argued in this study that 10:2-5 are not refuting a hyper-sacramentalism in Corinth, the mention of the sea as "baptism into Moses" and the description of the "supernatural food" are express parallels to Christian practices. It is likely that this was another way to show the relevance of Israel's experiences to the Corinthians.

(3) The description of the rock following Israel as Christ (10:4) has been much discussed, especially in seeking to find Paul's hermeneutical approach (133-138). That concern is beyond the scope of the present study. But apart from locating precise interpretive categories, this equation does prove the relevance of the Exodus events to Corinthian Christianity.

(4) The most direct claims of the significance of these Old Testament events are in 10:6 and 11. Here Paul is explicit: "Now these things are warnings for us, not to desire evil as they did." "Now these things happened to them as a warning, but they were written down for our instruction, upon whom the end of the ages has come." Again, apart from specific hermeneutical categories and details, the *function* of this appeal

---

he says that Christians should not only follow their conscience, but they must also consider the brother. In 1 Cor 8, 10 the conscience which counts is that of the other person. Schrage, 152f., is also mistaken in equating συνείδησις in 1 Cor 8:7; 10:12, 25f. with πίστις in Rom 14. In Rom 14 the faith which permits one to eat is his own faith; in 1 Cor 8, 10 the conscience which prohibits eating is that of the other person.

to Old Testament events is clearly to encourage the Corinthians in their own situation.

What is Paul's purpose, specifically, in showing these Old Testament events to be relevant? The structure shows that in the first five verses Paul sets forth his exposition, and then in 10:6-10 he admonishes the Corinthians directly. Paul's real interest in these Exodus happenings is to warn the Corinthians strongly about idolatry. This is stated in 10:14, "Wherefore . . . flee idolatry!"

Paul's concern with the real danger of idolatry at Corinth also comes out in 10:12, "Therefore, let the one who thinks he stands watch out lest he fall!" The Corinthian majority felt that in participating in pagan cult meals they were not in danger. Their position was not based on an exaggerated view of Christian sacraments but on their knowledge of the one God and the non-being of idols (8:5, 6). Therefore, after Paul refutes their arguments in 1 Cor 8, in 10:1-13 he begins to convince the Corinthians of the real danger they face by involvement with idols. This emphasis on the possible forfeiture of one's place with God in 10:1-13 follows Paul's similar warning based on his own situation (9:24-27). Whereas in 9:24-27 this danger is documented by Paul's personal experience, in 10:1-5 it is documented by scripture.

1 Cor 10:1-13 is the most obvious and explicit appeal to the salvation history in this discussion. However, there are four other passages in this section which at least allude to this motif: 8:3; 10:22, 26, 33.

In 1 Cor 8:3 Paul addresses the role of "knowledge" in Christian decision-making. This was an issue raised by the Corinthians in their slogan, "We know that all of us possess knowledge" (8:1). Paul warns against conceit in their attitude (8:2) and goes on to stress that what really counts is not what knowledge believers possess but that they are known by God (8:3).

In the exegesis it is argued (pp. 78-81) that the phrase "known by God" refers to God's electing love. It recalls a motif already familiar in the Old Testament that God "knows" his people.[38] An instructive parallel is Gal 4:9, where Paul describes Christians as those who "know God" (γνόντες θεόν) then quickly corrects himself to say "rather known by God" (μᾶλλον δὲ γνωσθέντες ὑπὸ θεοῦ). This shows that the allusion in 1 Cor 8:3 to being known by God is a part of the theme of salvation history, although it also relates to the motif of ecclesiology discussed below.

A second implicit reference to salvation history is found in the

---

[38]Bultmann, "Γινώσκω," 706.

rhetorical question of 10:22, "Shall we provoke the Lord to jealousy?" It was shown in the exegesis (214-215) that the most probable source of this question is Deut 32:21. In the context in Deuteronomy the idea of provoking the Lord is explicitly related to idolatry (clear in the LXX), which is also a danger in Corinth. The Deuteronomy passage is located in a rehearsal of the salvation history of Israel (it is the "Song of Moses") and is a warning to Israel. Thus the original context makes it an especially pertinent passage for the Corinthian situation.

It is possible, although unlikely, that Paul felt that the Corinthians would catch his allusion to the Song of Moses and thus know the appropriateness of the original context. It is more probable that the context of Deuteronomy directly influenced Paul's own course of thought. Whether he expects the Corinthians to perceive this is uncertain. Still, the salvation history recorded in Deut 32 has been influential in shaping Paul's perception of the Corinthians' involvement with pagan cult meals, and has indirectly affected his phrasing of the rhetorical question in 10:22. This makes clear that in Paul's mind the Corinthian interest in the pagan cult meals is an idolatrous provocation of God and a danger to their status as his people.

A third allusion to salvation history is 1 Cor 10:26. There God's role as creator is set forth as a justification for Paul's instruction to eat freely of meat sold in the public markets (229f.). It is somewhat unexpected that the creator role of God, a salvation history theme, is not more explicit in 1 Cor 8-10, as it is in Acts 10:9-16, another discussion of permissible eating by Christians. In 1 Cor 10:26 the theme of creation is a positive argument for eating. In 1 Cor 8:6 the theme of creation also occurs in the form of an early Christian confession. It is argued in the exegesis, however, that this creed comes from the Corinthian argument to Paul (pp. 84-87). Perhaps the prior use of the motif of creation by the Corinthians to justify their eating sacrificial meals explains Paul's own reticence to employ this concept. It has been preempted in the service of his inquirers.

The references to Christ's death in 1 Cor 8:12; 10:16 are certainly allusions to salvation history, and the reference in 10:32 to the "church of God" may be. However, these are best discussed in connection with the ecclesiological motif which is found in these chapters.

C. Christian Community

Several recent studies of Paul's ethical thought have given an emphasis to the role played by his doctrine of the church.[39] W. D. Davies, who himself argues that the key to New Testament ethics is Christology, also notes that: "It is the morality of a community born of the grace of the resurrection." He continues, "The New Testament knows nothing of a solitary religion and it knows nothing of an individual morality: it points to a community with a life to live."[40] Whether or not that is the case for the New Testament as a whole, it is certainly true for Paul.

Perhaps where Paul is most distinct from the Corinthian Christians in the issue of freedom to eat in pagan temples is in their views of Christian community. The Corinthians stress the individual: his knowledge, freedom, and rights. Paul stresses the mutual responsibility of Christians to each other by virtue of their corporate relationship to Christ. Wendland is entirely justified in terming Paul's ethic a "Gemeinde-ethik."[41] Paul's ethic works from the church as its presupposition and is directed toward the church rather than the world. This communal focus comes out in Paul's images of the church, in many direct appeals to the church, and even in Paul's use of "we" in ethical exhortations.[42] This community dimension affects how one decides who must be considered in decisions, how one is held accountable for one's decision, and how Christians relate to those outside their community.

Although Paul does not set out a theory of how the Christian decides right and wrong, he does often suggest that the context for making such decisions is the church. "Paul never pictures the believer as confronting alone the bewildering complexity of various possible courses of action."[43] As Wendland notes, Paul knows nothing of the ethical autonomy of the individual, a prominent theme in modern ethics.[44]

This communal context may be considered restrictive, and perhaps it was so considered by the Corinthians. But Paul regards it as positive. The individual's actions are never a private matter before God; rather, the

---

[39]Schrage, *Einzelgebote*, 174-78; Wendland, *Ethik*, 64-65.

[40]W. D. Davies, "The Moral Teaching of the Early Church," *The Use of the Old Testament in the New and Other Essays*, ed. James M. Efird (Durham, NC: Duke University, 1972) 323.

[41]Wendland, *Ethik*, 51. He notes that this distinguishes Paul's ethic from Stoic ethics, which claim universality of applicability.

[42]Ibid., 64.

[43]Furnish, *Theology and Ethics*, 233; cf. Schrage, *Einzelgebote*, 174.

[44]Wendland, *Ethik*, 65.

church is involved.[45] In 1 Corinthians this is explicit in the matter of incest (5:1-5) and personal lawsuits (6:1-8), as well as in more generally recognized vices such as intercourse with prostitutes (6:12-19). It means that even one's work habits are a matter of community ethics (2 Thess 3:6-18).[46]

This communal motif is present in 1 Cor 8-10 in several ways. A simple but important manifestation is the description of the injured Christian in 8:16 as "brother" (ὁ ἀδελφός) and the warning of sinning against "the brethren" (8:12, εἰς τοὺς ἀδελφοὺς).[47] The ecclesiological motif also appears in more extended forms: "building up" (οἰκοδομή), "fellowship" (κοινωνία), the Lord's Supper, and Christian exclusivism. Each of these expressions of the ecclesiological dimensions of ethics needs to be reviewed.

1. *"Building Up."* The motif of "building up" (οἰκοδομή, οἰκοδομέω) in the discussion of idol meat first occurs in 1 Cor 8:1, where Paul corrects a Corinthian slogan stressing knowledge by ἡ δὲ ἀγάπη οἰκοδομεῖ. Similarly, in 10:23 he corrects another Corinthian slogan, πάντα ἔξεστιν, with ἀλλ' οὐ παντα οἰκοδομεῖ. This verse repeats an argument found in 6:12, although there the issue addressed is different. Thus in 8:1, 10:23 and 6:12 the idea of "building up" is used to correct Corinthian conduct.

It was shown in the exegesis (pp. 72-78) that for Paul the idea of "building up" has a corporate focus. It is not the individual believer increasing his/her own Christian faith or knowledge, but what benefits the church as a whole which is properly called οἰκοδομή.[48] Paul's communal understanding of edification, in contrast to an individualistic understanding, is seen most clearly in 1 Cor 14 where he treats the issue of Christian worship. The Corinthians' individualism valued tongues above other charismata. But Paul favors prophecy above tongues, precisely

---

[45]Schrage, *Einzelgebote*, 178.

[46]William Neill, *The Epistles of Paul to the Thessalonians* (MNTC; New York: Harper and Brothers, 1950) 196, rightly comments, "A man no longer lives for himself once he has entered the fellowship; he is responsible to God and to his brothers in Christ." Roetzel, *Judgment*, 178, notes how conduct of individual believers reflects back on the body, thus bringing forth God's judgment. "If the old dominion governs the Christian's style of life, the whole church is implicated by his malfeasance."

[47]Murphy-O'Connor, 564.

[48]Conzelmann, *1 Corinthians*, 176.

because it builds up the church (14:5, 12). Indeed, Paul unfavorably contrasts seeking to build up one's self (14:4) with the proper goal of strengthening the community as a whole (14:5). Paul's guiding principle for Christian worship is, "Let all things be done for building up" (14:26).

It is characteristic of οἰκοδομῇ that it seeks the good of others first (Rom 14:19; 15:2). That is why it is such an important criterion to use in replying to the Corinthians' individualism, whether the problem is eating in temple shrines (8:1; 10:23) or proper conduct in worship (14).

2. *Fellowship.* A second way the need to consider the community is set forth in Paul's discussion of idol meat is by κοινωνία. This word has been the object of considerable study and debate. In the exegetical section it is argued that in 1 Cor 10:16-21 κοινωνία refers to the mutual obligations which accrue to those who share a communal alliance. This is true whether the κοινωνία under discussion is Christian, Jewish or pagan. The designation of such relationships as κοινωνία accords with Greek practice in social-religious fraternities.[49]

The idea of κοινωνία is a major motif in Paul's reply to the Corinthians. It is the unifying theme of 10:16-21. Today a prominent interpretation of this section takes κοινωνία to refer to a special relationship between the believer and the Lord (variously termed personal, mystical, even metaphysical).[50] If this approach is followed, then κοινωνία is properly an aspect of soteriology rather than ecclesiology. But it has been shown above that such an interpretation of κοινωνία fails to do justice either to the parallel cases of Jewish and pagan κοινωνία or to the understanding of Christian κοινωνία which is involved in the Lord's Supper.

It is true that Christian κοινωνία as noted in the traditional formula cited in 10:16, does derive from the sacrificial death of Christ. However, this κοινωνία is not some private appropriation of Christ's death. The sacrifice of Jesus established a new covenant (1 Cor 11:25; 2 Cor 3:6-14) and thus a new people of God.[51] Κοινωνία then refers not only to the death of Christ, which is the basis of this new covenant people, but also to the relationship of mutual obligation which exists

---

[49]This may also be found in Judaism. See B. W. Dombrowski, "YHAD in 1 QS," *HTR* 59 (1966) 293-307. He argues that the Qumran community saw itself as a religious κοινον and their self-designation יחד is equivalent to τὸ κοινον.

[50]Héring, *First Epistle,* 94. See also supra, 130-132.

[51]Shedd, 147, suggests that the allusions in 11:25 to a new covenant reflect Isa 42:6 and 49:8.

among its members who benefit from Christ's sacrifice. In this way κοινωνία denotes the community context of Christian life and the relationship of a common alliance among Christians. The relationship with each other, as well as with the Lord, is included in κοινωνία.

Other Pauline uses of κοινωνία confirm this community interpretation. In 1 Cor 1:9 Paul says Christians are "called" (ἐκλήθητε) into the κοινωνία of God's son. Rather than referring to each Christian having a share of Christ, this passage actually describes becoming a member of the church, the people of God (209f.). Even the Pauline collection, also termed κοινωνία (2 Cor 8:4; 9:13), is really a visible manifestation of the common alliance belonging to those in Christ's community.

3. *Lord's Supper*. In 1 Cor 10:16ff. Paul refers to the Lord's Supper in connection with the motif of κοινωνία. Thus really the Lord's Supper is a part of his treatment of κοινωνία. In the Lord's Supper the communal reality of κοινωνία is experienced and expressed. In 1 Cor 11:17-34 the excessive individualism of the Corinthians in their divisiveness at the eucharist is a denial of the meaning of the meal. Accordingly, those interpretations of 1 Cor 10:16-21 which see Paul's argument as based on "sacrament" are misleading. Paul is not arguing about the sacramental or non-sacramental character of the eucharist.

Johannes Weiss has objected that in 1 Cor 10:16, 17 Paul conducts his argument about eating sacrificial meat on a lower basis than a genuinely ethical consideration of brotherly responsibility (such as in 8 and 10:22ff.).[52] It was this alleged difference in approach, really conflicting approaches, between sacramentalism and brotherly love which led Weiss to deny the integrity of 1 Cor 8-10.[53] Even Hans von Soden's well-known defense of the intergrity of these chapters continues to regard 10:16-22 as organized around "sacrament."[54] In the exegetical section of this study which dealt with 10:16-21 it was argued that not only is there no opposition here, but even the categorizing of 10:16-21 as "sacramental" is mistaken.[55]

---

[52]Weiss, *Earliest Christianity*, 1.325ff.

[53]Ibid., 1.327.

[54]Von Soden, "Sakrament und Ethik," 23-31.

[55]See in this study 215-220. For example, E. J. Tinsley, *The Imitation of God in Christ* (London: SCM, 1960) 159, citing Héring on the ethical significance of the Lord's Supper as a sacrament, says: "Through the Eucharist Christians are in the process of becoming in actuality what they are in virtue of Baptism: dead with Christ to self and sin, and risen with Christ to sit with him in the heavenlies!" There are many question-

If one understands the Lord's Supper in 10:16, 17 to be κοινωνία in the sense of a communal activity which celebrates and maintains bonds of allegiance among members of the church, then it is clear that this approach is consistent with the appeals in chapters 8 and 10:23ff. There Paul urges his readers to consider the brother in their actions. Shedd's understanding of the Lord's Supper is helpful:

> The meal is a commemorative representation of the sacrifice by which Christ inaugurated the New Covenant which constituted the New Israel. As such it is a confessing of the covenant bond which makes the Community the People of God, while at the same time it produces a fellowship among those who partake of the elements in common.[56]

The communal bond established in the Lord's Supper is the community aspect of the Lord's Supper seen from its ecclesiological perspective. This is what Paul sets forth as the significance of the meal in 1 Cor 10:16-21, not only with the Christian meal, but also with Jewish and pagan ones. Since Paul had previously taught the Corinthians regarding the Lord's Supper, they probably had heard this explanation before, even if they had not understood it. However, since pagan associations also had communal meals, and these were sometimes called κοινωνία, the Corinthians may have understood the Christian meal apart from any demand for an exclusive loyalty to the one God (a point obvious to Jews).[57]

4. *Christian exclusivism.* The exclusivism demanded by allegiance to Christ was obvious to Paul (10:21) but not to the Corinthians. His motive in citing examples of cultic meals is not only to show that reli-

---

able assertions in these words, here I limit myself to disagreement with the "sacramental" importance of the Lord's Supper as a basis of Christian ethics.

[56]Shedd, 191. He continues: "It is preferable here to see Paul's conception of the unity of the Church as covenantal ... rather than sacramental."

[57]Whether one can justifiably use the word "sacrament" in speaking of the Lord's Supper depends, of course, on the operative definition of "sacrament." I have no objection to the term itself, except that its history and familiar meaning may obscure Paul's own interests. Walter, "Christusglaube," 432, n. 50, rightly says that we can speak of "sacramentalism" in Paul in the sense that participation in the Lord's Supper is an act of preeminent importance with the greatest consequences.

gious communities have such meals but to argue that these meals are exclusive in their loyalty.

In both 8:4-6 and 10:19 Paul acknowledges the non-being of idols. The Corinthians certainly would have agreed; indeed 8:4-6 may have come originally from the Corinthians. However, Paul and the Corinthians draw different conclusions from the truth of the non-being of idols when it comes to the matter of participating in meals at their shrines. The Corinthians argue that the meals of non-existent idols are innocuous. Paul, who beings with a more corporate understanding of the church, sees danger in these meals because they represent other allegiances and thereby endanger Christian loyalties (190-192).

In our discussion of the community motif of κοινωνία especially in the Lord's Supper, the theoretical aspect has been stressed. Nonetheless, there was an experiential aspect of this community life which was also certainly important. Bousset has graphically pictured this experiential side of the reality of fellowship in the eucharist:

> . . . here in the gatherings of the fellowship, in worship and cult, there grew up for the believers in Christ the consciousness of their unity and peculiar sociological exclusiveness. During the day scattered, in the vocations of everyday life, in solitariness, within an alien world abandoned to scorn and contempt, they came together in the evening, probably as often as possible, for the common sacred meal. There they experienced the miracle of fellowship, the glow of the enthusiasm of a common faith and a common hope; there the spirit blazed high, and a world full of wonders surrounded them.[58]

Thus, as Paul experienced it, Christian exclusivism had both theological and sociological supports.

D. Imitation of Paul

In the discussion of 1 Cor 8 and 10 Paul twice specifically sets forth his conduct as a guide in the question of whether to eat sacrificial meat.[59] In each case the reference to his conduct appears as an abrupt

---

[58]Bousset, *Kyrios Christos*, 135.

[59]Of the many important works on this theme, recent ones are: Hans Dieter Betz, *Nachfolge und Nachahmung Jesu Christi im Neuen Testament* (BHTh 37; Tübingen: J.C.B. Mohr [Paul Siebeck], 1967), esp.

and unexpected shift in the argument.[60] Paul says in 1 Cor 8:13, "There-fore if food is a cause of my brother's falling, I will never eat meat, lest I cause my brother to fall." While he does not explicitly demand the Corin-thians follow his lead in this proposal, it is obvious that Paul is encourag-ing them to do so. He is not simply stating how he himself would behave (see 108-109). In 1 Cor 11:1 Paul does specifically summon the Corin-thians to follow his example: "Be imitators of me." Of course, 1 Cor 9 features Paul as an example, but consideration of that evidence should follow an examination of *imitatio Pauli* in 1 Cor 8:13 and 11:1.

Much of the debate on the call to imitate Paul has concerned the *content* of the imitation urged. The content is directly tied to the idea of imitation of Christ, which Paul explicitly connects with imitating himself in 1 Cor 11:1 and 1 Thess 1:6, 7 and which he seems to allude to in 1 Cor 4:16f. and 1 Thess 2:14. At issue is whether this imitation is only general, that is, "be a Christian," or has more specific content.

The most thorough presentation of the position that Paul's sum-mons to imitation is only general and non-specific is given by Michaelis. He says that the imitation called for in 1 Cor 11:1 (and 4:16; 1 Thess 1:6) is simply to be obedient. He says of 11:1: "Μιμηταί μου γίνεσθε has the meaning: be told, take it to heart, keep to it, be obedient."[61] Even when Paul's conduct is explicitly named (2 Thess 3:7, 9 and Phil 3:17), the only content is to be obedient as Paul is obedient.[62] Michaelis specifically denies that Paul is urging himself as an object of imitation, or that Christ is such a model, "in either individual features or *total impress.*"[63]

Similar approaches to Michaelis' are taken by Eduard Lohse and

---

153-169; W. P. deBoer, *The Imitation of Paul* (Kampen: J.H. Kok, 1962); Eduard Lohse, "Nachfolge Christi," *RRG*[3] cols. 1286-12; W. Michaelis, "Μιμέομαι," *TDNT* 4 (1967) 666-674; D. M. Stanley, "Become Imitators of Me: The Pauline Conception of Apostolic Tradition," *Biblica* 40 (1959) 859-877; Tinsley, *Imitation.* A good, succinct review is Furnish, *Theology and Ethics,* 218-223.
[60]DeBoer, 156, citing a study by E. Gidem, "Imitatio Pauli," *Teologiska Studier Tillägnade Erik Stave* (Uppsala: Almquist & Wiksells, 1922) 67-85.
[61]Michaelis, 669, 673.
[62]Ibid., 671f. He finds this especially true in 1 Cor 11:16 (668).
[63]Ibid., 672 (italics mine). It is true that there is slim evidence that Paul appeals to the individual actions of Jesus such as are now found in the gospels. However, as is urged in this study, the total impress (the *gestalt*) of Jesus's life is important.

Hans Conzelmann. Lohse says that the absence of the concept of dis-
cipleship in Paul is supportive of an absence of any consideration of Christ
as a pattern, or a suggestion that Christians should live like him. For
Lohse also imitation, whether of Paul or Christ, is simply obedience.[64]
Conzelmann says that Paul is important as a transmitter of Christian
teaching, and the imitation of Christ refers to his saving work.[65]

The other extreme in interpreting the content of the *imitatio Pauli*
suggests that Paul is asking Christians to model their lives upon specific
characteristics of the life of Jesus, as Paul himself does. This is the view
taken by W. D. Davies[66] and W. B. deBoer.[67] In some ways it is also the
approach of Tinsley,[68] however his study seeks an even greater role for
the imitation motif by seeking to make it a normative theme for New
Testament theology.

It is hard to avoid the conclusion that both extremes have obscured
the issue by overstating their case. In view of Paul's scant appeals to the
words and deeds of "the Lord" it is hard to argue that he saw in the specifics of the life and work of the earthly Jesus a pattern for Christian
living. This is true apart from how one explains this absence of direct
references to the details of Jesus's life. Yet the other extreme in interpretation also seems mistaken also when it tries to limit the meaning of
μιμέομαι and μίμησις to "obedience." A third option is needed, not just
to seek a presumably laudable middle path, but because the evidence
seems to demand it.

DeBoer is correct when he observes that Paul's appeals summoning
his readers to imitate him, including the one in 1 Cor 11:1, accentuate
humility, self-giving and self-sacrifice for the sake of others.[69] Certainly
in 1 Cor 11:1 and also in 8:13 Paul is asking for the same prime concern
for others which guides his own conduct (and was characteristic of Jesus).
In a few words, Paul is asking the Corinthians to follow the path of ἀγάπη,
the better way (12:3-13:7).

Focusing on 1 Cor 11:1, it seems that Paul is asking for a specific
manner of Christian conduct consistent with his own conduct. He does

---

[64]Lohse, 1287f.

[65]Conzelmann, *1 Corinthians*, 179f.

[66]Davies, "Conscience," 671-676.

[67]DeBoer, especially 207-240.

[68]Tinsley, *Imitation*, 65-180.

[69]DeBoer, 207. Most doubtful is his next step attempting to prove
that in urging these qualities/actions Paul has in mind specifics of Jesus's
life.

not begin with his conduct but with an appeal to "do all to the glory of God" (10:31). This is subsequently explained as "giving no offence to Jews or to Greeks or to the church of God" (10:32). Paul claims that this is his own resolve and that it is motivated by his desire to serve others for their good (10:33). Therefore the appeal which follows, "Be imitators of me," means concretely: act to the benefit of others rather than for your own. This is the way of Christ himself (11:1b; cf. Phil 2:4-7).

The summons to act in the best interest of others (11:1) is substantially the same as the conduct Paul proposes for himself in 8:13 (and implicitly urges for others). The best commentary on both 8:13 and 11:1 is 9:19-23 where Paul stresses his willingness to forego any privileges for the good of others.[70]

The chapter division at 11:1 is misleading because 11:1 should be taken with what precedes it (esp. 10:31-33)[71] rather than what follows.[72] 1 Cor 10:31-11:1 serves as the recapitulation of the theme of Christian responsibility to others.[73] In this way it serves to summarize and conclude the discussion of chapters 8-10.

It is probably accurate to say that the final phrase of 11:1, "even as I am of Christ" (καθὼς κἀγὼ Χριστοῦ) does not have any additional significance. It is not the case that Paul is urging imitation of himself and of Christ, but of himself as a slave of Christ.[74] However, this is not because Paul sees his role as that of a necessary intermediary, as if to establish some hierarchy of imitation.[75] In Rom 15:1-3, a striking parallel to 1 Cor 11:1, Paul does call for an imitation of Christ (Rom 15:3, cf. 15:8) precisely in Christ's self-giving life for others.[76]

---

[70]Stanley, 874, says: "The phrase [in 1 Cor 10:33] πάντα πᾶσιν ἀρέσκω is an epitome of his whole apostolic career."

[71]Robertson and Plummer, 1 Corinthians, 225: "There is no connection with what follows."

[72]As does Conzelmann, 1 Corinthians, 179f., when he says: "v2 then emphasizes that which is essential and exemplary is the teaching (his italics) which he has transmitted to the Corinthians." Conzelmann is led to this position by his conviction that Paul does not set forth himself as a model, but only his teachings.

[73]This point is made by Robertson and Plummer, 1 Corinthians, 225f.; Maurer, "Grund und Grenze," 634f.; Furnish, Theology and Ethics, 223; and Tinsley, Imitation, 136.

[74]Stanley, 873f.

[75]Rightly Barrett, 1 Corinthians, 246; contra, Stanley, 874.

[76]Furnish, Theology and Ethics, 220. A similar approach occurs in Phil 2:1-10.

An important consideration in examining the theme of the imitation of Paul is why Paul employs this motif at all. Why does he add 10:33-
11:1 to 10:31, 32 which are complete and cogent arguments and would
have served well to cap his discussion? Why conclude his assessment of
the Corinthians' defenses with an abrupt personal example (8:13)? Finally,
what purpose does chapter 9 serve within the overall argument? Indeed,
many have concluded it serves no purpose and have argued on that basis
for partitioning the letter.

Paul's appeal to imitate him is not a means to effect indirectly a
change in the Corinthians.[77] Nor is it a way to remind them of his teaching, as would be the case if he is only asking for obedience to what he has
taught them. There are two reasons why Paul appeals to the Corinthians
to imitate him.

First, Paul stands in a very special relationship with the Corinthians because he is their "father" in the faith (4:14-17, cf. 3:10; 9:1, 2).
They owe their Christian existence to Paul.[78] It is probably significant
that Paul appeals for imitation only from those churches which he had
founded and thus has a unique relationship with in the gospel.[79]

Second, Paul can summon imitation of himself because he is an
apostle of Christ, whose life is conformed to Christ's life (Phil 4:10-12).
Indeed, Paul's life is Christ's (Gal 2:20, cf. 1 Cor 15:10). Paul does not set
himself forth as an exceptional Christian (if such a concept would have
been understood by him) but as one who by word and deed sets forth the
gospel (1 Thess 1:4-6; 2 Cor 1:5, 6). Furnish says this well:

> . . . it is clear that Paul regards himself not only as a bearer
> of *traditions* (e.g., 1 Cor 11:2; 1 Thess 4:1-2) but also as a
> bearer of Christ (e.g., 1 Cor 11:1, cf. Phil 4:9). What this
> means is most succinctly indicated by II Cor 13:4: Paul's
> suffering and serving as an apostle are to be regarded as a
> sort of "parable" of Christ's own saving death and resurrec-
> tion.[80]

The selflessness of Paul is consistent with and becomes a presenta-

---

[77]Such as is argued by Murphy-O'Connor, 568.

[78]DeBoer, 214, gives a strong emphasis to the "father" role of Paul
in the imitation motif. "In calling for imitation Paul is nurturing his
children in Christ." Similarly, Stanley, 872.

[79]Stanley, 872.

[80]Furnish, *Theology and Ethics*, 222f.

tion of his *theologia crucis*. This is not because Paul is the object of his own preaching (2 Cor 4:5), but because Paul's perception of Christ's work as essentially shaped by the cross guides his own life (2 Cor 4:7-14; Phil 4:12). Therefore Paul's speech and conduct are characterized by weakness (1 Cor 2:1-5, cf. 1 Thess 1:4-6), in which the power of God is at work (2 Cor 12:9, 10; 13:4).

The sufferings of Paul are only an extreme example of the fundamental truth of the gospel that God's power is manifest in weakness. Like his Lord, the apostle lives in loneliness and weakness.[81] Even an apparently personal choice, such as preaching without pay from his hearers, is for Paul a manifestation of his *theologia crucis*.

In conclusion, it should be clear that Paul's call to imitate himself is an important theme in 1 Corinthians 8-10. It is explicit in 8:13 and 11:1, and set forth forcefully in 1 Corinthians 9. Paul's summons to follow his example is not devoid of specific content. It is a summons to conduct one's life always giving first consideration to the effects on others. In the context of 1 Corinthians 8-10 this argument is directed toward the Corinthians in order to restrain their participation in cult meals. The context, then, gives a concrete focus to the underlying appeal of Paul's example, act in consideration of others. This means, of course, that one should act in love.

E. Love

1. *The Importance of Love in 1 Cor 8-10*. The characteristic New Testament word for love, ἀγάπη occurs only twice in 1 Cor 8-10. In 8:1 ἀγάπη is contrasted with knowledge by the effects each one has. In 8:3 the verb ἀγαπάω is used in one of the rare instances where Paul says Christians "love God." But the importance of the *motif* of love is not to be limited to the occurrence of the word for love. Furnish has shown how love is really the pulse of 1 Cor 8.[82] In fact, love is perhaps the most important motif in 1 Cor 8-10, because many specific admonitions and encouragements in these chapters depend upon love. As Schrage has observed, the command to love is not only the highest norm, it is the law of Christ. The command to love is often formulated as concrete, specific warnings.[83]

---

[81]Maurer, "Grund und Grenze," 630.

[82]Furnish, *Love Command*, 111-114.

[83]Schrage, *Einzelgebote*, 255f. This is, of course, the thesis of

Indeed, one can say that love is the primary consideration of all Christian life. Again Schrage is on target: "Die Liebe ist *conditio sina qua non* allen christlichen Verhaltens. Ohne sie is *alles* nichts, durch sie allein gewinnt *alles* seinen Wert. Alle Dinge sollen darum in Liebe geschehen (1 Cor 16:14)."[84] Love is so fundamental because it is not one act among many but is the substratum of all Christian actions.

Although Paul can state the appeal to love explicitly (Rom 13:8f., Gal 4:1, 1 Thess 4:9) he more often expresses this motif in concrete admonitions directed to specific situations.[85] Schrage points to 1 Cor 8 as a good example of how Paul both works *from* love and *to* love as a general principle.[86] This inclusive character of love is well illustrated by 1 Cor 10:31-11:1 where Paul urges the consideration of the other person.

The importance of love in Paul's ethical instructions arises from its close relationship to his Christology.[87] The shape and character of love for Christians arises in God's loving gift of his son (Rom 5:6-8). Christian love, either of God or others, is a reflecting and passing on of God's initial love in Christ.[88] There are many places where this Christological basis of ἀγάπη is stated in Paul. For example, in Phil 2:5ff., the apostle grounds his appeal for consideration of others in Christ's concern for others expressed in his self-denial and humility.[89] Also in Gal 2:20 Paul closely relates his ministry to Christ's self-sacrifice which he describes as his love.

In Rom 12:5ff., Gal 2:20, and Rom 5:6-8 the love of God in Christ is said to be evident in the cross, the clearest example of the selflessness of love. The same appeal to love and the death of Christ occurs in 1 Cor 8:11 (cf., Rom 15:3, 7). It is not that Christians are asked to repeat

---

Schrage's study, which he has amply documented in the total Pauline corpus. He also argues this thesis with specific consideration of 1 Corinthians 8-10. Furnish, *Theology and Ethics,* 212f., rightly argues that it is not possible to reduce all of Paul's ethical thought to the norm of love. Nevertheless, it is a very crucial motif in 1 Corinthians 8-10.

[84]Schrage, *Einzelgebote,* 254.

[85]Wendland, *Ethik,* 80, 85. He notes that the same appeal to love and consideration of the brother is behind the appeal in 1 Cor 6:1-11 to avoid lawsuits with other Christians.

[86]Schrage, *Einzelgebote,* 124; Wendland, *Ethik,* 59.

[87]Furnish, *Theology and Ethics,* 216ff.

[88]Schrage, *Einzelgebote,* 249.

[89]Wendland, *Ethik,* 60, also notes a connection to 1 Corinthians 8.

Christ's death,[90] but the death of Christ is proof of the meaning of love. The same motif is seen in Paul's selflessness in 1 Cor 10:31-33 (cf. 8:13, and frequently in 9), which is being urged by others.

Just as love is grounded in Paul's Christology so also it is expressed in his ecclesiology. In fact, Paul's ecclesiology is not separable from his Christology. When he calls for the church to "build up" others, it is the body of Christ which is being built up (this is clear in the discussion of charismata in 1 Cor 12 where the church is described as the body of Christ in an extended discussion, and subsequently one is urged in 1 Cor 14 to "build up" the church).[91] In 10:16-21 the discussion of κοινωνία is basically an ecclesiological idea; it is what love demands of those within the alliance of faith.

2. *Love and Freedom.* The relationship of love and freedom has already been examined in the study of 1 Cor 8. But before looking at some specific ways the motif of love is expressed in 1 Cor 8-10, it is useful to review the question of love and freedom.

In spite of various attempts to make "freedom" the hallmark of Paul's gospel,[92] Paul usually speaks of freedom either in the socio-economic sense of slavery and freedom (1 Cor 7:21f.; Gal 3:28) or in a polemic against a legalistic form of Christianity ("Judaizing," Gal 4:26-31; Rom 7:3). Certainly in these ways and others, a freedom is given through the act of Christ which Paul does regard positively.[93] Nevertheless, it is misleading to regard freedom as a primary category of Paul's gospel.

It is probable that the idea of "freedom" (ἐλευθερία) or "rights" (ἐξουσία) in regard to eating sacrificial meats originated with the Corinthians. Based on their Christian knowledge and faith, they argued that they had liberty to eat such meat. This means that "freedom" as a term of discussion in 1 Cor 8-10 did not begin with Paul. The Corinthians differed from Paul on freedom in two major ways. First, they gave the

---

[90]Merk, *Handeln aus Glauben,* 238.

[91]Ibid.

[92]Most recently, Richardson, *Paul's Ethic of Freedom.* In most of his comments in 1 Corinthians 8 and 10 there is substantial agreement with the exegetical parts of the present study. However, I question whether "freedom" is a major ethical category for Paul, and especially the implication that it is to be a first consideration unless limited by love.

[93]Barrett, "Things Sacrificed," 147. Schlier, "Ἐλεύθερος," 498f., has a good, succinct discussion of the basis of Christian freedom "through the act of Jesus Christ," how it is conveyed "through the call which comes to man in the gospel," and how the Spirit works in Christian freedom.

primary stress to freedom,[94] while Paul gave it to love (seen most clearly
in 1 Cor 13). Second, the Corinthians understood freedom very individualistically; Paul understood it (and love!) in a corporate sense.

Most interpretations of Paul's treatment of love and freedom argue
that Paul valued freedom highly yet was willing to restrict it in love. In
connection with 1 Cor 8-10 this leads many to say that Paul agrees with
the Corinthians who felt free to eat yet, unlike them, was willing to
forego his beliefs on occasion for the sake of the community.[95]

However, even this reasonable interpretation of the relationship of
freedom and love must be challenged. It is not a minor point to contest
the view that Paul favors freedom but he limits it with love. Rather for
Paul love is an act of freedom. Only the person whose life is guided by
the needs of others, who does not seek privilege for himself, is truly
free. Christians are "free for" their neighbors, free not to seek their own
good (10:24).[96] This way, of course, is the way of love (1 Cor 13) and
Christ's own way (Rom 15:7, 8). Furnish is correct in concluding on this
basis, "The 'strong' do not *lose* any of their freedom thereby [in the
service of others], but will be *using* it in love and thus affirming the
reality of their new life in Christ."[97]

3. *What Love Does.* We have already noted that "love" (ἀγάπη)
occurs only twice in 1 Cor 8-10. But the motif of love is important
beyond this statistic. The normative role of love is set out repeatedly in
1 Cor 8-10 in diverse way.[98] Positively, love seeks the good of others,

---

[94]Thus the Corinthians wrongly viewed freedom as *autonomy*. See
Schrage, *Einzelgebote,* 109. Contra Friedrich, "Freiheit und Liebe," 81,
who inexplicably suggests that Paul shares the view that Christians are
self-ruled.

[95]See in the present study 115-117, where several examples of this
viewpoint are noted. See also Schrage, *Einzelgebote,* 157f.; 257, who says
that love is the limit of freedom and knowledge. Similarly, deBoer, 155,
says that Christians must balance freedom on the one hand and acting in
love on the other.

[96]Noted by Wendland, *Ethik,* 57.

[97]Furnish, *Love Command,* 118. He is speaking here of Romans
15:3-8, but the observation is equally appropriate to 1 Corinthians 8-10.
Furnish also notes, 114, that the Christian should employ his freedom (in
this case, one's freedom either to *eat* or *not* to eat) to serve the neighbor
(Gal 5:13, 14).

[98]Schrage, *Einzelgebote,* 256f., rightly notes the importance of
love being frequently expressed by other terms.

their benefit, how to please them. It seeks to build up the church.[99] Conversely, negatively, love is not puffed up, and it places no stumbling block before the other person. I conclude this discussion of the motif of love in the eating of idol meat by reviewing quickly the ways in which love is manifested as a criterion of Christian conduct in 1 Cor 8-10.

Paul's first response to the Corinthians' defense of eating sacrificial meat is that "love builds up" (8:1). The term οἰκοδομέω may have been in the Corinthians' letter, or Paul himself may have coined the ironic use in 8:10. "Building up," as we have seen, is an important theme for Paul. It is how he understands his work as an apostle (1 Cor 3:10-15; cf. 2 Cor 10:8; 12:19).

The idea of "building up" combines the motif of love with ecclesiology. Love is the hallmark of the church; "building up" is the expression of that love within the church.[100] This appeal is explicit in 1 Cor 8:1; 10:23 and is the major theme in the discussion of spiritual gifts in 1 Cor 14. Stated epigrammatically, love demands, "Let all things be done for edification" (14:26).

In 1 Cor 8:1 Paul describes love's work as "building up," a description he repeats in 10:23. In 10:23 he adds the parallel thought that love is "helpful" (συμφέρω). From this parallelism it is clear that οἰκοδομῆ and συμφέρω have the same intent.[101] Both refer to love which benefits the community of faith by strengthening it. It is love which "seeks the advantage" (σύμφορον) of the many (10:33).

A third way in which the motif of love finds expression in 1 Cor 8-10 is in the appeal to "seek the good of others." This is explicit in 10:24, "Let no one seek his own good, but the good of his neighbor."[102] The theme is restated in 10:31-33. The connection between love and seeking the good of others is explicit in 13:5, "Love seeks not its own."

When Paul gives himself for the advantage of others, he does so

---

[99] Ibid., 53. Schrage notes that Paul's ethic is not only one of intent, but also of action. He points to such active verbs as: πράσσειν, ποιεῖν, κατεργάζεσθαι, and ἐργάζεσθαι.

[100] Vielhauer, *OIKODOME*, 99.

[101] Friedrich, "Freiheit und Liebe," 94, notes that the criterion of what is "useful" (σύμφορον) in deciding actions is a corporate concern.

[102] Richardson, *Paul and Freedom*, 118f., says that the principle of seeking the good of the neighbor (1 Cor 10:24) is summarized by love.

from love (2 Cor 12:14). This is the essence of his whole ministry (9:19-23), of which renouncing his right of financial support is only a concrete instance (9:15-18). Seeking the benefit of others can also be described as "serving" (δουλεύω). Thus Christians are urged, "Through love be servants of one another" (Gal 5:13; 1 Cor 9:19).[103] It is "pleasing" others (10:33, cf. 12:25, 26; 9:19-23; Rom 15:1, 2). In this Christ is the pattern for love, for he "did not please himself" (Rom 15:3).

---

[103]Schrage, *Einzelgebote*, 252; Richardson, *Paul and Freedom*, 119.

Bibliography

STANDARD REFERENCE WORKS

Bauer, Walter. *A Greek-English Lexicon of the New Testament and Other Early Christian Literature.* Second Revision by William F. Arndt, F. W. Gingrich, and Frederick Danker. Chicago: University of Chicago Press, 1979.

Blass, Frederich and DeBrunner, Alfred. *A Greek Grammar of the New Testament and Other Early Christian Literature.* Translated and Revised by Robert W. Funk. Chicago: University of Chicago Press, 1961.

Buttrick, George A. *The Interpreter's Dictionary of the Bible.* 4 vols. Nashville: Abingdon Press, 1962. s.v. "Conscience," by W. D. Davies.

Crim, Keith, ed. *The Interpreter's Dictionary of the Bible, Supplementary Volume.* Nashville: Abingdon Press, 1976. s.v. "The Apocalypse of Adam," by George MacRae; "Conscience," by Robert Jewett; "Corinth," by Cynthia Thompson.

Farnell, L. R. *The Cults of the Greek States.* 5 vols. Oxford: Clarendon Press, 1909.

Frazer, J. G. *The Golden Bough.* 13 vols. London: MacMillan and Co., 1911-1915.

Galling, Kurt, et al., ed. *Die Religion in Geschichte und Gegenwart: Handwörterbuch für Theologie und Religionswissenschaft.* 7 vols. Tübingen: J. C. B. Mohr [Paul Siebeck], 1957-63. 3rd ed. s.v. "Nachfolge Christi," by Eduard Lohse.

Hastings, James F., ed. *Encyclopedia of Religion and Ethics.* 13 vols. New York: Charles Scribner's Sons, 1908-21. s.v. "Sacrifice, Introduction," by E. O. James; "Sacrifice (Greek)," by L. R. Farnell; "Sacraments, Primitive and Ethnic," by J. A. MacCulloch.

Kittel, Gerhard, ed. *Theological Dictionary of the New Testament.* 9 vols. Grand Rapids: Wm. B. Eerdmans, 1964-74. Various articles and authors consulted.

Klauser, Theodor, ed. *Reallexikon für Antike und Christentum, Supplement.* Stuttgart: Hiersemann, 1976. s.v. "Genossenschaft," by Peter Hermann, et al.

Liddell, Henry George and Scott, Robert. *A Greek-English Lexicon.* 9th ed. rev. Oxford: Clarendon Press, 1940.

Moule, C. F. D. *An Idiom Book of New Testament Greek.* Cambridge: University Press, 1967.

Moulton, James H. *A Grammar of New Testament Greek.* Edinburgh: T. & T. Clark, 1908.

Moulton, James H., ed. *A Grammar of New Testament Greek.* Edinburgh: T. & T. Clark, 1963. Vol. 3: *Syntax,* by Nigel Turner.

Moulton, James H. and Milligan, George. *The Vocabulary of the Greek Testament: Illustrated from the Papyri and other non-literary Sources.* Grand Rapids: Wm. B. Eerdmans, 1930.

Pauly, August Friedrich von and Wissowa, Georg. *Realenzykopädie der klassischen Altertumswissenschaft.* 24 vols. Stuttgart: A. Druckenmuller, 1894ff.

Strack, Hermann L. and Billerbeck, Paul. *Kommentar zum Neuen Testament aus Talmud und Midrasch.* 3rd ed. Munich: Beck, 1924-61.

ANCIENT TEXTS AND SOURCES

Behr, C. A. *Aelius Aristides and the Sacred Tales.* Amsterdam: Adolf M. Hakkert, 1968.

Dindorf, Wilhelm. *Aristides.* Hildesheim: Georg Olms, 1964.

Dittenberger, Wilhelm. *Sylloge Inscriptionum Graecarum.* 4 vols. 3rd ed. Leipzig: S. Hirzel, 1914-1924.

Dodds, E. R. *Euripides; Bacchae.* 2nd Revised Ed. Oxford: Clarendon Press, 1960.

Edelstein, E. J. and L. *Asclepius: A Collection and Interpretation of the Testimonies.* 2 vols. Baltimore: Johns Hopkins Press, 1945.

Eitrem, S. and Amundsen, Leiv. *Papyri Osloenses.* Oslo: Det Norske Videnskaps Adademi, 1936.

Engelmann, Helmut. *The Delian Aretalogy of Sarapis.* Vol. 44 of Études Préliminaires aux Religions Orientales dans L'Empire Romain. Leiden: E. J. Brill, 1975.

Epstein, Isidore, ed. *The Babylonian Talmud.* 35 vols. London: Soncino Press, 1938.

Etheridge, J. W. *The Targums of Onkelos.* New York: KTAV Reprint, 1968.

Foucart, Paul. *Des Associations religieuses chez les Grecs.* Paris: Klineckseick, 1873.

Grenfell, Bernard P.; Hunt, Arthur S.; and Hogarth, David C. *Fayum Towns and Their Papyri.* London: Oxford Press, 1960.

Grenfell, Bernard P. *Oxyrhynchus Papyri.* London: Oxford Press, 1912--.

James, M. R. *The Biblical Antiquities of Philo.* London: S. P. C. K., 1917.

Johnson, J. DeM.; Martin, Victor; and Hunt, Arthur S. *Catalogue of the Greek Papyri in the John Rylands Library.* Manchester: University Press, 1915.

Kern, Otto. *Die Inschriften von Magnesia am Mäander.* Berlin: W. Spemann, 1900.

Kirk, Geoffrey S. *The Bacchae of Euripides.* Englewood Cliffs, NJ: Prentice-Hall, 1970.

Loeb, James, et al., ed. *Loeb Classical Library.* Cambridge: Harvard University Press. Various texts and editors.

Meyer, Eduard. *Der Papyrusfund von Elephantine.* Leipzig: J. C. Hinrichs, 1912.

Mitteis, Ludwig and Wilken, Ulrich. *Grundzüge und Christomathie die Papyruskunde.* 2 vols. Hildesheim: Georg Ulms, 1963. Vol 2: *Christomathie,* by Ulrich Wilken.

Oates, J. F.; Samuel, A. E.; and Welles, C. B. *Yale Papyri in the Beinecke Rare Book and Manuscript Library.* Vol. 1: American Studies in Papyrology, no. 2. New Haven: Yale University, 1967.

Poland, Franz. *Geschichte des griechischen Vereinswesens.* Leipzig: Teubner, 1909.

Sokolowski, Franziszek. *Lois Sacrees des Cites Grecques, Supplement.* Paris: E. de Boccard, 1962.

Vandoni, Mariangela. *Feste Pubbliche e Private nei Documenti Greci.*
Teste e Documenti per so Studio Dell 'Antichita: Serele Papyro-
logica, no. 8. Milan: Instituto Editoriale Cisalpino, 1964.

Youtie, H. C. and Pearl, O. M. *Tax Rolls from Karanis: Michigan Papyri,*
Vols. 4-6. Humanistic Studies, Vols. 42-45. Ann Arbor: University
of Michigan, 1939.

Ziebarth, Erich. *Das griechische Vereinswesen.* Leipzig: Teubner, 1896.

COMMENTARIES ON 1 CORINTHIANS

Barrett, Charles, Kingsley. *The First Epistle to the Corinthians.* HNTC.
New York: Harper & Row, 1968.

Bousset, Wilhelm. "Der erste Brief an die Korinther." *Die Schriften des
Neuen Testaments neu übersetz und für die Gegenwart erklärt.*
Vol. 2. Edited by Wilhelm Bousset and Wilhelm Heitmüller. Göt-
tingen: Vandenhoeck & Ruprecht, 1917, 1918.

Conzelmann, Hans. *1 Corinthians.* Hermeneia. Philadelphia: Fortress
Press, 1975.

Georgi, Dieter. "I Corinthians," *Interpreter's Dictionary of the Bible,
Supplementary Volume.* Nashville: Abingdon Press, 1976.

Grosheide, F. W. *A Commentary on the First Epistle to the Corinthians.*
NICNT, No. 7. Grand Rapids: Wm. B. Eerdmans Co., 1955.

Héring, Jean. *The First Epistle of Saint Paul to the Corinthians.* London:
Epworth Press, 1962.

Lietzmann, Hans. *An die Korinther I, II.* Rev. Werner Georg Kümmel,
HNT 9 (Tübingen: J. C. B. Mohr [Paul Siebeck], 4th ed., 1949.

Moffatt, James. *The First Epistle of Paul to the Corinthians.* MNTC.
New York: Harper & Brothers, n.d.

Morris, Leon. *The First Epistle of Paul to the Corinthians.* Grand Rapids:
Wm. B. Eerdmans, 1958.

Orr, William F. and Walther, James A. *I Corinthians.* AB No. 32. Garden
City: Doubleday, 1976.

Parry, Reginald St. John. *The First Epistle of Paul the Apostle to the
Corinthians in Revised Version with Introduction and Notes.* The
Cambridge Bible for Schools and Colleges. Cambridge: University
Press, 1926.

Robertson, Archibald and Plummer, Alfred. *A Critical and Exegetical Commentary on the First Epistle of St. Paul to the Corinthians.* ICC. New York: Charles Scribner's Sons, 1911.

Schlatter, Adolf. *Die Korintherbriefe.* Stuttgart: Calwer, 1962.

Thrall, Margaret E. *I and II Corinthians.* Cambridge Bible Commentary. Cambridge: University Press, 1965.

Weiss, Johannes. *Der erste Korintherbrief.* KEK 5. Göttingen: Vandenhoeck & Ruprecht, 1910.

Wendland, Heinz-Dietrich. *Die Briefe an die Korinther.* NTD 7. Göttingen: Vandenhoeck & Ruprecht, 1936.

ARTICLES

Aalen, Sverre. "Das Abendmahl als Opfermahl im Neuen Testament." *Novum Testamentum* 6 (1963) 128-152.

Bandstra, A. "Interpretation in 1 Cor 10:1-11." *Calvin Theological Journal* 6 (1971) 5-21.

Barrett, Charles Kingsley. "Things Sacrificed to Idols." *New Testament Studies* 11 (1965) 138-153.

Betz, Hans Dieter. "The Mithras Inscriptions of Santa Prisca and the New Testament." *Novum Testamentum* 10 (1968) 62-80.

Boak, A. E. R. "The Organization of Guilds in Greco-Roman Egypt." *Transactions of the American Philological Association* 68 (1937) 212-220.

Bourke, Myles M. "The Eucharist and Wisdom in First Corinthians." *Studiorum Paulinorum Congressus Internationalis Catholicus* (= *Analecta Biblica* 17, 18; 1961) 367-381.

Broneer, Oscar. "Hero Cults in Corinth." *Hesperia* 11 (1942) 130-161.

_____. "Paul and the Pagan Cults of Isthmia." *Harvard Theological Review* 64 (1971) 169-187.

Bultmann, Rudolf. "Gnosis." *Journal of Theological Studies* n.s. 3 (1952) 10-26.

Cadbury, Henry J. "The Macellum of Corinth." *Journal of Biblical Literature* 53 (1934) 134-141.

Cameron, A. "Latin Words in the Greek Inscriptions of Asia Minor." *American Journal of Philology* 52 (1931) 232-262.

302   Idol Meat at Corinth

Conzelmann, Hans. "Korinth und die Mädchen der Aphrodite." *Nach-richten von der Akademie der Wissenschaft in Göttingen* 8 (1967-68) 247-261.

Dombrowski, B. W. "Yahad in 1QS and *to koinon:* An instance of early Greek and Jewish Synthesis." *Harvard Theological Review* 59 (1966) 293-307.

Dow, Stirling and Gill, David H. "The Greek Cult Table." *American Journal of Archaeology* 69 (1965) 103-114.

Dugmore, C. W. "Sacrament and Sacrifice in the Early Fathers." *Journal of Ecclesiastical History* 2 (1951) 24-37.

Ellis, E. Earle. "A Note on First Corinthians 10:4." *Journal of Biblical Literature* 56 (1957) 53-56.

Elmslie, W. A. L. "The Mishna on Idolatry: 'Aboda Zara.'" *Texts and Studies* 8 (1911).

Farnell, L. R. "Sacrificial Communion in Greek Religion." *Hibbert Journal* 2 (1904) 306-323.

Faw, C. E. "On the Writing of First Thessalonians." *Journal of Biblical Literature* 73 (1952) 207-225.

Fee, Gordon D. "II Cor vi.14-vii.1 And Food Offered To Idols." *New Testament Studies* 23 (1977) 140-161.

Ferguson, W. S. "The Attic Orgeones." *Harvard Theological Review* 37 (1944) 61-140.

_____. "The Salaminioi of Heptaphylai and Sounion." *Hesperia* 7 (1938) 1-76.

Findlay, George. "The Letter of the Corinthian Church to St. Paul." *The Expositor* 6th ser. 1 (1900) 401-407.

Forbes, C. A. "Ancient Athletic Guilds." *Classical Philology* 50 (1955) 238-252.

Ford, J. M. "Hast Thou Tithed Thy Meal? and Is Thy Child Kosher?" *Journal of Theological Studies* 17 (1966) 71-79.

Friedrich, Gerhard. "Freiheit und Liebe im ersten Korintherbrief." *Theologische Zeitschrift* 26 (1970) 81-98.

Gill, David. "*Trapezomata:* A Neglected Aspect of Greek Sacrifice." *Harvard Theological Review* 67 (1974) 117-137.

Goppelt, Leonhard. "Paul and Heilsgeschichte: Conclusions from Romans 4 and 1 Cor 10:1-13." *Interpretation* 21 (1967) 315-326.

Grant, Robert M. "Pliny and the Christians." *Harvard Theological Review* 41 (1948) 273-274.

Gressmann, Hugo. "Η ΚΟΙΝΩΝΙΑ ΤΩΝ ΔΑΙΜΟΝΙΟΝ." *Zeitschrift für die neutestamentliche Wissenschaft* 20 (1921) 224-230.

Harris, B. F. "ΣΥΝΕΙΔΗΣΙΣ (Conscience) in the Pauline Writings." *Westminster Journal of Theology* 24 (1962) 173-186.

Healy, Robert F. "A Sacrifice Without a Deity in the Athenian State Calendar." *Harvard Theological Review* 57 (1964) 153-159.

Hicks, E. L. "A Sacrificial Calendar from Cos." *Journal of Hellenistic Studies* 9 (1899) 323-339.

Hinnells, John R. "Christianity and the Mystery Cults." *Theology* 71 (1968) 20-25.

Horsley, R. A. "The Background of the Confessional Formula in 1 Kor 8:6." *Zeitschrift für die neutestamentliche Wissenschaft* 69 (1978) 130-135.

_____. "Consciousness and Freedom Among the Corinthians, 1 Corinthians 8-10." *Catholic Biblical Quarterly* 40 (1978) 574-589.

_____. "Pneumatikos vs. Psychikos: Distinctions of Spiritual Status among the Corinthians." *Harvard Theological Review* 69 (1976) 269-288.

_____. "Wisdom of Words and Words of Wisdom in Corinth." *Catholic Biblical Quarterly* 39 (1977) 224-239.

Jourdan, George V. "ΚΟΙΝΩΝΙΑ in 1 Corinthians 10:16." *Journal of Biblical Literature* 67 (1947) 111-124.

Karris, Robert J. "Romans 14:1-15:3 and the Occasion of Romans." *Catholic Biblical Quarterly* 35 (1973) 155-178.

Koenen, L. "Eine Einladung zur Kline des Sarapis." *Zeitschrift für Papyrologie und Epigraphik* 1 (1967) 121-127.

Laeuchli, Samuel. "Urban Mithraism." *Biblical Archaeologist* 33 (1968) 73-99.

Lock, Walter. "I Corinthians VIII.1-9: A Suggestion." *Expositor*, 5th ser. 6 (1897) 65-74.

Lohse, Eduard. "Zu 1 Cor 10:26.31." *Zeitschrift für die neutestamentliche Wissenschaft* 47 (1956) 277-80.

Loisy, Alfred. "The Christian Mystery." *Hibbert Journal* 10 (1911) 44-64.

Merritt, Benjamin. "Greek Inscriptions." *Hesperia* 11 (1942) 275-303.

Metzger, Bruce M. "Considerations of Method in the Study of Mystery Religions." *Harvard Theological Review* 48 (1955) 1-20.

Milne, J. G. "The Kline of Sarapis." *Journal of Egyptian Archaeology* 2 (1925) 6-9.

Minear, Paul S. "Paul's Teaching on the Eucharist in First Corinthians." *Worship* 44 (1970) 83-92.

Murphy-O'Connor, Jerome. "Freedom or the Ghetto (1 Cor. viii, 1-13; x, 23-xi.1)." *Revue Biblique* 85 (1978) 543-74.

Nabers, Ned. "A Note on *Corinth* VIII, 2, 125." *American Journal of Archaeology* 73 (1969) 73-74.

_____. "The Architectural Variations of the Macellum." *Opuscula Romana* 9 (1973) 173-176.

Nilsson, Martin P. "Second Letter to Professor Nock on the Positive Gains in the Science of Greek Religion." *Harvard Theological Review* 44 (1951) 143-151.

Nock, A. D. "The Historical Importance of Cult-Associations." *Classical Review* 38 (1924) 105-109.

Robertson, Noel. "How to Behave at a Sacrifice: Hesiod *Erga* 755-56." *Classical Philology* 64 (1969) 164-169.

Smith, Dennis E. "The Egyptian Cults at Corinth." *Harvard Theological Review* 70 (1977) 201-231.

Stanley, D. M. "Become Imitators of Me: The Pauline Conception of Apostolic Tradition." *Biblica* 15 (1959) 859-887.

Theissen, Gerd. "Die Starken und Schwachen in Korinth." *Evangelische Theologie* 35 (1975) 155-172.

Thrall, M. E. "The Pauline Uses of ΣΥΝΕΙΔΗΣΙΣ." *New Testament Studies* 14 (1968) 118-125.

Tod, M. N. "NVGAE EPIGRAPHICAE." *Classical Quarterly* 23 (1929) 1-6.

von Dobschütz, Ernst. "Sakrament und Symbol im Urchristentum." *Theologische Studien und Kritiken* 78 (1905) 1-40.

Walter, Nikolaus. "Christusglaube und heidnische Religiosität in paulinischen Gemeinden." *New Testament Studies* 25 (1979) 422-442.

Williams, C. K. II and Fisher, J. E. "Corinth, 1971: Forum Area." *Hesperia* 41 (1972) 143-184.

Westermann, W. L. "Entertainment in the villages of Graeco-Roman
Egypt." *Journal of Egyptian Archaeology* 18 (1932) 16-27.

Wright, Kathleen S. "A Tiberian Pottery Deposit from Corinth." *Hesperia*
49 (1980) 135-177.

Youtie, Herbert C. "The *Kline* of Sarapis." *Harvard Theological Review*
41 (1948) 9-29.

MONOGRAPHS

Angus, Samuel. *The Mystery Religions and Christianity.* New York:
Charles Scribner's Sons, 1925.

Attridge, Harold W. *The Interpretation of Biblical History in the Antiquitates Judaicae of Flavius Josephus.* Harvard Dissertations in Religion, no. 7. Missoula, MT: Scholars Press, 1976.

Bacon, B. W. *The Story of St. Paul.* Boston: Houghton, Mifflin and Co.,
1904.

Barrett, Charles K. *The Second Epistle to the Corinthians.* HNTC: New
York: Harper & Row, 1973.

Bartchy, S. Scott. ΜΑΛΛΟΝ ΧΡΗΣΑΙ: First-century Slavery and the Interpretation of 1 Corinthians 7:21. SBL Dissertations, no. 11. Missoula,
MT: Scholars Press, 1973.

Barth, Karl. *The Resurrection of the Dead.* London: Hodder and Stoughton, 1933.

Bartsch, H. W. "Der korinthische Missbrauch des Abendmahls." *Entmythologisierende Auslegung.* Theologische Forschung, no. 26. Hamberg-
Bergstedt: H. Riech, 1962.

Behr, C. A. *Aelius Aristides and the Sacred Tales.* Amsterdam: Adolf M.
Hakkert, 1968.

Betz, Hans Dieter. *Nachfolge und Nachahmung Jesu Christi im Neuen
Testament.* BHTh, no. 37. Tübingen: J. C. B. Mohr [Paul Siebeck],
1967.

Bevan, E. R. *Later Greek Religion.* Boston: Beacon Press, 1950.

Bjerkelund, Carl J. *Parakalō*. Oslo: Universitets Forlaget, 1967.

Bonsirven, Joseph. *Exegese rabbinique et exegese paulinienne*. Bibliotheque de theologie historique. Paris: Beauchesne et ses fils, 1936.

Boobyer, George H. *"Thanksgiving" and the "Glory of God" in Paul*. Leipzig: Robert Noske, 1929.

Bornkamm, Günther. "Lord's Supper and Church in Paul," *Early Christian Experience*. New York: Harper & Row, 1969. 123-160.

_____. "The Missionary Stance of Paul in 1 Corinthians and in Acts." In *Studies in Luke-Acts*, 194-207. Edited by L. E. Keck and J. Louis Martyn. Nashville: Abingdon Press, 1966.

Bousset, Wilhelm. *Kyrios Christos*. Nashville: Abingdon Press, 1970.

_____. *Die Religion des Judentums im späthellenistischen Zeitalter*. HNT no. 21. Tübingen: J. C. B. Mohr [Paul Siebeck] , 1926.

Bultmann, Rudolf. *The Theology of the New Testament*. New York: Charles Scribner's Sons, 1951.

Caird, G. B. *Principalities and Powers*. Oxford: Clarendon Press, 1956.

Campbell, J. Y. "Κοινωνία and its cognates in the New Testament." In *Three New Testament Studies*, 1-28. Leiden: E. J. Brill, 1965.

Cerfaux, L. *The Church in the Theology of St. Paul*. New York: Herder and Herder, 1959.

Colpe, Carsten. *Die religionsgeschichtliche Schule*. FRLANT, no. 78. Göttingen: Vandenhoeck & Ruprecht, 1961.

Conn, Walter E. *Conscience: Development and Self-Transcendence*. Birmingham, Alabama: Religious Education Press, 1981.

Craig, Clarence T. "Soma Christou." In *The Joy of Study, 73-85*. Edited by Sherman E. Johnson. New York: MacMillan Co., 1951.

Cranfield, C. E. B. *The Epistle to the Romans*. 2 Vols. ICC. Edinburgh: T. & T. Clark, 1979.

Cullmann, Oscar and Leenhardt, F. J. *Essays on the Lord's Supper*. Ecumenical Studies in Worship, no. 1. Richmond: John Knox Press, 1958.

Cumont, Franz. *The Mysteries of Mithra*. Chicago: Open Court Publishing, 1903.

_____. *Oriental Religions in Roman Paganism*. Chicago: Open Court Publishing, 1911.

Currie, Stuart D. "Koinonia in Christian Literature to 200 A.D." Ph.D. dissertation, Emory University, 1962.

Davies, W. D. "The Moral Teaching of the Early Church." In *The Use of the Old Testament in the New and Other Essays*, 310-332. Edited by James W. Efird. Durham, NC: Duke University Press, 1972.

deBoer, W. P. *The Imitation of Paul: An Exegetical Study*. Kampen: J. H. Kok, 1962.

Deissmann, Adolf. *Light from the Ancient East*. London: Hodder and Stoughton, 1927.

Dibelius, Martin. *Die Geisterwelt im Glauben des Paulus*. Göttingen: Vandenhoeck & Ruprecht, 1909.

Dodd, C. H. *According to the Scripture*. Digswell Place: James Nisbet, 1952.

_____. *The Bible and the Greeks*. London: Hodder and Stoughton, 1935.

Dodds, E. R. *The Greeks and the Irrational*. Boston: Beacon Press, 1957.

Dupont, Jacques. *Gnosis. La connaissance religieuse dans les epitres de S. Paul*. Universitas Catholica Lovaniensis, Dissertationes in Facultate Theologica, 2.40. Louvain: Nauwelaerts, 1960.

Ehrenberg, Victor. *The People of Aristophanes*. Oxford: Basil Blackwell, 1951.

Ehrhardt, A. A. T. "Social Problems in the Early Church: I. The Sunday Joint of the Christian Housewife." In *The Framework of the New Testament Stories*, 278-290. Manchester: University Press, 1964.

Elert, Werner. *Eucharist and Church Fellowship in the First Four Centuries*. Saint Louis: Concordia, 1966.

Ellis, E. Earle. "How the New Testament Uses the Old." In *New Testament Interpretation*, 199-219. Edited by I. Howard Marshall. Grand Rapids: Wm. B. Eerdmans, 1977.

_____. *Paul's Use of the Old Testament*. Edinburgh: Oliver and Boyd, 1957.

Enslin, Morton Scott. *The Ethics of Paul*. Nashville: Abingdon Press; Apex Books, 1962.

Forbes, C. A. *Neoi. A Contribution to the Study of Greek Associations.* Philological Monographs, no. 2. Middletown, CN: American Philological Association, 1933.

Furnish, Victor Paul. *The Love Command in the New Testament.* Nashville: Abingdon Press, 1972.

_____. *Theology and Ethics in Paul.* Nashville: Abingdon Press, 1968.

Gnilka, J. "2 Cor vi.14-vii.1 in the Light of the Qumran Texts and the Testaments of the Twelve Patriarchs." In *Paul and Qumran,* 48-68. Edited by Jerome Murphy-O'Connor. Chicago: Priory Press, 1968.

Goodenough, Erwin R. *Jewish Symbols in the Greco-Roman World.* 13 vols. New York: Pantheon Books, 1953-1968.

Goodenough, Erwin R. and Kraabel, A. T. "Paul and the Hellenization of Christianity." In *Religions in Antiquity,* 23-68. Edited by Jacob Neusner. Supplements to Numen, no. 14. Leiden: E. J. Brill, 1968.

Goppelt, Leonhard. "Kirchengemeinschaft und Abendmahlsgemeinschaft nach dem Neuen Testament." In *Koinonia,* 24-33. Edited by Friedrich Hübner. Berlin: Lutherisches Verlaghaus, 1957.

_____. *Typos: Die typologische Deutung des Alten Testaments im Neuen.* BFTh 2.43. Gütersloh: Bertelsmann, 1939.

Grant, Robert M. "Hellenistic Elements in I Corinthians." In *Early Christian Origins,* 60-66. Edited by Allen Wikgren. Chicago: Quadrangle Books, 1961.

Griffiths, J. Gwyn. *The Isis-Book: A Commentary on Apuleius' Metamorphoses Book 11.* Leiden: E. J. Brill, 1976.

Grundy, Robert H. ΣΩΜΑ in Biblical Theology. SNTSMS no. 29. Cambridge: University Press, 1976.

Guthrie, W. K. C. *The Greeks and Their Gods.* Boston: Beacon House, 1950.

Halliday, W. R. *The Pagan Background of Early Christianity.* London: Hodder and Stoughton, 1925.

Hanson, R. P. C. *Allegory and Event.* Richmond: John Knox, 1959.

Harrison, Jane Ellen. *Prolegomena to the Study of the Greek Religion.* Cambridge: University Press, 1903.

_____. *Themis.* New York: World Publishing, 1912; Rev. ed. Meridian Books, 1962.

Hatch, Edwin. *The Influence of Greek Ideas on Christianity.* New York: Harper, 1957.

Heitmüller, Wilhelm. *Taufe und Abendmahl bei Paulus.* Göttingen: Vandenhoeck & Ruprecht, 1903.

Höfler, Anton. *Der Sarapishymnus des Ailios Aristides.* Berlin: W. Kohlhammer, 1935.

Hurd, John C., Jr. *The Origin of 1 Corinthians.* New York: Seabury, 1965.

James, E. O. *Sacrifice and Sacrament.* New York: Barnes and Noble, 1962.

Jeremias, Joachim. *The Eucharistic Words of Jesus.* New York: Scribners, 1966.

_____. "Zur Gedankenführung in den paulinishcen Briefen: (3) Die Briefzitate in 1. Kor 8.1-13." 273-76. *Abba.* Göttingen: Vandenhoeck & Ruprecht, 1966.

Jewett, Robert. *Paul's Anthropological Terms.* AGJU, no. 10. Leiden: E. J. Brill, 1971.

Jonas, Hans. *Gnosis und spätantiker Geist.* 2 vols. Göttingen: Vandenhoeck & Ruprecht, 1964, 1966.

Judge, E. A. *The Social Patterns of Christian Groups in the First Century.* London: Tyndale, 1960.

Kane, J. P. "The Mithraic cult meal in its Greek and Roman environment." In *Mithraic Studies,* Vol. 2:313-351. Edited by John R. Hinnels. Manchester: Manchester University Press, 1975.

Käsemann, Ernst. *Leib und Leib Christi.* BHTH, no. 9. Tübingen: J. C. B. Mohr [Paul Siebeck], 1933.

_____. "The Pauline Doctrine of the Lord's Supper." In *Essays on New Testament Themes,* 108-135. SBT 1.41. London: SCM, 1964.

Kent, John H. *Corinth VIII, part iii, The Inscriptions 1926-1950.* Princeton: American School of Classical Studies, 1966.

Knox, W. L. *St. Paul and the Church of the Gentiles.* Cambridge: University Press, 1939.

_____. *Some Hellenistic Elements in Primitive Christianity.* London: Oxford University, 1944.

Köhler, Ludwig. *Old Testament Theology.* Philadelphia: Westminster Press, 1958.

Kümmel, W. G. *The New Testament: The History of the Investigations of Its Problems.* Nashville: Abingdon Press, 1970.

Laeuchli, Samuel, ed. *Mithraism in Ostia.* Chicago: Northwestern University Press, 1967.

Latte, Kurt. "Opfer und Gebet." In *Römische Religionsgeschichte,* Vol. 4, Handbuch der Altertumswissenschaft. Munich: Beck, 1960.

Lehmann, Paul. *Ethics in a Christian Context.* New York: Harper & Row, 1963.

Lietzmann, Hans. *Mass and Lord's Supper.* Leiden: E. J. Brill, 1953ff.

Lindars, Barnabas. *New Testament Apologetic.* Philadelphia: Westminster Press, 1961.

Lindsay, Jack. *Daily Life in Roman Egypt.* London: Frederick Muller, 1963.

_____. *Leisure and Pleasure in Roman Egypt.* New York: Barnes and Noble, 1965.

Longenecker, Richard. *Biblical Exegesis in the Apostolic Period.* Grand Rapids: Wm. B. Eerdmans, 1975.

MacMullen, Ramsay. *Roman Social Relations 50 B.C. to A.D. 284.* New Haven: Yale University Press, 1974.

Manson, T. W. "The Corinthian Correspondence (1)." In *Studies in the Gospels and Epistles.* 109-209. Edited by Matthew Black. Philadelphia: Westminster Press, 1962.

Maurer, Christian. "Grund und Grenze apostolischer Freiheit." In *Antwort: Karl Barth zum siebsigsten Geburtstag,* 630-41. Edited by Ernst Wolf, Ch. von Kirschbaum and Rudolf Frey. Zollikon-Zurich: Evangelischer Verlag, 1956.

Merk, Otto. *Handeln aus Glauben.* Marburger Theologische Studien, no. 5. Marberg: N. G. Elwert, 1968.

Michel, Otto. *Paulus und seine Bibel.* BFTh 2, 18. Gütersloh: C. Bertelsmann, 1929.

Montague, George T. *Growth in Christ.* Fribourg, Switzerland: St. Paul's Press, 1961.

Munck, Johannes. *Christ and Israel.* Philadelphia: Fortress, 1967.

Mylonas, George E. *Eleusis and the Eleusinian Mysteries*. Princeton: Princeton University Press, 1961.

Nabers, Ned Parker. "Macella, A Study in Roman Archaeology." Ph.D. dissertation, Princeton University, 1967.

Neill, Stephen. *The Interpretation of the New Testament: 1861-1961*. London: Oxford University, 1964.

Neill, William. *The Epistle of Paul to the Thessalonians*. MNTC. New York: Harper and Brothers, 1950.

Neuenzeit, Paul. *Das Herrenmahl: Studien zur paulinischer Eucharistieauffassung*. SANT, no. 1. Munich: Kösel, 1960.

Nickle, Keith. *The Collection*. SBT 1.48. London: SCM, 1966.

Nilsson, Martin P. *Cults, Myths, Oracles and Politics of Ancient Greece*. Lund: C. W. K. Gleerup, 1951.

_____. *The Dionysiac Mysteries of the Hellenistic and Roman Ages*. New York: Arno Press, 1975.

_____. *Geschichte der griechischen Religion*. 2 vols. Handbuch der Altertumswissenschaft. Edited by Walter Otto. Munich: C. H. Beck, 1941.

_____. *Greek Folk Religion*. New York: Harper & Row, 1940; Harper Torchbooks, 1961.

Nock, A. D. *Early Gentile Christianity and Its Hellenistic Background*. New York: Harper Torchbooks, 1964.

_____. *Essays on Religion and the Ancient World*. 2 vols. Edited by Zeph Stewart. Cambridge: Harvard University Press, 1972. Selected articles.

Norden, Eduard. *Agnostos Theos*. Leipzig: Teubner, 1913.

Otto, Walter F. *Dionysus: Myth and Cult*. Bloomington, IN: Indiana University Press, 1965.

Pearson, Lionel. *Popular Ethics in Ancient Greece*. Stanford: University Press, 1962.

Peters, F. E. *The Harvest of Hellenism*. New York: Simon and Schuster, 1970.

Peterson, Erik. Εἷς Θεός; Epigraphische, formgeschichtliche, und religionsgeschichtliche Untersuchungen. FRLANT, no. 41. Göttingen: Vandenhoeck & Ruprecht, 1926.

Pfleiderer, Otto. *Primitive Christianity*. 2 vols. New York: G. P. Putnam's Sons, 1906.

Pierce, C. A. *Conscience in the New Testament*. SBT 1.15. London: SCM, 1955.

Rahner, Hugo. *Greek Myths and Christian Mystery*. New York: Harper & Row, 1963.

Rankin, Edwin Moore. *The Role of the ΜΑΓΕΡΟΙ in the Life of the Ancient Greeks*. Chicago: University Press, 1907.

Rauer, Max. *Die 'Schwachen' in Korinth und Rom nach dem Paulusbriefen*. Biblische Studien, no. 21. Freiberg: Herder, 1923.

Reitzenstein, Richard. *Hellenistic Mystery Religions*. Pittsburgh Theological Monographs, no. 15. Pittsburgh: Pickwick Press, 1978.

Rengstorf, Karl Heinrich. *A Complete Concordance to Flavius Josephus*. Vol. 2. Leiden: E. J. Brill, 1975.

Richardson, Peter. *Paul's Ethic of Freedom*. Philadelphia: Westminster Press, 1979.

Robinson, John A. T. *The Body: A Study in Pauline Theology*. SBT 1.5. London: SCM, 1952.

Roebuck, Carl. *Corinth XIV, The Asklepieion and Lerna*. Princeton: American School of Classical Studies, 1951.

Roetzel, Calvin J. *Judgment in the Community*. Leiden: E. J. Brill, 1972.

Rohde, Erwin. *Psyche*. 2 Vols. New York: Harcourt, Brace and World, 1925.

Sahlin, Harald. "The New Exodus of Salvation According to St. Paul." In *The Root of the Vine*, 81-95. Edited by Anton Fridrichsen. New York: Philosophical Library, 1953.

Sawyer, W. T. "The Problem of Meat Sacrificed to Idols in the Corinthian Church." Th.D. dissertation, Southern Baptist Theological Seminary, 1968.

Schenke, H.-M. *Der Gott 'Mensch' in der Gnosis*. Göttingen: Vandenhoeck & Ruprecht, 1962.

Schmithals, Walter. *Gnosticism in Corinth*. Nashville: Abingdon Press, 1971.

Schrage, Wolfgang. *Die konkreten Einzelgebote in der paulinischen Päranese.* Gütersloh: Gütersloher Verlagshaus, Gerd Mohn, 1961.

Seesemann, Heinrich. *Der Begriff* KOINΩNIA im Neuen Testament. BZNW, no. 14. Giessen: Alfred Töpelmann, 1933.

Selwyn, Edward George. *The First Epistle of St. Peter.* London: MacMillan and Co., 1946.

Sevenster, J. N. *Paul and Seneca.* NovT Sup., no. 4. Leiden: E. J. Brill, 1961.

Shedd, Russell P. *Man in Community.* London: Epworth Press, 1958.

Smith, W. R. *The Religion of the Semites.* Cambridge: A. C. Black, 1889.

Stacey, W. David. *The Pauline View of Man.* New York: MacMillan and Co., 1956.

Thornton, L. S. "The Body of Christ in the New Testament." In *The Apostolic Ministry,* 53-111. Edited by K. E. Kirk. London: Hodder and Stoughton, 1946.

_____. *The Common Life in the Body of Christ.* London: Dacre Press, 1942.

Tinsley, E. J. *The Imitation of God in Christ.* London: SCM, 1960.

Tod, M. N. *Sidelights on Greek History.* London: Blackwell, 1932.

Vielhauer, Philipp. *OIKODOME: Das Bild vom Bau in der christlichen Literatur vom Neuen Testament bis Clemens Alexandrinus.* Karlsruhe-Durlach: Tron, 1939.

Vermaseren, M. J. *Mithras, the Secret God.* New York: Barnes and Noble, 1963.

Vermes, Geza. *Scripture and Tradition in Judaism.* Studia Post-Biblica, no. 4 Leiden: E. J. Brill, 1961.

Von Rad, Gerhard. *Old Testament Theology.* 2 vols. New York: Harper & Row, 1962.

von Soden, Hans F. "Sakrament und Ethik bei Paulus." In *Marburger Theologische Studien,* Vol. 1.1-40. Gotha: Leopold Klotz, 1931.

Weiss, Johannes. *Earliest Christianity. A History of the Period A.D. 30-150.* 2 vols. New York: Harper Torchbooks, 1965.

Idol Meat at Corinth

Wendland, Heinz-Dietrich. *Ethik des Neuen Testaments: eine Einführung.* NTD, no. 4. Göttingen: Vandenhoeck & Ruprecht, 1970.

West, A. B. *Corinth VIII,2: Latin Inscriptions, 1896-1926.* Cambridge: University Press, 1931

Wibbing, Siegfried. *Die Tugend-und Lasterkataloge im Neuen Testament.* BZNW, no. 25. Berlin: A. Töpelmann, 1959.

Wiseman, James. "Corinth and Rome I: 228 B.C.-A.D. 267." In *Aufsteig und Niedergang der römischen Welt, 2.7.1.* Edited by H. Temporini and W. Haase. Berlin: Walter de Gruyter, 1979.

Witt, R. E. *Isis in the Greco-Roman World.* Ithica: Cornell University Press, 1971.

Wuellner, Wilhelm. "Greek Rhetoric and Pauline Argumentation." In *Early Christian Literature and the Classical Intellectual Tradition: In Honorem Robert M. Grant,* 177-188. Edited by Wm. R. Schroedel and Robert L. Wilken. Theologie Historique, no. 53. Paris: Beauchesne, 1979.

Yerkes, Royden Keith. *Sacrifice in Greek and Roman Religions and Early Judaism.* New York: Charles Scribner's Sons, 1952.

Zuntz, Günther. *The Text of the Epistles.* London: Oxford University Press, 1953.

Index

MODERN AUTHORS

INDEX OF SCRIPTURE CITATIONS
(apart from 1 Corinthians 8 and 10)